Communicating in Groups and Teams

S H A R I N G   L E A D E R S H I P

Communicating in Groups and Teams

SHARING LEADERSHIP

Gay Lumsden

Donald Lumsden

Kean College of New Jersey

WADSWORTH PUBLISHING COMPANY

Belmont, California

A Division of Wadsworth, Inc.

Communications Editor:	Holly Allen
Development Editor:	John Bergez
Editorial Assistant:	Katherine Hartlove
Production:	Cecile Joyner, The Cooper Company
Print Buyer:	Diana Spence
Designer:	Janet Bollow
Copy Editor:	Peggy Tropp
Permissions Editor:	Jeanne Bosschart
Photo Researcher:	Sara Hunsaker
Technical Illustrator:	John Foster
Cover Design:	Janet Bollow
Cover Photo:	© Eric Meola, The Image Bank
Signing Representative:	Jeff Wilhelms
Compositor:	G & S Typesetters, Inc.
Printer:	Malloy Lithographing, Inc.

The photograph on pages 1, 51, 103, 189, 257, and 329 by Howard Grey, © Tony Stone Worldwide, is used with permission.

Case study materials from Environmental Defense Fund/McDonald's Corporation Waste Reduction Task Force used with permission from Environmental Defense Fund.

Material from Hastings, C., Bixby, P., and Chaudhry-Lawton, R., *The Superteam Solution: Successful Teamworking in Organisations,* Aldershot, England: Gower Publishing Co., Limited, 1986, is used with permission.

Concepts, ideas, and figures similar to material in G. Lumsden and D. Lumsden, "Problem Solving with Information and Analysis"; and D. Gallaro, M. Knight, G. Lumsden, and D. Lumsden, "Empowerment and Teamwork in the Quality Organization," chapters in T. D. Connors, ed., *Nonprofit Organizations Policies and Procedures Handbook* (in press), are used by permission of John Wiley & Sons, Inc.

 This book is printed on acid-free paper that meets Environmental Protection Agency standards for recycled paper.

1 2 3 4 5 6 7 8 9 10—97 96 95 94 93

Library of Congress Cataloging-in-Publication Data

Lumsden, Gay.
 Communicating in groups and teams : sharing leadership / Gay Lumsden, Donald Lumsden.
  p. cm.
 Includes bibliographical references and index.
 ISBN 0–534–19068–5
 1. Communication in organizations. 2. Work groups. I. Lumsden, Donald L.
II. Title.
HD30.3.L86 1992
658.4′036—dc20   92-18605

You may love working in groups, or you may hate it. Whichever way you feel, you can be certain of two things: First, you have company, because teamwork can be both gratifying and mind-boggling. Second, no matter how you feel, you *will* work in groups and teams extensively.

We've written this book because we know that your life and your career, whatever it may be, will involve you in cooperative group efforts. Organizations—big and small, private and public, profit and nonprofit—use groups and teams for everything from designing and implementing projects to managing to improving quality. That's because cooperative groups can be more effective than individuals at many tasks. When a team brings together people with different experiences and backgrounds to focus their attention on an issue, their diversity carries the potential for a wider range of ideas and approaches. Groups also have the potential, however, for breakdowns and misunderstandings; it takes wisdom to make them work.

You can develop the wisdom to make your groups and teams work effectively as you learn to understand them and as you hone your communication skills. A cooperative group or team is more than the sum of its parts; with several people interacting, communication among members multiplies in complexity. Members need strong communication skills to make their ideas clear, to understand others, to build a team, and to work together through the task processes of collaborative problem analysis and decision making.

This book will help you learn how to create good team experiences. It will help you most effectively if you know how we've designed it. We want to tell you, therefore, about the philosophical premises on which it's written; what we assume about you, the student; features that may help you learn; and how the book is organized.

Philosophical Premises

By philosophical premises, we mean beliefs that are basic to every part of this book. Let's begin by listing several of these.

A cooperative group should become a team. An effective task group builds a team by using the best abilities and talents of every member in a process that serves the needs of the individuals and of the task concurrently. This involves mutual commitment to vigilant, collaborative analysis as well as to team building.

Leadership is every member's responsibility. Each person must take responsibility for influencing the team's transactions and tasks. Each serves as member, facilitator, contributor, participant; each has a responsibility for the quality of group transactions and achievements, for the satisfaction of the members, and for ensuring that the functions of leadership are served.

A designated leader is more than a manager. Leaders guide their teams over obstacles; they empower team members to take leadership; they activate quality contributions, interaction, and responsibility-taking within the team; and they link the team to parent organizations and outside systems.

The team is a system within a system. Teams today frequently cross departments, organizations, or public institutions to weave a number of systems, subsystems, goals, and objectives together in cooperative efforts. Learning how to do this can help you to bridge and to heal some of the chasms in your world.

The team is a microcosm. People of both sexes and of many sociocultural and racial backgrounds interact in groups. Diversity contributes to quality teamwork when members appreciate differences, actively seek different points of view, and understand that communication behaviors and norms are influenced by gender, culture, and expectations.

The team is an ethical system. Groups must consider ethical dimensions both in a dialogical ethic of team transactions and in the decisions that they make. Principled members and leaders who focus attention on ethical questions and their potential impact at every stage of a team's development and work will make better decisions and realize healthier consequences than those who do not.

Assumptions about Students and Approaches to Learning

We think of you as one of our own students. We assume that, like our students, you have natural curiosity, an interest in becoming an effective group communicator, a desire to succeed, and some ideas about what teamwork is like.

You certainly have your own learning style; everybody does. You may also be like most people in that you learn best when you connect with the material in some real way. In the words of a Chinese proverb: "What I hear, I forget; what I see, I may remember; what I do, I understand."

These and other assumptions about you influence the features we have chosen to include in this book.

Features

This book is user-friendly. It is written for you, the student. It starts with you and your experience because we know that people learn, as Aristotle pointed out, from the known to the unknown. Learning works best when it starts where you are, with your experiences and your life.

The writing is directed to you and designed for your use. Throughout the book are clear checklists that will help you focus on exactly what works to make groups effective. Plenty of explanations, definitions, and examples clarify the ideas. Many of these come from our own experiences with students and with teams in organizations. If you interact with them, by creating your own examples and applying the definitions and concepts, the information will become more real to you.

The emphasis is on making your groups and teams effective. Theory and research are not emphasized for their own sakes, but are included as needed to make concepts clearer, to make a point, or to show relationships among different areas. The references contain excellent sources to which you can refer if you want to follow up on ideas for a research project.

Learning strategies are varied and interesting. We believe in varying learning experiences to meet a range of students' learning styles, so we've used a range of approaches. Because we also believe that learning about teamwork should be put in an applied perspective, the book has some real-life materials to show you how people are currently using what you are learning. Some of these are included in the text as examples, but some are in special formats.

Boxes   Brief, inset boxes provide excerpts and synopses from newletters and articles, as well as teamwork examples from corporations and from nonprofit, public, media, and political organizations.

A Serial Case Analysis   In many chapters, inset boxes give you a series of steps in how the Environmental Defense Fund/McDonald's Corporation Waste Reduction Task Force developed its recommendations to McDonald's. This innovative cooperative venture, which completed its landmark work in 1991, tells you much about what intergroup cooperation can do. You can follow the case throughout the book.

Other Case Studies   Other case studies are included in exercises and with pictures throughout the book, so you can analyze them, discuss the questions, and make recommendations.

Exercises   Exercises at the end of each chapter provide opportunities for you to:

Observe and evaluate others, in class and in outside situations, as they work in groups and teams. Most chapters include forms for observation and evaluation of groups to help you apply the information in the exercises.

Participate in group and team experiences that focus on the content of the chapter.

Reflect upon and analyze your own experience and skill in relationship to the chapter's content.

Write about your observations and experiences.

These exercises will make your learning real and applicable.

Glossary Important concepts are printed in boldface so you will know that they are in the glossary at the end of the book. As you read, if you can't remember precisely what a term means from a previous chapter, you can refer to the glossary for a reminder.

Instructor's Manual Your instructor will doubtless use his or her own assignments and methods in the course. In addition, an instructor's manual contains assignments, exercises, case studies, evaluation forms, and test questions to help you work through the material in and out of class.

Organization

Learning *information* about groups and developing *skill* in working with them require you to deal with many things at once, and that presents a dilemma. Ideally, as students, you would know everything covered in the textbook before you began applying it. That isn't possible in a communication class. You must practice skills from the first moment of the semester, but information you need about these skills may be presented late in the book.

A textbook goes step by step through information that is intricately related throughout, and that doesn't always fit the way an instructor arranges the course. Your professor may well rearrange the book to suit the way your course is designed. In whichever order you use the chapters, however, it will help to know how they are arranged.

Part One (Chapters 1 and 2) starts with where you are—with your experiences in previous groups. It moves on into your future in groups and teams, your personal leadership responsibilities and roles, and the impact of ethics on your participation in groups and teams. This gives you a *thinking* foundation for the course.

Part Two (Chapters 3 and 4) introduces you to team processes—setting goals, getting the work under way. It also shows you a vision of an excellent team, and what you need to do to get one started. This part gives you a *doing* foundation— it gets you and your classmates started on activities and projects—and introduces you to what a developing team will experience.

Part Three (Chapters 5 through 8) guides you and your teammates through the task processes of goal setting, agenda design, team inquiry, critical and creative thinking, problem solving, and decision making. This part focuses your thinking and your work on vigilance and collaboration.

Part Four (Chapters 9 through 11) develops verbal, nonverbal, listening, and questioning skills for team communication. This includes assertive, confirming behavior that contributes to developing dialogue and healthy team climates. These chapters help you weave the transactional processes that make a team.

Part Five (Chapters 12 through 14) addresses some sophisticated, and critical, problems and challenges in group interactions and thinking. These include issues of deviance and conformity, competitive communication, groupthink, conflict, and problems with members and meetings. This part gives you tools to deal with problems all teams might face.

Part Six (Chapters 15 and 16) guides you through team projects and reports—planning public meetings, and preparing and presenting written and oral reports. This part provides the key to finishing up course assignments effectively; it is also a valuable resource for future projects in other courses and your career.

The epilogue, finally, brings together what you have learned and suggests ways that teams can complete their experiences and say good-bye.

Acknowledgments

Our approach to this book is influenced by our own research and learning about group communication, and that started in a class such as yours. We have been fortunate in having excellent professors and mentors to guide us along the way. We take this opportunity to express thanks to Dennis Gouran who, when he was at Indiana University, influenced the way we think about group communication and directed Gay's dissertation in group leadership. He continues to provide his sage advice and, occasionally, consolation. We also are indebted to the late Martin Andersen for immersing us in the study of groups during our years at California State University at Fullerton. Our thanks, too, go to Juliette Venitsky of Cerritos College for helping us develop our early understanding of the communication discipline we have come to love.

It is important for us to acknowledge here the influence of a person we never had the opportunity to meet and know. Henry Ewbank, who taught for years at the University of Wisconsin, had an enormous impact on our educational experiences through his writings and, especially, through his students whom we later encountered as our professors. Jeff Auer, Bob Gunderson, Ray Smith, and Martin Andersen modeled for us, as Dr. Ewbank clearly had done for them, a love of scholarship and, even more important, human concerns for students, teaching, and learning. He is, to us, an academic grandfather who died before our "births." Ours is a rich heritage.

We also appreciate those who worked directly to help us write this book. Wadsworth team members were helpful throughout the project. Jeff Wilhelms was graciously persistent in urging us to undertake the task, and Kris Clerkin's encouragement kept us going through the early stages. Holly Allen's enthusiastic support and guidance as the communication editor energized our efforts, and we could always count on editorial assistant Kathy Hartlove's effective responses to our many questions and needs. We also gained insight from John Bergez's skillful eye as a developmental editor and the coaching from Joanne Fraser's chapter review. Jerry Holloway kept us linked with the right people through the production stages, and Cecile Joyner was delightful and efficient in her production work—transforming our typewritten pages into a book. Janet Bollow's design beautifully solved the problem of accommodating our multiple formats. And we were blessed to have Peggy Tropp as our editor; her work on our copy enhanced it immeasurably.

Although responsibility for the content is ours, several communication colleagues across the country reviewed drafts at various stages of development. They helped us keep perspective on the book's material and on students as its readers. These included David E. Butt, Penn State University; Patricia Comeaux, University of North Carolina–Wilmington; Isa Engleberg, Prince George's Community College; Charles Griffin, Kansas State University; Joan Holm, Northern Virginia Community College; James A. Jaksa, Western Michigan University; William E. Jurma, Texas Christian University; Matt Seeger, Wayne State University; and Brant Short, Idaho State University. Also, Freda Remmers, our colleague at Kean College, read an early draft and gave us excellent suggestions for changes. They are proof that multiple perspectives can lead to an improved final product.

Additionally, our thanks go to Allan Margolin and John Ruston from the Environmental Defense Fund (EDF) for helping us develop the case study materials relating to the EDF/McDonald's task force. Finally, Mary Palmiter of Kean College's library contributed enormously by securing many materials for us through interlibrary loans.

We dedicate this book to our families, friends, students, colleagues, and to each other. All have added to our understanding of the importance of communicating in groups and teams.

BRIEF CONTENTS

DETAILED CONTENTS

pg 99
Guidelines
for "Team"
Dev. a "Team"

10 Nonverbal Cues and Meanings: Enhancing Team Messages 214

11 Listening and Questioning: Developing Team Dialogue 236

PART FIVE   CHALLENGES TO LEADERS AND LEADERSHIP   **257**

12   Teams and Designated Leaders: Fulfilling Role Expectations   259

Your Roles in Groups and Teams

Groups and Teams:
Communicating for Success

"I'd really rather work alone. . . ."
Forget it, the twenty-first century works in groups.

We're going to put this right up front: group and teamwork will be not only important but unavoidable in twenty-first-century life. Sometimes, when we introduce group communication, either in the college classroom or in corporate training, people beam enthusiastically. Often they wince. It all depends on their backgrounds and experiences.

That's what we have to build on—your background and experiences. In this chapter, we start with groups and teams you have experienced, how you felt about them—for better or for worse—and the factors that may have influenced your feelings. We go on to examine your future in various types of groups and teams, the power of teamwork, and contemporary trends in the workplace. Finally, we give you some tips to get started on your work for this class. Thus, our goals for this chapter are to help you:

1. Understand how and why group experiences may both satisfy and frustrate you and other group members.

2. See how and why groups and teams will be involved in your future life and career.

3. Understand a set of basic group and team concepts used in this book.

4. Become aware of how communication operates in group settings.

5. Get started on your experiences for this class.

Let's start with where you've been—and move forward to where you'll be going.

Your Past Group and Team Experiences

From day one of your life, you were in a group—your family—and this set your expectations of how people act when they are together. Along the way to the present, you've added to your experiences. Perhaps you've been in study or support groups or worked with special problem-solving groups, management or staff committees, or quality groups. Any of these may have been connected with larger organizations—school, work, the community, or a religious group. You may have competed on a team in areas as diverse as scholastics, livestock judging, basketball, or automobile racing. Many students have formed their clearest vision of what a group or team should be from these experiences.

Your vision of groups and teams may be shiny or dim. On the shiny side, it's a great feeling to be part of a winning team or even a committee that does its job well. It can be more fun, more stimulating, and more motivating to work with other people than alone. Belonging to a group can feel pretty good. The dim picture, however, is that working in a group can be a pain. It's demanding. It requires you to work on many levels at once—with people, with relationships, with information, with ideas—and anything can go wrong. It takes leadership and commitment to make a group work well.

As you look back, how do you feel about your experiences? We want your future groups and teams to give you great success and satisfaction, so it's worth considering what some of the factors behind those feelings might be.

Expectations. People tend to generalize from experiences—to decide that what was true of one will be true of all. These expectations color future events for them. If, for example, the members of a study group were both expert and helpful to you, the experience probably helped your grade and your self-esteem. As a result, you may look forward to participating in other groups. In contrast, you may have been on a project team when others didn't do their work so you had to pick up the slack. Perhaps your grade or your income was damaged by the incompetence or irresponsibility of others. The loudest groans in our classes come from students who have had these negative experiences and who do not want to repeat them.

Investment. Previous groups may have taught you that the more people involved, the more time, energy, and money the job takes. For a corporate team, each person's salary and work time—as well as space, materials, and other resources needed for the group—factor into the costs of the team. Group projects represent investments for the members and their organizations.

Pressures. Group work can create stress in many ways, including the pressure of the work and pressures from the group. Sometimes people conclude an experience with, "The pressure was so great that I just didn't say what I really thought." A group that is closed to dissent may exert extreme pressure on members to give in to majority thinking. This can lead to dishonest, unethical, or at least foolish decisions. It takes leadership and wisdom to keep the group open and to eliminate the dangers of team conformity.

Personal characteristics and preferences. Each individual brings a personal approach to work. You're an individualist, perhaps, a "loner," confident, creative, and competent in doing things by yourself. You may not really trust a group of people to do as well. In fact, you may agree with the old line that "a camel is a horse put together by a committee." At the other extreme, you could dislike working alone and find the social interaction of a group more motivating and stimulating for your own thinking or creativity.

Gender. Although male and female role expectations are changing rapidly, there do seem to be some differences. Males are more likely to approach groups with a competitive, let's-get-it-done task orientation, whereas females may be more cooperative and concerned with the well-being of the group (Pearson, Turner, & Todd-Mancillas, 1991, pp. 218–219). Both approaches are important, no matter which gender contributes them.

Culture. Cultural influences are vitally important, but generalizing about them is risky. Even characteristics shown to be generally true of a culture may be untrue of a subculture or of individuals within that population. The point is not to stereotype individuals, but to recognize that different cultures do understand groups in different ways. For example, individualistic Europeans and North Americans may be easily frustrated by group communication; Latin Americans like working in groups as a method of supporting each other and improving outcomes (Triandis, Brislin, & Hui, 1988, p. 269); Japanese rely on groups to achieve agreement and commitment among workers (Cathcart & Cathcart, 1986, p. 186). A team of diverse people, therefore, presents some challenges. The good news is the rich gold mine of ideas and creativity each makes available. The bad news is the minefield of interpersonal frustrations and conflicts that can occur among diverse human beings who are just being human.

You have, no doubt, experienced these factors in some of your group experiences—and they've contributed to what those experiences have been like for you. That's your starting point for the work ahead.

Your Future in Groups and Teams

Unless you plan to become a hermit or a highly eccentric and wealthy genius, you will work—occasionally, often, perhaps constantly—in groups and teams. Despite all the pitfalls, cooperation is the way almost everything happens these days.

This is true even in your private life. There's the family, of course—and all the activities families have. You often hear the complaint that parents are "nothing but chauffeurs" for the kids: Little League, dance theater, scouts, soccer team, gymnastics team, 4H. Not only are the children involved in multiple group activities, but so are the parents: advisory groups, planning groups, support groups.

There are group activities in the community, in recreation, even—especially—in places of worship. More and more, churches, synagogues, mosques, and temples have special groups and teams of members to serve their needs. We know a church

WHAT EMPLOYERS WANT YOU TO KNOW

For employers, the basic workplace skills challenge has been coming into focus for some time. In addition to the basic skills of reading, writing, and math, the following are essential:

Learning to learn
Listening
Oral communication
Creative thinking
Problem solving
Self-esteem
Goal-setting/motivation
Personal/career development
Interpersonal skills
Negotiation
Teamwork
Organizational effectiveness
Leadership

Organizations are composed of individuals with differing opinions and operating styles. Whenever people work together, successful interaction depends upon effective interpersonal skills, focused negotiation, and a sense of group purpose (teamwork). Of course, diversity inevitably results in conflict from time to time. In today's workplace, the move toward participative decision making and problem solving inevitably increases the potential for disagreement, particularly when the primary work unit is a peer team with no single person taking on the role of decision maker (that is, supervisor or manager). All this puts a premium on developing employees' group effectiveness skills.

Excerpt from A. P. Carnevale, L. J. Gainer, and A. S. Meltzer (1990), *Workplace Basics: The Essential Skills Employers Want*. San Francisco: Jossey-Bass, pp. 2 and 31. © 1990 by Jossey-Bass Inc.. Publishers. Used with permission.

member who is on an interdenominational task force to provide housing for the homeless, a special corps of lay people who help with family crises, the church planning committee—and more. This man also serves in community groups and works with teams in his profession as a sales representative.

The probability is that your private life and your work life—whatever your career—will involve you in groups and teams. First, let's look at some examples of teamwork in various career areas, then describe some different types of groups and teams on which you might serve, and finally take an overview of the power of teamwork and current trends in the workplace.

Careers and Teamwork

Consider your future career. You may have your sights set on a communication, scientific, or medical field; on archaeology, history, or meteorology; on a technological field, or sales, or agriculture, or the arts. In any of these, you are likely to work with teams of others in your field or in special groups that bring diverse specialties together.

If you're a communication major, your career may be in mass communication, telecommunications, or media; organizational communication; public communication or public relations; or, possibly, performance. And in this, as in the other majors, you could become a teacher or pursue a career in management, in business, in research, or in a helping profession.

To get a hint of how groups and teams might be a part of your future, let's look at some applied career examples.

∎ A mass communication, telecommunications, business, art, or electronics graduate might work on a team to design a communication system for a corporation, or on a task force to develop guidelines for local, state, or national advertising. A media, marketing, art, or education major might work on teams to design, produce, shoot, edit, and market training tapes, advertising tapes, and so on. Some of our recent graduates followed precisely this path and now operate their own media business—as a team.

∎ An organizational communication major could work on a corporate team to design and implement training programs—one of which might be to train managers in how to work effectively in teams. Another of our graduates followed this path in a large corporation. He began with producing training materials; soon his responsibilities expanded to coaching executives in communication skills.

∎ A political science or public communication major might work on a team to design and implement a campaign. One graduate, passionately interested in animal rights, has made her career designing campaigns against animal abuse.

∎ A public relations graduate cooperates closely with team members to coordinate advertising, public appearances, press relations, and legal responses for his or her client. A recent graduate began her career as a public relations intern for a pharmaceutical company, moved on and up into another company, and recently served as part of a special team to introduce to the market a product on which she had worked, from its inception, as an assistant account executive.

∎ A performance major, in radio, television, film, or theater, works constantly in a team situation. Just ask an actor or a director who has worked in a repertory situation what it was like, and you will hear a glowing account of a true team. One graduate, a dancer, went to work in a small, tightly organized children's theater troupe. Her team does everything from planning publicity, selling tickets, and making sets to performing at schools and parties.

∎ An education major, as a teacher, cooperates in close groups with administrators, other teachers, support staff, students, and sometimes parents to create and implement programs and policies. Another graduate became a history teacher and soon created and led a team of faculty and parents to design an entirely new curriculum for his school.

∎ Many majors (business, communication, science, technology, liberal arts, psychology, English) may become managers, working in teams with other managers and with numerous other groups and teams of superiors, subordinates, and related departments. One of our graduates works on a management team for a retail store and concurrently is developing her own small business. She's succeeding because she's forged a tight employee team that makes her business work.

▮ Many majors go into business. A businessperson serves in groups of service organizations, other businesses, and community organizations to help design special community projects or, perhaps, to lobby the state government for more favorable tax laws. That same businessperson may create teams within his or her organization to work on issues such as quality and production.

▮ Graduates from a wide range of majors—communication, liberal arts, behavioral sciences, sciences, marketing—become researchers engaged in teams of other researchers, of clients, and of representatives from related areas. A marketing researcher, for example, might be testing the market for a new product in coordination with departments of research and development, finance, sales, production, and advertising.

▮ Some majors enter a helping profession or health profession. A health or social worker, for example, works on many teams, frequently comprised of all professionals relevant to the care of one client.

All of these people will use their understandings and their communication skills in numerous other group and team situations. And so will you.

Types of Groups and Teams

Your private and work life will put you in many different types of groups and teams, each with a distinct purpose and mode of operation. Let's take a look at some of these types.

Informal groups. You may have just come from or be preparing to attend a meeting of some kind of group. It may be an informal group of friends or of people with similar interests. Football fans who get together for tailgate parties and games may be an informal group. Whatever structure their party planning may follow is informal, loose, and probably variable.

Ad hoc groups. Ad hoc means "to this" in Latin. When people set up a meeting to focus specifically on one issue, it is an **ad hoc** meeting. For example, you may be angry because of a new college policy so you call together a few other students. You share your information, discuss the issue, and think of a way to put pressure on the college to change it. Your initial ad hoc meeting may be your only one, or you may create an ongoing ad hoc group to lobby for this issue.

Study and support groups. Both of these are ongoing groups of peers who get together to help each other to help themselves. The **study group** focuses on learning information or skills; the **support group** focuses on learning to cope. These groups may be self-starting and self-governing, or they may be sponsored by larger organizations. Meetings of such groups address the specific needs of their members, whether it be getting through a course in biochemistry or getting through life with an alcoholic parent or mate.

Staff groups. A **staff group** consists of people who work together in some capacity and meet periodically to discuss information and policies. In many organizations, staff meetings have some systematic organization and approach; in others, they may be loose and unstructured. When they are badly run, people complain about how much time and energy are wasted. When they are well run, they contribute to an excellent organization and strong satisfaction and cohesiveness among members of the group.

Task forces. Similar to an ad hoc group, a **task force** brings people together to work on a specific problem. Frequently the members are appointed to represent a variety of interests or areas of expertise within an organization, or sometimes from multiple organizations. Usually the task involves investigating an issue, gathering information, and making proposals that other groups may (or may not) implement. As a rule, such groups meet a number of times and have specific goals to accomplish.

Governance groups and committees. The gears of a democratic system are **governance groups and committees**. These are people who represent larger populations or organizations and subgroups of those representatives. They meet on a regular basis to consider issues, gather information, make proposals, and report to larger groups. You may have participated in or observed such groups. If not, tune in C-SPAN on a cable television channel and watch your government at work, or attend a meeting of your student organization or your faculty senate. Their processes grind slowly and they embody all the problems of group communication and of bureaucracies, but these groups are the way we protect our rights and strive for justice in this society. Maybe we can't live with them, but we won't live without them, either.

Self-managing teams. These teams demonstrate a relatively new concept in U.S. organizations, corporate or otherwise. A **self-managing team (SMT)** is a group of people who work together in any area—media production or an assembly line, for example—and are responsible for all aspects of their efforts. This includes everything from personnel decisions and budget allocations to planning projects, coordinating with other teams and departments, and assessing their own success.

Management teams. These teams are becoming more important as managers increasingly are responsible for coordinating various employee groups, including self-managing teams, who participate in directing their own activities. A **management team** consists of managers of various departments and areas who meet on a regular basis to coordinate their efforts, make decisions, allocate resources, and so on.

Quality circles. A **quality circle** is a group of employees, drawn from different departments and areas of an organization, who work together to improve quality in any area of the organization. Quality circles can be used at any level of any organization, public or private, large or small.

Project teams. A **project team** is a group of people of varied backgrounds and skills who work together to accomplish a specific task from beginning to end. A project could be developing a new product, getting it manufactured, and marketing it; moving an organization from one area to another; or establishing a corporation-wide training system.

Creative teams. This approach is growing as creative work becomes more expensive and riskier to produce. In a **creative team**, people who have specific talents work together to do necessary research, formulate ideas, and carry through an entire creative project. A creative team might include a marketing research analyst, a public relations professional, a writer, an artist, a director, and a producer, who design and produce a television commercial for a product or a political candidate. One of the all-time most famous creative teams developed one of the all-time most popular television series, "M*A*S*H." The high energy and sharp wit of the program were the result of intensive, intimate teamwork among all members of that team (Hastings, Bixby, & Chaudhry-Lawton, 1986, p. 68).

Health care teams. Teams are becoming a potent force in delivering care to patients, bringing together the entire range of professionals necessary to an individual's treatment and rehabilitation. Although you may or may not serve on a **health care team**, chances are that you and people you love will be the clients of one. One team we observed included: geriatric, infectious disease, heart, and cancer specialists; nurses at various levels of specialization and care; physical, occupational, speech, and respiratory therapists; a nutritionist, a chaplain, and a social worker. Their tightly coordinated diagnoses and care saved the life of their patient. At the same time, each of them served on other teams to provide life and rehabilitation to other patients. Their teamwork was the key to their success.

All these groups and teams have one thing in common: they have specific goals and objectives or tasks toward which their members work. That's what this book is about: groups and teams that have tasks to accomplish.

The Power of Teamwork

Teamwork is a powerful concept, because it can accomplish powerful things. Of course, there are times when one individual can do a better job than a group in solving a problem. If it's a math problem, and you have just one mathematical genius available, don't bother with a group. Let the genius do it. Likewise, if a group is composed of members who are incompetent, unmotivated, and untrained in group communication skills, that group probably cannot do any better than its best member could do alone. It might even drag the performance down.

When you have competent, motivated, and trained individuals working as a team, however, you have a more powerful instrument for problem solving than any one of those individuals alone. A recent study found that such groups outperformed their best member 97 percent of the time (Michaelson, Watson, & Black, 1989). Two factors can increase a team's performance: (1) having sufficient diversity among members to think from a number of angles, and (2) having the commitment to develop ideas together.

Diversity   Groups often achieve goals better than individuals because people together multiply their information, skills, and abilities to go beyond the limits of everyday thinking. Just as people who study in groups learn more and do better in their classes, people working together can increase creativity when one mind sparks another. In a playful exploration of possibilities, wild and crazy ideas emerge. Some of those ideas go to the vast dumping ground of wild and crazy ideas, but from others, brilliant and effective solutions are identified.

The more varied and diverse the members of a group are, the more angles from which they can see a problem. It has become a cliché to say that the United States is no longer a "melting pot" (if it ever was) but a "salad bowl." The cliché has some truth to it. Reflect on how boring and unnourishing is either a melted mess of glop or a salad of plain lettuce. It is the diversity of ingredients that makes it interesting, creative, and healthful.

Teams that include people of various talents, abilities, backgrounds, and cultures profit from the different perspectives these people bring to the group. Similarly, teams comprised of both males and females profit from the different approaches men and women sometimes take to group communication (Wood, 1987). A variety of perspectives can assist tremendously in creating a new and more productive process for a group that welcomes and uses those diverse perspectives. Fortunately, this society has a wonderful mix of cultures and perspectives from which to draw.

Commitment   A range of ideas and insights is only useful when team members can listen to and process those contributions. Diversity—whether of culture, race, gender, or opinion—requires members to work harder at understanding each other than if they were all the same. When teams do listen to divergent viewpoints, as compared to those that listen primarily to the majority, they tend to find more and better strategies for solving problems and to arrive at better solutions (Nemeth & Kwan, 1987).

Because a variety of people bring different thinking styles and value systems to the discussion, they are able to evaluate ideas from a number of points of view. The result is likely to be a better analysis of the logic, the evidence, and the ethics of the questions faced by a team than a single individual or a group of very similar people could possibly produce. When people think alone, or with others who are very similar, they don't have as many thinking tools to check assumptions or to ask hard questions. A team that knows how to do that together, and brings a spectrum of viewpoints to the process, can produce more rational and more ethical results.

Trends in the Workplace

The emphasis on teams and teamwork is increasing rapidly in the United States. It's a sort of teamwork revolution, as all segments of society have had to recognize that the United States isn't doing so well in comparison to other economies and societies. Teamwork seems to be the key to opening up new doors for learning and advancement.

TEAM EXCELLENCE AT XEROX

Since 1984 Xerox Corporation has recognized outstanding team performance through its Team Excellence Award, which involves a formal recognition ceremony and a monetary award shared equally by team members. For the purposes of the award, a team is defined as "a group of Xerox employees, normally two to twelve in size, who have clearly understood and shared goals, who work together using quality tools and processes, and who achieve results."

One recent winner was a group that called itself the "Fly-by-Nites," who used quality improvement to reduce spending on overnight air shipments and to reverse customer dissatisfaction with current service levels. . . . The results have been impressive. Some 82% of deliveries are now made by 9 a.m. compared to less than 20% in 1988; . . . freight expenses were reduced by $1.9 million. . . .

"As a result of this team's efforts, Xerox overtook a prime competitor and is now the industry benchmark in timely deliveries to critical locations," says CEO Paul Allaire. "We believe in the power of teamwork; 75% of all Xerox employees are actively involved in quality-improvement or problem-solving projects."

Excerpt from J. G. Bowles, "The Human Side of Quality." Reprinted by permission from a paid advertising section in *Fortune* magazine, September 24, 1990.

The potential power of group communication has been recognized for a long time. Research going back more than fifty years has fully documented how effective cooperative groups can be. In the United States, business and education have developed ways to use participatory management and cooperative group learning for two reasons: (1) these methods yield better ideas and productivity; and (2) participants involved in doing their own learning and making their own decisions are more satisfied and committed to the group's decisions. When people know, probably more thoroughly than if they had worked alone, why and how a decision was reached, they achieve greater consensus and satisfaction (Gouran, 1969).

These concepts are basic to a movement sweeping the country today. The "total quality movement," or TQM, advocates full participatory involvement of teamed employees throughout all elements of an organization. These ideas, originally developed in the United States, were adapted by W. Edwards Deming to help Japan get on its feet after the Second World War (Walton, 1986, pp. 10–21). Only now is the United States catching on and catching up with the vital recognition that every organization—whether a school, a television station, or a multinational corporation—performs better when its people work as fully participative teams at every level of data gathering, problem solving, decision making, and assessment of the institution.

You may well be involved in an organization that's working on a TQM program—possibly even at your college. You may be asked to work in a group to identify ways to improve some service or activity. For a while, quality circles fell into some disrepute because they were used poorly. Problems arose because the teams were used manipulatively, because the members weren't trained, and because they weren't adequately supported. When used well, however, quality circles have been quite successful, and there are indications that they have a strong future as a team approach to employees' participation in developing quality organizations (Berman & Hellweg, 1989).

Key Concepts

Your work in this course—and your effectiveness later—rests in part on understanding some key concepts as we use them in this text. All of these ideas will be explored in greater detail in later chapters, but a few basic terms and definitions will help get you started.

Groups and Teams

A group is more than a bunch of people in the same place, and a team is more than a group.

A basic definition of a **group** is "two or more persons who are interacting with one another in such a manner that each person influences and is influenced by each other person" (Shaw, 1981, p. 8). There are three important issues in understanding groups and teams: the nature of the relationships among members; the processes they use; and the purposes for which they are together. If you brainstormed terms that defined each of these aspects, you might start with:

Relationships. Interacting, influencing, sharing, cooperating, interdepending.

Processes. Communicating, organizing, leading, supporting, developing, analyzing, thinking, creating.

Purposes. Goals, vision, tasks, activities, outcomes.

You can think of more, but these are a beginning. A group may have varying kinds and degrees of each of these components, and its purposes may range from having a good time together to creating a plan for universal peace.

Is a team different from a group? Yes and no. According to Dennis Kinlaw (1991, pp. 10–12), teamwork consultant to corporations and government agencies, ordinary work groups and teams are functionally and qualitatively different. A team starts out as a group, but, according to Kinlaw, it reaches a new level of quality, it develops special feelings among its members, it creates critical work processes, and it reflects leadership for its own development and performance. "Every work group," says Kinlaw, "can become a work team and every work team can become a superior work team" (p. 12).

A **team** can be defined in terms of the following characteristics:

A team is a diverse group of people. In a team, more than in a casual group, specific and different resources and abilities are needed from each individual to accomplish the task.

Members share leadership responsibility. They help the group interact and move along the task. Because of the diversity of contributions and the specificity of the task, every member must guide the team whether there's a designated leader or not.

A team creates an identity. Much more than an ordinary group, a team develops a particular identity, a self-image, that becomes a cohesive and motivating force for the team.

Its efforts are interconnected. The team constantly weaves and coordinates the contributions of each member to develop a tighter energy and focus than most groups have.

Members work to achieve a mutually defined goal. Members communicate intensively to develop a consensus as to goals and how to achieve them. Larson and LaFasto (1989) count a "clear, elevating goal" as a distinguishing feature of a successful team.

The team works within the context of other groups and systems. A team affects and is affected by the context, the environment, and the system within which it works. Although this often is true of other groups, the relationship among the team, the task, and other systems is more likely to be critical to the team's functioning.

Putting all these factors together produces the following definition: *A team is a diverse group of people who share leadership responsibility for creating a group identity in an interconnected effort to achieve a mutually defined goal within the context of other groups and systems.*

To visualize this definition in simplified form, take a look at the model in Figure 1.1. To make this model clearer, we've assumed a team with only three mem-

FIGURE 1.1

Model of a three-member team using transactional and task processes to reach team goals

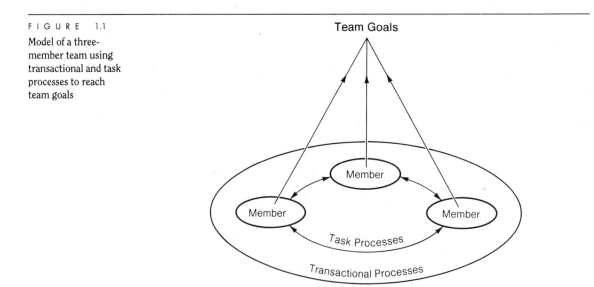

bers, although most have more than that. Each individual is focused on a goal that the members have set together. To reach that goal, the members communicate and work together through task and transactional processes, defined and discussed in the following section.

Task and Transactional Processes

These concepts are, essentially, what this book is about: they are the processes that make the relationships among people work, enabling them to achieve their goals. Task and transactional processes carry, develop, and focus on the give-and-take of communicating in task groups and teams.

Before we define the concepts, think about this example. A team is to design a policy recommendation for a new college center. Sean has brought in some statistics, gleaned from a local newspaper, that indicate college populations are shrinking. The team needs to decide (a) whether the statistics are valid and (b) whether they apply to the team's goal and, if so, how. That discussion moves through a task process.

The transactional process, however, determines the *way* members discuss it. And that affects the approach the team takes to analyzing the statistics, the thoroughness of the discussion, the amount of supportiveness or defensiveness the contributing member feels, and—for good or for ill—future transactions in the team's work. Suppose Rhonda says to Sean, "You want us to believe something printed in *that* rag?" and Todd says, "Sean, is that the best you can do?" and Sean comes back, "Hey, I don't see anybody else with data!" What then?

Although the topic of these comments is Sean's information and relates directly to the group's task, the messages carry other sets of implications about Sean and his competence—and he reacts to those by defending himself. The transactional processes, therefore, have made the task processes ineffective. Task processes are a specific, focused, interactive set of behaviors, but they work within the flow of transactional processes (see Figure 1.1).

Task processes are specific interactions that focus on the job at hand. These include gathering and sharing information; analyzing problems; designing solutions; analyzing and testing evidence and reasoning; making, implementing, and evaluating decisions. In task processes, the roles and functions of the members are focused on the work.

Transactional processes are give-and-take interactions that carry communication about three possible topics concurrently: messages about individuals, messages about the team, and messages about the task processes. In transactional processes, the members use verbal and nonverbal communication to develop the climate and identity that creates a team. Transactional processes that are positive make it possible for members to take the necessary risks in communication, to share information and ideas, to develop new ideas and approaches with others, to analyze ideas, to make decisions. Where transactional processes work poorly, the task processes are diverted by the tides of negative messages.

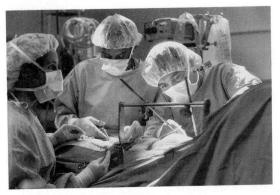

What characteristics of groups and teams do these three groups have in common? What are some differences? How do they reflect diversity in membership? In what ways would each group relate to a larger system? (*Photograph top left* © 1990 Barbara Alper/Stock, Boston; *top right* © 1991 Susie Fitzhugh/Stock, Boston; *bottom* © T. DelAmo/H. Armstrong Roberts.)

Traditionally, group theory talks about two kinds of one-way messages: group-maintenance and task-maintenance messages. These concepts are similar to transactional and task processes, but we prefer the idea of transactional processes as involving the interactive messages, feedback, and adaptations that members go through to establish meanings about themselves, their relationships to each other, and their tasks.

Transactional processes require leadership, role-taking, and communication skills of all members. At the same time, they make possible every interaction and accomplishment of the team.

Communication in Groups and Teams

If transactional processes make it possible to accomplish task processes, then communication makes it possible for transactional processes to work. Knowing how to communicate in a group is the foundation. **Communication** is *the process of using verbal and nonverbal cues to negotiate a mutually acceptable meaning between two or more people within a particular context and environment.*

Process suggests that understandings constantly develop and change through transactions. When people communicate they engage with a dynamic, moving set of variables that have been interacting and will continue to interact. If you had a fight at home, it colors your transactions in your team.

Verbal and nonverbal cues rely on the language and uses of voice, body, face, space, touch, and other personal cues. Sharing the same language does not ensure understanding, for each person has different connotations for even simple words and gestures. These may be cultural, subcultural, or just individual perspectives. You introduce yourself to a new member, looking her in the eye and touching her arm as you say, "I'm glad you've joined us—this is a really exciting project." To you that may be open and welcoming. But she may have been brought up to believe that direct eye contact and touching are invasions. To top it off, she may think the project is boring. Even though you speak to her in her language, the way you put the message and the way she "hears" it may be very different.

Negotiate a mutually acceptable meaning between two or more people indicates that communication is *not* the transfer of meaning or information from one person to another. Whatever an idea starts out as with one person is changed by the time it is perceived by the other. To negotiate, members give and take bits of meaning to and from the other until each believes the other understands enough of the original intent.

A particular context means that any communication is defined in terms of circumstances and situations. "How's the job going?" has a different meaning if you ask it of someone who just landed the first big job or of someone who suspects she or he will be fired soon.

Environment refers to the physical, social, and emotional conditions within which the communication occurs. "How's the job going?" is different in the physical setting of a crowded elevator or an intimate private office. Equally, the social and emotional climate affects the nuances of a message. It may be whispered out of the boss's earshot in a workplace that is permeated with distrust, or it may be shouted across the room in a workplace where openness and friendliness are the norms.

Take all of the communication variables and processes, visualize them compounded by numbers of people, and you have communication in a group. If you make a statement, there are as many possible interpretations as there are possible interactions between and among people in the group. Add to that the influence each other person in the group may have on a given individual's understanding of your message and you begin to see how very difficult sending and receiving clear and acceptable messages can be. A quantitative analysis of possible relationships in a group, starting with one relationship between two individuals, found that with seven people in the group there are 966 communication relationships (Kephart, 1950). Even these numbers do not convey the full complexity of the situation, however, because each individual in the group brings in and takes out information, opinions, attitudes, beliefs, values, and interpretations to and from other individuals and groups. The number of interactions among people and groups is truly incalculable.

Risk in Group and Team Communication

The concept of risk is critical to understanding all human communication, but particularly communication in groups and teams.

Communication often presents a dilemma between need and fear. One side of the dilemma is that human beings absolutely need to communicate for physical and emotional survival. The opposite side, however, is that when you communicate you take a risk. The risk may be very small, but it's there. "I have to tell her the meeting time's been changed. She's going to be mad at *me*." This dilemma may not present heavy consequences, but it is still a risk. Maybe you really hate being snapped at.

Sometimes, though, the risk is greater. A person who speaks up may risk rejection, ridicule, perhaps failure. You may want very much to speak up for what you believe in, but you fear the team will think you're silly—dumb—whatever. So you keep silent, or perhaps phrase your thoughts in vague, ambiguous terms; that way, if you feel the team is rejecting them, you can back off with minimal damage. That's one response to the dilemma.

In a group, the extent of the risk is compounded by the number of people and possible interpretations and interactions that can result from communication. If one person might reject your ideas, what might seven do? This personal dilemma becomes critically important to transactional and task processes because it may cause a person to censor what she or he should say. And what that person should say may be important.

This is a problem with groups: it is much too easy for members to talk themselves into ignoring moral or ethical issues or even into rationalizing immoral or unethical choices. If members, because they fear rejection or ridicule, are so afraid to address these issues that they keep silent—or, worse, pretend to agree with the majority—then the team may make mistakes the members will regret.

Understanding this dilemma, in yourself and in others, can help you in two ways: (1) to comprehend and have patience with the risky give-and-take process of negotiating a shared meaning, and (2) to ensure that transactional processes in your team enable people to think for themselves, take risks, and express their thoughts freely.

Systems and Subsystems

A team usually works within an organization and with other units—and this affects everything the team does. A good way to understand these effects is in terms of **systems theory**. It's easy to understand by using the analogy of a family.

Each member is his or her own intrapersonal system, a **subsystem** of the family. Each individual subsystem plays various roles in the family system. The mother or father may have primary responsibility for decision making, but other members may influence decisions and family interactions as well. The members are interdependent; they work for mutual goals; they support each other; they have conflicts and problems. The family has unwritten definitions of how relationships, responsibilities, power, and influence are conducted and by whom.

Outside of this family system are other systems and subsystems—other families, friends, schools, workplaces, community—to which members of the family relate. Influences to and from those other systems are carried by family members as they interact with other members of the family system.

Basically, that's what systems theory describes. Applied to a team, it shows us the system within the team, its relationships with other teams and systems, and its relationships with its parent organization and outside organizations.

These internal and external relationships are easier to understand in terms of the following six concepts:

Interrelationships and interdependency. A decision made within any part of a system may affect other parts of the system. If it is made without considering those relationships, the effect may be negative. If the Marketing Department, for example, distributes product samples without consulting the Production Department, the production people could be annoyed when inventory suddenly plummets without explanation.

Linking communication. The relationships among the subsystems are created and maintained by the communication flow. Without these connections, each unit functions as independent, not interdependent.

Open systems. Information, ideas, and influences flow into and out of the system. Efforts to keep it closed, or exclusive, only make it insensitive to its environment and insulated from information it needs. Closed-off systems often go awry and cannot be repaired. The consequences can be disastrous.

Norms. Accepted ways of doing things govern systems and subsystems. People live by norms as if they were rules: members of the system know when and how to behave and when and how to communicate because of the norms in the group. For example, if you invite a friend to visit your political task force, she or he may ask, "How should I dress?" You know the answer to the question, because you know how the group dresses. It's a norm.

Roles. Roles are ways of behaving or contributing that individual members play in the transactional processes and task processes of the team. Roles may be positive, facilitating behaviors, or they may be negative, blocking behaviors. The unit or subsystem also may have roles that it serves in the larger system.

Cybernetic processes. Feedback and assessment methods help open systems with their own development and improvement. A **cybernetic** process is like that used by a thermostat to assess whether the temperature is correct and, if not, to adjust it to the right level. It's different from simply reading the temperature, as a thermometer does. Another analogy might be receiving back a paper with only a grade on it as opposed to one that also has comments and suggestions for improving the next one. The grade is a thermometer; the comments are the cybernetic thermostat—that is, of course, if you use the information for improvement.

A Team Processes Model

Remember the model of a team we showed you (Figure 1.1)? How that team acts as a subsystem of a larger system is illustrated in Figure 1.2.

The three cone-shaped figures represent separate teams within an organization (remember each team consists of members using transactional and task processes to reach a mutual goal). Each team has a goal that works toward the vision of the parent organization, and it functions within the organizational culture. As the arrows in and out of the teams indicate, they communicate back and forth with one another and with their parent organization.

The arrows to and from government, community, other organizations, and people indicate the influence that flows constantly back and forth between outside systems, the teams, and the parent organization. Any given organization may have many teams, interacting with departments, management, and numerous outside systems. You can see how important communication can be to making all that teamwork effective.

FIGURE 1.2

Model of teams as subsystems interacting with the larger system and with other systems and subsystems

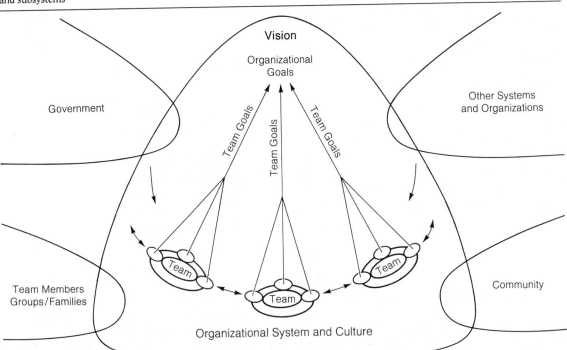

Preparing for Teamwork

This chapter has introduced you to concepts of groups and teams that are essential to understanding this course. Now it's time to get started on your actual work. If you skipped reading the preface, please go back and read the sections outlining the philosophical and learning premises of this book and its main features, including the exercises, case studies, and special boxes that are included. This overview will make it easier and more productive for you to use the book.

With that bit of homework done, it's time to get started on your group experiences in this class. The key to success, early on, is to start thinking about transactional and task processes. Those processes begin the moment you and your teammates first sit down together. Here are some specific hints for getting started:

1. Be interested in each other.
   ■ Get acquainted.
   ■ Find areas of compatibility and interest.
2. Take time to figure out what the group is to do.
   ■ Is there a task or a goal?
   ■ Do you know what the learning objectives are?
   ■ Or will you discover the learning objectives from the experience?
3. Plan a systematic approach to reaching your goal.
   ■ Estimate how much time you will need.
   ■ Decide what steps you will take.
4. Plan ahead if the assignment will take more than one meeting.
   ■ Exchange telephone numbers and schedules.
   ■ Assign work among members.
   ■ Set next meeting time and place.
5. Help each other to meet your goals.
   ■ Fulfill your personal responsibility.
   ■ Be on time, prepare materials, share ideas.
   ■ Support each other in the work.

As you can see from this checklist, creating a good team starts with goodwill and common sense. Developing your team and achieving your task, complicated as some of the processes may be, depend mostly on more goodwill and common sense. Keep that in mind, and you'll succeed.

Summary

In your private life and in your work, you will participate in group and team communication. Your experiences, personal preferences, characteristics, culture, and gender all may affect how you feel about working with others. Although groups can involve frustration and conflict, commitment of resources, and pressure to conform (possibly to unethical and harmful positions), they can also have enormous advantages.

You may work in a wide variety of groups and teams. The power of teamwork is that it takes advantage of the diversity of group members to develop creativity and exploration, encourage logical and ethical examination of questions, and achieve good solutions with high member involvement, group identity, and commitment. Trends in the workplace emphasize teamwork because organizations know that participatory-management and cooperative groups can achieve better quality, maximize the participation of diverse members, and lead to greater employee satisfaction and commitment.

Key concepts to understand include how groups and teams involve interdependency, interaction, mutual influence, and mutual goals, and how teams develop more intensive goal orientation and image. You need

to know how task processes (which convey messages about the work) are carried by transactional processes (messages about individuals and the team). Working in a team requires that you understand communication as a necessary, risky, dynamic process involving the perspectives of individuals and their verbal and nonverbal skills in complicated contextual and environmental situations. Because risk of rejection can keep people from discussing important ethical issues, transactional processes must keep discussion open. You also need to understand the team as a system within, interacting and interdependent with, other systems.

Exercises

1. Think of the best and worst groups you've ever experienced (work, school, church, sports, etc.) and rate the best and the worst on Form 1.1. With a few other students, discuss what characteristics you found in common that distinguish "best" and "worst" groups. Together, create a list of five to ten

---

CASE ANALYSIS 1.1

On August 1, 1990, the McDonald's Corporation and the Environmental Defense Fund (EDF) joined forces in a unique collaborative project. In this effort, the nation's largest quick-service restaurant and one of America's leading environmental research and advocacy organizations worked together to find ways to reduce McDonald's solid waste.

(From the final report, McDonald's Corporation/Environmental Defense Fund Waste Reduction Task Force, April 1991, p. i. All case study materials from Environmental Defense Fund/McDonald's Corporation Waste Reduction Task Force are used with permission from Environmental Defense Fund.)

The work of forming this task force actually began in July 1989, when EDF proposed to McDonald's that they meet to discuss its materials and packaging and its solid waste disposal. McDonald's had a commitment to reducing its packaging and waste disposal; EDF had scientific expertise and a mission to make an impact. Fred Krupp, executive director of EDF, met with Ed Rensi, McDonald's U.S.A. president. Staff-level meetings followed, leading to a proposal to create the task force.

The agreement forming the joint task force provided a charge and objectives. It set parameters for the work that "would allow both sides to maintain their flexibility, independence, and credibility," including provisions that each would pay its own members' expenses and that McDonald's would not use the relationship in its marketing. Also, either side could end the relationship at any time.

A *Chicago Tribune* editorial headlined the task force announcement the "environmental odd couple" and pointed out that "both have a lot at risk." McDonald's opened itself to an unprecedented level of scrutiny by an outside,

Leadership and Responsibility: Influencing Your Teams

"I'm not a leader—I'm a follower!"
Wrong. You have a leadership role, even when you are not "the leader."

You may not be the designated leader. You may not want to be. Yet you have personal responsibility for providing leadership to your team.

Imagine this: you are on a jury that must decide an accused person's guilt or innocence. The foreman and two others loudly assert the guilt of the accused. You are disturbed by the leader's "railroading," and you believe some of the evidence was biased. Yet because you are not the leader, you raise neither of these issues. No one else raises them, either. You all go along with what you assume is the majority view. A possibly innocent person is convicted —not because the jury fully agreed on the verdict, but because the members did not exert their leadership to make sure the process was just.

An extreme example? Yes. Can it happen? Yes. That's why this chapter is so important. It lays the foundation for leadership—leadership that can avert disappointment, frustration, or even guilt from bad team experiences and wrong decisions. You, as a good team member, can gain the understanding and skills to help a team move through work and ethical decisions with credibility and confidence.

Developing that foundation starts with knowing the differences between being the leader and leadership and recognizing how your leadership affects you and your team. Leadership develops as you focus on your responsibilities to integrate ethical principles in team processes and decisions and as you consciously practice the necessary skills.

Through your work in this chapter, you will enhance your ability to:

1. Perceive team leadership as your responsibility.

2. Understand how your leadership affects your success and that of your team.

3. See how your leadership helps your team with transactional and task processes.

4. Identify and adapt roles for better leadership.

5. Use your leadership to ensure ethical group processes and decisions.

6. Understand how your leadership is related to your credibility.

7. Start developing your credibility, your confidence, and your leadership effectiveness.

What Leadership Means

Leadership is a central focus of this book. We're going to explain why in terms of (1) the differences between leadership and being the leader and (2) your responsibilities as a team member.

Leadership versus "Being the Leader"

Let's begin by clarifying the differences between providing "leadership" and "being the leader." The first is a set of behaviors; the second is a position. One must be developed and exercised; the other can be elected or conferred. One implies responsibility and influence; the other may rest on some degree of status and power.

Designated leaders should, of course, carry the qualifications of both "leader" and "leadership." Sometimes they do; sometimes they don't. Even when the designated leader provides strong leadership, that alone is not enough for a team to function well. Certainly, when you have confidence in the leader and the team, you engage actively in helping to reach team goals. When you simply "follow" a leader because of his or her position, however, you may abdicate responsibility for what happens. That can lead to stupid, sometimes harmful, decisions and actions. Businesses and bureaucracies often initiate time-wasting and people-frustrating policies because no one dares point out weaknesses when policies are proposed. Followers do what "Simon says." At a far more deadly level, lynch mobs and riots occur when forceful leaders emerge to exploit people's baser motives and their inclinations to follow mindlessly.

To prevent such consequences, every member of a group or a team must be responsible for what happens—for both members' interactions and group decisions. What, then, do we mean by leadership?

Leadership is *verbal and nonverbal communication behavior that influences a team's transactional and task processes in achieving members' and the team's needs and goals.* This definition recognizes that communication is the means by which leadership is exercised; that transactional and task processes are the means by which needs and goals are met; and that both individual members' interests and team interests are important.

Leadership and Responsibility

To influence someone or something is to provide motivation, direction, orientation; it can cause change, modify attitudes, or affect actions. Leadership, as we use the term, assumes the ability and right of each individual to think and to make choices. It also assumes responsibility. In a team situation, mutual respect and influence among members should create the best possible transformation of individual responses into team choices and actions. Thus, each person on a team has the *responsibility* to share leadership, to affect actively the thinking of others, and to have an impact on the team's processes and outcomes.

The concept of shared leadership is not new. Back in 1948, Benne and Sheats saw "the leadership role in terms of functions to be performed within a group in helping that group to grow and to work productively. No sharp distinction," they wrote, "can be made between leadership and membership functions, between leader and member roles" (p. 41). In 1976, Potter and Andersen defined effective group communication as "the systematic, purposeful, primarily oral exchange of ideas, facts, and opinions by a group of persons who *share in the group's leadership* [emphasis added]" (p. 1).

In the 1990s, we know that leadership is every individual's responsibility because group communication is complex, because one leader cannot see or do everything that needs to be done, and because members rely on one another in working toward their goals. Dennis Gouran (1982) pointed out that many individuals must provide leadership to counteract problems that block a group as it works along the path toward its goal. When such leadership is absent, groups often make bad decisions and take harmful actions (p. 148). That's why your leadership counts.

Leadership and You

Your leadership is important to you, personally. It's important in your short-term success with your team; it's also important to your long-term success in your life and career.

Short-Term Success

In the short term, you may simply want to get through a project as efficiently and smoothly as possible. If you take responsibility for making sure the team works effectively, you will avoid frustration. You also will gain satisfaction from being part of a mutually supportive, creatively functioning team that gets results.

One of our students, irritated with teammates who were not doing their job, said, "I used to think I was a follower. From now on, I'm using my own leadership so I don't have to go through this frustration any more." After she made that decision, her team improved, the project turned out well, and her grade was an "A."

When your team wins, you win. Almost any work group serves some larger organization or the community, so your team may have at least three sets of goals. Some of those serve the larger interests of the organization; some serve the group itself; some serve you, personally.

For example, if you are part of a creative team designing an advertising campaign, your client's goal is, obviously, to sell the product. Your team, as part of an agency, shares the client's goal and, further, would like to impress other clients through this campaign's success. Each team member has personal goals to make the client and the agency happy and, by so doing, to further his or her career, to get a raise, to increase self-esteem, and possibly to reach many other goals. When you share the team's leadership, your influence can help to achieve all levels of success.

Long-Term Success

In the long term, you build a foundation for your future effectiveness in teams and career opportunities. Almost every request for a letter of recommendation we, as faculty, receive includes a space for evaluating the "leadership skills," "interpersonal skills," and "communication skills" of the applicant. Although corporations, businesses, service institutions, and graduate schools are interested in any activity in which you actually served as the leader, that isn't what they mean by "leadership skills."

People who might hire you or admit you to their graduate program are looking for a leadership orientation—for motivation, thinking, and communicating skills that you can offer. Ironically, your entry-level career position may give you little opportunity to exercise those skills, but they become apparent in how you work with others, how you problem-solve, how you take responsibility. When you demonstrate these skills, you are marked for advancement and opportunity.

The working world emphasizes leadership so much that many organizations put potential managers into simulated team situations and observe how they perform. A candidate's leadership thus becomes a key to advancement.

Leadership and Teamwork

As you share the team's leadership, you have to be able to do several things at once. You need to understand the roles people fill in groups; be able to facilitate task and transactional processes; and overcome obstacles to leadership.

Roles People Play

You play **roles** all the time, of course. A person plays a role by behaving in specific ways that seem to distinguish his or her function or character in a situation. People have definitions, often unconscious, of how to behave as "wife," "husband," "son," "daughter," "student," "teacher." Sometimes they have character roles: "I'm a comedian," "I'm a helper." People also have role definitions of how they behave in groups. These roles may overlap. For example, a "life of the party" person may take a distracting role in a work team. An individual who is in the habit of being "the boss" may take a dominating role in a group. Perhaps an individual who thinks of herself or himself as a "parent" carries that role into the team and nurtures everybody else to death.

Individuals' ideas of their individual roles are, however, only part of the story. Many roles serve task or transactional needs. Some are obvious: "She took the role of leader." "He was the secretary." In this sense, a role is a job or a function that an individual fills, formally or informally.

Some roles are more process-oriented than job-specific: they simply influence the transactions among the members. One leadership skill is recognizing needs and being able to adapt your role to meet those needs. Another is helping others to switch their roles to eliminate problems and facilitate processes. These skills require you to be able to identify various role options.

Traditionally, role definitions are divided into three groups: those that serve "group building and maintenance," "group task," and "individual" needs. Group-building roles, focusing on feelings and harmony, include: the encourager, harmonizer, compromiser, gatekeeper and expediter, standard-setter, group observer/commentator, and follower (Benne & Sheats, 1948). Although these roles were defined long ago, today's students have identified similar leadership behaviors (Pavitt & Sackaroff, 1990) in encouraging participation, harmony, and discussion, as well as in managing conflict.

Task roles focus on doing the job. They include: initiator/contributor, information-seeker, opinion-seeker, information-giver, opinion-giver, elaborator, coordinator, orienter, evaluator/critic, energizer, procedural technician, and recorder (Benne & Sheats, 1948). Today's students, right on track, identified stating the group's procedure, summarizing, keeping the discussion organized, and playing devil's advocate as leadership behaviors (Pavitt & Sackaroff, 1990).

Some roles, however, are not part of leadership. These individual roles, played at the expense of the group, include: aggressor, blocker, recognition-seeker, self-confessor, fun-seeker, dominator, help-seeker, and special-interest pleader (Benne & Sheats, 1948).

If you think about groups you've seen in action—even informal groups of friends—you will recognize people you know in some of these roles. One person may consistently be the compromiser or the harmonizer. Another may serve so regularly as information-giver that everyone counts on him or her for that function. Yet another may invariably take up everyone else's time with personal problems, or repeatedly block the group's progress for some undisclosed agenda.

Perhaps the most useful aspect of these role definitions is that they can help you to diagnose a group situation. At the end of this chapter, you'll find a condensed list of these roles, with definitions, and an observation form to use in analyzing a meeting. You may want to observe a small group and use those categories to identify the roles each person plays.

Team Processes

You may have noticed that "group building and maintenance" and "group task" roles are related to transactional and task processes. That is, the roles reflect individual behaviors that influence the two types of processes. But those processes are much more dynamic and interdependent than you would think if you looked exclusively at the roles people play in them.

A given transaction, for example, may carry a message about the task; but it may also confirm or disconfirm an individual and, thereby, build or diminish the team. Suppose a member says, "I found these incredible statistics . . . " and another says, "Doesn't anybody ever look at whether statistics are valid or not?" Although the statement is related to the task, the slam is directed to the individual—and both the individual and the team are hurt. Transactional processes are carried on within, through, and around task processes.

It may seem that transactional processes take time away from getting the task done; but you can't accomplish the goal without the processes. If transactions involve individual roles and they upset or alienate people, that interferes with pursuing the task; if transactions help people to feel excited about their teamwork, that advances the task. If the task is frustrating and seems unattainable, transactions among people reflect that pain; if the task is exciting and achievement is high, transactions are easier and more rewarding. It's up to every person to provide the kind of leadership that enables the group to have positive transactional *and* task processes.

Transactional Processes   Transactional processes carry the task processes by working through the communication, negotiations, and understandings among the team's members. When transactional processes work well, they develop a climate in which group-building and task functions can be served, in which individual and team needs are met, and in which problems created by individual roles can be handled in such a way that they do not damage the team's effectiveness.

Your leadership in moving transactional processes along depends on your being intensely involved and highly committed to the team process and, at the same time, able to see the interactions from enough distance to know what needs to be done. That sounds difficult, and it is challenging, but it is a skill that you can develop. We'll work on the necessary verbal, nonverbal, and listening skills in later chapters, but the following list gives you a start on how to use your leadership in transactional processes.

Suggest and encourage positive norms. Establish an expectation of openness, mutual concern, cooperation, and responsibility. Openly state your preference for this climate and ask for agreement from other members.

Encourage the involvement of each member. Ask for information, ideas, opinions, and feelings; support others with agreement or open questions; confirm the worth of others through your verbal, nonverbal, and listening communication.

Encourage trust and openness. Take a few risks and disclose a little about yourself. You can state norms for confidentiality, expect it, and protect confidentiality and support for others.

Help manage conflicts. When conflicts arise, remind the team that conflict is normal; recognize that it can be helpful; stay objective; find ways to support negotiation and compromise.

Make connections. Help people to support each other; look for things they have in common, state your appreciation for others' contributions. Encourage open-mindedness and interest in others' points of view.

Create a sense of "teamness." Orient members toward mutual goals; support team process; discuss the ways in which the team works and comment on what it does well; suggest positive ways to assess and improve the quality of teamwork.

Work actively to deal with team stress. Acknowledge stressful situations; help to diagnose causes of stress and find ways to relieve it; use humor, "time-out," and negotiation to ease conditions.

Task Processes   Task processes focus specifically on the job at hand. Transactions that produce information, cooperative analysis, critical and creative thinking, problem solving, decision making, and task achievement are part of these processes.

In an effectively functioning team, task processes are characterized by the use of an appropriate agreed-upon structure, by flexibility and adaptability, and by clarity of goals and objectives. The team has the commitment and ability to acquire and use necessary information and resources, and it maintains a norm of openness to creativity and critical analysis. Members use a variety of problem analysis and decision-making approaches, and they constantly evaluate and re-evaluate their progress.

To make such a process work, every member must provide leadership through specific behaviors. The following guidelines will help you get your team started on solid task processes:

Orient the team toward task processes. When attention wanders, call it back. Summarize what's been done, suggest next steps, check to see if people agree before moving on.

Be sure meetings are organized. Suggest and confirm meeting arrangements, agendas, records, and assignments. Remind people when the discussion gets too far off track.

Discuss and confirm team goals. State goals for the team and ask for confirmation that everyone agrees with them.

Identify what the team needs for its work. Suggest that the team consider needs for information and resources and propose ways to get what's needed.

Help the team to divide the work. Guide discussion of expertise, information needs, and interests; suggest ways to divide up research and other outside work.

Make sure information is shared. Request, summarize, review, and analyze information; ask for others' analyses and opinions, too.

Provide information and ideas. Take responsibility, get good information, and bring it to the team with clear explanations.

Contribute creativity and critical thinking. Help others to get ideas, ask questions, and make suggestions. Use your analysis to evaluate logic, reasoning, and proposed solutions.

Test conclusions for ethicality. Ask questions that stimulate thinking about the ethics of team considerations and decisions. Examine the value and acceptability of suggestions, decisions, and actions.

Obstacles to Leadership

It may be up to every person to provide leadership, but we all know that it doesn't necessarily happen that way. Some members may sit there, virtually silent, and do nothing to guide or encourage the development of a team. You may have done that yourself at some time.

Although a few of the silent ones may simply be uninvolved, uncommitted, and uncaring, many are probably none of these things. Often people are blocked by obstacles to their participation.

When any member is excluded, or excludes herself or himself, the team loses. It loses information, ideas, insight, analysis; it loses a point of view. A team *needs* every member. You can exercise leadership by recognizing and overcoming obstacles that may stand in the way of your own or other people's participation.

Recognizing Obstacles   People are often blocked by other members' perceptions—and/or their own perceptions—of who they are and what roles they should play. These perceptions stereotype, label, and put people into boxes—and it's hard to exercise leadership from a box. Some common pigeonholes are:

The shy box. Shy people may be thought to be uninterested, or dull. They may be able to provide good leadership, but nobody makes an effort to find out.

The point-of-view box. This encloses someone whose political, religious, or professional point of view is in the minority. Others just ignore or put down the individual until she or he remains silent.

The different box. This one is reserved for people whose race, culture, or ethnic traditions are different from others'. Majority members may not even consider that a "different" individual could provide some leadership.

The too-much-effort box. If it takes a little extra effort to communicate with someone who's disabled, for example, or who speaks with an accent, members often won't bother.

"Well, gentlemen, since we all seem to agree . . ."

The gender box. Despite recent changes, it's still harder for women to provide leadership no matter how much they have to offer. In fact, when men are in the group, some women of high leadership ability often fail to assert their leadership roles (Carbonell, 1984).

The disapproval box. A group may cut off leadership from a person because he or she lives a different lifestyle. Even if the group is open and receptive, some people (gay or lesbian, orthodox religious, punk rockers—anyone whose lifestyle is a little off the norm) may withdraw because previous experiences have made them fear stereotyping and labeling.

Please note that none of this assumes there is anything wrong with the person who is boxed in. Nor does it assume you have to approve of or like everyone in a group. What it does assume is that every member may be able to contribute something important, no matter who or what she or he is. One of your leadership responsibilities is to help overcome these obstacles—for yourself or for others.

Overcoming Obstacles   People erect these obstacles to leadership, consciously or unconsciously, because their stereotypes and expectations are deep-rooted. Someone—either the boxed-in member or another person—has to do something. Some possible approaches are:

Confront the obstacle. Confrontation can be tough. It takes tact, determination, and guts to work through an issue like this one, but sometimes it's the only way. (We talk about conflict management and confrontation in Chapter 13.)

Persuade the group. Call attention to the norms of the group, discuss them, and suggest ways of changing them. You may want to talk to members outside of the meetings, getting their cooperation in changing norms and attitudes that exclude an individual.

Act as a mentor. Help the restricted member connect with the group. Encourage, coach, and help the person to understand the team and how it works. Others may follow your example. The individual will become more confident and credible as she or he contributes, a bit at a time.

Ethics and Leadership

From the moment a team is formed, from the first words you exchange, you are invested in the team and its outcomes. It's an investment of self and of conscience. Your **ethics** are involved. Ethical issues, according to Johannesen (1992), "focus on value judgments concerning right and wrong, goodness and badness, in human conduct" (p. 30). Choosing between right and wrong can be difficult, however, particularly with a group of people.

As effective as a really good team can be, by its very nature a mix of people has in it areas of quicksand. In fact, the realities of group communication can make it compelling to follow ideas or actions that an individual probably would not accept alone. The enthusiasm of others, the sense of being part of something beyond oneself, and the pressure to conform can sometimes separate people from personal responsibility and conscience.

Philosophers since Plato have probed the implications of one person's influence upon another, and communication has long been examined for the ethical questions it involves (see, for example, Arnett, 1987). Weaver (see Johannesen, 1990, pp. 4–5) has suggested that language is "sermonic"; that is, whenever you speak, your language is chosen to influence, to persuade, to instruct another person. You make internal right-wrong choices about what you will say and how you will say it. ("Is it truthful if I say it this way? But will it have the effect I want?") In a dialogue, more choices among ideas or phrasing evolve as the other person addresses his or her sermonic language to you.

Team processes involve making choices—individual choices and group choices. When leadership guides analysis of those decisions to include ethical concerns, all members stay on more solid ground. The old expression, "If you don't stand for something you'll fall for anything," applies to groups as well as individuals. It's complicated in a group because ethical questions highlight differences among group members—differences in likes and dislikes, values and priorities. Brown (1990) has summarized the problem as follows: "Discovering value judgments and evaluating them can create sharp disagreements in groups. Perhaps that is one reason people ignore value judgments as much as they do. In any case, for ethical analysis to really work in organizations, we need to learn how to handle disagreements" (p. 4).

It takes guts to speak out against the majority, even when you think the majority is wrong. It takes tolerance and understanding to try to comprehend another's point of view. It takes patience to handle the disagreements that ethical analysis creates. That's why it takes excellent leadership to ensure that you and all other team members understand ethical obligations and how to fulfill them.

In order to fulfill those obligations, you need to identify ethical dilemmas and conflicts and to protect the ethics of individuals, team processes, and team decisions.

Ethical Dilemmas and Conflicts

Not all choices have ethical consequences. Whether a report has a blue or green cover may involve conflicts over preferences, but not necessarily over values. But what if you must choose between including information in the report that advances a worthy cause but is not quite accurate, or information that is accurate but does not support the cause?

Toffler (1986, p. 20) makes an important distinction: an *ethical issue* is one that can be considered in abstract, right-or-wrong, good-or-bad terms; an **ethical dilemma** is a situation in which we must apply standards and make decisions between two real choices. Those choices, even for an individual, may present a dilemma between conflicting needs, desires, and ethical criteria. For a team, they may present multiple dilemmas among individual and team ethics.

Teammates may conflict over distinctly different values, deeply held within their respective cultures. Such differences can be extreme. What does a team do—what do you do—when ethical positions conflict? Suppose you must choose between two alternatives, neither of which meets your ethical standards? Or either of which meets some standards, but not others?

Hackman and Johnson (1991) point out that "standards vary from culture to culture, but the dilemma of establishing the measure of right and wrong remains constant" (p. 282). To recognize and solve a team's ethical dilemmas entails raising questions of right and wrong, good and bad; it requires discussing the implications and consequences of an action in terms of how they affect the team, the task, and others on the outside. You have to strip away the emotional language, focus on the issues, and allow others to have their perspective at the same time that you defend your own.

Say you're a member of a campus group that can get access to the answers on an exam. Those answers would give members a definite edge in passing the class with good grades. Some members, including you, oppose cheating; they don't want to compromise their ethics, and they don't want their group to, either. Other members justify it by pointing out that the professor is unfair anyway, and getting the answers will just equalize the situation. Still others can't imagine what the big deal is; they don't even think of it as cheating.

What do you do? You lay the cards on the table; you discuss the issues; you listen; you learn to understand where the others are coming from; you try to persuade them. In the end, you may have helped to forge a team with an ethic that includes honesty. You will have learned something about how others think, and you may have managed to teach them something, too.

But what if the majority still favors cheating? Do you necessarily accept their decision? Do you cheat? Do you refuse to cheat, but still remain a member of the group? Do you leave the group in protest? It depends. You'll make those decisions based on your own strength of character; the group's importance to you; the degree to which you share its other values; and whether you hope to help the group evolve ethical standards more acceptable to you.

Jaksa and Pritchard (1988) make what is, to us, a very important point: you can tolerate disagreement without giving up your own standards. "Tolerating differences of choice and refraining from automatically labeling opposite choices as immoral are essential. At the same time, seeking exact points of difference can help solve disagreements by eliminating false distinctions and evasions" (p. 9).

Some people fear that listening to and respecting differences in values and ethics means that they must take a relativistic point of view—that they can never take a stand. Jaksa and Pritchard (1988) point out that people can be nonrelative—that is, they can believe that something is right or wrong, good or bad—and still be tolerant, still see shades of gray in issues, and still have respect for others' beliefs and ways (pp. 11–13).

Ethical Issues for Teams

If making choices with ethical implications is so much a part of a team's work, then understanding and analyzing ethics are incredibly important to team processes and outcomes. The reasoning is as follows:

1. Teams are made up of individuals, each of whom applies his or her own moral/ ethical standards to making choices and interacting with other people.
2. Communication choices and interactions involve ethical questions of good and bad, right and wrong.
3. In a team, individuals interact and influence each other to make many group choices and decisions.
4. The ethical systems and standards of individuals, used to assess and determine team choices and decisions, frequently come into conflict.
5. Ethical/moral/value questions can be ignored or overlooked in the midst of transactional and task processes.
6. Individuals can lose sight of or abandon ethical standards under pressure in group processes.
7. Unethical decisions can be made or unworthy actions taken in the name of the team.

Ethical concerns of groups, then, involve making mutual choices amid differing morals and standards—choices about sources of information and quality of analysis; choices about the transactional processes of the group; choices about the impacts of decisions; and choices about the freedom of each member to dissent. The list is endless.

With all those choices, it is possible to override or distort ethical decisions. There also is the possibility of exerting superior analysis and making better ethical decisions because shared leadership examines issues from a wider perspective, bringing to bear more points of view than one individual could.

As a team member, you have three broad sets of leadership responsibilities for dealing with ethical choices and dilemmas. One is to protect your personal standards; the second is to develop an ethic of team processes; and the third is to guard the ethics of team decisions and outcomes.

Personal Standards   It's difficult enough to make decisions that affect you alone. When you work with a group, it's all too easy to be pushed in directions you would not choose, so it's important to think about what your ethics are, to get a perspective on how they influence you.

The *standards*, or criteria, you apply to making your own choices are complicated; they relate to your value system, to learnings from your earliest childhood. Some of them you know consciously and could write as a list; some are unconscious assumptions about the way things should be.

Standards may be clear moral rules: tell the truth, be fair, don't cheat. Others may be ethical guidelines for how you behave and make choices: always do your best, be positive, be kind; perhaps, be smart, win, be the best.

People get their ethical standards from a variety of sources. Religions teach perspectives on life and moral "thou shalts" and "thou shalt nots." Families and cultures, through examples and norms, teach their ways of doing things. Even subcultural or professional groups develop rules and codes of honor that distinguish their particular images. Any or all of these may influence how you approach your ethical choices.

These influences help mold a person's ethical point of view—the perspective from which he or she makes ethical judgments. There are many ways to describe points of view. We will look at three that are most important to teamwork: legalistic, situational, and philosophical.

The *legalistic view* uses some code or set of rules as the basis for decision making. In this view, if it isn't illegal, it isn't unethical; if it isn't legal, then it is unethical. Legalistic views may be based on statutory law, on a religion, or on a code of ethics. The American Bar Association, the Public Relations Society of America, the American Association of Advertisers, the Speech Communication Association—each has a code of ethics formulated by its members.

Laws and rules are essential to a society, but they are not sufficient for ethical choices. The problem with relying exclusively on a legalistic point of view is that it assumes that all ethical issues are included and that the law is inevitably right. Such a position legally kept African-Americans as second-class citizens until Martin Luther King, Jr., argued effectively that our body of laws included some that were "just" and others that were "unjust." He established clear criteria to identify which was which, and proposed that just laws should be obeyed, but that unjust laws should be broken. Conscience finally overcame the irrational rationalization of law.

The *situational view* is ad hoc: every ethical question is weighed in terms of the context and the situation. A number of viewpoints may come into play. For example, a member of a communication training team was asked to provide stress management training for a cosmetic company's customer relations representatives, who were under fire from animal rights activists because the firm tested products on animals. The trainer, though not an activist, believed that unnecessary animal testing was wrong. Although neither her religion nor the law would have prevented her from providing the training, her personal ethical standards created a dilemma. She was sympathetic toward the stressed representatives and wanted to help; but she would also have been helping a corporation she believed was cruel to helpless animals. She and the team decided to put the issue up front with the company and, after examining the situation, decided to forego the contract.

The situation might have been much more difficult had she desperately needed the income. Would she still have foregone the opportunity? Situational ethics are not considered in a vacuum; they are considered in terms of real situations and issues. The more complicated the circumstances, the more difficult are the decisions.

The *philosophical view* may draw from a person's religious, cultural, family, political, professional, and life experiences. It rests on assumptions about human beings, about their position in the universe, about governments, about God. Often, these sources are intertwined in the ethical structure of a society.

The philosophies of the men who drafted the U.S. Constitution and the Bill of Rights, for example, influenced the content of those documents. Their assumptions then influenced the development of the American political system. That system, in turn, influences the assumptions that Americans make about what is right or wrong in political decisions, and also in personal decisions.

The consequence is a society in which people can take diametrically opposed positions that are ethically right to them, along with a social imperative to discuss, evaluate, and decide on best alternatives for the society as a whole. We cannot, it seems, get away from the philosophical point (or points) of view in ethical decision making.

Processes   Ethical questions are easy to see in task processes, such as using good data and making correct decisions. They are equally important in transactional processes, but perhaps even more complex. Transactional processes involve standards—moral choices about how people treat one another, about how they help one another to communicate, to learn, to develop, to be a team. Only through those processes are the ethics of task processes and decision making made possible.

Our philosophical point of view is described by Johannesen (1992) as a dialogical perspective on communication. This approach is especially important to ethical processes in groups. Think of dialogue in contrast to monologue. Monologue occurs when a person's communication is centered on himself or herself as the

AN ETHICAL DILEMMA

When the *Village Voice* was offered a free-lance article last month that purported to expose the homosexuality of a high Pentagon official, editors of the radical New York City weekly decided to reject the piece as an unwarranted invasion of privacy. Last week the same editors permitted a *Voice* columnist to summarize the allegations, complete with the official's name. The rationale for the turnaround: the man's identity had been so widely circulated by other news organizations that continued restraint would have been "a futile exercise."

But at the Washington *Post*, editors chose to cover the controversy without citing the official by name. Explained Karen DeYoung, the *Post*'s assistant managing editor for national news: "Our policy is that we don't write about personal lives of public officials unless the personal aspects begin influencing the way they perform their jobs." The paper canceled a Jack Anderson column, normally a featured item, because it named the man, even though editors assumed many of Anderson's 700-plus clients would run the story, making the *Post*'s discretion largely symbolic.

The hottest ethical issue for journalists these days is where to draw the line between two colliding rights, the individual's right to privacy and the public's right to know—and then, having drawn the line, how to avoid being pulled across it by cunning manipulators or by the competitive urge on a breaking story.

Excerpt from W. A. Henry III, "To 'Out' or Not to 'Out': The press wrestles with a thorny issue—When is it appropriate to reveal the private lives of public officials?" *Time*, August 19, 1991, p. 17. Copyright 1991 The Time Inc. Magazine Company. Reprinted by permission.

giver, but not receiver, of ideas. Dialogue involves commitment, give-and-take, listening, and negotiating new meanings between and among people.

This view considers the attitudes of people toward each other in dialogue "as an index of the ethical level of that communication. Some attitudes are held to be more fully human, humane, and facilitative of personal self-fulfillment than are other attitudes" (p. 35).

A dialogical ethic creates a climate in which people are enabled to be authentic about who they are; to include and confirm the worth of others; to be "present" (accessible and attentive); and to share a spirit of mutual equality (Johannesen, 1990, pp. 62–64). The dialogical view describes the values and assumptions teams must integrate when they establish their ethics for team processes. Brown (1990) points out that when teams evaluate information or ideas, "members must know that their views will be taken seriously and that the analysis will focus on the strengths and weaknesses of their arguments rather than on their character. For differences to become productive, participants . . . need to become mutually engaged in an open inquiry into the materials that all members contribute to the discussion" (p. 7).

In a team with this ethical perspective, everyone has equal responsibility. Members act in ways that fulfill that responsibility, and encourage others to do the same. Each member believes in the rights and worth of every other member, and works for the best results for every member and the team as a whole. The team rejects the concept that any individual must win points or triumph at the expense of others, but values each member for his or her unique qualities; members listen to and encourage one another to share those qualities. It takes every member's leadership to create and maintain this dialogical ethic of team process, thereby enabling the team to make ethical choices and decisions about its task.

As you work in a team, you can assess your processes by asking some questions suggested by Gouran (1982):

1. Did we show proper concern for those whom our decision, if enacted, will affect?
2. Did we explore the discussion question as responsibly as we were capable of doing?
3. Did we misrepresent any position or misuse any source of information?
4. Did we say or do anything that may have unnecessarily affected any participant's sense of self-worth?
5. Was everyone in the group shown the respect due him or her? (p. 227)

We will talk more about these attitudes throughout the book; for now, we hope you'll think of them as guidelines for how your team conducts its transactions and accomplishes tasks together.

Team Decisions   Throughout this section we've talked about how important ethics are to the decisions your team makes. Behind every decision are many choices—small and large—that may have ethical implications. Those choices may be important to the individual, to the team, and/or to someone on the outside. A team needs to know what criteria it will bring to bear on those dilemmas.

It may seem fairly simple to know what your team's ethical criteria are. People frequently assume that others' ethics are the same as theirs. Not so. Each individual brings his or her set of ethical assumptions and guidelines.

To recognize and solve a team's ethical dilemmas suggests raising questions of right and wrong, good and bad; it requires discussing the implications and consequences of an action in terms of how they affect the team, the task, and others on the outside.

Say you are on a creative team working on a television sitcom episode. Suppose the team decides to go with a dialogue that uses a racial stereotype for humor. The "bit" will affect the self-perceptions of members of that race and other-perceptions of members of other races. We believe that would be an ethically indefensible choice, even though the bit may have been good for a laugh.

But what if the team has decided that its highest priority is profit, and this will be profitable? Perhaps your team uses a purely legalistic ethic: if it isn't against the law, it's okay. Maybe, with that criterion, the team won't even mind the public protests that follow.

Still, team members each have some religious, social, and/or cultural system of ethics. Some may include criteria as to how you treat other human beings. Someone's standards may be in conflict with a code that permits the team to go with a stereotyping, dehumanizing episode. Your leadership could influence your team to examine the dilemma and, we hope, find it cannot make a choice that hurts people. This example, of course, reflects our ethical code and our own perspective.

Leadership Development

This entire book is written to help you, as a now-and-future member of groups and teams, to develop leadership skills. Obviously, you have to start somewhere. The best place to start is by developing your credibility and your confidence.

Developing Credibility

What do you think of when you say someone is credible? Honesty? Accuracy? Competence? Likability? Whatever it is, it determines how you respond to his or her influence. **Credibility** is a set of perceptions existing in the minds of those with whom you interact. What kind of perceptions are they? What is it about you that makes you credible? How do you make those perceptions positive?

What Credibility Is   As you read about credibility, you will notice how strong the relationship is between it and the ethics we just discussed. An historical clue to the relationship is the Greek word *ethos*, used by Aristotle to describe credibility.

When Aristotle talked about ethos as the foundation for persuading others, he identified three perceptions listeners would have of the credible communicator: good character, good sense, and goodwill. After more than 2000 years of practice, observation, and research, we know more about credibility, but the empirically derived factors of credibility are remarkably similar to Aristotle's. They are: competence, objectivity, trustworthiness, coorientation, and dynamism (Whitehead, 1969; Tuppen, 1974).

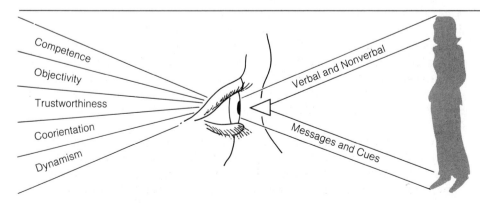

Competence
Objectivity
Trustworthiness
Coorientation
Dynamism

Verbal and Nonverbal
Messages and Cues

FIGURE   2.1
How a person perceives another's credibility

Competence is the degree of expertness, qualification, authoritativeness, and skill a person demonstrates. It is an essential component of teamwork, in which each member must contribute some expertise, information, analysis, and creativity to solving the problem.

Objectivity, like Aristotle's concept of "good sense," is the ability to look at both sides of an issue; to suspend personal biases; to be reasonable and dispassionate; to examine evidence, reasoning, and value questions before taking sides. In Western societies, where discussion and debate are the means by which issues are decided, the ability to be an objective judge is particularly crucial.

Trustworthiness is how consistent and honest a member's behavior is understood to be. In the classical sense, it is "good character." It is other people's confidence in your sincerity and in your ability to behave ethically even under pressure.

Coorientation is other people's sense that you are similar to them; that you are concerned for their well-being; that you share their interests, values, objectives, and needs. They can identify with you, because you can identify with them. It is similar to Aristotle's "good will." Credible communicators care about how their actions might affect others, not only about their own personal objectives. Someone who wants a team to excel so he or she will "look good" is perceived by members with far less credibility than one who wants all members of the team to succeed.

Dynamism refers to the vigor, the intensity, the compellingness with which an individual gets and maintains other people's interest. Although dynamism can make a difference in influencing others, it is a tricky element of credibility. It can be disagreeable, negative, and intense behavior that leads a group to perceive a dynamic individual as maintaining influence, at least in the short term, even though the effect of that influence is to diminish consensus and group satisfaction (Lumsden, 1972, p. 78).

An individual's culture may affect how she or he perceives another's credibility. Many Native American and Asian people view their elders as imbued with great wisdom from life experiences, whereas other cultures tend to dismiss them as "too old." A strong, loud voice may seem credible and authoritative to a North American; to a Thai, it may seem angry (Dodd, 1991, p. 221).

Stereotypes may also affect the way other people perceive a person's credibility. In a number of studies, the *same messages* were attributed to high-status (Anglo-American, male) speakers and to low-status (female or minority) speakers. Subjects rated the high-status persons as having higher credibility (Pearson, Turner, & Todd-Mancillas, 1991, p. 225).

As women and minorities take more leadership roles and advance further in society, their credibility will increase; this already is happening. In the process, however, they have to work harder, be better, and be prepared to prove their credibility more thoroughly than those whose position in society is more dominant.

How to Develop Credibility   Given what you now know about these five elements, you can start developing your own credibility, both in your self-perception and in the perceptions of others. Let's look at each component.

Competence   One key to being perceived as competent is to *be* competent. Start by recognizing the competencies you have. You may be excellent in math but mediocre in analysis of literature; you may be strong in face-to-face communication but terrified and bumbling in a presentation. You may have a lot of expertise on the Spanish-American War, but little on World War II. Everyone is more competent in one area than in another; that's why "more heads are better than one."

Think of competence in terms of content and process. In *content*, if you have knowledge of the subject, organize it and share it with the team. If you do not already have knowledge, get it. Do research, learn about the subject, organize your information, and present it to the team. You may not be an expert, but you are seen as worth listening to because you have something to contribute.

For *process* competence, develop your skills in careful listening, thinking, questioning, observation, and analysis. As you do this, you help the team and you establish your competence.

Objectivity   Developing your objectivity is really a matter of disciplining your thinking and phrasing your thoughts. It's something you can practice even as you read or interact with people in a social situation.

Try to look at every issue from more than one side. Even when you feel strongly, anticipate how a person who feels differently might argue or justify his or her position. Look for reasons and evidence to support various points of view. What you are doing is developing a habit of open-mindedness and fairness.

In dialogue, listen receptively to what others have to say, and phrase your own statements to acknowledge their points of view. As you develop these habits, you will become more objective and be perceived as objective by others.

Trustworthiness   To be trusted, one must be trustworthy. Trust—such a fragile commodity—is essential to relationships in general and leadership in particular. It can be measured in some very specific and easily violated ways. You can evaluate your own trustworthiness by looking at how you communicate it:

1. Do you live up to what you say? Can you be trusted to follow through on a promise or commitment?
2. Do you protect another's confidentiality? If you hear a rumor, do you pass it on or stop it? If someone tells you something personal, do you keep it to yourself? If you observe something embarrassing or distressing to someone else, do you share it with the world or keep silent?
3. Do you speak up for the trustworthy, ethical action when choices are to be made? Do you waver between advising the ethical path and taking the easy one?

4. Do you consistently give the most truthful information you can? Do you choose the truth when a lie would be easier?
5. Is your communication straightforward and open? Do you try to avoid manipulating others? Do you deal with issues in a straightforward manner?

Examining your own behavior can help you evaluate how trustworthy you are, and how trustworthy others perceive you to be. Using these guidelines can help you to be trustworthy—and to be trusted.

Coorientation   Your coorientation with other team members starts with the common interests that bring you together. It goes beyond common interests, however. To see you as credible in this regard, people need to sense that you care about them; that your values and your attitudes are similar to theirs; that, in some way, you and they are part of the same picture. Here are some ways to start:

1. Look at things from the other members' points of view. Try to understand who they are.
2. Find ways in which you and the others in the group *are* similar. Examine backgrounds, attitudes, values, beliefs, and goals to find areas of agreement.
3. Find ways to express that coorientation; confirm your common goals and common feelings.
4. Express your opinions and ideas in ways that connect with those of others.
5. Listen carefully to others and express your support, if not your agreement.
6. Confirm statements that reflect others' coorientation with you.
7. Show, verbally and nonverbally, the kind of openness, friendliness, and supportiveness that says, "We're part of the same team, and we have the same vision."

Such communication carries a sense of mutuality that makes coorientation easy. We do not mean you should pretend. We mean you should express concern for others' positions and similarities when there are genuine bases for them. This may seem like a very obvious thing to do, but often people take the things they share for granted. People assume that others know they sympathize with a point of view, when the other person may not know that at all.

Dynamism   We have already noted that dynamism can be important to credibility, but that its impact is hard to predict. If you are competent, objective, trustworthy, and cooriented with the team, dynamism is probably not too important. Some very soft-spoken, gentle people are powerful group members.

Our advice is simply to be as open and naturally enthusiastic as you can. Be sensitive to others' feedback, and adjust to it. If the group needs energizing, express your feelings with a little extra strength; use humor to enliven or energize a discussion; allow yourself to use gestures and vocal variety to give your communication energy and expressiveness; use eye contact and body language to connect with others and intensify your messages.

If you think you're a little too low-key, work on these skills to come across as more dynamic. If being dynamic is natural and easy for you, be careful. Watch for responses. Don't bowl people over; don't dominate; don't keep the emotional pitch of the team at a constant high. The idea is to let dynamism energize your messages, not overwhelm the team.

Building Confidence

Nothing is more important to your leadership than to believe in it. You may, at this moment, be very comfortable with leadership. If so, keep it up; continue adding to your skills and looking for objective feedback on areas you can develop. If you're not confident yet, you will be soon.

We suggest an approach to building confidence that we know to be successful; it involves visualizing yourself the way you want to be and practicing what you visualize.

Visualization   Visualization is one of the most important techniques a person can learn. Actually, you already do it, though perhaps not the way we hope you'll do it in the future. You use it to tell yourself you're good at something, or to tell yourself you're bad. Furthermore, you believe yourself; you see yourself as being the way you have described. Then you go forth and do what you've predicted.

The human mind is incredibly powerful. You can make yourself sick and make yourself well. When you want to become good at something—or better—or best—using the power of your mind and your imagination can help develop that ability.

An excellent technique for using your mind to develop a skill and to increase your confidence in it is to visualize the way you want to be. **Visualization** involves forming a mental picture and fulfilling it with **self-talk**, or messages to yourself about who you are and what you do. We're looking for positive visualizations and self-talk, of course.

Try using these techniques to build confidence in your leadership:

1. View yourself as you would be in a leadership role, seeing transactional and task needs, stepping in and filling those needs with credibility. Paint yourself a mental picture. Hear yourself speaking and others responding to you.

2. Write down, in a sentence or two, an affirmation of how you feel and act in that picture. An affirmation is a statement that is positive, present tense, and descriptive. For example: "I feel confident about my ability, and I give the team good, direct information about the topic we are discussing. I listen carefully to be sure I understand my teammates accurately. I answer questions confidently and easily because I know what I am talking about."

3. Keep picturing yourself in that positive scene, and occasionally read your affirmation to yourself. Use positive self-talk. You will begin to act in accordance with the visualization in your mind. You make it happen.

In a letter to the *New York Times Magazine*, Shane Murphy (1991), Sport Science and Medicine Division of the United States Olympic Committee, notes that "interventions based on techniques like goal-setting, relaxation training, visualization and self-talk are effective in helping about 80 percent of athletes" (p. 8). Sports organizations and businesses, too, currently employ people to train their managers and workers in visualization techniques. We've seen self-talk and visualization improve the communication and leadership of many people, and we know it has worked for us. It can work for you, too.

Practice   The obvious next step is to practice those skills. If you find it easy, forge ahead. If it's more difficult for you, take small responsibilities in your team, but start. If you use self-talk to describe what you want to do, and visualize what you will be like, you will find yourself doing it.

It may be helpful to identify one or two leadership characteristics to develop at a time, rather than trying to change too many habits at once. You may decide, for example, to improve your task process skills by periodically summarizing a group's discussion more effectively. Then, look for opportunities and try it in your group. Ask the members for feedback to see if you have adequately described the ideas. Your leadership practice has many benefits. Among them: your team is more effective, you are more effective, and—definitely—your teamwork is much more fun. Leadership is gratifying and rewarding.

Summary

Although you may not be the designated leader, your responsibility in a team is to provide leadership by understanding and influencing transactional and task processes. To do that effectively you must understand the group, task, and individual roles people play in these processes. Your leadership affects your own short-term and long-term satisfaction and success, as well as the team's processes and its success.

Through leadership you can help eliminate obstacles to others, as well as to yourself, such as the stereotyping "boxes" into which people are sometimes put because of culture, race, or gender. You can also protect your personal ethics, help develop a dialogical ethic of team process, and influence the ethics of team decisions. These ethical issues are crucial because groups face conflicts and dilemmas among ethical choices in their task and transactional processes.

Developing leadership begins with developing credibility, which includes the factors of competence, objectivity, trustworthiness, coorientation, and dynamism. One way to work on your competence, as well as build confidence, is to use self-talk and visualization to "see" yourself influencing the transactional and task processes of your team.

Exercises

1. Assess your leadership skills, using Form 2.1. Make an extra copy of the form. On one copy, rate how you perceive yourself; on the other, ask a friend to rate your behavior.

   Discuss the completed forms. What does your friend see that you do not? How can you use that feedback? List your strengths and the skills you'd like to develop.

2. Select one behavior from the leadership survey that you think you could use more often. For a couple of weeks, consciously use the new behavior in meetings of groups or classes. Keep a journal of

FORM 2.2   ▮   OBSERVATION OF MEMBERS' ROLES

Observe a small group meeting. Enter the name of each member at the top, and tally each time someone acts as facilitator for transactional or task processes or acts as a process blocker by playing individual roles. Where possible, record specifically which role is involved. The next page provides descriptions of these roles.

MEMBERS' NAMES

TASK PROCESSES FACILITATOR							
Initiator/contributor							
Information/opinion seeker							
Information/opinion giver							
Elaborator							
Coordinator							
Orienter							
Evaluator/critic							
Energizer							
Procedural technician							
Recorder							
TRANSACTIONAL PROCESSES FACILITATOR							
Encourager							
Harmonizer/compromiser							
Gatekeeper							
Standard setter							
Observer							
Follower							
PROCESS BLOCKER							
Aggressor/blocker							
Recognition seeker							
Self-confessor/help-seeker							
Player/fun-seeker							
Dominator							
Special interest pleader							

Discuss:

How did roles seem to combine for each member?

In what ways did role behaviors contribute to the leadership of the group?

⟋⟍Which members provided leadership? What roles were they filling?

How/when did members take roles to balance the roles others were taking?

⟋⟍When and if members played blocking roles, how did others respond?

How did roles people took reflect ethical issues or decisions?

TASK PROCESSES FACILITATOR'S ROLES

Initiator/contributor . . . . Proposes ideas or solutions

Information/opinion seeker . . . . Asks for facts, information, opinions, values, clarification

Information/opinion giver . . . . Offers facts, statistics, examples, opinions, beliefs

Elaborator . . . . Develops examples, extends ideas

Coordinator . . . . Pulls ideas, relationships together

Orienter . . . . Summarizes, calls attention to task

Evaluator/critic . . . . Analyzes data, reasoning, conclusions

Energizer . . . . Tries to motivate the group

Procedural technician . . . . Runs errands, distributes materials

Recorder . . . . Keeps records

TRANSACTIONAL PROCESSES FACILITATOR'S ROLES

Encourager . . . . Gives understanding, support

Harmonizer/compromiser . . . . Smooths, suggests ways to manage conflict

Gatekeeper . . . . Encourages participation, curbs excess

Standard setter . . . . Sets standards for tasks, ethics, goals

Observer . . . . Observes, gives feedback on processes

Follower . . . . Goes along with others

PROCESS BLOCKER'S ROLES

Aggressor/blocker . . . . Puts down others, takes issue, bulldozes, is negative

Recognition-seeker . . . . Uses group to boost his/her ego

Self-confessor/help-seeker . . . . Unloads personal woes, uses group for sympathy

Player/fun-seeker . . . . Uninvolved in group, creates distractions

Dominator . . . . Manipulates, tries to control

Special interest pleader . . . . Uses team to serve own or another group's interests

Based on K. D. Benne and P. Sheats, "Functional Roles of Group Members," *Journal of Social Issues, 4* (1948), 41–49.

Leadership to Create Teamwork

The "Work" in Teamwork: Starting the Process

"Okay, here we are. Now what do we *do*?"
Yes, indeed. The second word in teamwork is *work*.

Work—it's a four-letter word! Some people don't mind it. "I'm not afraid of work," they say, half-joking. "I can sleep very comfortably right alongside it." Americans have been accused of having "lost the work ethic." We don't think so, but people in this individualistic society are accustomed to rolling up their shirt sleeves and tackling a hard job alone. Frequently, when these individuals get together on a task, they don't really know how to work as a team. Our mission, therefore, is to show you how.

In this chapter, we start with the groundwork for success: getting to know one another—your strengths, your values, your personal agendas—and deciding whether or not to designate a leader at the outset. Then we examine your team in its context of systems and subsystems, organizational responsibilities to the team, and team members' responsibilities to one another, the team, and the organization. This leads to the first steps toward the actual task: setting goals and objectives in terms of the parent organization's charge and purposes for the team; establishing standards and procedures for the team's work; setting norms regarding time and commitment; deciding approaches to meeting times, places, and formality; and designing and using agendas that will accomplish your meetings' purposes.

The actual work of a team involves a lot of pieces, and they do not all fit together in a nice, neat, straight line. In fact, the work of a team has many dimensions. You will find yourself looping back and forth, to and from all of the task "steps" discussed in this and future chapters.

By the end of this chapter, you will be ready to start teamwork toward accomplishing a task, whether that task is to be concluded at the end of a classroom period or at the end of the semester. Our goals are for you to:

1. Know the initial steps in working together.

2. Understand the context in which your group was formed and how that affects your work.

3. Know procedures for developing team goals.

4. Be familiar with methods for setting work standards and procedures.

5. Learn approaches to planning and conducting your work meetings.

Groundwork for Success

Members of a new team are entering into a relationship in which they will collaborate to achieve certain goals. To do that, they must develop some understanding of how the others work and how best to interact. That can be difficult, at times.

Your team has to invest time to build rapport, to get to know one another, to understand what special strengths and abilities each may bring to the task. Team members need to share their values and perspectives enough to see how those viewpoints might affect their interactions on the task. And they need to air their personal agendas—what they want from the group. As you do this, you start to share information that will help the team to develop and work toward its goals.

Get to Know One Another

A group that meets just once may have only five minutes for making connections among the members, but even those five minutes are important. For a team that will meet for weeks—or, perhaps, months or years—taking enough time and effort to get to know one another can be absolutely essential. We suggest that you make a conscious—and conscientious—effort to move the group through a getting-acquainted process.

1. *Start the process.* If the new group seems to be moving too fast toward the task, you can provide leadership by suggesting that the group take a few minutes for introductions. Say something like, "Could we take time to find out something about each other? I think we'll work together better if we do."

2. *Make a genuine effort to learn one another's names.* A name, after all, is the first step to seeing another person as a distinct individual. This may seem obvious, but how many classes have come to the end of the semester with your still designating another student as "you know—the smart senior who sits over there in the front?" If you had gotten to know "smart senior," she or he might have helped you with those sticky concepts that knocked your grade down a full point.

3. *Create a dialogue.* You can take some of the stiffness and formality out of the discussion by asking people questions and showing some interest in them. Start, of course, with basic information, such as where you're from, what you do, what your major is. This can lead to disclosing bits of personal information—people's likes and dislikes, attitudes, and opinions—and *that* can begin building interpersonal credibility and trust.

4. *Make connections.* Soon team members begin to make connections among themselves on similar interests. As in any initial conversation, you and your teammates are feeling your way toward coorientation, but you're doing it as a group, and you're laying the foundation for a mutual task.

When you start on the work of the team, you'll know better how to talk to one another and how to work together.

Identify Special Strengths

Each individual brings particular strengths to the group. These may be everything from access to resources, to interests and talents that relate to the task, to skills in research, analysis, organization, writing, creative projects—almost anything. Many individual attributes emerge naturally from the "getting acquainted" discussion, but it's also possible to bring the subject up by saying something like, "Why don't we each make a list of what we think we can do for this team? I mean, for example, I have some contacts with people who can give us information on the subject."

Exploring individual possibilities will help members recognize what they can do early enough to do it. It's infuriating to get to the end of the task and hear someone groan, "I just realized I could have made a great visual for our presentation on my brother's computer." Too late! So explore the strengths early in the game.

Consider these people as meeting in a group for the first time. What type of group could they be? What will they need to learn about one another to proceed effectively with their task? What should they do to get started? (Photograph © American Stock Photography.)

Share Your Values

Individuals start out with a set of personal feelings about the team and its task. These may relate to how much time they have to put into it and how important the work is to them; their particular needs or wants; and their expectations about how they want to interact.

These feelings and expectations often reflect members' values. As a team develops, those values will affect transactional and task processes again and again. An early sense of what people believe and value will provide a starting point for members to understand one another and to communicate about value-laden issues. At this early stage, exploring values can focus on questions such as: What do you think is important about the issues facing the team? What kinds of ethical issues will we face? How will we deal with them?

By tentatively exploring these basic issues, members can begin to understand one another's perspectives. This does not mean that everyone will see values in precisely the same light; in fact, diversity of membership assures that they will not. What it does mean is that later, when the team inevitably faces conflicts, knowledge of one another's values will make it easier to manage those conflicts.

Air Personal Agendas

Some issues, however, are harder to detect at the beginning. Team members bring their own **personal agendas**, or individual goals and objectives. Often, these agendas are hidden, based on motives that the individual would rather not talk about but that will affect every moment of interaction in the team.

Understanding personal agendas helps your team to meet members' needs and achieve its goals. One of our students, at the first meeting of her project team for the semester, looked her teammates in the eyes and said, "I want an 'A' out of this project. I hope you all do, too." Naturally, everyone agreed. Knowing this member's personal agenda helped later when the team had to confront problems with two members who were slacking off on their share of the work.

Unfortunately, people frequently do not want to get their objectives out into the open—or, perhaps, aren't even fully aware of what they are. One of us worked on a team in which one member blocked every idea. After months of frustration and conflicting undercurrents, the team finally found out that he was angry at the organization because he felt he had not received a deserved promotion. When we got it out in the open, the team members were empathic and gave him support. He stopped throwing boulders in our way and started participating as a team member. If his personal agenda had been discussed early on, we would have conserved a lot of wasted time and energy.

Although people do not always know what it is they want and need from a group, an early discussion of individual issues and expectations can start the connections that make it possible to deal with issues when they arise. Often, it can start a process that allows the team to meet both individual and team needs throughout the life of the team. How do you do this at the beginning? First, suggest that team members discuss what each person wants to accomplish from the experience. Second, understand and state your own agendas as honestly as you can. And finally, listen carefully to others and ask intelligent, nonthreatening questions.

Decide about a Leader

Your team may already have a **designated leader**. It may even have more than one. If you're working in an organizational structure, for example, your team may be one of a group of self-managing teams supervised and coached by an outside manager whose goal is to lead the teams until they can lead themselves (Manz & Sims, 1987). Within the team, management may appoint a manager, supervisor, or team member as leader. In many cases, however, you may be starting your team without a designated leader.

If that's the situation, we urge your team to discuss the advantages and disadvantages of immediately selecting a designated leader and make a decision—or decide not to decide.

Reasons for and against Designating a Leader   Some people believe that starting out with a designated leader is essential to a group's effectiveness. One argument is that time will be wasted if someone does not immediately take charge of organizing meetings, getting resources, representing the team, and helping members stay motivated and focused on the job. Certainly, some member or members must do these things. These responsibilities, however, could be distributed among members and shared.

A stronger argument for a designated leader rests on the specific problems a given team might face. That is, a designated leader may be important when the task is very complex; or the members are so different that conflicts seem inevitable and someone must take responsibility for managing them; or the team's relationships with a parent organization and other systems are so complicated that the team needs a strong spokesperson.

One argument against starting out with a designated leader is that it may be difficult to select the right person; it may take time to assess individuals' abilities to fulfill leader functions. In a work team, it also may be unfair to saddle one person with the bulk of administrative work—paperwork, representing the team in outside meetings, following through on decisions, and so on—when she or he also works full time at a job. Finally, it may be too easy for a team to leave all responsibility up to the leader and fail to do the kind of work needed to develop a real team.

Your team must weigh the disadvantages, the advantages, and the alternatives to make a decision. Do you want to designate a leader immediately, do you want to choose an alternative, or do you want to postpone the decision?

Alternatives   If your team has talked about what kinds of needs and preferences you have for a leader, then it might consider these alternatives:

1. Designate a leader immediately.
2. Distribute leader functions among team members according to their inclinations and talents, or use distributed leadership for some functions and share responsibilities for others.
3. Take turns as primary leader according to a specific schedule. Often self-managing teams do this so the administrative tasks of leading do not weigh too heavily, for too long a period of time, on one person.
4. Share leadership among members, relying on good mutual planning and communication to fulfill the functions.
5. Wait and allow a leader (or leaders) to emerge as the team works together over time. Frequently someone emerges in the role by filling leader functions and gaining the members' confidence. That individual then becomes the acknowledged leader of the group.

Decision Modes   If your team decides it does need to designate a specific leader right away, there are two basic ways to make that decision: consensus or election. From the outset, it may be that everyone feels a particular person is the best choice. The members discuss their choice with the person in question, and he or she agrees to take the position. The decision is made: the team has selected its leader by **consensus**.

If the team doesn't see a consensus candidate but still thinks the immediate need for a leader is critical, the standard solution is to nominate and discuss candidates and then bring the decision to a vote. Consensus is a far better approach, because members give more cooperation and commitment to a leader on whom they've all agreed. Sometimes, however, voting is the only way to get the job done.

Teams and Their Contexts

Teamwork doesn't happen in a vacuum. It's a focused, collaborative effort within a specific context. Even though a group or a team might have been put together five minutes ago, it works within some context that affects everything the team does—its input, its transactional and task processes, its output.

Rarely can a team wait to learn everything about its context before moving on with its task. You will learn many things as you proceed. At the outset, however, you can make some observations about the larger system, or organization, within which your team functions. You can examine the relationships of your team to other subsystems, including the interdependencies and problems that may arise. You also need to examine responsibilities—those of the organization to the team, including sufficient support and autonomy to do its job, and those of the team members to each other, to the team, and to the organization.

THERE'S MORE THAN ONE KIND OF TEAM

There actually are three kinds of teams in American business.

The first is the *baseball team*. The surgical team that performs an open-heart operation and Henry Ford's assembly line are both "baseball teams." The players play *on* the team; they do not play *as* a team. They have fixed positions and are best when the sequence of actions is thoroughly understood so the team is inflexible. Every position does its own job in its own way. Everyone can operate separately, can be a star, can be evaluated and rewarded individually.

The second kind of team is the *football team*. The symphony orchestra and the hospital rescue unit are "football teams." The players also have fixed positions but they play *as* a team rather than on the team. It's flexible, but it needs a "score," whether it's a play the coach signals to the huddle or the Mozart symphony everyone puts on the music stand. So the word of the coach is law.

Third is the *tennis doubles team*. It is the kind of a team in a jazz combo, the team of senior executives, or the team most likely to produce a genuine innovation like the personal computer 15 years ago. Players have a primary rather than a fixed position; they "cover" their teammates, adjusting to their teammates' strengths and weaknesses and to the changing demands of the "game." The tennis doubles team has five to seven members at most. They have to be trained together and must work together for quite some time before they fully function as a team. Only the team "performs"; individual members "contribute."

All three are true teams. But one kind of team can play only one way.

Teams, in other words, are tools. Team work is neither "good" nor "desirable"—it is a fact. Which team to use for what purpose is a crucial, difficult, and risky decision that is even harder to unmake. Managements have yet to learn how to make it.

Condensed from Peter F. Drucker, "There's More Than One Kind of Team," *The Wall Street Journal*, February 11, 1992, p. A16. Used with permission.

Analyze the System

Most groups and work teams are created by some higher authority. That means they function within a system and have responsibilities to it. Often, they also work interdependently with other systems and subsystems.

In a work team, some relationships are obvious. Members who represent other groups or departments, for example, bring a set of connections and responsibilities to others that affect their work with the team. It should be equally clear that when other teams or departments are working on related goals, it's imperative for these units to communicate and cooperate. Sometimes, however, it's not quite so obvious, and your team has to do some careful analysis of possible interdependencies.

Interdependence among systems even affects your work in this class. Your student groups function within the larger system of the class; that makes the class your parent organization and, we suppose, it makes the professor the Chief Executive Officer (CEO).

Suppose your group wants to do a student survey. If it's okay with the CEO, can you simply go out and do it? Maybe. The class operates within a larger system, the department, which functions within the college and interacts with other academic departments, schools, and support systems. The college also functions within and interacts with other systems—the state and federal systems, various accreditation systems, legal systems. Each system and subsystem affects other systems. Your survey could be affected by any one of those relationships, depending upon what kind of survey you want to do and how you want to do it.

It is critical for your team to be aware of the importance of systems relationships and to identify significant ones early. As your work continues, the team will consider how and in what ways other outside resources and relationships might be important to its goals.

Identify Responsibilities

The interdependence of teams in systems underscores an omnipresent issue: teamwork is about responsibility. It's about the parent organization's responsibilities to the team, giving it the support it needs and sufficient autonomy to do its job. It's also about the team members' responsibilities to one another, to their team, and to the parent organization.

Organization's Responsibilities   The system that creates a team has a responsibility to do it right. That doesn't mean, sad to say, it always will. But you hope it considers two questions in creating your team:

1. What degree of autonomy does the team have in doing its work?
2. What support will it receive from the organization?

A work team has the greatest chance for success when it has the freedom—the autonomy—to do three things (Cummings, 1978):

1. Define its task as different and distinct from those of other groups.
2. Control both its physical and its social conditions without interference from outside management.
3. Choose its processes for accomplishing and assessing its job.

Such autonomy is important because people who have the opportunity *and* the responsibility for creating their own work are stimulated to use their abilities, talents, skills, and energies to do just that. They are more creative, more energetic, and more committed—and they do a better job (Hackman, 1982).

Of course, no team can be entirely autonomous; neither can an individual or an organization. To use teams effectively, however, an organization must be willing to take risks, allow teams to make choices, and trust them to make the right ones. When an organization shows its commitment to teams in this way, its teams are more likely to make the risks pay off for themselves and for the organization.

Teams that flourish almost always have sufficient support to develop the team and do the job. An organization that provides that support starts by carefully planning and selecting the team. It understands that time is needed for a team to develop, and it supports the process. It gives the team leadership and training. It provides necessary physical resources—time, money, space, technical support. It gives the team trust, encouragement, and high visibility.

Knowing the degree of autonomy and support your team has can be helpful in four ways. It can help you:

1. Ensure that the team is properly autonomous and supported from the start.
2. Diagnose problems when a team is in trouble.
3. Clarify team needs and, if necessary, compensate by finding alternative sources of support.
4. Negotiate improved conditions and support for your team.

Team Responsibilities   Autonomy and support enable the team to function and do its work as the members think it should be done. With all freedoms, however, come responsibilities. A team's responsibilities may be tied to various relationships, some of which may be easy to overlook—and overlooking them can lead to trouble. If the team does miss some of its obligations to others, it may lose the confidence of the parent organization, teammates, or other groups. It's important, therefore, to discuss and identify the various responsibilities your team must fulfill. Some of these are:

To one another and the leader. Members have a personal responsibility for preparation, participation, and leadership to one another as individuals and to the designated leader, if there is one.

To the team. Members have responsibilities to develop a real team, to ensure that transactional processes are dialogical and ethical, that task processes are thorough and analytical, and that decisions are ethically defensible.

To other groups. Individual members who represent separate departments or other groups also have responsibilities to them. They may be expected to represent the group's interests to the team and to report back on the team's actions.

To the parent organization. The team's responsibility to its founder is threefold: (1) to develop its own strength as a team in ways that justify the organization's support and trust; (2) to fulfill its task; and (3) to report its progress and outcomes.

When you have examined and accepted your team's responsibilities, you are ready to take on the work that lies ahead.

Team Goals

We all need to know where we're going in order to know if we got there. Even when we change destinations in the middle of a trip, knowing where we *were* going gives us a point of comparison for where we wound up.

Any work team has three important reasons to set its **goals** very early on:

1. To clarify what the parent organization expects.
2. To develop a plan, a strategy, for doing its work. Even though every good plan is flexible, it also maps the route specifically to a result.
3. To develop strategies for evaluating the team's processes and outcomes.

When a team sets goals, it starts by identifying the purposes for which the team was created. On that basis, it can define its goals. But *even goal setting is not a linear, step-by-step process.* As your team continues to work toward its goals, it may reassess and change them based on new information or new insights. Initial goals, nonetheless, need to be understood clearly and early in the life of the team.

Identify the Team's Purposes

The first step toward setting goals is to identify who created your team and for what purposes. In your class, the founder may have been the professor. In a public institution or private corporation, it may have been the CEO, a task force, or a management team. Perhaps you and some other people organized your group for reasons of your own.

The founder may have put together a team for any of a number of purposes. They usually fit into one or more of these broad categories:

Information gathering. This charge asks for research and investigation focusing on a specific problem or issue, and usually involves preparing a report. **Information gathering,** as a process, is usually a necessary step for all other team purposes.

Problem analysis. You might be on a task force to investigate a specific problem, to determine its scope and the seriousness of its impact. This charge of **problem analysis** requires careful thinking about the relationships of causes and effects, and may include recommendations about possible solutions. In a college setting, a problem-analysis team might focus on anything from the parking problem to plagiarism. A report with recommendations probably would conclude the work of the team.

Decision making. This charge takes the team another step. The team charged with **decision making** usually goes through the full range of information-gathering and problem-analysis processes to arrive at specific decisions that will be implemented. The team might carry through its decisions, or it might pass them along to other teams and groups to implement.

Quality improvement. The charge might be to "identify areas where quality can be improved, and find ways to improve it." With this deliberately vague charge of **quality improvement,** the team, possibly a quality circle, might select any area of the organization, study it, develop ideas for improving quality within it, and carry those ideas through to implementation and assessment.

All of these are legitimate and desirable uses for teams. Unfortunately, organizations can use, misuse, or abuse groups. Organizations may initiate groups purely for political, and sometimes unethical, purposes. They may create teams to deceive people into believing they are participating in decisions management has already made. Eventually people catch on and become cynical, and everybody loses.

QUALITY   CIRCLES   HELP   SHARPEN   COMPETITIVE   EDGE

As our world and our business become more and more competitive, quality becomes an increasingly important factor. That's why we're striving to make quality a company-wide obsession through a network of Quality Circles. . . .

All Quality Circle team leaders receive training on how to conduct a successful meeting, prepare an agenda of discussion topics, and brainstorming, which encourages everyone to talk about their ideas. . . .

Henry Lam, manager of Quality Assurance, provides the training and helps the groups along the way. "Typically, the first few meetings of a Circle involve some griping and complaining," Henry explains. "As people become more familiar and comfortable with the purpose of the Circle, which is to solve problems, they soon catch on and begin to discuss what needs to be improved and offer their ideas for solutions."

Success follows quickly. . . . By giving people who do the job the power to solve problems, Quality Circles are helping All-state sharpen its competitive edge.

Condensed from "Quality Circles Help Sharpen Competitive Edge," *The Scorpion*, The official All-state Legal Supply employee publication, Winter 1991, p. 1. Used with permission.

Sometimes organizations establish groups only to soothe angry people or to defuse a crisis. We've seen institutions create task forces to "study the issue" when enough people got mad, but they built in restrictions—in timing, resources, support, personnel—that created obstacles to the task forces' progress. You can't help but distrust the organizations' motives in these cases.

These abuses of group purposes are, to us, unethical and reprehensible. If your team is being misused and abused, however, don't panic. You may feel your best ethical choice is to refuse to serve. It's possible, however, that your team can accomplish excellent results despite the manipulative intent. To turn it around, you and your teammates need to understand both the legitimate and illegitimate purposes of the team's creation so you can choose ways of transforming an unethical start into an ethical ending. You can make lemonade out of the proverbial lemon on occasion, but you need to know early that it's a lemon and not a peach.

Define the Team's Goals

The people who put your team together presumably told you the purpose. Usually a team gets a task description, often called the "charge." It may or may not be specific. On a college committee, the charge may be to "look into the problem of insufficient library resources." On the job, you're assigned to a task force with a charge to "interface with the academic community." With equal specificity, your church asks you to participate in a group to "improve human relationships."

In each of these instances, the statement gives some overall purpose or hopes, but does not give your team a concrete set of tasks to accomplish. So the team must define the goals for itself.

To define those goals, your team examines its purposes; the charge to the team and the expectations behind it; the final products the team wants to achieve; and its criteria for success. These steps enable the team to phrase—clearly and measurably—its goals and the instrumental objectives it must achieve to reach the goals. Then, and only then, can the team commit to the goals it has set.

Terms in the Charge   A first step is to look carefully at the language of your charge. Let's take the previous job-based example—a task force to "interface with the academic community."

How would your team define this charge? What does your boss mean by "interface"? Does it mean communicate? Might it be defined as collaborate? Perhaps it could mean "develop mutually beneficial, cooperative programs." Who is to interface with whom? What does "academic community" mean? A local university? Colleges? High schools, junior highs, elementary schools? And what elements of the "academic community" are included? Teachers? Students? Support personnel? Administrators?

You go back to the person who prepared the charge and ask for some clarification. Can she or he tell you more specifically why the team was created and what it is to do? The team should outline its understanding of the task. Then the members, or a representative, present the goals they have defined to the founder and say, "We've talked about these goals; are they consistent with your perspective?"

Expectations behind the Charge   You may get more of an overview than a direct answer. "Well, more and more corporations are reaching out to schools, helping with programs, even influencing curricula; we just thought it was time for us to start doing *something* with the local schools. Which ones? Well—I guess we could start with colleges."

What your team has at this point is a general purpose: find ways to "help" with colleges. Your parent organization has some goals of its own—perhaps "improve community relations," "influence college programs," or "employ better-prepared graduates." The more you find out about these expectations, the better prepared you will be to write your goals.

Final Products   Once you have an idea of what's expected, your team should try to specify the final product or products of its work. Again, your founder may or may not be very specific in what she or he wants. "We want a report." On what topics? "I don't know—what other companies are doing, what the colleges want, what colleges need to do to prepare their students for jobs with us . . . oh, and some ideas for things we could do." A written report or an oral report? "Yes." Yes, what? "Yes, both."

What your team has to do is boil that down into some possible goals. Your discussion should lead you to a sketch of what your work will accomplish by the end. It might look like this:

1. Prepare a written report.
2. Prepare an oral report.
3. Get information on current "interfacing" between business and academia.

4. Get information on what colleges see as a helpful corporate role.
5. Find out what businesses want colleges to do better.
6. Suggest ideas for what your company can do.

You now have six goals: three information-gathering tasks, one problem-analysis, idea-generating task, and two reporting tasks. Now you want to work each goal out so that you can reach it.

Criteria for Success   To write your goals well, you need to plan how you will measure your achievement of them. These measures are your criteria—your clear statements of what the team will see as successful accomplishment of those goals. Taking the written report as an example, ask yourselves:

1. What do you want the report to *do*? Provide complete information? About what areas? Document information clearly and accurately? How?
2. What do you want the report to be *like*? Present information professionally? Be well written, clear, readable?
3. When do you want the report to be submitted? To whom?
4. How long should the report be?

The answers to these questions give you some criteria for measuring goal attainment; now it's time to work out the wording. That may be more touchy than it sounds, because everyone's agreement with the goal is essential to the tight teamwork needed to attain it.

Phrasing Goals   The perfect goal statement is clear, unambiguous, and measurable. Thus, the written-report goal might be stated something like this:

Major goal. On October 1, to present to Ms. Sorensen, Director of Community Relations, a written report on the investigation and recommendations of the V.V. Video Company Task Force on Corporate and College Interfacing.

Criteria. The report will be approximately twenty pages, complete, well written, documented, and professionally prepared.

Even with these criteria, we can guarantee that people will assign very different meanings to adjectives such as "well written," "documented," and "professional." You can start with these criteria, but very quickly the team will need to look at examples of written reports so you can agree more specifically on what the criteria mean. And that's just for one of your six goals.

Instrumental Objectives   The final goals are often called **terminal objectives** because they conclude the work. Along the way are any number of **instrumental objectives**, or steps that must be taken to reach the goal. Identifying these is critical to create a path to the goal.

For example, for the goal of finding out what colleges and corporations are now doing, three instrumental objectives might be:

1. Design a survey.
2. Survey local organizations and institutions.
3. Analyze the results of that survey.

Each instrumental objective should be constructed just as carefully as the major goal.

Some of these instrumental objectives emerge in the course of the team's work, but you need to plan ahead as much as possible. We've seen teams do all the work for a survey, including duplication, and then discover they skipped the instrumental objective of getting institutional permission to do it. That meant delays in time and, often, rewriting the survey to meet requirements. The more attention you give to the objectives at the outset, the fewer times in the course of the team's work will you slap yourselves on the forehead and ask each other, "Why didn't we see that before?"

It helps to prepare a timeline for achieving the instrumental objectives that shows the path to the terminal objectives. Figure 3.1 shows a schedule a group might use to create a videotape as a class project. Notice how each step is identified in relation to the other instrumental objectives necessary to reach the goal. This view also lets you evaluate other aspects of the overall plan. For example: What is left out? Is enough time allowed for each step? Where should more time be built in for contingencies?

Understanding and Commitment   It is critical to confirm the team's commitment to its goals. You start to work, believing that members are standing together, and suddenly come to the rueful realization that your feet aren't even on the same planet.

FIGURE 3.1

The path of instrumental objectives to goal achievement

Instrumental Objectivies

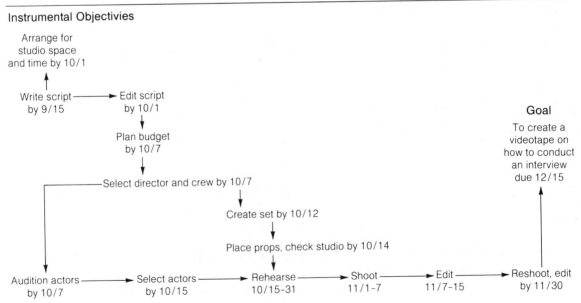

Sometimes you have to confirm both members' mutual understanding of what the goals are and their commitment to achieving them. Some ways to confirm understanding are:

Paraphrasing the goals and discussing whether the paraphrase covers the meaning. Sometimes the discussion will unearth differences you didn't know were there; other times it confirms that everyone has a similar understanding.

Hypothesizing interpretations, examples, or applications for the goals. One member might say, "Okay, we've said we want this report to be well documented. Would an annotated bibliography be one way we'd do that?" Someone else might say, "Good grief, no! I thought we'd just list any sources we used!"

When everyone can express close to the same ideas about what the goals state, you've negotiated a meaning. But you may still need to negotiate everyone's commitment to those goals. If some people believe the goals are worth working for and some do not, or if some people can give great time and energy to them and some are willing to commit only a little, the team's effort is diminished.

You get commitment in two ways: by asking for it, and by building it into the norms of the team as you go along. You need both.

At this stage of goal setting, you can check commitment with a *census-taking* technique, asking each member to what extent she or he can commit to achieving these goals. We are not suggesting loyalty oaths here. Every member has his or her own needs and approach, and you'll never have a total match among members. All you want to do is be sure everyone's on the same boat with approximately the same rowing pace.

CASE ANALYSIS 3.1

The task force established the following goals:

1. To develop recommendations and options for McDonald's to gain a maximum reduction in materials use and waste.
2. To make proposals consistent with McDonald's business practices and future growth.
3. To create a model approach to waste reduction that others could apply.

Issues for Your Consideration

1. Based on these goals, how would you identify the task force's purpose in terms of the types of purposes discussed in this chapter?
2. What sources and influences do you suppose the task force considered in developing this set of goals?
3. Apply the criteria for goals provided in this chapter. In what ways do these statements meet the criteria? In what ways do they not?
4. Identify some instrumental objectives the task force would have to attain in order to reach these terminal goals.

Degrees of commitment often increase with performance. As the members work together and begin to see some success in their efforts, they become more involved in the entire process and more committed to its outcomes.

Standards and Procedures for Work

As your team works through its goals, the members may feel they are well focused on the specific tasks necessary to get started. You may feel comfortable about working together and excited about your plans. But you need to think about how you'll work through the transactional and task processes that lie ahead. Groups often don't think about this. They "just grow." They don't realize that the norms they establish in the beginning affect how satisfactorily the team manages its time and its commitments in the long run. They also don't anticipate their frustration if they fail to plan their approaches to meetings and agendas. Your team can make its experience infinitely better if it attends to these issues early.

Basic Norms

A team that works together for a while will develop norms—for everything from ways of dressing to ways of thinking to ways of interacting—and members will behave in accordance with those norms. These may be useful norms, or they may not. We suggest, therefore, that a few norms be proposed, discussed, stated, and agreed to at the beginning. As the group develops, you may need to reassess and modify norms now and then, but at least you'll have a good start.

The norms we're talking about can affect your processes significantly. They concern time commitments and responsibilities to the team.

Time Commitments   Imagine that you've knocked yourself out for several weeks and then some other member justifies her or his lack of attendance, or constant lateness to meetings, with "Well, I just don't have the time," or, even more endearing, "But I'm always late—that's just the way I am!" An early discussion of time can help to avert these blockades to progress.

First, the team needs to find out:

1. How much time (per day, per week, per month) can each member reasonably commit to meetings? And to outside work?
2. What time problems does each member have to solve? Family or work conflicts? Habits of lateness or last-minute work?
3. How much time is each member willing to give?
4. How can team members fit their schedules together to produce feasible blocks of mutual free time to work as a team?

Second, the team needs to:

Agree on team norms for time—being on time to meetings, not missing meetings, meeting work deadlines.

Agree on ways of dealing with exceptions—communicating among members, taking responsibility for sharing information.

Specific norms have to be worked out through the team's exploration of the issues and ideas for dealing with them. To develop these understandings, your teammates need to really listen to one another and understand the issues that may affect members' abilities to conform to the norms your team sets. You may have to work out some inventive compromises. The *transactional* process of doing this—together with the statement of and agreement to a few specific norms—can begin to create an effective *task* process for your team.

Responsibility Commitments   A sensitive but important set of understandings relates to members' responsibility to the team. Many issues and conflicts in teams arise because of individuals' differing backgrounds and expectations. The team needs to discuss members' expectations of leadership, of behaviors, and of structure. Question each other, understand these expectations, and where they suggest an important working norm for the group, state that norm.

A team we knew fervently wished they had set out some norms on these issues when, nearing the end of the project, they discovered that one member had "just assumed" that other members would "pick up" the work he had not done. He missed meetings and never communicated with the other members of the team. In the end, the team managed a good project because the other members pulled together, but it was with no thanks to the errant member. Frustration could have been avoided if the team had stated and followed up on two firm norms:

1. Whenever one member is absent, another contacts him or her immediately.
2. The team has a system for sharing work at each stage of the task, instead of waiting until the end.

Meeting Times and Places

If there's anything that can make or break a team, it's the meetings. At the first session, members need to discuss the times and places of their meetings.

Meeting times. Scheduling meetings is worth every second you put into it. We suggest that you share your schedules and identify potential meeting periods. Next, set specific meeting times, with a few alternatives in case of unforeseen glitches, for the entire stretch of the team's work. Ask members to put those meeting times on their calendars, but also get someone—the leader, the secretary, or a volunteer—to send out reminders. They limit absences caused by forgetfulness, and they eliminate excuses.

Meeting places. Where you meet affects the processes of the group. Consider variables such as accessibility for all members, comfort, resources that you might need, and the "feeling" of a place. If someone offers her or his living room, will the homey comfort facilitate discussion, or will it be so comfortable it gets you off the task? If you meet in a classroom, will the accessibility of the library and a blackboard be advantages? Or will everybody be so burnt out with school that the classroom ambience will be deadly?

The more specifically you can set up your meeting times and places, the better. People will be more likely to attend, and you can plan meetings with a clearer picture of when, where, and how they'll be conducted.

Agendas

An **agenda** is simply a plan to guide a meeting. It can be simple and straightforward, or creative and artful. Its purpose is to structure transactional and task processes to ensure that members have the opportunity to discuss, freely and openly, the important issues.

Almost every meeting should have some form of agenda. Whether formal or informal, an agenda needs to be designed, ordered, and phrased so that it facilitates the purposes, member interactions, issues, and time needs of the meeting. In most cases, it's a good idea to distribute the agenda before the meeting, but expect to modify it if necessary at the meeting.

Formal Agendas   Some agendas are structured in terms of a traditional, formal set of procedures. One reason may be the comfort level of members. Some personalities and cultural backgrounds prefer an established, predictable structure. These people need and want to know exactly how things are going to work. For other people, structure is a pain in the neck. Thus, you need to discuss structural issues and decide what your team prefers.

Sometimes the decision is influenced by the kind of organization in which the group functions. Large organizations often use parliamentary rules such as the most recent revision of *Robert's Rules of Order* (1990). These rules guide how bylaws should be written, how officers should be elected, when and how motions can be made and discussed, what kinds of motions take precedence over others, how votes are conducted, and so on. The rules are established with the realization that democratic bodies are set up on adversarial, political premises; that members can engage in every possible means of persuasion; and that their interactions must be guided by rules or the weakest voices will not be heard and their meetings will be bedlam.

Even when the meeting is of a small subcommittee of a parliamentary organization, the group is often required to submit a record of its actions and votes, with its minutes, to the parent organization. That requirement imposes a more formal approach and agenda on the committee, regardless of its members' preferences.

The formal, parliamentary agenda follows a predictable format, although the content under each category varies from meeting to meeting:

1. Meeting called to order by chair or president.
2. Minutes distributed or read by secretary.
3. Approval of minutes.
4. Committee reports from standing committees and special committees.

5. Old business (motions being discussed when the last meeting adjourned).
6. New business (motions not previously introduced).
7. Announcements by members or officers.
8. Adjournment.

This type of agenda works as a guide for meetings where there are officers, regular committee reports, and a variety of issues or plans to discuss and bring to a vote.

Informal and Special Agendas   An informal or special agenda may follow some modification of a formal agenda, but it does not necessarily follow specific rules of procedure. It is custom-designed for the purposes of the meeting, which could be anything from an ad hoc, one-time meeting to a workshop extended over several days. As you acquire experience with meetings, you develop a keen sense of how to put together and use an agenda effectively.

A special case is when you meet on an ad hoc basis without previous preparation, as when you're asked to do a classroom exercise with a group of students. You have a limited amount of time, and you've been assigned a specific task. Under these circumstances, people rarely talk about their agenda—they just start. That's a mistake; the first thing the group should do is discuss what it's going to do and how to do it. You might think of an agenda like this for your unplanned meeting:

1. Introduce yourselves.
2. Ask someone to take notes if necessary.
3. Ask someone to lead if necessary.
4. Decide on your goal or goals—what you must have accomplished by the end of the meeting.
5. Plan steps to reach the goal.
6. Get all information about your task on the table.
7. Work through the process to the goal.
8. Summarize what you've accomplished.

Although this agenda must be adapted according to the meeting's purpose, using it as a checklist helps your group work through its task efficiently.

Creating an Agenda   A team that meets over a period of time usually needs more specifically designed agendas for the various purposes of its meetings. Considerations to keep in mind include:

1. Purposes of the meeting.
2. Participants—who will be at the meeting and what each individual may want from it.
3. Issues—what, when, by whom they will be raised.
4. Time, place, and conditions for the meeting.

Suppose, for example, that this is the second meeting of your team. You've gotten to know one another and set some norms at the previous meeting. The team has asked you to lead this meeting. The purpose is to open discussion and set goals. Your team doesn't yet have conflicts, personal-agenda issues, or problems you expect to have to address. Your agenda might include:

1. Reviewing the background and the charge to the team.
2. Brainstorming to identify possible goals.
3. Drafting and revising specific goals.
4. Discussing members' agreement with and commitment to those goals.

This agenda has only four items, but that is enough for the purpose.

Suppose, on the other hand, that you've been working together for eight weeks and a major conflict has arisen. You could have a meeting with one agenda item: to negotiate a mutually acceptable way to manage the conflict.

Planning the agenda, then, requires understanding exactly what needs to be accomplished by the end of that meeting. It also will be heavily influenced by the participants.

As members of the team, their preferences are important. Some may have particular issues that you know they will want to raise. Sometimes, people block progress and discussion because of their own agendas. If you take the probability of individuals' behaviors into account, you can build an agenda that provides freedom of discussion and, at the same time, helps to control individual problems.

The issues to be discussed are, of course, paramount to creating a good agenda. You have to estimate how many issues are pending; how straightforward or complex each one is; and how much discussion, how much heat, and how much debate are going to be required to resolve each of them.

Finally, time is crucial in several respects. How much time do you have for the meeting? What is the group norm for people being late, socializing, having coffee? What needs will there be for breaks? When you know the time in which you have to work, you can examine each issue and approximate how much time it will take. Can you do it all in one meeting? If you cannot, can you eliminate or postpone some of the discussion to the next meeting?

With this information, you are ready to think about the content and order of the agenda.

Developing the Order   Each of the items we've discussed helps you decide the order of your agenda. You need to weave it carefully for transactional processes and task processes. Suppose, for example, you know these facts about your meeting:

Purposes

To decide Issue A; extremely controversial.

To decide Issue B; not controversial.

To decide Issue C; not controversial.

To discuss, perhaps decide, Issue D; not controversial.

To discuss, perhaps decide, Issue E; not controversial.

To discuss, perhaps decide, Issue F; not controversial, but Lynn's pet project and Lynn is feeling alienated because this has been postponed several times already.

To discuss, perhaps decide, Issue G; mildly controversial but not urgent.

To discuss, perhaps decide, Issue H; not controversial.

Time frame

Meeting time: two hours.

Socializing: half an hour.

Actual work time: 90 minutes.

You know 90 minutes is not enough to resolve all these issues. You know Issue A is going to take time because opinions on it are strong. It must be resolved at this meeting, but if you put it at the beginning of the agenda, it will take so much time you will not get to Issues B and C—and they must be resolved, too. Items D, E, F, G, and H could be postponed—but Issue F involves a member's feelings and can affect the team's transactional processes. It would not be wise to delay this one.

What you might do is postpone all but the three issues that must be resolved at this meeting and the one issue that is of special concern to the miffed member, Lynn. Your agenda would then look like this:

1. Discuss and decide Issue B (about 10 minutes).
2. Discuss and decide Issue C (about 10 minutes).
3. Discuss and decide Issue A (about 50 minutes).
4. Discuss and decide Issue F (about 15 minutes).
5. Confirm next meeting time, place, and assignments (about 5 minutes).

You've set it up to make the three essential decisions, but you've put the two less controversial issues first and suggested time limits of 10 minutes each for discussing them. The team will understand that, because the controversial one is next, allowing 50 minutes for discussion. The last issue, which does not have to be decided at this meeting but is important to Lynn, has its specific place at the end of the agenda. You can probably cover it, but even if you don't, at least the team has acknowledged its importance, and you can put it first for the next meeting. Thus, your agenda facilitates both transactional and task processes to achieve the purposes of the members and the meeting.

Phrasing the Steps   The phrasing of agenda items can take any number of approaches. In Chapter 8 we develop steps that guide problem-analysis and decision-making processes. Here, we're going to mention just two approaches: topical format and question format.

If everyone has a clear sense of where you're going, and your purpose is only to review and discuss some information, then all the agenda needs to do is provide the order of discussion and reminders of the topics. A simple *topical format* will do; it can be terse and to the point:

1. Review info from last meeting.
2. Report from Bob.
3. Report from Jan.
4. Discuss info relating to Dale's proposal.
5. Set up next meeting.

If, however, your purpose is to think through the implications of a proposal, you might use a *question format* to stimulate discussion and thinking:

1. How well does the proposal meet our goals?
2. What are the advantages of the proposal?
3. What are the disadvantages?
4. What are the ethical implications?
5. What are the legal implications?

Several other questions are possible, but you get the idea. The question format guides the order and kicks off the discussion, but it leaves wide open spaces for thinking critically and creatively.

An agenda can be very creative or very dull. Sometimes creative agendas can be fun and stimulating—and sometimes dull agendas can be absolutely to the point and just fine. Again, it depends on what best facilitates the processes for your purposes, people, issues, and time.

Distributing Agendas   People often feel much more organized and much more secure with an agenda, but only if it's prepared, clear, and available. A team needs to decide how it will be prepared and distributed so that it's most useful to the members.

Who designs the agenda. If you have a designated leader, the responsibility usually belongs to him or her. If you don't have a designated leader, the team can choose someone to prepare the agenda, or the members can take turns.

How and when the agenda should be distributed. Knowing what is to be covered really helps team members "do their homework" and prepare for the meeting. A good agenda can save a lot of wasted effort and time if people have it early. The team may want to make it a rule that the agenda is put together and copies sent out to the members a specific amount of time before each meeting. Some organizations' bylaws specify a time for distributing agendas. For small groups and teams, a simple statement of policy is usually sufficient.

Modifying the agenda. It should be a norm that the agenda can be modified at the beginning of a meeting. A member might say, "I'd like to add something to the agenda . . ." or "I think we should modify the agenda because something came up just this morning." The agenda, after all, should facilitate team processes, not stifle them. There needs to be room for spontaneity and adjustment; modifying the agenda is one way of providing that.

In a way, everything we've talked about in this chapter informs and facilitates creating an agenda, because an agenda provides a strategy for a meeting that advances the goals of the team.

Summary

The "work" in teamwork begins with getting to know your teammates—their strengths, their personal agendas, their perspectives. It requires making decisions about leaders—shared, emergent, distributed, turn-taking, or designated—so that the functions of the team can best be served.

The team's work is based, in part, on its context—how it interacts with other systems and subsystems and how the organization's responsibilities for giving the team autonomy and support affect its task. The team's work also requires understanding the responsibilities of the members to one another, to groups they may represent, and to building the strength of the team, as well as the team's responsibilities for self-leadership, task fulfillment, and reporting to the founder.

A team's first steps include understanding its purposes, analyzing its charge, and examining special issues, expectations, and final outcomes in order to develop a set of specific goals. Defining goals requires careful development of criteria for success and clear, unambiguous phrasing of instrumental objectives as well as terminal goals. To achieve those goals, members must confirm their understanding of and commitment to them.

Teamwork requires, too, that members establish standards and procedures for their meetings and for outside preparation. Team members must agree on basic norms about time and responsibilities. They also need to think about when and where they will meet, how formal or informal they will be, and how they will use agendas.

Considerations behind agendas include the purposes of a meeting, its participants, issues, and time. The agenda order can control individual blocking behavior while maximizing the opportunity for free and open discussion of issues, so that transactional processes and task processes work effectively together. Agendas should be distributed before meetings and modified at meetings when necessary.

Exercises

1. As a team, locate a working committee or task force (your college has faculty and student organizations and committees). Using Form 3.1 as a guide, find out all about the group from someone connected with the committee—founder, leader, and/or member. Get permission, if you can, to observe a couple of meetings. How do aspects of the group's development seem to affect the meetings? How effective do you think the group is, and why? Report what you've learned to the class.

2. Meet with a group of students. Assume you work for Families, Inc., a nonprofit organization that tries to keep troubled families together with counseling, seminars, activities, and financial assistance.

   The president has assigned your task force to investigate how Families, Inc., can cooperate with businesses and colleges to reach more families in trouble. Using Form 3.2, set goals, instrumental objectives, and criteria for your task force.

3. Your job is to create an agenda for a future meeting of your class. The purpose of that meeting is to create a list of test questions that could be included in a special examination for high school teachers who work with student groups. Don't make the list—just create the agenda for the class meeting. Use Form 3.3; be realistic about information, resources, time limitations, etc.

4. Critically analyze a task group meeting in which you've participated. How well did the group understand its relationships to other groups and systems? To what extent were the goals, and criteria for reaching them, clear to members of the group?

   How did the goals affect transactional and task processes? How did they affect accomplishing the task? What were the group norms? Did they facilitate or impede the group's work?

   How was the meeting? Was there a written agenda? Did it work? Did it help people to focus on the task and discuss issues effectively? What worked well? What would have made the meeting better?

FORM 3.1 ▮ TEAM IDENTIFICATION ANALYSIS

To identify the who-what-why-where-when-how of your team, complete the grid with this information:

Reasons   For members, why they were chosen for the team; for others, what their relationships to the team might be.

Goals   For members, what each would like to get from the teamwork; for others, what they expect the team to produce.

Resources   For members, what each can contribute (talents, skills, abilities, resources, etc.); for others, what they can/will provide for the team's work.

Limitations   For members, how each may be limited (time, resources, etc.); for others, how their involvement may be restricted.

	REASONS	GOALS	RESOURCES	LIMITATIONS
Members				
Founder				
Related Teams or Units				

Note below any other history, circumstances, or comments that are important to understanding the team and its context:

FORM 3.2 ▌ TEAM GOALS ANALYSIS

Together, set the *goals* for the team's work. Then identify the *instrumental objectives* the team must accomplish to reach each goal and the *criteria* the team will use to judge its success in reaching the goal. (Duplicate this form for additional goals.)

Goal # 1

_____

_____

Instrumental objectives for goal # 1

_____

_____

_____

Criteria for reaching goal # 1

_____

_____

_____

Goal # 2

_____

_____

Instrumental objectives for goal # 2

_____

_____

_____

Criteria for reaching goal # 2

_____

_____

_____

FORM 3.3 ∎ A G E N D A   P L A N N I N G

Step One: Survey these planning data before creating the agenda.
Purposes of the meeting

_____

_____

_____

Special concerns of members

_____

_____

_____

Time limitations

_____

_____

Special equipment/resource needs	Persons responsible for arranging for/obtaining item
_____	_____
_____	_____
_____	_____

Step Two: Using the above data, arrange your agenda to allow time for members to discuss issues and arrive at their goals. If an individual is responsible for reporting a given item or facilitating discussion, indicate that responsibility on the form. Be sure to include time for preparation for the next meeting.

	PERSON RESPONSIBLE	APPROXIMATE TIME
Item # 1		
Item # 2		
Item # 3		
Item # 4		
Item # 5		
Item # 6		
Item # 7		

Notes to remember for the meeting:

CHAPTER 4

The "Team" in Teamwork:
Bringing Individuals Together

"Make a team out of *this* group? Nah—can't be done!"
Sure it can. You just have to "get it together."

It's one thing to "get a group together," and quite another to forge that group into a team. We've all completed a series of meetings feeling ho-hum about the whole thing. Or sometimes we've left muttering, "Not on pain of dismemberment and death will I *ever* work with those people again." Such group experiences, in which you never feel a sense of "teamness," are not pretty pictures.

In this chapter we start off with a different picture—a model of the "superteam" for which to strive. Then we take you through the processes of building a team. A team starts developing in the context of an organizational culture. It is comprised of individual members whose characteristics and motivations help to shape it. It begins creating its own team attributes as it goes through phases of development, and it guides and nurtures its own development by using feedback.

At the end of this chapter, you should:

1. Have a mental picture of the "ideal" team.

2. Know how organizational culture affects a team's development.

3. Understand how individual members' motivations and characteristics affect a team's development.

4. Know the ways in which a team develops its own characteristics.

5. Understand the phases a team goes through as it develops.

6. Know how to get and use feedback to help a team develop.

A "Superteam" Model

Sometimes when writers get started on the "ideal," it begins to sound like metaphysical hocus-pocus or, worse, pure hype. A lot of writing about teams today gives the impression of "rah, rah, sis boom bah" cheerleading for the good old team concept.

That's *not* what we want to do here. What we want to do is show you a model of what you're working to create in future teams. This picture of superteams comes from observations by a British consulting group (Hastings, Bixby, & Chaudhry-Lawton, 1986). Superteams, they say, "weave together a rich fabric of competencies, experience, attitudes and values which create a tightly woven, integrated cloth suitable for many purposes" (pp. 10–12).

Hastings and his colleagues identified characteristics of such teams. We have rephrased and subdivided these into qualities of transactional processes, task processes, and systems relationships, to place them in the context of this book.

In terms of *transactional processes* superteams are:

Success-driven. They have energy, excitement, and commitment and thrive on the recognition that success brings.

Active. They are quick to respond, positive, optimistic even when the going gets tough; they make things happen.

Committed to quality. In team and task, they have very high expectations of themselves and of others.

Leader-valuing. They value leaders who maintain direction, energy, and commitment. They expect the leader, with their help, to fight for support and resources.

Tenacious and inventive. They confront people and issues and remove obstacles in their paths.

Flexible. They work best with principles and guidelines rather than rules.

Consistent. They maintain communication and momentum; their teamwork continues apart as well as together.

People-valuing. They respect knowledge, competence, and contributions over status and position.

Cooperative. They always try to work with others, rather than for or against them.

Never satisfied. They understand why they are successful but constantly look for ways to "do things better."

In terms of *task processes,* superteams are:

Vision-driven. Their vision of what they are trying to achieve gives them a sense of purpose and direction, a realistic strategy for turning the vision into reality.

Goal-oriented. They are persistent, obsessive, yet creatively flexible, continuously asking, "What are we trying to achieve?"

Analytical. They distinguish priorities and choose flexible, creative, or routine approaches appropriately.

Creative and innovative. They take legitimate risks to achieve significant gains.

With respect to *systems relationships,* superteams are characterized as:

Networking. Builders of formal and informal networks, they include people who matter to them and who can help them.

Visible and accessible. They communicate what they are and solicit feedback and help from outside the team.

Understanding. The larger system's strategy and philosophy, or that part of it important to success, influences their decisions.

Committed to success. They want to achieve the parent organizations' goals. They thrive in an open culture where responsibility and authority are delegated to them to produce agreed-on results.

Mutually influential. With their organization, their influence is based on credibility rather than authority.

We've seen members of highly motivated, strong teams turn to each other and say, almost out of nowhere, "Damn, we're good!" That's mostly a positive outcome, because it motivates members to drive on to bigger and better things.

A superteam needs to recognize the negative side, however: "Superteams sometimes seem arrogant—and this can be the cause of their downfall!" (p. 12). Feeling too good, being too cohesive, can lead to excesses of ego, blind spots, declines in productivity, and, yes, to arrogance. We examine the dynamics of that phenomenon, and what to do about it, in Chapter 13.

With that said, we see an accurate image emerging from this list. It's a team that achieves its goals, and then some. It's something for which to strive, but getting there takes understanding and work. A superteam doesn't just happen.

Context and Organizational Culture

Did you notice how the last five characteristics of superteams are influenced by the way the organization as a whole *feels* to people? That's because every organization has a culture of its own, and teams develop within the context of that culture.

In an **organizational culture,** observes Ott (1989), "as in *all* cultures, *all* facts, truths, realities, beliefs and values *are what the members agree they are*—they are perceptions." As people work together, they create a culture and pass it along to new members through telling and retelling "organization myths, stories, and sagas, complete with heroes, crises, and happy endings" (p. vii).

Organizations develop norms, expectations, and responses that become part of their culture; these guide the way people act and what they do. Recently we observed the organizational culture in a large hospital. It was unmistakably one of care and concern; no matter how rushed or exhausted from twelve-hour shifts people were, they spoke with compassion and focused on the patients' well-being. We were startled when one nurse was abrupt and rude; later we found out she was not a permanent employee. This hospital's culture was so strong that we, as outsiders, could tell when one individual simply wasn't part of it.

Although teams create their own cultures, they tend to be in tune with the parent organization and to work toward a common vision. When the culture of the organization changes, so do roles and circumstances of its subsystems. A dramatic example occurred following the breakup of the Soviet Union and elimination of the Communist party. The Soviet military, a subculture of the defunct Soviet organization, was thrown into massive confusion. Almost immediately, a group of Soviet military leaders was sent to the John F. Kennedy School at Harvard University to study the role of the military in a democracy. The major changes in the organizational culture of government had an impact on other parts of the system, and the military leaders had to be retrained.

The type of organizational culture can make or break the ability of groups and teams to function within it. Walton and Hackman (1986) identify two distinct types of organizations: control strategy and commitment strategy. In between these two is the mixed-strategy organization, one in transition from control to commitment. Familiarity with these types of organizational cultures can help you understand what's happening to a team.

A **control-strategy organization** is status and power driven, hierarchical, and tightly controlling. It has an adversarial, nontrusting relationship with its people and the union. You find few formal groups or teams; management simply doesn't trust people to work in groups.

A **commitment-strategy organization** deliberately reduces layers of authority and control, commits to quality, and adopts methods to make the culture open, receptive, and participative. It uses teams extensively, gives them support and autonomy, trains and nurtures members, and empowers them to make decisions and create quality results.

A **mixed-strategy organization** is trying to shift from control to commitment. Management, aware of newer approaches, is trying them out. Because old habits of mistrust and control die hard, management may appoint teams but give them little training, support, or autonomy. Frustration may be high, and the organization may have to work through periods of adjustment and learning.

Teams perform more effectively in commitment-strategy organizations because they can be more creative, more satisfied, and more productive. In an old-fashioned control-strategy organization, teamwork is limited to what people can create with co-workers, on the job, and without organizational help.

You may well find yourself, however, in a mixed-strategy organization. Teamwork in your future may involve helping such an organization develop good teams, understanding the difficulties of the transition, and providing leadership.

The way an organization sees its culture inevitably affects how a team sees itself. If it is controlling, suspicious, and mean, it's hard for the team to get beyond

ASPIRATIONS STATEMENT: LEVI STRAUSS & COMPANY

We all want a company that our people are proud of and committed to, where all employees have an opportunity to contribute, learn, grow, and advance based on merit, not politics or background. We want our people to feel respected, treated fairly, listened to, and involved. Above all, we want satisfaction from accomplishments and friendships, balanced personal and professional lives, and to have fun in our endeavors.

When we describe the kind of Levi Strauss & Co. we want in the future, what we are talking about is building on the foundation we have inherited: affirming the best of our company's traditions, closing gaps that may exist between principles and practices, and updating some of our values to reflect contemporary circumstances.

What type of leadership is necessary to make our aspirations a reality?

New Behaviors: Leadership that exemplifies directness, openness to influence, commitment to the success of others, willingness to acknowledge our own contributions to problems, personal accountability, teamwork, and trust. Not only must we model these behaviors but we must coach others to adopt them.

Diversity: Leadership that values a diverse work force (age, sex, ethnic group, etc.) at all levels of the organization, diversity in experience, and diversity in perspectives. We have committed to taking full advantage of the rich backgrounds and abilities of all our people and to promoting a greater diversity in positions of influence. Differing points of view will be sought, diversity will be valued and honesty rewarded, not suppressed.

Recognition: Leadership that provides greater recognition—both financial and psychic—for individuals and teams that contribute

to our success. Recognition must be given to all who contribute: those who create and innovate and also those who continually support the day-to-day business requirements.

Ethical Management Practices: Leadership that epitomizes the stated standards of ethical behavior. We must provide clarity about our expectations and must enforce these standards through the corporation.

Communications: Leadership that is clear about company, unit, and individual goals and performance. People must know what is expected of them and receive timely, honest feedback on their performance and career aspirations.

Empowerment: Leadership that increases the authority and responsibility of those closest to our products and customers. By actively pushing responsibility, trust, and recognition into the organization, we can harness and release the capabilities of all our people.

Used by permission of Levi Strauss & Company.

those barriers. If the culture of the organization is caring about people and daring about progress, the team will be able to be that way, too.

Individual Members

Regardless of where a group starts—an organization, athletic program, community, or academic institution—it requires changing a loosely connected bunch of individuals into something that has a life, a culture, and characteristics of its own. A "team" is shaped, consciously and unconsciously, by the individuals who are drawn together from across some system or organization. What is it about individuals that induces them to join groups, and what attributes do they bring to creating a team?

Why People Join Teams

You and your teammates find yourselves on a team for a number of reasons, and those individual reasons affect your interactions. Sometimes a specific personal interest or attraction spurs you to become a member, or the group helps to meet needs, to reduce drives, or to provide rewards for you.

Interests and Attractions   People join groups for a lot of reasons. You may be in a group or a team because you've been assigned to it; for this class, you may be assigned to a project team or work groups. In your career, you may join, form, or be assigned to many teams. You may join a sports team because you want to play, a study group to succeed in a class, or a support group for help in coping with some heavy burden. You may form a coalition to achieve some community or political purpose because you feel deeply about the goal. You may even join a particular group just because you are attracted to the members—you like them.

What attracts you to other people? Their physical appearance? Their likes and dislikes, intellect, sense of humor? The degree to which they are like you? The degree to which they are unlike you? Most people are attracted to others by physical appearance and/or similarity (Krebs & Adinolf, 1975). They measure others by standards of beauty and style acquired through a lifetime of socialization. People also feel safer with others who seem like themselves because there are fewer unknowns, fewer surprises, about similar people.

Attraction and similarity may become less important as you get to know others (Zajonc, 1968). It's possible, after a period of time with a group, to discover that you really respect and enjoy a person you thought was boring to begin with, or that you dislike someone you originally found attractive.

Drive Reduction   Interests and attractions aren't the only motivators for group activity. Deeper needs and motivations can initially draw people to groups—and then shape and drive the way those members interact. Knowing something about human drives helps enormously in understanding—and reducing frustrations—in transactional processes.

Suppose, for example, you're on a community task force whose job is to make recommendations for changes in police coverage for the town. Among the members are a representative of a city-supported housing project and the principal of an elementary school on the "better side of town." You notice that the housing-project representative keeps saying the town needs more police protection and seems not to want to hear anything else; the school principal keeps insisting that the task force must produce a truly high-quality report. Neither person understands the other. What's going on?

It's possible that the housing-project resident is terrified by crime in the area. The school principal, who lives and works in a secure, affluent part of town, may be more concerned that the task force reflect well on its members. These two people may have joined the task force for very different reasons; understanding those diverse needs can affect how they listen to and talk with one another.

One way to understand people's motives is in terms of **drive reduction theories,** which suggest that people are motivated to act in ways that help them reduce the drives they feel. Abraham Maslow's (1943) theory could account for the motives of each person in our example. Maslow believes an individual moves up a ladder of needs, driven to satisfy one level before being able to notice the next. The steps go like this:

1. *Physiological* needs for food or sleep. Once these needs are met, the person can attend to:

2. *Security* needs for safety and predictability. (Our housing-project representative is probably at this level and can't think about anything but whether the family is safe at home.) With security satisfied, it's possible to feel the need for:

3. *Love and belongingness* with other people. Social interactions with others are motivators here. Once one is comfortable with relationships, then attention can go to:

4. *Self-esteem.* At this level, people need to feel good about themselves. (That's probably where the principal is.) With a strong sense of self-esteem, an individual can attend to:

5. *Self-actualization*—an unlimited drive to develop oneself, to reach beyond present accomplishment to achieve full potential. (Not many people are here; most mortals are struggling up the prerequisite steps.)

Another insight comes from Schutz (1966), who sees *control* (along with inclusion and affection) as a motive driving interactions with others. Control needs show up often in groups. They may motivate people to join, to lead, and to dominate other members, and people may interact with others to balance their own control needs. For example, a member of your team may try to force his or her opinions down others' throats; she or he may have a strong need to control. If others need to *be* controlled, they may accept that direction comfortably. If, on the other hand, they don't like being controlled, or if they want to control the group themselves, watch out. They may lock horns in a power struggle.

Another drive that affects team membership and transactions is the *need to achieve*. This need is similar to Maslow's self-esteem need. People who have a high need for achievement, according to McClelland (1989), "set moderately difficult, but potentially achievable goals for themselves . . . setting challenges for themselves, tasks to make them stretch themselves a little . . . but they behave like this only if they can influence the outcome by performing the work themselves" (p. 86).

A high achiever can set a standard and help to motivate others, leading them to create a high-achievement team, seeking challenges and improvement for the sake of the growth they provide. We've experienced such teams, and we liked them.

Did you come from a family who believed that anything could be accomplished with hard work? Then, chances are that philosophy is a basic tenet of your management style.

Did your family solve problems through consensus by holding a family meeting? If so, that may be one reason why you seek the opinion of your group before making a final decision.

Did your family insist on cooperation among the members, that siblings help each other to finish chores faster? That may be why a team approach to problem solving is one you choose.

As these examples illustrate, your family history—who you are and how you were raised—can affect how you approach your job. . . .

High Expectations   Some families expect the best from their sons and daughters—high marks in school, artistic talent, athletic prowess. While setting high goals for children can be inspiring, it can also be demoralizing when any attempt falls short of the mark. A series of misses may result in an individual developing low self-esteem, something that can carry over into a career.

Low Expectations   Families who failed to encourage their children produce workers who are ambivalent about success. . . . Someone who does achieve success may suffer the "imposter syndrome" and be unable to accept that success. . . .

Make Negatives Positives   A perceived weakness may be an area of strength if applied properly. Your family may not have appreciated your penchant to pursue a task doggedly until completed. But that habit could be used to your advantage at work.

Condensed from *Working Smart: Personal Report for the Executive*, September 1, 1990, pp. 1–2, published by National Institute of Business Management, Inc. Used with permission.

Each of these views provides insight into why people join groups and why they behave as they do. The important concepts to remember from these drive-reduction theories are:

1. Motivational drives may be, as Maslow believes, hierarchical. Recognizing these levels of needs can help you understand how another member can start from assumptions so different from yours.
2. The need to control may be, as Schutz proposes, balanced or imbalanced in interactions between or among people. Recognizing that can help you understand some seemingly strange affiliations and conflicts among people in groups.
3. The need for achievement, described by McClelland, explains why individuals have certain expectations that can be met through their involvement on the team. Recognizing those expectations helps you understand their goals and suggests ways you can help lead a team to higher achievement.

Reinforcement   Another explanation for the way people choose groups and interact in them is the reinforcement, or rewards, they can provide. **Reinforcement theories** propose that people do things for some reward, and don't do things because of some threat or punishment. If I make a joke and the team laughs, that's a reward; if I make a joke and the members glare, that presumably is a punishment. Theoretically, the reward causes me to continue making jokes, whereas the punishment keeps me from doing it again. Immediately, of course, you think of the individual who seems to love being glared at and who turns right around and offends you again.

Rewards and costs are perceived individually. You could look at this example in terms of both drives and reward. If my drive is for love and I can't seem to get it from being "good," perhaps getting attention from being "bad" is reward enough. I'll just keep on playing the "fun-seeker" role in my team—preventing work, frustrating people, but getting the attention I need.

People may weigh the possible results of their actions, either consciously or unconsciously. Kelley and Thibaut (1978), in their **social exchange theory**, propose that people weigh three factors when selecting their behaviors:

1. How they predict the interaction will come out. Will the rewards outweigh the costs?
2. How that result would compare to what they minimally will accept.
3. How it would compare to other possible choices.

Suppose you're trying to decide whether or not to join the debate team. You're motivated to join because you'd feel good about yourself and you believe you would win trophies and/or opportunities (rewards). You also know it would take an enormous amount of time and energy (costs). You compare the expected satisfactions to the amount of time you dare give up from your schedule (comparison level), and decide the rewards outweigh the costs. Now you compare the rewards of joining the team to those you've calculated for taking an extra job (comparison level for alternatives). The debate team seems to promise more rewards, so you decide to go with it.

You have gone through a social exchange process—computing your possible rewards and costs, aligning those comparisons with your motivations and needs—and you've come up with a decision that you predict will be a good one for you.

Although some people see drive-reduction and reinforcement theories as mutually exclusive, we do not. Both are useful for understanding what influences a person to join a group and what influences the ways in which she or he participates.

What Individuals Bring

A variety of personal motives cause people to join groups, but when you are *selected* for a team, it's specifically for what you, as an individual, can bring to it. The diversity individuals bring to their team can become a strength that ensures its success, or it can create barriers to the team's effectiveness. The outcome depends, in large part, on understanding how differently people can perceive and how important the richness of diverse backgrounds can be.

Ways of Perceiving   Picture this: You and a teammate have the same magazine article in your hands. You see it as supporting your position; your teammate sees it the opposite way. Who is right?

Try this one: Your team is stymied. You've worked on a report for hours, and you just can't seem to make it clear. Then one member exclaims, "Map! We'll draw a map showing how the data lead to our conclusions." Of course! What you couldn't do with words alone, you can do with a diagram. How come one member saw it when others did not?

One more: You are uncomfortable with a teammate because you believe she doesn't like you. Then another member tells you privately that the person you thought didn't like you believes *you* don't like *her* and she's hurt because you avoid her.

Perception is a funny thing. It's the way people do (or do not) pay attention to a stimulus and how they interpret it for themselves. These examples point to three facts about the ways people perceive that are particularly important for transactional and task processes:

People perceive selectively. When their motives, needs, drives, wants, and experience get in the way, they may actually not see things that are unacceptable or unknown to them. They may find, in a ten-page essay, the one and only statement that supports their biases. It isn't just a matter of consciously ignoring something, although people do that, too. They may not even know that a message has been given; they've screened it out.

People perceive what their backgrounds permit them to perceive. Culture, language, gender, experience—all affect the way a person can see and think. The teammate who thinks of a map that no one else imagined may be more visually oriented than others—perhaps an artist, or maybe a chemist who sees things in structures. Once, for example, one of us gave a report on Aristotelian logic. A classmate, recently arrived from Japan, looked puzzled. After class, he explained, "In my culture we do not think this way. We have no 'logic' in the way you use the term." He was a very competent, bright person, but our backgrounds prepared us to perceive things in different ways.

People multiply their misperceptions in regard to other people. Just as you cannot really be sure how another person perceives objects or ideas, neither can you be sure how teammates see you; nor can they be sure how you see them; nor can they be sure how each of them perceives each of the others. The same person may be perceived as creative by one member; flaky by another; weird by another; bright by yet another. One member may have selectively screened the individual out, and can't even think of her name. Furthermore, the individual in question undoubtedly perceives each of those other people differently and misunderstands how *they* perceive *her*.

What a member selects and perceives affects what she or he believes to be true—about ideas, facts, people. Another member's reality, based on his or her perceptions, may be different. Each member's perceptions interact with all other members' perceptions to affect the team's transactional and task processes.

Abilities and Backgrounds   You find yourself in a group with people who see things, and each other, in a wide variety of ways. What on earth inspired someone to put you all together? A discussion of whom to assign, or invite, to a team may go something like this:

"Let's put Bobbi on the team; we need her expertise." "That's true, but she's so abrasive." "Right. Well, what if we ask Ron to be on it? He's good at smoothing out the rough edges." "Okay, great . . . yeah, he really is. But sometimes he smoothes things out so well you don't get at some of the problems." "True. What if we add Janet? She can go straight to the heart of an issue—great critical analysis—and she also gets along well with Bobbi. . . ." A team with different, but complementary, abilities and backgrounds begins to form.

Some considerations that go into creating teams are:

Specific talents, abilities. The point is to meet needs for task and transactional processes.

Resources. Individuals may be selected for their knowledge, networks, or specific qualifications.

Differences of background and experience. Variety in ways of perceiving can provide more creativity, better critical thinking, greater success in achieving goals.

Representation. The team may include women, minorities, special interest groups for diverse perspectives and insights.

Control, authority, and/or status. A manager, administrator, or person with "clout" may be appointed to lead the team or influence it. In some cultures, such as France, this is essential.

The rationale for membership affects both task and transactional processes. A manager who is there to make the final call, for example, may inhibit the way the team considers ideas. If someone is there because she or he has a strong legal background, the team may look to that person exclusively on legal issues. Interactions also can be affected by expectations of an individual as a representative of some other group.

It can be tough, for example, if you're the only African-American member. Your teammates may expect you to speak for the entire race and to know precisely what every African-American thinks about every issue. Outside people may expect you to move the entire team in the direction of their thinking. You may feel shut out of the chance to make observations about anything that is *not* seen as an "African-American issue," because anything else is not perceived as your role, no matter how relevant and important your analysis may be. Such pigeonholing seriously limits your potential contributions.

An aware and effective team enables members to fulfill the unique purposes for which each was appointed. At the same time, it empowers all members to go be-

CASE ANALYSIS 4.1

The task force had four members from McDonald's and three from EDF. The McDonald's members were:

1. Director of operations development department involved with new operating systems and improvements worldwide; began as a crew member at a local McDonald's and worked up to this position over 17 years.

2. Environmental affairs consultant, government relations department; involved in research on recycling and source reductions issues and a corporate spokesperson to environmental and government groups.

3. Director of environmental affairs from the company that purchases packaging and materials for McDonald's from a large number of suppliers.

4. Director of communications; responsible for managing McDonald's interaction with the media, and provides communications counsel, support, and training throughout the company; also has specific responsibility for environmental issues.

The EDF members were:

1. Senior scientist with a Ph.D. in molecular biophysics and biochemistry; specializes in hazardous and solid waste management issues.

2. Staff scientist who conducts research on solid waste issues, including recycling technologies and the use of life-cycle assessments in evaluating consumer products.

3. Economic analyst with a master's degree in city planning, with a specialization in environmental policy; works on issues linking economic development and environmental quality.

Issues for Your Consideration

1. For what reasons do you think each was put on the team? Do any members seem unnecessary? Would people with other backgrounds and abilities be helpful?

2. Are there ways in which background differences might affect the team's work positively? Negatively?

yond expected roles, to contribute the full range of their talents and abilities, and to exercise leadership in the process of developing a strong team.

Team Attributes

Just as individuals have unique characteristics, so do groups. As individuals work together—as they bring their complementary abilities into play—they start to develop the traits that bring their team closer to the ideal picture of the superteam, creating a group culture, image, vision, syntality, synergy, and cohesiveness.

Team Culture

We've talked about how a team is affected by the organizational culture within which it functions. When you develop a new team, you also develop a **team culture**. It is a newly woven fabric of threads from the larger society, from the parent organization, and from the various cultures or subcultures of the members.

Team members, different though they may be, develop shared values, beliefs, and assumptions. They create mutually understood and accepted rules and norms that influence their behaviors in, and often outside of, the group. They develop a team ethic that governs their transactions and influences their tasks.

Does a team's culture, for example, encourage open exploration of ideas? Or does it stifle members' efforts to look at various viewpoints? Does the culture emphasize honesty and equity in decision making? Or does it communicate that the highest value is profit or advantage? Does the team culture encourage dialogue, trust, and cooperation—or does it foster competition and suspicion?

As your team develops, keep an eye on the myths, stories, images, and symbols that seem to distinguish your team's culture. They are a measure of its quality. Do people, for example, tell stories of moments that the team pulled together and created something positive? Or do they exult in taking advantage of another group or in playing "dirty tricks"? What do these clues indicate about the team culture's ethics?

Shared Image

A team that works together for any period of time develops, as part of its culture, a **team image**—a strong sense of its own identity that helps motivate and direct the members, just as a strong sense of personal identity may shape an individual's behaviors.

An excellent team can identify its own positive self-image. It may not deliberately create the image, but it can encourage its development. The foundation often consists of moments of humor, bits of fantasy, or metaphors that people use to describe how they feel about the team's task or work. One way of providing leadership is to be alert to such moments and help build on them, to create mutual symbols for the team's experience.

For example, if in a meeting someone says, "I feel like I need spikes on my shoes, we're climbing so many mountains," another might respond, "Yeah! I've got my little pick and rappel rope handy." A few more comments, and the team has created an image of a carefully coordinated team of skillful climbers, mutually dependent on one another, scaling a difficult peak, determined to plant its flag at the top. The image becomes a metaphor for the entire experience, and the symbols become refined through frequent reference. Sooner or later someone says,

"Wait a minute—I've got to get my spikes in," and everyone knows exactly what that means.

Such an image is positive, mutual, and healthy. When problems must be overcome, this team is more motivated to overcome those challenges—to get to the top of their mountain—than is a team with a weaker image. However, it is possible for teams, like individuals, to develop negative or destructive self-images. Good leadership detects and discourages negative or weak images; but it senses and seizes moments to encourage the team's mutual development of a strong and healthy team image.

Sometimes the culture of a small group can be so strong, and its image so clear, that nonmembers can identify a member of that group without any information other than the person's behavior, dress, or speech. You see this in fraternities, sororities, professional groups, sometimes in departments of an organization. We're not suggesting that this is necessarily a good thing; it *can* lead to the arrogance we mentioned earlier and to excessive conformity. But it does indicate how strong a group image can become and how important it can be.

Shared Vision

People who have experienced excellent teamwork feel that they shared a **team vision** of what they were doing and where they were going. This vision is more holistic than the goals and objectives; it is something total the team sees ahead as the result of its work.

The principle is closely akin to visualization, described in Chapter 2. When an individual has a clear mental picture of what she or he is striving for, both the goal and the steps to be taken become more vivid and more attainable. Just as visualizing a goal and strategies for achieving it helps individuals, it also helps groups to know what they're striving for and to behave in ways that will get them there.

As a team develops a culture, an image, and a vision the interactions among team members begin to take on characteristics of their own. Group theorists call these characteristics syntality and synergy (Cattell, 1948).

Syntality

Syntality is to a group what personality is to an individual. Your personality reflects who you are to yourself and to others; your team's syntality communicates what that team is to itself and others. It includes what people have created in the way of a team culture, ethic, image, and vision, as well as what they themselves are. You can't "add up" the personalities of each member and come out with the team's syntality; the whole is much more than the sum of its parts.

Your team's syntality reflects the entirety of its traits: the way members interact, the way they share ideas and solve problems, the way they feel and respond to one another. Teams can be introverted or extroverted, open-minded or close-minded. The entire approach to transactional and task processes is reflected in the group's syntality.

Synergy

As members work together, their energies and talents fuse into a special kind of energy. **Synergy** is the energy that moves your team; it is a combination of the drives, needs, motives, and vitality of the members. When all members are committed to the team and its vision, and when their individual needs and drives motivate them to work for the goals of the team, then the interactions of the team create synergy. It is synergy that actually makes it possible to be a team and to do the work of the team.

It's easy to see how important synergy is to a team's effectiveness if you look at a group in which its qualities seem poor or nonexistent. Some members drag the team back with their negative energy. Other members, motivated to do well for a grade or a promotion, work themselves to a frazzle, do other people's work for them, and meet frustration at every turn. They function as loose-knit individuals, not as a team.

Cohesiveness

Good teams have a sense of being more than just a bunch of people. A team's **cohesiveness** is the degree to which its members are attracted toward one another and the group; it is a team's esprit de corps, "groupness," or team pride. Cohesiveness involves loyalty, commitment, a certain like-mindedness, and a willingness to sacrifice for the group. It is the glue that sticks members together.

The quality of a group's performance is related to the degree to which a team is cohesive. Obviously, you want your team to develop cohesiveness, a "one for all and all for one" good feeling about your team and your work. It helps you do great things.

It's important, however, to distinguish the positive from the negative effects of cohesiveness. It can give members an unrealistic view of things; keep them from thinking for themselves and from investigating issues; and lead to illusions and bad decisions. Cohesiveness is something to think carefully about as we work through this book. It comes up again in Chapter 13.

Phases of Development

All the characteristics that team members must create together develop over time. Not every team grows in precisely the same way as every other team, but some predictable patterns can give you an idea of what to expect before you start. We'll look at some typical phases and then examine some ways to help your team work through them.

"Now, now, folks—we're just going through a phase . . ."

Tuckman and Jensen (1977) identified five stages of interaction and work development that many groups go through. Your team will not necessarily go through them in this order, but you can almost bank on experiencing each of them at some time:

1. *Forming.* Initially, members get organized and oriented to one another and the group.
2. *Storming.* Conflict among members arises when the honeymoon is over. Some groups have an intense, prolonged struggle; others a brief skirmish.
3. *Norming.* A sense of team emerges in the third stage, along with norms for handling conflict and transactional and task processes that work.
4. *Performing.* In this stage, the team completes the work, and members reinforce one another in feeling a sense of accomplishment.
5. *Adjourning.* The team ends its functions, and members find ways of saying good-bye to the team.

How a team experiences these phases is influenced strongly by the type of team it is and by its purposes. Gersick (1988) observed project teams, fund-raising committees, corporate and health care teams, and university teams. All had specific projects and tasks, used shared leadership, and met for an extended period of time. Thus, Gersick's observations relate directly to the kinds of teams most people experience.

Each team had distinctive patterns of development, depending on its purposes and members, but they all experienced a **punctuated equilibrium**—that is, periods of seeming inertia broken by bursts of energy and change. For every team, *precisely at the midpoint of its life*, a period of crisis struck. This is consistent with our own observations of a **midpoint crisis**: members suddenly wake up and realize that half the time's gone and only half is left to get the job done. Sometimes they panic; then they get down to work.

Gersick found a general pattern that went like this:

1. At their first meetings, teams' activities varied with their respective tasks.
2. Several meetings (Phase One) dealt with conflicts, getting information, and working through issues.
3. The midlife crisis meeting was focused according to the team's purpose. Various teams dealt with decisions about goals, revising drafts of reports, outlining programs, or managing conflicts. One team even dissolved, reconstituted, and redefined itself at this meeting. It was a point of tension, management, and direction. The same kind of crisis and change period hit each team at precisely the midpoint of its experience.
4. After this transition, teams went through another series of meetings (Phase Two) to work out details of their tasks.
5. This led to the final completion meeting, in which each team finalized its work according to the type and purposes of the team.

If you can identify what your team is going through, you'll be able to help the process along. As you exercise leadership in this way, keep in mind:

1. The emotional highs and lows—storming, norming, conflicting—are normal in group development.
2. Developmental stages are important. If the group abbreviates a stage because it is too anxious to get the problem solved, or because the members aren't willing to work through their conflicts, or because they simply won't take the emergence of the group seriously, the team and its quality may be torpedoed.
3. Your team may go through periods of inertia as it fumbles around with its conflicts and its tasks; that's normal, too. And it probably will hit an essential midpoint crisis before it really gets to work.

If you understand what's happening, then the team can use its "midlife crisis" as an effective fulcrum to promote creative, productive fulfillment of the goals of the team.

Feedback Approaches

One way to help a team develop through all these processes and phases is to use a mirror. Healthy teams use the cybernetic processes introduced in Chapter 1—feedback, observation, discussion—to see what they're doing and to modify it as they go along.

As we discussed earlier in this chapter, one person's perception can differ greatly from another's. "Gee," one member might say, "that was a terrific experience! Did you notice how so-and-so came out of his shell?" It sounds good, until so-and-so tells you privately that the group was a nightmare. It's only natural for people to judge things based on their own limited perceptions.

Teams need systematic approaches for getting feedback and using it to assess and improve their accomplishments. In this section we talk about principles, sources, and uses of feedback to improve a team's processes and outcomes.

Principles

There are two critical principles for feedback: it must be nonthreatening, and it must be team-generated (Lumsden, Knight, & Gallaro, 1989). All members must plan and want the feedback before they can use it freely. That means it has to be exclusively for the team's use.

If you are working on a corporate team, for example, and your organization uses evaluations of your team to decide pay raises or promotions, there is no way you and your teammates can view that feedback as something you want or something you will use; you can only see it as reward or punishment. In such a case, your team needs to generate its own separate feedback for its own private use.

As a team, establish expectations that you will collect information on how you're doing. Decide that, as a team, you will choose your methods, timing, and use of that feedback. Then the cybernetic process belongs to, and serves to benefit, your team.

Sources of Feedback

You need feedback all through the life of the team from all relevant sources; everyone involved with the team can help. A constant feedback loop can get information from the parent organization (or "boss" or teacher), from team members, and from related sources (other teams or departments, clients, customers, depending upon the type of team). You can seek feedback on the ways in which team members actually conduct both transactional and task processes, how the team interacts with other systems and subsystems, and the effectiveness or quality of the outcomes.

Here are some useful techniques for assessing what is happening in team transactional and task processes:

Feedback forms. Members regularly complete short questionnaires about their teamwork individually, then analyze them together. Feedback forms can focus on any aspect of the team experience: individual, transactional, or task.

Objective process observers and consultants. An outside person can observe and analyze the team as it works. She or he can then help members process the observations and design ways to improve their quality. In a classroom, the observer may be a member of the class. For an organizational team, a consultant with expertise in team communication may come from a corporate training and development department or be hired from outside.

Videotaping or audiotaping. Taping a session and playing it back for discussion can help team members see how they are working together. It highlights both strengths and weaknesses—and it can be played back as many times as needed.

If these methods are combined, a very clear idea of what's working and what's not working can emerge.

Uses of Feedback

It's critically important for all members to participate in getting and analyzing feedback because it takes mutual commitment for any changes to be effective. Teams can use the following guidelines to make feedback work most effectively:

1. Focus on the team's successes and accomplishments. Identify those processes that are working well and the positive feelings members have about the team's work. All teams do some things well, and starting with this perspective provides a foundation on which to build future successes.

2. Discuss what the feedback means to the team. Is it valid? Was the technique used to gather it objective, complete, and consistent? Is the information supported by and consistent with other knowledge the team has of itself? Does it indicate important insights into the way the team is functioning?

3. Design a method for implementing the insights gained from the feedback. The method could be structural—changing the format, location, or times of meetings; it could be constitutional—modifying the team's task, adding or deleting members, or changing the leader; or it could be transactional—changing specific communication behaviors, such as agreeing to be more assertive.

4. Agree on a method for achieving the change. Methods may require getting outside support or resources, adopting new procedures, supporting and helping each other with behavioral changes.

5. Agree on times and methods for reassessing the issue to see if it is resolved or improving. That could mean simply repeating the original method of feedback and comparing it, or it could mean adding new evaluation methods to the process.

6. Agree to implement and support the changes and to be open in giving and receiving feedback in the process of improvement.

Here's an example of the process: A consultant has observed four meetings of a corporate work team and noted that of the seven members, only three talked—an executive and two managers. In discussing this observation, the team notes that it was consistent over all four meetings, that it is objectively supported by video-tape and the observer's notes, and that it conforms with the members' own observations and evaluations.

Is this information important? In discussing the subject, with the facilitation of the consultant, the four usually silent members—a supervisor and three workers—finally speak up. It seems that they all had information to contribute but were intimidated by the status of the three more talkative members. The more dominant three are shocked: they thought they *had* to talk because the others would not. Now they have an insight that may help. For it to make a real difference, the team and its consultant should explore how the team can change the imbalance of contributions and liberate the silent members.

After working out ways of changing their transactions, the team members will have to practice their new behaviors. At an agreed-upon point in the near future, they should reassess their transactions to see if they are working better. They might use feedback forms and discussion, or they might bring their consultant back in, depending on what the team feels it needs to do at that point.

Does this kind of feedback, assessment, adaptation, and reassessment happen in the "real world"? Yes, although not often enough. Too often organizations wait until the harm is done and then provide team training and feedback. The point, of course, is to avoid the problems by using feedback as you go along. You'll have that opportunity in this class and, we hope, in teams in your future.

Summary

When you start to develop a team, you're working toward an ideal superteam. Such a team is created in the context of an organizational culture that has developed its own ways of being and ways of doing things. The organizational culture may reflect a commitment, control, or mixed strategy.

Individuals join teams for many reasons: shared interests, attraction to the group and its members, and/or personal drives, needs, and motivations for reward and reinforcement. Individuals are assigned to teams because of their specific attributes. They bring diversity in ways of perceiving, thinking, and doing to their transactions within the team.

As members work together, they develop a team culture—influenced by the organizational culture and by their own cultures and subcultures—which includes a team ethic, team myths and symbols and beliefs, team ways of doing things. They also develop, over time, a team image and a team vision. The group develops a syntality—the personality of the team as a whole; and synergy—the combined energies and drive of all members. Through these elements, the team develops cohesiveness.

In the process of developing, teams typically go through phases. These vary according to the type and purposes of the team, but all teams seem to hit a midpoint crisis in their development, leading to refocused work and completion. To guide its development through these phases, a team should use feedback, adaptation, and improvement for all of its processes and outcomes. To be effective, these processes must be team-generated and used by the team for its own benefit.

Some overall guidelines for developing a successful team are summarized in Figure 4.1.

Guidelines for Developing a Team

FIGURE   4.1
Guidelines for develop-
ing a team

1. Get to know one another.
   ▮ Who's on the team?
   ▮ What does each person want from the experience?
   ▮ What attributes does each person have to offer the team?

2. Look for ways to "connect" members.
   ▮ What can members find in common?
   ▮ How can the team share experiences, create bonds?
   ▮ What can members do to enjoy one another as people?
   ▮ How can members support one another?

3. Start to develop a vision.
   ▮ What is the team striving to accomplish?
   ▮ What will be the qualities of that accomplishment?
   ▮ How does the team's vision relate to the vision and goals of the parent organization?

4. Help the group develop its own character.
   ▮ What norms and expectations will develop a strong, positive team culture?
   ▮ How can you reinforce positive ways that create a strong syntality and synergy for the team?
   ▮ How can you share stories, approaches, traditions that make the team "special"?
   ▮ What ethical standards will be part of the team's culture?

5. Make the team safe for participation.
   ▮ What can members do to value and use their diversity?
   ▮ How can members find shared values and orientations?
   ▮ What norms will help members manage disagreements?
   ▮ How will each member share leadership?

6. Discuss phases as the team goes through them.
   ▮ How can the team identify phases and work through them?
   ▮ What will the team do to handle inertia?
   ▮ How will the team deal positively with a midpoint crisis?

7. Develop transactional and task processes.
   ▮ What will keep communication open, clear, supportive?
   ▮ How can the team develop strong, analytical task processes?

8. Use cybernetic processes for self-assessment and improvement.
   ▮ How will the team work out feedback approaches?
   ▮ How will the team use information from feedback?

9. Celebrate the team and its accomplishments.
   ▮ How will the team accomplish its vision?
   ▮ What can the team do to recognize and reinforce its achievements?

Exercises

1. Your executive team at Foods, Inc., which handles farm products of all kinds, is meeting to decide on criteria for selecting a team from both inside and outside the company. That team will design strategies for educating schoolchildren about foods.

   What types of expertise should the members possess? What backgrounds, motivations, and special perspectives or abilities does the team need? Do any of your criteria conflict with other values? Are there ethical issues involved? What similarities and differences among these members could cause misunderstanding or disagreement—or contribute to better thinking and valuing? Report your decisions to the class.

2. As a follow-up to the previous exercise, consider how the characteristics of your executive committee members affected your team processes. Then do this individually:

   Label a separate piece of paper or index card for each person in your group. Make a list of the individual attributes you think she or he can contribute to a team. Think of how that member interacts with others, approaches a task, thinks, values—anything that seems relevant to transactional and task processes.

   On another piece of paper or card, list the attributes you believe *you* contribute to a group.

   Now exchange lists. Give each person the list you made for him or her; keep the list of your own attributes, along with the lists others have made for you.

   Still working individually, look over the lists to see what attributes people seem to agree on. What trends do you see? How do others' perceptions of you agree with your own?

   Now, as a group, discuss what you've found. Look for clarification, and talk about how you can develop and maximize your best qualities.

3. With a group of students, design a model or a picture that shows the characteristics of a team; include culture, image, vision, syntality, synergy, and cohesiveness.

4. Use Form 4.1 to assess a group or team with which you're presently associated. What strengths do you see? What problems? How do you think the problems could be corrected, the strengths maximized?

5. Using the guidelines listed in Figure 4.1 (p. 99), analyze the same team in terms of its development. What aspects has it accomplished well? What remains to be done? How do you see the team doing those things?

FORM 4.1   ▮   EVALUATION OF TEAM SYNTALITY

After watching a team's transactional and task processes over a period of time, rate how true each statement is of that team.

	VERY	SOMEWHAT	NOT AT ALL
1. Members feel unified.	☐	☐	☐
2. Members bring diverse ways of thinking, valuing, seeing.	☐	☐	☐
3. The team has norms, beliefs, its own ways of doing things.	☐	☐	☐
4. Members of the team know what the team's vision is.	☐	☐	☐
5. The team has an image that members and others can identify.	☐	☐	☐
6. The members are motivated for team success and achievement.	☐	☐	☐
7. The members are cooperative in critical problem analysis.	☐	☐	☐
8. Members support each other.	☐	☐	☐
9. Members work for the team when apart as well as together.	☐	☐	☐
10. Members share responsibility.	☐	☐	☐
11. The team analyzes ethical issues.	☐	☐	☐
12. The team maintains open communication with outside systems.	☐	☐	☐
13. The team has credibility with other systems and subsystems.	☐	☐	☐
14. The team seeks and uses feedback to improve transactional and task processes.	☐	☐	☐

In a few words, try to describe the team's syntality (use metaphors, images, analogies):

Leadership through Task Processes

Task Questions and Resources: Launching Your Inquiry

"Well, maybe we could—like—do a video project . . ."
That's the end. How about starting at the beginning?

It's a temptation, when you have a final goal in mind, to jump right to a plan without paying an iota of attention to what's in between the start and the finish. When people do that, they tend to "fill in" the middle as best they can and call it a job. They overlook important information, don't think of alternative possibilities, and miss serious drawbacks—leading to flimsy thinking and poor results.

A team's potential superiority over individuals in processing information lies in members' exploring together all available facts, ideas, and opinions. Data, without benefit of analysis in light of the group's ideas and opinions, could be circulated among the members without even meeting. Ideas and opinions without benefit of facts on which to base them only "pool the group's ignorance," leading to biased and unsupported decision making. Quality decisions depend on quality evidence.

Information gathering begins with a team strategy to understand the issues and get the facts. That includes seeing the overall plan of which information gathering is a part; analyzing and differentiating among questions of fact, value, policy, and prediction; and phrasing questions in ways that promote inquiry and discussion. From that base, a team needs to identify the scope and types of information necessary for its task, and consider resources from which the information can be obtained. The group needs a plan for conducting the research and ways to share findings among team members that keep them focused and well informed.

This chapter is designed to help your group develop the information base necessary for effective analysis and decision making by strengthening your abilities to:

1. Develop a work plan for your team's approach to its task.

2. Analyze questions for a clearer understanding of the issues involved.

3. Phrase questions to focus on the issues.

4. Identify data needs and resources to create an information base.

5. Assign responsibilities among members to maximize research efforts.

6. Share information with team members in clear, useful ways.

Planning the Team's Inquiry

The process that intervenes between setting a team's goals and reaching them usually determines the success of that final achievement. Individuals work through a task process together better than they do alone, but only if they know what they're doing.

Nobel prize winner Herbert A. Simon (1977) has worked extensively on decision making in organizations. He divides the process into four broad phases, or categories, that are useful for analyzing what people actually do when they have to work through to a conclusion.

Intelligence—the process of recognizing a need (or an opportunity) for a decision and gathering the necessary information to analyze the situation.

Design—the process of developing alternative possible solutions.

Choice—the process of analyzing, weighing, and selecting a plan of action.

Review—the process of assessing the effectiveness of a choice and adopting appropriate adjustments or changes.

For the moment, think of these four stages as an outline for a team work plan. The team divides its work into these four broad stages, but within each it makes other divisions.

Your team receives an assignment; you see that the assignment will require decisions; you set your goals. You gather the information you need—the "intelligence" phase. You start thinking of ideas and possible plans and tentatively work each of them out to see how it would fit your goals—the "design." Then you go through critical analysis, debate the pros and cons of each alternative, choose a decision, and implement it—that's "choice." Finally, in the "review," you look at your implemented decision to see if it's working well, assess it, test it, and fix whatever isn't working the way you intended. Thus, the team plan carries you through the entire process.

This chapter concentrates on the intelligence phase; the next three chapters focus on the other categories. Keep this overview in mind, however. Your group might be in the middle of design, for example, and realize suddenly that you need more information. So you scurry back to the intelligence phase for that information and bring it back into the design. That's as it should be, and Simon's phases help you to know where your loops are taking you.

Identifying Questions for Analysis

Teams deal with a wide range of issues over the entire life of the team. What we're concerned about here are the *types* of issues or questions that may arise. Frequently, discussions are confused because team members do not recognize underlying questions that are related to, and entangled with, tasks and purposes. Much like the Russian dolls, one question is frequently nested inside another question, and you have to open them one at a time. Opening them up is simpler when you know how to separate out questions of fact, value, policy, and prediction.

Questions of Fact

Questions of fact are questions that can be answered by data that prove, or support the acceptable probability, that a statement is true or untrue.

When is a "fact," in fact, a fact? Discussions constantly proceed on ideas that people assume are facts because something always used to be true, or it always seems to be true, or it certainly ought to be true. To make good decisions, however, you need to know what *is* true. For many decisions, you need to know what is true about multiple issues. That may require your team to spend extensive time gathering and analyzing information for facts.

We'll talk about how you analyze information and assess its quality in Chapter 6. Suffice it to say here that as you explore questions of fact, you need to look carefully at the evidence. Is the source objective or biased? Is it credible? Is the fact 100 percent true? Not too many are. To be universally true, there must be no exceptions to the "fact." This means you will have to decide whether a fact is *probably* true. But what probability that a "fact" is true will the team accept? Is it true 90 percent of the time? Or 80 percent? Or 50 percent? Are you 75 percent sure that it is ever true?

Questions of Value

Questions of value are questions seeking answers about the worthwhileness, ethicality, and relative importance of a concept, act, or policy.

Questions of value are intrinsic to every task a team takes on. Sometimes they are very small questions, to be sure. "Is it okay to use Fred's boss's duplicating machine without permission?" is a question of ethics, and ethics are grounded in moral and value assumptions. It might not rock the world; nonetheless, it reflects a value choice that the team might make.

At a more elevated level, a team may be trying to draft a policy recommendation for the way social service agencies handle abusive parents. A value question might be: which is more important, keeping a family together or protecting a child from possible harm?

Here you begin to see the relationship between questions of fact and questions of value. Questions of fact: "Is there a probability the child will come to harm? How strong is the probability?" Questions of value: "What risk is acceptable? How important is the child's safety? How important is it to the child to be with its parents?" As you consider these questions, you begin to play the third against the first two, conflicting value questions. Combined with a number of other questions of fact and value, they begin to illuminate a question of policy.

Questions of Policy

Questions of policy seek answers to what positions or actions should be adopted, enacted, or implemented.

Think of "policy" as something that guides or structures the behavior of a group or organization. A policy question might involve laws, rules, or guidelines to be enacted by a governmental body, a public institution, a private corporation, or a smaller organization or group of any kind. Policies on student aid could include, for example: broad policies of the federal and state governments on higher education; laws enacted by Congress about repayment of student loans; scholarship policies of the community relations office at the local telephone company; college policy governing financial aid counselors' interactions with students; or a policy of your sorority or fraternity to help incoming freshmen fill out applications for financial aid.

These questions are not about what policies *exist;* that is a question of fact. They don't ask whether existing policies are *good;* that is a question of value. The key terms to look for in policy questions are *should* and *ought to.*

Every policy question has a number of questions of fact and questions of value within it. One reason it's so hard to get people to agree on a policy is that it is so filled with conflicting data and conflicting values. Another reason is that it's difficult to predict what will happen in the future.

Questions of Prediction

Questions of prediction ask to what degree a given condition or policy will, in the future, fulfill conditions of fact, value, or policy.

When present facts and values are discussed, prediction questions may arise as to the probability of their effects or conditions in the future. "How will the present ozone problem develop in the next twenty years?" asks for a prediction of probable fact.

When policies are drafted, too, the drafters attempt to predict their effects. Will they be practical? Will the results be desirable? Will they have the hoped-for effect? These questions can only be answered in terms of probability, yet they are the questions on which policy adoption turns.

Prediction questions address fact, value, and policy: "Will the proposed policy manage the need?" (fact prediction); "Will the policy produce worthwhile results?" (value prediction); "Will future policies contradict the present effort?" (policy prediction).

Let's take the earlier example of child abuse to look at the way questions interweave in a discussion. We'll start with a value assumption. We assume no one in his or her right mind would say that child abuse is okay, so we begin this policy discussion with that value held in common. From there, the questions to be answered might interrelate as shown in Figure 5.1.

Such a diagram helps you visualize the relationships among the fact, value, prediction, and policy questions with which your team must work. In the end, a policy decision is the one the team decides is *probably* best, based on value choices, on facts that they believe are probably true, and on predictions of probable effects and outcomes. Every insight the team can get to help it raise the right questions also helps it make the best decision.

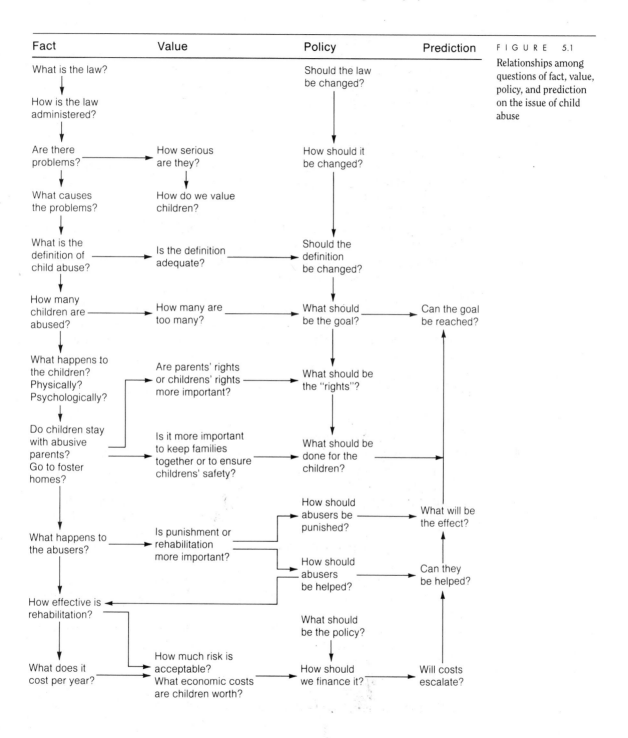

Fact	Value	Policy	Prediction

FIGURE   5.1

Relationships among questions of fact, value, policy, and prediction on the issue of child abuse

Phrasing Questions for Discussion

Often questions of fact, value, policy, and prediction arise without anyone ever phrasing them as such—you just find yourselves discussing the issues. Sometimes that's fine. At other times, however, the questions need to be phrased more pointedly.

Sometimes the team finds itself discussing one kind of question as if it were something else. In this case, it helps to clarify exactly what you *are* talking about. For example, you're discussing demographic data that indicate middle-class students cannot get financial aid. This is a question of fact. As you discuss it, though, there seems to be a lot of anger in the air, and words such as "unfair" are getting tossed around. This tells you there really are two questions at issue: (1) "What are the facts about financial aid for middle-class students?" (2) "How fair is financial aid for middle-class students?" By clarifying and separating the questions, you get a clearer, more pointed, and more effective discussion than if you let the two continue to interweave and overlap.

Another situation that calls for specific phrasing of questions is when you want to use them as focus items for an agenda for either private or public discussion. Careful selection and wording of questions helps a group to focus its analysis. Some guidelines for phrasing and disentangling discussion questions are:

1. Focus on one idea per question.
2. Phrase unambiguously and clearly.
3. Phrase objectively.
4. Phrase open-endedly.

When the question focuses, clearly and unambiguously, on just one subject, it's easier by far to keep the discussion on target. When it's open-ended, it's easier to stay open-minded and think creatively because it reduces the yes-or-no, right-or-wrong responses fostered by closed-ended questions.

Sometimes a closed-ended question is okay, if you're really dealing with exclusive alternatives. The problem is that dichotomies are often artificial. Take, for example, "Is the campus policed by municipal or campus security?" If it's really just one or the other, that's okay. The question, however, overlooks the possibility that each group has different responsibilities or that another off-campus security organization does part of the work. Generally, you're better off with an open-ended question such as, "What group or groups are responsible for policing the campus?"

There are a few "tricks of the trade" to creating questions that meet the criteria of unitary focus, clarity, unambiguity, and open-endedness for each kind of question.

For All Questions

1. Use terms that keep it open-ended: "what," "in what ways," "in what respects," "to what extent," "how," "how much," "where," "when," "who," and "why."

2. Keep the question short.
3. Keep the language simple and concrete.

For Questions of Fact

1. Ask about things that can be measured or proved.
2. Ask about things that can be answered in numbers.
3. Ask about things that can be answered by historical record.
4. Ask about things that can be answered by empirical research.
5. Ask about things that can be answered by expert testimony.
6. Avoid adjectives; they introduce other value and fact issues and bias it with conclusions about secondary questions.

For Questions of Value

1. Ask about the degree to which something is worthwhile.
2. Ask about how concepts and actions should be prioritized.
3. Ask about the degree to which an idea is consistent with moral, ethical, and value criteria.

For Questions of Policy

1. Ask questions that contain "should" statements.
2. Ask questions about possible actions as solutions to problems.
3. Ask questions that subsume both value and fact ideas.
4. Avoid adjectives; they introduce other value and fact issues and bias it with conclusions about secondary questions.

For Questions of Prediction

1. Ask questions of fact, value, or policy that may arise in the future.
2. Ask questions that must be answered in probabilities.

Careful analysis of your questions helps to avoid confusion. Too often, people include values and facts in one long question or statement, and it takes a great deal of talk to straighten out which is which.

Consider this question: "How should the college control the appalling lack of respect for college property?" This question assumes a policy decision—the college should control the problem—and meets the criteria for policy questions: it contains "should" and asks about solutions. But it also assumes a question of fact—that there *is* a problem—and it biases the issue by using a value-laden adjective, "appalling." Finally, it makes a prediction assumption—that the college *can* control the alleged problem.

What you need is all four ideas in separate sets of questions:

Fact. "What harm is being done to college property? How much harm is being done to college property? By whom is the harm being done?"

Value. "How important is the harm being done to college property? How do we weigh the harm as compared to other issues requiring college resources?"

Policy. "What should be the policy of the college in regard to protecting its property?"

Prediction. "To what extent will the proposed solution control damage to college property?"

When you separate the questions like this, you begin to see other questions, too, and you're on your way to getting information with which to address the issues.

Identifying Information Needs

Walton (1986, p. 96), writing about the Total Quality Movement, starts her chapter on data with, "In God we trust. All others must use data." That about sums it up.

Questions are answered with information. People must have material from which to draw ideas and with which to make decisions. Hirokawa and Scheerhorn (1986) note that "a group's information base is directly or indirectly tied to all phases of the decision-making process. Therefore, any errors occurring within the base are likely to contribute to faulty decision-making" (p. 74).

Some teams start out with the information they need and immediately start applying it to problems and solutions. Some teams are formed strictly for fact-finding purposes. Most teams, whatever their purposes, find they need more information than they have. A quality circle, for example, may need to get data about employee satisfaction before it can make recommendations for company policy. Members of a task force may need to develop personal learning—about a topic, about skills, about other members' viewpoints—in order to proceed with their job.

An early task, then, is to talk about what information your team needs to do its work. The kinds of information you need might come from historical, empirical, critical, or opinion research.

Historical information. Teams need historical information for background about issues, events, people, and processes. The information may go back thousands of years or one day. Historical data are summations and analyses of what has happened, according to written and oral records, to people and events. Even the simplest historical question can be important.

Empirical research. This is scholarly, specific investigation of ideas or behavior. Sometimes it's reported as specific studies on limited variables; sometimes it's combined into theories about causes, effects, and relationships. Empirical research starts with questions or hypotheses to be answered or tested; it follows research designs that (one hopes) are carefully selected to give the most specific and focused information possible. The data drawn from empirical research are

∎ TEAM BUILDERS

One of the great wonders of Habitat for Humanity is that it has built close to 13,000 houses around the world, almost entirely with volunteer laborers. Most of these volunteers are unskilled. Many have never hit a nail, or even raised a hammer, before their encounters with Habitat. But the homes they build are safe, sturdy and secure.

How can that be? The answer is quite simple: Habitat is an Each-One-Teach-One ministry, and we've got some great master teachers. Across the country, professional plumbers, roofers, carpenters and other skilled tradespeople donate their expertise, both to train Habitat novices and to serve as quality control managers. Millard Fuller, Habitat's founder and president, likes to quote humorist Will Rogers that "everybody is ignorant, just on different subjects." *The secret is in organizing the diversely skilled volunteers into an effective team* [italics added].

Excerpt from *Habitat World*, February 1992, p. 1. Published by Habitat for Humanity International, Inc. Used with permission.

presented in terms of probabilities, not absolute truths. They contribute to further questioning, hypothesizing, testing, and development of theory and often are applied in decision making about policies and actions.

Critical analysis. In critical methods, researchers analyze and judge qualities and effects of written or oral materials or processes. The critical analysis may be of a play, a speech, a social movement, or policies and procedures. It should be conducted with objectivity and competence; provide clear definitions of the criteria used; and offer new insights into the subject of the research.

Opinion research. Research on opinions may investigate what experts or laypeople (nonexperts) believe about a subject. Experts provide bases for interpreting, drawing conclusions, and evaluating circumstances and facts. Laypeople cannot provide expertise, but if you want to understand what ordinary people are feeling or thinking, or you want to know about their personal experiences and observations, then lay opinions are valuable.

Suppose you're on the campus Multicultural Task Force. Your goal is to increase multicultural sensitivity and awareness. What information do you need? You might have a list that goes something like this:

1. Historical background and definitions of multiculturalism in the United States and other societies, on campuses in general, and on your campus in particular.
2. Empirically researched information about how people's attitudes are formed and how they can be changed.
3. Opinions from experts—anthropologists, sociologists, psychologists, and others—who have researched issues of multiculturalism.
4. Lay opinions from people on campus whose personal experiences might speak to the issues.
5. Critical analysis of events, communication, and activities on campus that relate to cultures and multiculturalism.

"Norman just hates to be confused with facts."

This list is a good starting point. Next, your team would break it down further, into specific units of research. Then you'd figure out where to get the information.

Identifying Information Resources

After you discuss the kinds of information your team will need, the group has to obtain that information efficiently and thoroughly. If you can identify possible resources, that will help get you started.

When you start planning your research, keep in mind the differences between primary and secondary sources. A **primary source** is direct. It may be an expert or layperson in an interview or letter; usually it is the first printed source in which an item was published. It could be an in-depth news analysis, a research study in a journal, or an original news report in the newspaper. When you can get primary sources, that's what you want. You can trust them more than you can trust secondary sources.

A **secondary source** is one that paraphrases, repeats, and/or quotes information from another source. Thus, it is at least one step removed from the original source. The distinction can be important for two reasons. First, secondary sources often present an item as "new news" when it's not. Research quoted in a magazine may be years old and obsolete; the date and context may not be given. Second, every time information is abstracted, summarized, and presented in a secondary publication, it changes. The secondary source may "put a spin" on the information that distorts it in some way. Secondary sources are usually easier to find, and you can't avoid using them—but watch them carefully.

With these points in mind, you can start planning your research. You will want to draw from your team's expertise, use external research sources for information, and develop a plan detailing responsibilities for every team member.

Information from Team Members

Information gathering begins "at home." In a work team, the members are there partly because of their expertise and competence in specific areas. They already have knowledge that will help the team; they just need to share it. Even in a group whose membership is less specifically selected for expertise, each individual brings personal knowledge, information, understanding, and resources to contribute.

An initial exploration, therefore, includes examining what people know, what they can do, and how they can share their expertise. Keep your antennae up for the unexpected or unusual resource in an individual. We remember, in a group discussion of language acquisition, the sudden discovery that one woman thought of American Sign Language as her "first" language and spoken English as her second. She had learned sign first, even though she was a hearing child, because her older sister was hearing impaired. The entire family used signing from her earliest memories. An incredible range of insights about language acquisition became available to all of us from this woman's personal experience.

Information from Team Research

In most instances, a team will need to do some research, although the kind of research varies according to the team's purpose and task. We'll look first at research from public resources and then at ways to get information from people who have pertinent backgrounds.

Public Resources   The potential of print and media sources is enormous—and growing. Libraries are changing rapidly, as new technologies make more information more readily available. You might be surprised at what your library and others can offer. Public offices, museums, and archives are helpful, too.

In addition to the old card catalog, most college libraries have computerized databases and index disks that can give you quick printouts of sources for an extremely wide variety of subjects. You will find indexes, some on disk, covering a wide range of academic disciplines and for many special types of publications. An index called *Books in Print,* for example, lists every book published on any subject. Other indexes list all kinds of organizations and millions of government sources on every subject imaginable.

Many libraries also have outstanding collections of special or antique books; historical artifacts; letters and documents from historical figures; music, art, or drama; or collections of books, documents, videotapes, and artifacts dedicated to a major era or event in history.

Another rich source of information can be specialized museums or special collections in general museums. There are museums dedicated to broadcasting, to baseball, to the Holocaust, to women writers—to almost anything of interest to anybody. The curators have enormous knowledge, and usually stacks of information, that they are more than willing to share.

Public offices, too—local, state, and federal government, nonprofit organizations, and corporate offices—often have information on a wide range of topics and are happy to share it with you.

Human Resources   People can sometimes be your best resources—experts or laypeople, depending on your needs.

For experts, brainstorm a list of people you know, or have heard of, who may be able to provide data. Whether you're serving on a work team at your job, on a campus task force or committee, or on a project team—even one for this class—many experts on various subjects are easily within range of a telephone call or a short visit.

If you don't know any "experts," consult the faculty list at your college (most college catalogs list faculty, with their degrees and areas of expertise, in an index at the back). Or use a two-step process: ask people in the community or in the college if they know of someone.

Here are a few tips on interviewing an expert:

1. Call well ahead of time; make an appointment; confirm the appointment.
2. Do your homework. Be familiar with the subject; plan a rough outline of what you want to know.
3. Be on time.
4. Use a tape recorder *if the respondent is agreeable,* or take notes. Ask probing questions; verify what you hear.
5. Leave before your welcome is worn out.
6. Write a thank-you note. Call to verify any information of which you are uncertain.

Sometimes an interview gives you not only excellent information, but contacts that might be invaluable in your future. Use it well.

To get the opinions, attitudes, or views of ordinary people (students at your college, co-workers at your job), your team may want to take a survey, distribute questionnaires, and/or conduct interviews. Once again, here are some guidelines:

1. Be clear on what you want to find out.
2. Select a sample of the population you want to know about.
3. Make your questionnaire, survey, or interview questions clear, unambiguous, easy to answer, and easy to tabulate.
4. Ask respondents logically, courteously, and persuasively to help you out; take as little of their time as possible; conclude courteously; and tell them how they can find out the results of your research if they want to know.

GET INFORMATION FROM THE EXPERTS

How do you convince experts to give you the exact data you need over the telephone?

Easy enough, if you follow these simple steps:

Find the right source. Make sure the person you reach is the person you want.

Identify yourself. State up front your name, your company, the information you need, and why.

Set up an appointment to talk. If it's not a good time for the expert to talk, ask how soon you can schedule an interview.

Be specific. Don't expect an expert to discourse endlessly on a broad topic over the telephone. Instead ask pointed questions.

Hold off on tough questions. If you have a difficult or, worse yet, sensitive question to ask, wait until later in the conversation when the expert has relaxed somewhat.

Know the basics. Your expert will be annoyed if you display total ignorance of the subject. But don't hesitate to ask for clarification. The information you get will be useless if you don't understand the terms or abbreviations being used.

Be nice. Remember that the expert is doing you the favor. Solicit other sources. Ask for names of others to talk with. That ensures your next interview will get off to a good start because you can say, "Mr. Smith from ABC Institute suggested that I call . . ."

From *Working Smart*, March 15, 1990, p. 6. Published by National Institute of Business Management, Inc. Used with permission.

5. Tabulate your responses as clearly and honestly as you can, and draw only reasonable conclusions from them.

Information Research Plan

We have looked at the kinds of questions and issues your team can expect to deal with, the types of information you may need, and resources from which you can get it. Now it's time to divide up the information-gathering work and start doing it.

You've already explored what each member might be able to contribute personally as a resource and in contributing to other research needs; go back over these and identify areas for each person to cover. Consider each person's talents, interests, contacts, and time—but also, as a team, consider equity and balance in getting the work done.

Agree on how and when the work will be done. This is where many groups slip up. Everybody gets an assignment; half of the people do it, half don't. Of the half who do it, half do it halfway and the other half do it well. By the time those who do it halfway get what they've learned back to the team, you can cut it in half again. The team winds up without the information it needs, and that undermines its effectiveness. What's the answer?

Before anyone leaves the room, do two things:

1. Establish guidelines for presenting the information to the team.
2. Set deadlines.

CASE ANALYSIS 5.1

The team had extensive expertise relating to this project, and the members individually read books and materials to gain information about the other organization's operations. For additional background, the team used the approaches described in the following statement, condensed from the task force report, to enhance its knowledge.

> Team members spent numerous hours in various McDonald's restaurants to understand operations. Each EDF member worked a day in a restaurant. McDonald's and its suppliers opened their doors for a review of operations. The team toured facilities of two McDonald's food suppliers, five packaging suppliers, and one of McDonald's largest distribution centers. They also visited a polystyrene recycling facility and a composting facility. Most visits included tours, formal presentations, and extensive question and answer sessions with top management and technical experts. McDonald's brought in experts from various departments to discuss issues in depth. Likewise, additional EDF staff as well as experts from other environmental organizations provided background on issues beyond solid waste. (p. iv)

Issues for Your Consideration

1. Review the team member descriptions in Chapter 4. In how many different ways could the director of the operations development department serve as a team resource? Identify other special contributions each member might make.
2. Considering the team members' expertise, for what reasons would this team have to spend so much time gathering additional information?
3. In addition to the personal learning experience, what special benefits for team development might be gained from the EDF members' working a day in a McDonald's restaurant?

Guidelines for presenting information can be simple; your team can identify its own needs. But here a few things we know can help:

1. Get full documentation for sources—author, date, title of article, title of book or journal, edition, publisher, page numbers. This is essential for two practical reasons, and one ethical one. For practical purposes, documentation shows the credibility of your source; in addition, if you need to go back to the source for further information, you'll know where to find it. The ethical reason is that documenting your sources is the way you avoid plagiarism. When you state something you've learned elsewhere without stating its source, you're plagiarizing it. People fall into this ethical trap without ever meaning to do so, and all it takes to keep out of it is documentation.

Information Planning Form					
What information is needed?	Resource location	Reporting format	Possible resources	Date needed	Person(s) responsible

FIGURE 5.2

Information planning form

2. Get full data for experts you've interviewed—correct name, academic degrees, position held, accomplishments relevant to the topic. This is another form of documentation; it, too, supplies credibility and enables you to trace information.

3. Provide the team with brief, concise handouts that clearly summarize the critical information.

4. Include brief, clear glossaries for new terms.

5. If a member runs across information that would be useful for someone else on the team, bring that person a full bibliographic citation, or a duplicated copy.

If all members know and accept the guidelines the team has set up, they are more likely to bring back information that the team can work through, organize, and use in the amount of time available. Much time, and valuable information, can be lost simply because people don't organize it and record it in a usable way.

When you know who will do what and how they will report it, create a work plan that includes assignments and deadlines. Within the period before the final project or report, calculate the time available for research, discussion, and planning. *Leave room for the unexpected.* The only thing you can count on is that you can't count on anything. Set specific deadlines for having each piece of work completed and ready to report to the team.

Another practical hint: *Make a complete list of assignments*—who is doing what and, if you're doing the work in subteams, with whom and by when. Use Figure 5.2 to create a worksheet on which you fill out all responsibilities and deadlines. Give everyone a copy.

Sharing Information as a Team

Information in a file folder is not much help. Nor is information just "spilled out" in quantity. If people have been thorough, they may well wind up with a wheelbarrow full of "stuff." Now they must be well organized and competent in selecting and presenting it. The team needs to establish some expectations as to how information will be shared. There are good reasons why team members need to work through information together, and there are excellent methods for sharing information with the team to gain members' attention and understanding.

Work through Information Together

When your team meets to share information, that well may be the only item on your agenda. You need to be very clear about why you're meeting, get everyone's commitment to be there, and share that information as clearly and usefully as you can. Follow the guidelines suggested earlier—documenting, condensing into handouts, keeping information easy to follow.

This may seem obvious, but it's a point teams sometimes overlook, and the results can be painful. Be sure that every member of the team understands the information that each member has uncovered. Work it through; allow time for feedback and questions. Even if different people are responsible for discrete parts of the task, even if specific members have individual expertise that others do not share, be sure that all members' understandings are woven together with the major informational threads.

This is important for two reasons. First, if there is a change in membership or some personal crisis occurs—who knows?—it's far easier for the team to pick up the threads and weave the work back together. Second, information is essential not only to achieving the goals, but also to developing the vision and cohesiveness of the team. When information is shared and understood by all, the team's base is strengthened, and the synergy of the group has a more consistent focus. It's one of the ways you become a superteam.

Make Clear Reports

Reporting to your team requires the same skills as presenting to a full class or other large group. It means organizing the material carefully, presenting it in an interesting and direct manner, and supporting what you say so that it is both clear and believable. Chapter 16 provides suggestions for preparing both written and oral team reports; you may find it helpful to look ahead to those topics.

In a large audience, it may not matter if a few people don't understand you. In a team, all the members need to understand all the information well enough to analyze it, draw conclusions from it, and use it to achieve the team's goals. They must be able to talk about it together. When members share information with their teams, therefore, they need to keep everyone's attention focused. When team members discuss ideas, you want them all to be "on the same page."

Some special techniques for handling information can help keep the team focused. The same principles apply to larger group presentations, but they are essential in teamwork. The idea is to *post* information—that is, display it visually so that everyone can see it while you're talking about it. Let's look at some general principles and then at some specific techniques for posting information.

Principles for Posting Information   Human beings are easily distracted by competing stimuli. If a person's hearing *and* vision are involved, his or her senses are used more fully. This makes it easier to pay attention and to resist distraction.

A second advantage of visual stimuli is that different people process information differently. Some learn more readily through hearing a lecture; others through "hands-on" experience; still others through visual input. When an individual receives a variety of stimuli, it's more likely that one will "click" for that person than if she or he is given only one method of delivery.

A third reason for using visual displays along with verbal explanations is that people are able to share specific visual stimuli in a way they cannot share the hearing and interpretation of words. When the data are in front of people, they can discuss them, point to them, and understand them in a more directly shared frame of reference than if they're working exclusively with words.

All this is true, of course, only if the visual display is done well. Note that we don't mean fancy. If you're reporting to your parent organization, you want to be as professional and polished as you can. If you're reporting the information you've found back to your team, you don't need to be elaborate—just good. To be good, a visual display needs to follow a few very important rules:

1. Eliminate extraneous information.
2. Keep messages big and easy to see.
3. Keep messages brief.
4. Keep language clear.
5. Use only a few (seven at most) items per grouping.
6. Use vivid comparisons or contrasts.
7. Use rounded-off numbers.
8. Use the most effective method for the purpose.

Methods for Posting Information   There are various ways of presenting information visually, but we focus here on those that help you report information to your team so you can work with it together. These displays can be on printed handouts, overhead projectors, or flip charts.

Facts or conditions can be presented in line or bar graphs, and in matrices and grids. They are familiar territory and easy to read for almost anyone because they enable the viewer literally to see the data. They make the information vivid, clear, and memorable.

A line graph displays the interaction between two things. It's excellent for visualizing trends or changes across periods of time. If your self-managing team is trying set up its personnel assignments to cover the work load, for example, you might use the line graph in Figure 5.3 to help decide how many people need to be on duty each day.

A bar graph is another easy way of visualizing how one thing relates to another. You draw bars vertically or horizontally to demonstrate distinctions between units of time or categories. They often work well for showing trends and contrasts in statistical information or populations by time or by some other variable.

One specific type of bar graph is called a histogram. You find histograms in many reports, because they show vividly how frequently something has occurred within certain brackets of time or circumstances. If your team is investigating the fund-raising activities of charitable organizations, for example, you might want

F I G U R E 5.3

A sample line graph

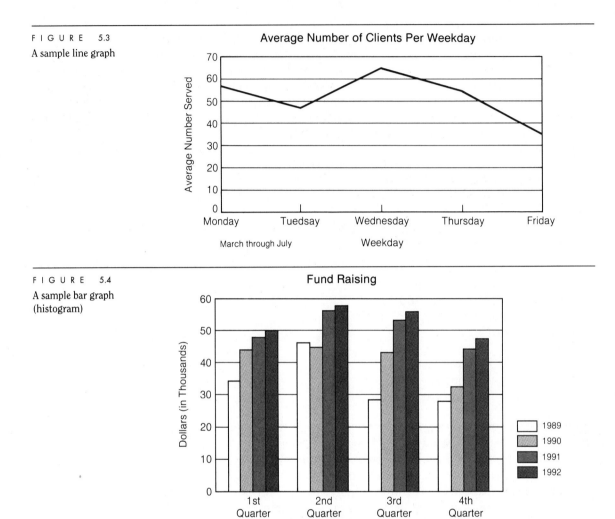

F I G U R E 5.4

A sample bar graph
(histogram)

to present data on how much was contributed in each quarter over a four-year period. The histogram in Figure 5.4 shows you how that visual would look.

Matrices and grids help in seeing relationships and remembering detail. They show information spatially, in related blocks or "cells," and this is a powerful aid to analysis. A matrix can be set up by hand to illustrate your information, or it can be computer-generated.

The variables that interrelate are labeled across the top of the grid and down the left side. Then each cell of the grid is filled in with the information about each variable. What emerges from this visual device is common relationships and interactions.

Figure 5.5 shows a grid created by a team investigating educational opportunities for southwestern Native Americans. After identifying the kinds of questions the team needed to answer, information needs were brainstormed and entered

TYPE OF INFORMATION	SUBJECT OF INFORMATION		
	System	Suppliers	Customers
QUANTITATIVE			
	Numbers of:	Numbers of:	Numbers of:
public records	schools	N.A. teachers	N.A. students
tribal records	tribal schools	Non-N.A. teachers	elem. school
	colleges near	N.A. support	middle school
		Non-N.A. support	high school
		N.A. admin.	college
		Non-N.A. admin.	post-grad
ratings	of each school	of teachers	students' scores
			% graduating
QUALITATIVE			
	Nature of:	Nature of:	Nature of:
Surveys,	schools	teaching	student achievement
interviews:	education	teacher prep	student motivation
personnel	support	teaching styles	learning styles
teachers			distractions
students			
families			lifestyles
tribal elders			traditions
Analysis:			values
stories			beliefs
documents			needs
legal code	Effects of:		expectations
federal regs.	laws, rules,		
Experts:	historical		
scholars	influences		
gov't.			
PERSONAL			
focus groups	school	N.A. community's	N.A. students' ideas,
community	personnel's	ideas, feelings,	feelings, opinions
forums	ideas,	opinions	
	opinions		

FIGURE 5.5

Sample information planning grid: information needed to study educational opportunity proposals for Native Americans into the appropriate cells of the grid. This provided a clear picture of what was needed and a way to see what might have been overlooked.

These specific forms for displaying information are presented here to help you share information with your team, but they are useful throughout your team's work. Anytime members explore ideas, it helps if they use a flip chart, a board, an overhead projector, or if the group is small enough, a pad that all can see. Then you can refer to a specific item or see relationships among ideas in ways that make it easier to keep everyone focused and recall what the ideas meant. We'll review some other specific visual techniques as aids to problem analysis and decision making in the next chapter.

Summary

In this chapter, we've suggested that using a systematic plan helps the team achieve success. Simon's four phases of group development—intelligence, design, choice, and review—provide a good basis, although a team will adapt these categories according to its purpose, task, and needs.

Analyzing and phrasing questions of fact, value, policy, and prediction that must be answered to reach the goal allows a team to begin identifying its information needs. The team may need both quantitative and qualitative data drawn from historical, empirical, critical, and opinion research.

The team should use members' expertise and necessary research. This requires setting up a complete work plan, including specific agreements as to who does what research and reports it to the team on what date. It also involves following guidelines for good reporting and sharing information with the team. The team should carefully work through the information together so that every member understands and can use it when working toward goals. Presenters need to select and organize information, using handouts and visuals to clarify data and help the team stay focused on the task.

Exercises

These exercises create a hypothetical team and goals. The activities can be used for your actual class team if you are working on a related assignment.

1. Analyze a topic. Your team is a community task force investigating health care for the elderly. You are trying to decide whether or not to urge the federal government to provide long-term health care for all elderly citizens.

   Consider the proposition, and figure out what *type* of discussion question it is. What other questions (of fact, value, policy, or prediction) will your task force have to examine in order to reach a decision about urging federal provision of long-term health care for all elderly citizens? See how many you can identify.

2. Examine all the questions you identified in Exercise 1. How could you phrase them to make them

appropriate questions for a discussion format? Write one well-phrased question of fact, one of value, and one of policy.

3. Plan your inquiry. As a group, identify sources to which you could go for information on the questions you have identified. Think of specific sources of each of these types:

Governmental agencies	Scholarly journals
Professional organizations	Newspapers
Periodicals	Experts

4. Using the information planning form in Figure 5.2 (p. 119), draft a plan for getting the information your task force would need. Consider how long your search might take, who would do what, and how members would report to the group.

Logical and Critical Thinking:
Analyzing Information

"We've got all this 'stuff.' Now, what do we do with it?"
That depends on whether it's garbage or gold.

It's a good feeling when you and your teammates have gone forth to do your research and brought back reams of data. You've made a good start. As we all know from any quick trip through a newspaper, however, not all information is equal. It takes analysis to separate the garbage from the gold.

Analysis involves thinking logically about information and the conclusions you draw from it. A team has an advantage over an individual: what one person misses, another might see. Sadly, teams don't always live up to their potential. Meyers's (1991) review of research shows that groups are often uncritical, approaching analysis as a social activity rather than a critical thinking task. In other words, teams'

transactional processes tend to create a climate for simply agreeing with one another rather than an atmosphere in which the task processes of cooperative critical analysis—including constructive disagreement—can take place.

Inadequate or inaccurate analysis can lead to wrong decisions. In 1976, for example, the federal government reacted to predictions of a swine flu epidemic by unnecessarily spending millions of dollars on vaccine that actually harmed more people than the flu probably would have affected. Neustadt and May (1986) identify illogical reasoning from the data as one factor leading to that expensive and embarrassing decision.

The potentially serious impact of analytical errors underscores the need for teams to develop climates and habits that foster critical thinking. Logical, critical analysis will not prevent all decision-making errors; hindsight always provides a clearer view. But when members, like a team of detectives, cooperate in critical analysis, they can track causes and connections that one individual might miss.

To help you become a good critical detective, this chapter spells out norms, criteria, and methods for evaluating information critically. Then it helps you analyze ideas by examining how people reason from data to conclusions. Finally, it provides ways of testing reasoning quality, identifying fallacies, and understanding people's underlying assumptions and values.

With these purposes in mind, our goals in this chapter are to enable you to:

1. Help your team set norms for critical analysis.

2. Analyze data to determine what makes it trustworthy and usable, or unacceptable and not useful.

3. Find the strong points and the weak points of ideas and reasoning.

4. Avoid illogical pitfalls and fallacies in thinking.

5. Detect how assumptions and values affect a team's cooperative analysis.

Evaluating Information Critically

No matter how bright and analytical a team may be, good analysis requires good information. If you draw conclusions from data that are incomplete, wrong, or false, you don't have much chance for complete, correct, or true results. Evaluating your information, therefore, is crucial. The entire team must be tuned in and tuned up for the process. It needs to set norms and criteria for its analysis.

Norms for Critical Analysis

We've talked before about norms that "just grow" and norms that are "set." By the time you've gone through the whole process of setting goals, identifying information needs, and establishing criteria for researching and reporting, your team may well have established a norm for critical analysis. It's so important, however, that a team be prepared to analyze critically (and creatively) that it's a good idea to discuss and agree on some specific norms. We suggest starting with these:

Quality of data is everyone's responsibility. All members share a mutual, hardheaded concern that any data the team uses must be of high quality and worthwhile.

Analysis is a collaborative activity. The team expects to analyze information and reasoning together; to look for connections, fallacies, and problems; and to listen to and extrapolate one another's ideas and insights.

Analysis is objective and not personal. Members focus on the information and reasoning; they avoid bringing personalities or blame into the equation.

Disagreement and mind-changing are part of cooperative analysis. Members expect to disagree on points—and sometimes to change their minds—as they work through their analyses. They probe the sources of disagreement and listen carefully to one another to arrive at the best interpretation.

The team owns all information. Data can take on an emotional character, creating a barrier to good analysis. Members start referring to "June's study" rather than to its source, "the Gallup Poll." The member feels forced to defend the information because, heaven help her, her teammates will attack as if the data were her own creation. Avoid "killing the messenger" by agreeing that, once information is reported, it belongs to the team. It can be quoted, praised, criticized, cut up, cut down, or shredded without ego involvement or defense by anybody.

Set these as norms, practice them, and you'll have a team that can handle information the way it ought to be handled.

Criteria for Analysis

You can't analyze data critically without some standard of measurement. "Uh— well—it just doesn't look right to me," is a start, but it's certainly not a finish. Team members need to discuss and share criteria in two areas: the source of the information, and the information itself.

Source   Jan brings in a tape and summary of her interview with an expert. To decide whether the source is good or not, you evaluate the expert. Dan brings in statistics from an article written by a free-lance reporter based on an interview with an expert and published in a magazine. Now you have three sources to consider: the expert, the writer, and the magazine. Fortunately, many of the same criteria apply to each of those sources, but the team must be aware that it can't overlook one as it analyzes the other.

We suggest three broad categories of criteria: (1) the external credibility of the source's expertise; (2) the habits of communication the source exhibits; and (3) the ethical inferences you can make from the content of his or her messages.

Expertise   If the credibility of your source relies, in part, on his or her expertise, you start with that. To examine the source's observable expertise, ask these questions:

> *Qualifications* Are the person's academic degrees, experience, and training sufficient? Are these qualifications relevant to the information in question? In other words, is the expert really expert on your issue?

> *Reputation* Is the person acknowledged and respected by other experts in the field? Do other experts refer to or quote this person as a source?

Habits of Communication   If the source of your information passes these tests, then you want to examine other aspects of the source's communication to assess his or her credibility. An excellent perspective is Karl Wallace's (1955) four criteria for examining a communicator's ethics. The following definitions and questions will help you apply these criteria:

> *Habit of search*—the knowledgeable, thorough presentation of sound information. Does your source document information? Prove assertions? Are the

It was a meeting of the minds at a crossroads of world trade.

In a Singapore ballroom, the British oil company head was about to reveal to managers from 37 countries the characteristics necessary for success in their global company. The audience squirmed in anticipation of the usual list of sensible-but-bland clichés about biases for action and putting people first.

"*Brains*," he said. "You need *brains*." And sat down.

How unexpected. How refreshing. How appropriate. Mental agility is essential when business itself is at a crossroads. . . .

In every sphere, it seems, received wisdom about categories, distinctions, and groupings is being challenged. Trying to conduct business while the system itself is being redefined puts a premium on brains—to imagine possibilities outside of conventional categories, to envision actions that cross traditional boundaries, to anticipate repercussions and take advantage of interdependencies, to make new connections or invent new combinations. Those who lack the mental flexibility to think across boundaries will find it harder and harder to hold their own, let alone prosper. . . .

Ellen Langer coined the term "mindfulness" for the ability to make aware choices, to pay attention to the essence and potential of things rather than to be blinded and inhibited by the categories applied to them. Research has associated integrative thinking with higher levels of organizational innovation, personal creativity, and even longer life. . . .

What matters most today is the ability to think *together*, not alone. To think imaginatively about matters of substance, incorporating many perspectives and reaching beyond conventional categories. To create new concepts that make new connections.

A bias for action is important in a fast-paced world of flux and change. But even higher on the priority list should be a bias for brains.

source's data complete, or is important information excluded? Is the source's habit of search ethically acceptable (e.g., not abusing the environment or animal or human subjects)?

Habit of justice—fairness in presenting information so an audience can assess it equitably. Is he or she known to be trustworthy, honest? Is the source normally clear and direct in dealing with issues and people, or is there a history of manipulation and strategy?

Habit of preferring public to private motivations—openly letting people know about her or his sources, plans, expectations. Are previous actions consistent and reliable? Do contradictions in behavior or quality put the source in doubt?

Habit of respect for dissent—the ability to remain objective, to dialogue with opposing arguments and positions. Does the source have a history of bias toward a political, social, philosophical position, or does she or he typically present and listen to more than one side of issues?

Ethical Inferences   Antczak (1991) suggests two additional bases on which to evaluate messages. One is the *vision* the message builds—its characterizations, arguments, language, effects on further discourse, reasoning, and assumptions. The other is the *character* of the message—its inclusivity or exclusivity for people, its relationship to the audience and the culture, and its implications for extension to or revision of the culture.

These criteria—the external credibility of a source's expertise, habits of communication, and inferences about vision and character—can help your team decide how much to trust that source's information.

Information   When you start to accumulate information, you make an interesting discovery: conclusions from data may be possibly true, probably true, but hardly ever absolutely true. As a team, you will want to know how probable something is. How do you assess probability?

As a team, you approach this question by weighing various pieces of evidence that seem to support or refute an idea. As you go through the various kinds of information, your team becomes judge and jury: you assess each piece in terms of its quality, and then you weigh contradictory pieces against each other.

The process is not that different from weighing evidence in a court of law or in a debate. What evidence seems to have the most convincing characteristics? Which evidence pertains most directly to the issue or question at hand? Which conclusion has the most evidence on its side? The best conclusion—the one that is most *probably* true—is the one supported by the preponderance of quality evidence. In other words, there are more credible data backing that conclusion than backing contradictory conclusions.

For most team purposes, the preponderance of evidence is enough to draw a conclusion. If you were on a criminal jury, you would have to be even more criti-

Perhaps we should clarify what we mean by "weighing the evidence."

cal in examining and weighing evidence. A criminal court requires a conclusion "beyond reasonable doubt." This criterion demands not just greater evidence, but leaves no room for any other possibility for which there are good reasons.

Most team decisions, however, rely on assessing the relative weight and value of the data. The criteria you use to evaluate information are similar—but not identical—to those used in evaluating a source. By way of illustration, let's take an example: Your team has been asked to improve the quality of student life. You've obtained the results of a survey conducted three years ago at another college. Here are some questions you might ask in analyzing that survey—and information in general:

1. Is the information valid? That is, does it measure what you intend to measure? Does it apply to the research questions or hypotheses? Specifically, does this survey measure the lives of the students concerned? Is it applicable to your campus? Would students today be different from those surveyed three years ago?

2. Are the data reliable? Reliability refers to the extent to which data are consistent with themselves or with other data. On this survey, if the question "Are you comfortable at ZU?" gets a strong "yes," but "Do you feel at home at ZU?" gets a strong "no," the reliability may be questionable.

3. Is the information truthful and objective? Does the report present more than one side of an issue? Were the data gathered objectively? If respondents to your survey were asked to "agree" or "disagree" with statements such as "ZU offers a range of activities" and "ZU offers activities that appeal to me," that's probably okay—you can differentiate between quantity and specific quality according to students' needs. But with biased questions such as "ZU should reduce its excessive fees for activities," you lose objectivity.

4. Is the information sufficient? How much information is enough depends on the questions you're investigating and what you need to know about them. Are the questions inclusive? Do they focus on facts, values, policies? What more might you need to know?

Reasoning Logically

We begin by spelling out three assumptions that represent our beliefs about the uses of analysis in this society, as well as in teams:

1. Careful, objective, cooperative analysis is the essential tool of a democratic society where people discuss, debate, argue, and try to persuade one another to make what they believe are "right" decisions. It is, therefore, the essential tool of effective teams.

2. Human beings can make rational decisions, even though much of what people do and feel seems to be unconnected to rationality. Techniques of analysis are ways to ensure ethics, to discipline thinking, and to achieve a measure of rationality in individual or team decisions.

3. The objective of critical analysis is to make ethical choices. According to Brown (1990), "the purpose of ethics is not to make people ethical; it is to help people make better decisions" (p. xi). Making ethical choices goes beyond just good behaviors: "An ethical perspective . . . looks for reasons that justify acts rather than explain behavior" (p. 16). Thus, ethical team decisions aren't matters of etiquette and avoiding wrongdoing; they are matters of choosing actions that are right.

With those assumptions stated, let's go on to examine how people draw conclusions from data and how we can assess the validity of reasoning.

Drawing Conclusions

A corporation's human resource division, which is responsible for monitoring the cost of employee benefits, has asked your team to prepare proposals for reducing health insurance expenses. You have data showing that insurance for Health Maintenance Organization (HMO) members costs less than individual coverage. Your team concludes that all employees should become members of an HMO.

In reaching this conclusion, the team simply looks at the data and draws its conclusion from it, as shown in Figure 6.1.

That's what people do. You can call this process "leaping to conclusions." The mind is a wonderful thing. People get some bit of data, and suddenly they've drawn a conclusion. Somehow, between the data and the conclusion, the mind makes an **inference**—a connection of which the individual may not even be aware. The line going from the data to the conclusion in the figure represents the inference. That quick, invisible arc of inference between a bit of information and a conclusion is how people reason.

In a team, every individual goes through internal, mental inferential processes constantly. The team's job is to bring those inferences together with some kind of coherency. Critical analysis demands that a team identify the inferences—the relationships between data and conclusions—and evaluate them. What you need are ways of seeing the invisible relationships.

Toulmin (1958), a British philosopher, has diagrammed ways to describe how people think. The diagrams used here are adaptations of his work. They help you visualize the processes of reaching a conclusion—or, in Toulmin's words, making a **claim**. When the steps are more visible, a team can use this approach to analyze the reasoning going on in its deliberations.

What influences our inferences? Why do we leap to any particular conclusion from a specific item of evidence or data? According to Toulmin, the thinking process includes a "because" clause—he calls it a **warrant**—that provides the rea-

---

(Inference)

HMOs cost less. – – – – – – – – – – – – – – – – – → All employees should join HMOs.

(Evidence/Data)   (Conclusion/Claim)

F I G U R E   6.1

Inferring a conclusion from data

FIGURE 6.2

Identifying reasoning
from data to conclusion

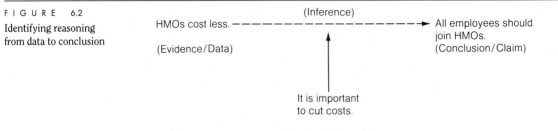

sons for the connection. The warrant in this example might be: it is important to cut costs. That certainly is consistent with the team's charge. Figure 6.2 shows how the warrant relates to the data and the claim, providing the reason for making the inference.

Analyzing Warrants   Warrants often are not stated out loud; sometimes they aren't even fully recognized. That's one way people make logical errors—by not recognizing their reasoning. In discussion, members may not have stated their reasons or examined them; they assume they share a common connection between data and claim, and they assume it is valid. The warrant is a critical segment for examining the logical processes members are using and for confronting the ethical implications of choices.

There may be a number of different reasons for using the same warrant. Examining the reasons frequently pinpoints ethical issues and dilemmas. Why is it desirable to have a health care delivery system that cuts costs? Obviously, it would save the company money. But consider these related issues:

1. Do other warrants or rationales have a higher priority than cutting costs? Would a change in systems reduce the quality of health care available to employees or result in higher out-of-pocket costs for them?
2. For what reasons is cost-cutting important? Would it reduce the need to lay off employees, provide more money for salary increases, provide money to redecorate the board meeting room, or provide a better return to shareholders?

Critical thinking requires you to look at these types of issues and examine them in relation to one another. By focusing on competing priorities for warrants and on the background for accepting any given warrant, you come face to face with ethical implications. Your team may want to recommend that cutting costs on health care is not a desirable thing to do. If you avoid examining warrants, you can make errors in logic and in judgment.

Identifying Reservations   For almost any claim, there are reservations to challenge it. A **reservation,** whether it is spoken or unspoken, recognizes the possible arguments against a claim. These may in some way refute the data, the warrant, or the reasoning. Even though the team might agree that employees should belong to HMOs because reducing costs is desirable, for example, some might add "*unless* cutting costs results in lower-quality health care." Another might think the data are too limited, and say, "Employees should join HMOs only if further data will support the claim that they're less expensive." If members of your team play devil's advocate and bring up all possible reservations, you can develop a better understanding of the reasons for and against accepting a claim as logically and ethically acceptable.

Qualifying Conclusions   What degree of certainty do you attach to a conclusion? We have indicated that most decisions are based on probability—the degree to which you can be sure that any conclusion is true. For this reason, conclusions need to be "qualified" to indicate a level of certainty. It is important that you use these **qualifiers** appropriately:

Possible means that the conclusion has only a small chance of being true, but it could be so.

Plausible implies a higher probability of truth than possible, but the conclusion is still not the most likely interpretation.

Probable applies to a conclusion that has a greater likelihood of truth than 50–50. But be careful with this one. Sound research methods recommend that levels of certainty should be in the 95 to 99 percent range to be accepted as probable.

Certain means that the conclusion is 100 percent guaranteed; in that case, you may simply eliminate qualifiers. Keep in mind, however, that if you don't qualify a conclusion, it implies certainty—and that's hard to arrive at for most claims.

Examining Complete Arguments   Let's go back to the diagram and add some of the elements we've been discussing. Figure 6.3 shows how the reasoning behind the warrant and a qualifier for the conclusion fit into the picture.

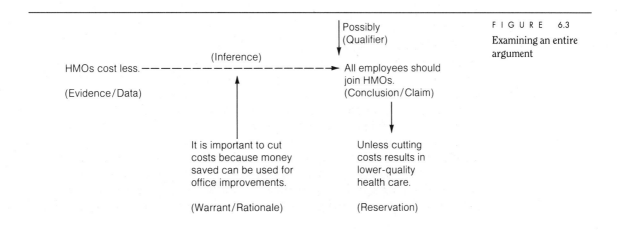

FIGURE   6.3
Examining an entire argument

▌DECISION-MAKING FLAWS

No matter how firm a grip you think you have on decision-making techniques, you could be tripped up by four fatal mistakes:

Overconfidence . . . usually the result of approaching a problem from a limited perspective. Suggestion: Search for and welcome contradictory evidence by seeking other perspectives on a problem before making your decision.

Anchoring. Studies show that people tend to rely too much on the first information they receive. They allow it to "anchor" them to first impressions, thereby overshadowing data and impressions that come later. . . . Suggestion: Awareness of the tendency is essential. Make a conscious effort to use it strategically, rather than automatically.

Rationalizing. When people see that their decision-making process is not working, or has already failed, the natural human tendency is to attribute the failure to anything other than their own flawed judgment. This prevents getting to the real root of the problem and seeking alternatives that will lead to a better decision. Suggestion: If you have objective viewpoints to balance your own, you will be more likely to see the error of your ways . . . ask for input and feedback.

Confirmation bias. It's human nature to automatically seek confirming evidence for an opinion, solution or hypothesis, rather than to look for other possibilities. . . . Suggestion: Always entertain other possibilities and test them out.

Condensed from "Decision-Making Flaws," based on an interview with Paul J. H. Shoemaker, associate professor of decision science and policy, University of Chicago Graduate School of Business, *Personal Report for the Executive*, February 15, 1988, pp. 5–6. Published by National Institute of Business Management, Inc. Used with permission.

When the team is aware of the warrants, it can more honestly decide how probable it is that the claim is justified. If you diagram a full argument or statement this way, you can visually track the thinking that went into it. This is helpful in several ways:

1. The warrant and the reservation show you how the inference connects the data and the claim; you can actually *see* the strength of the connection.
2. When you see the reasoning laid out, you may see other alternatives. Is this an either-or situation? Might other data and different warrants lead to a different conclusion?
3. You can see the degree of probability or possibility that modifies the argument. Is the claim probable enough to accept it?
4. You can assess the ethical priorities that go into a decision. Is the warrant one that your team evaluates as ethically acceptable or desirable?
5. You can examine the trustworthiness and competence of your sources. If you see that the data support only a "probably" or a "possibly" qualifier, and the source of your information has stated a conclusion as if it were absolutely true, then you have to question that source's honesty and/or analysis of data.

Diagramming the logical connections between data and conclusions can help you see the probability that the conclusion is correct. It also can help you see some of the common mistakes in reasoning and fallacies that we all commit.

Testing Reasoning

Everybody's "logical." It's just that sometimes their logic has holes in it. Mending the holes in that logic is much easier if you understand three types of reasoning that form some of the connections within the diagram we've been discussing. These three types—inductive, deductive, and cause-and-effect reasoning—are not mutually exclusive; people move constantly from one form of reasoning to another. Seeing the distinctions, however, helps in analyzing warrants. Let's take a closer look at these three ways of reasoning and at some of the fallacies people commit when they use them.

Inductive   Suppose your community water quality task force learns that two small farms have problems with polluted springs (the data) and concludes that there is an underground pollution problem. The warrant is: "If two springs are polluted, there is a general underground pollution."

Your team has used **inductive reasoning**. Inductive reasoning *draws a general conclusion from specific instances of an occurrence.* It relies on a sufficient accumulation of repetitive data to justify making a generalization from it—or it should. In this case, when your team examines its warrant, members may see that two polluted springs probably are not enough data from which to draw a firm conclusion. Figure 6.4 shows how a general conclusion is reached inductively from specific instances.

To check whether an inductive reasoning process leads to a valid general conclusion, you can ask these questions:

- Are there enough cases in the sample to justify a conclusion?
- Do the cases represent the same population as that to which the generalization will apply?
- Are there exceptions to the general conclusion?
- Can the exceptions be accounted for without weakening the conclusion?

Deductive   Suppose your water quality task force has established, after thorough investigation, that there is an underground pollution problem. On the basis of that general conclusion, you notify the Swensons that their spring is polluted. In this instance you have used **deductive reasoning.** Deductive reasoning *draws a*

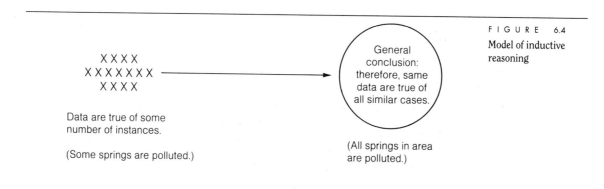

X X X X
X X X X X X X
X X X X
⟶
General conclusion: therefore, same data are true of all similar cases.

Data are true of some number of instances.

(Some springs are polluted.)

(All springs in area are polluted.)

FIGURE   6.4
Model of inductive reasoning

F I G U R E   6.5
Model of deductive
reasoning

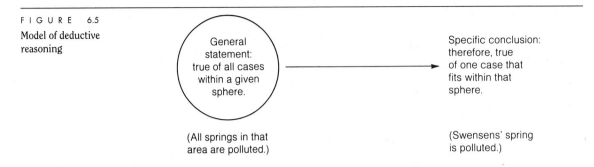

conclusion about a specific case from a general, or universal, statement. Figure 6.5 illustrates the deductive process. You move from a general premise (all
springs in the area are polluted) to a specific conclusion (the Swensons's spring is
polluted).

Deductive reasoning, too, may be invalid. Some questions you can ask to assess
its validity are:

▮ Is the general statement accurate? Should the general statement have a qualifier (some springs, most springs)? You may need to look at how the generalization was arrived at—that is, the validity of the inductive process.

▮ Is the instance to which you're applying the generalization really the same as
the ones covered by the general concept? (Is the Swensons's farm in the same
geographical area?)

▮ Do other characteristics make the specific instance less likely to be affected in
the way other instances are affected by the generalization? (Is their spring fed
from a different source?)

Cause and Effect   Suppose your water quality task force discovers that farmers
have been dumping waste into sinkholes (data). These land surface depressions
allow substances to move into and through a wide, underground limestone system (warrant). Your team concludes that dumping in sinkholes pollutes the
springs (claim). In this case, your team has used **cause-and-effect reasoning:**
dumping is the cause, pollution is the effect. Cause-and-effect reasoning *observes
a relationship between two occurrences and infers that one causes the other.*

Much of teamwork involves trying to analyze problems to discover their causes.
Few effects have single causes; the actual causes may be many and complex. Thus,
this analysis often demands very careful and detailed examination to discover
what the causes actually are and how to interpret both the causes and their effects.

Cause-and-effect reasoning is critical to problem analysis. Teams need to sort
through many possible connections to determine how various circumstances relate. Questions that help in determining causes are:

▮ Has the suggested cause happened every time before the effect, or are there
exceptions?

▮ Did the suggested cause happen concurrently with other events? Could the other events be causes?

▮ Do other causes, or multiple causes, seem more probable?

There also may be a variety of effects, or aspects of a problem, that result from one or more causes. Examining the effects involves questions such as:

▮ How extensive are these effects?

▮ Who is affected, to what extent, and under what circumstances?

▮ How significant are the effects?

▮ To what extent, and in what ways, are they harmful?

▮ Could these effects also result from some other cause?

As you see, these questions begin to get into issues of fact (data) and value (warrants); they may lead to reservations about the probability of a claim and possible rebuttals to those reservations; they may even lead to qualifying or changing the conclusion. To arrive at a policy decision that will correct a problem, you have to go through these analyses of causes and effects.

People tend to make quick inferences about causes and effects. If one occurrence is followed by another, it's easy to conclude a causal relationship between them. Many myths and bad decisions have come about because someone did not examine the relationship between causes and effects. "Fire the coach," says the alumni board. "The team didn't win enough games this season." In fact, they may be firing a great coach.

Fallacies   When people make mistakes in deducing a specific conclusion from a general premise—or when they irrationally draw a general conclusion from inadequate specific data—or when they mistakenly infer that one event has caused another—they are thinking fallaciously. A **fallacy** is *an inference from data to claim that circumvents sound, logical reasoning*. Here are some common fallacies, with tips for catching them:

Hasty generalization reasons from one example or instance to a broad conclusion. Team leaders sometimes assume that everyone is for a decision because two people spoke in favor of it (the "twofer" system of decision making). Then they're surprised when the rest of the team is unhappy. Watch hasty generalizations by checking the quantity and quality of the data on which the conclusion is based, and qualify claims with "probably, "possibly," or "perhaps."

Sweeping generalization, similarly, overgeneralizes from slim data, but it sweeps people in related categories under one, indiscriminate blanket. "You people are all alike" represents this fallacy. A management team might decide that tardiness is a problem and set up rigorous rules and penalties to deal with it. A thorough analysis might have shown that only one or two employees were chronically late. To avoid this fallacy, watch out for the terms "always" and "never" or other forms of unqualified conclusions. It helps to examine generalized ideas for exceptions to them and for their sources. Careful treatment of generalizations can avoid a lot of "isms"—racism, sexism, classism, handicapism—and open up possibilities for solutions to problems.

False analogies compare one thing to another because of similarities when, in fact, they also have significant differences. Your college holds "pep rallies" before games and shows enthusiastic school spirit; my college concludes, therefore, that it should hold pep rallies, too. Yours is a small, residential campus with an active athletic program; mine is a large, urban, commuter campus with a limited athletic program. Both are colleges, but the analogy breaks down from there. Avoiding false analogies requires identifying the differences. If the two don't compare on all significant issues, reject the analogy.

False dilemmas artificially divide an issue into an either-or choice when there may be other alternatives or both may be true. Discussions about distributing condoms in high schools frequently reveal this fallacy. One side, advocating abstinence, argues that "condoms don't work very well." The other side argues that "teenagers who are sexually active shouldn't be denied the protection of condoms." People tend to line up on one side or the other. But the two positions are not mutually exclusive; it's possible to believe both. The conclusion that condoms may provide "safer" rather than "safe" sex recognizes both arguments. Anytime you hear a dichotomous statement, or have an urge to make one, examine the alternatives to see what might lie in between.

Special pleading is giving special consideration to one entity over others because of bias, prejudice, or other preferential factors. It seeks to apply a different standard to similar situations. Related fallacies are appeals to pity or to ignorance as special reasons for treating one situation differently from another. The classic example is the man who kills his parents, then asks for leniency because he's an orphan. Though not all circumstances are the same, you need to weigh suggestions for preferential treatment against established criteria and precedents. You need to base decisions on the merits of the case and on ethical evaluation.

Red herring is a fallacy that diverts attention from the real issue by presenting arguments that are not really relevant to it. A paralyzed former police officer who had been shot in the line of duty made a dramatic entrance into the courtroom during an unrelated trial for another police officer accused of shooting a teenager. The judge was outraged because he believed that the paralyzed officer's appearance was intended as a red herring—an attempt by the defense to focus the jury's attention on a different situation rather than the merits of the case at hand. One way to examine this fallacy is to diagram the argument as Toulmin suggests. The lack of relationship among data, claim, and warrant reveals the red herring.

Circumlocution is reasoning that actually goes in a circle. Suppose we, as your authors, tell you that every word in this textbook is the final word on the topic. How do you know it's the final word? Because the authors say so in the book. How do you know the authors are correct? Because the book is the final word on the topic. (We would not make that claim, and we hope you wouldn't believe us if we did.) Using a Toulmin diagram is a big help here. If you can see that the claim and the data are the same, or the data and the warrant are the same, you know you have circumlocution.

Appeal to authority is linking an advocated position to someone or something that has higher status, whether or not that status has any relevance to the issue. A corporate team member may argue that an idea is superior because it comes from the firm's president. The president's point of view may be important, but it is not necessarily better just because of his position. To avoid fallacious appeals to authority, separate the issue from the appeal, and consider the issue on its merits.

Ad hominem, or personal attack, avoids the issue by attacking the individual or the information source. Labeling a newspaper as "that rag" or a person as a "reactionary" diverts the focus away from what the source has to say. In organizations, proposals may be labeled as "management" or "union" without considering the potential usefulness of the ideas. Try to focus on the issue, not its source. Disregard statements about individuals unless they are directly relevant to the credibility of the information and the issue at hand.

Avoiding fallacies in your own thinking, and catching them in others, requires a habit of analysis. It's an ability to separate issues, to remain objective, to isolate sloppy or deceptive thinking. It requires alertness and awareness of what you and others say and think. It requires separating the merits of an issue from the fallacies, because even fallacious thinking may lead to a conclusion that is reasonable on other grounds. It requires tact in confronting others' fallacies and maintaining open communication. The good part is that this process of analyzing thinking and spotting fallacies is energizing and challenging.

Examining Assumptions and Values

What individuals feel, and what they think they know, pervades every transaction between and among people; indeed, these issues permeate every aspect of cooperative analysis. We're talking about people's assumptions and values, which affect their reasoning and how they analyze issues and fallacies. We want to look at the nature and effects of assumptions and values and at how they are influenced by issues such as culture and gender.

Nature and Effects

Assumptions and values aren't the same thing, though sometimes people assume that they are. An **assumption** is *an untested belief, often unconscious and usually unstated, that something is a fact*. It can be a belief about data, values, people, actions—about anything. In our thinking processes, as we have seen, many warrants are simply assumptions. How many times in your life have you said, or heard someone else say, "But I thought you'd agree," "I just assumed we had enough money for the evening," or "I figured you knew I was going to do that"?

Actually, people couldn't get along without assumptions. There is too much to know, there are too many decisions to make, for a person to check every assumption before proceeding. The problem is that an assumption is often treated as if it were a fact. Furthermore, one assumption may be based on another: he not only assumed she knew he was going, but he also assumed that if she knew she wouldn't mind. The assumer believes the assumed fact is shared by others and, therefore, doesn't need to be discussed.

A **value** is different. It is *a personal, internal understanding about the worthwhileness and importance of an idea, an action, or a way of being.* It is a foundation for human behavior, and it takes on its character through the way a person ranks it or prioritizes it against other values and how an individual acts upon it. Like assumptions, values are often unstated and may be unconscious for an individual.

It's easy to confuse the two because frequently a person assumes that another person holds particular values. Members of discussion groups sometimes stare at each other in complete bogglement when they reach a point of decision and realize that they are coming at it from totally different value systems. They had assumed that they held basic values in common, but they were wrong.

Assuming values can work the other way around, too. People who know intuitively that they differ in their assumptions, may also assume that they have radically differing values. Sometimes they are shocked when they agree on value-motivated decisions.

Here's an example. A task force, comprised of corporate and nonprofit organizational representatives, is trying to develop a low-income housing program for the homeless. Among the team members are Ann, a corporate manager, and Bernard, a nonprofit organization worker. Ann assumes that Bernard's top value is making life easy for the poor, and that he doesn't comprehend the realities of life. Bernard assumes that Ann's top value is corporate profit, and that she doesn't understand the realities of life. When time for a decision comes, they find themselves agreeing on a plan for corporate sponsorship to help people rehabilitate condemned homes and buy them at extremely low prices.

They may both be surprised about agreeing with someone they assumed to be so different from themselves. What they don't realize is that they may be starting from different assumptions about the "realities of life," but not from such different values. The assumptions: To Bernard, corporations are indifferent to human deprivation and social injustice; to Ann, corporations are not indifferent and have a unique capability to intervene and counteract human and social incompetence. The values: Bernard doesn't know that Ann values opportunity for human beings even more highly than she values corporate success; Ann doesn't know that Bernard values opportunity for human beings very highly, and also values American entrepreneurship and independence. In this case, their values lead them to favor a plan that meets their priorities and allows both sets of assumptions and values to operate comfortably.

We could say that these two people live in different subcultures, and that they are engaging in a cross-cultural negotiation. If they listen to each other and examine some of their assumptions and values, they'll reach agreement faster and with much less pain.

Culture and Gender Influences

The influences on people's assumptions and values are multiple and complex, so it's hard to predict how they will affect team members and their transactions. It's clear, however, that cultural, subcultural, and gender factors influence people's assumptions and values and that these, in turn, influence the ways in which they analyze data, reason, and arrive at conclusions.

Many teams today are multinational, with government and business drawing together decision makers from across the world. Even small, local teams involve people of differing genders and diverse backgrounds. How do these factors influence the assumptions and values of participants?

Argyle (1991), after summarizing research on values in various societies, was able to derive a few generalizations:

In parts of India . . . status and glory were valued most, while wealth was not valued (being associated with arrogance and fear of thieves), nor was courage or power. The Greeks valued punishment (which was associated with justice) and power. The Japanese valued serenity and aesthetic satisfaction, and disvalued ignorance, deviation, and loneliness . . . Americans rated love and friendship as their most important life concerns, health as fifth; Koreans ranked these values as 12th, 14th, and 19th. (p. 41)

What do these differences mean? Suppose an international task force, charged with creating cultural connections among countries, is trying to choose between two proposals: one is to sponsor, in the capital of one country, an impressive International Plaza to exhibit art from around the world; the other is to create a long-term, well-funded cultural exchange program among the countries. The warrants (perhaps unspoken assumptions) might be "this action will reflect glory on the team" versus "this action will strengthen understanding among our nations." How might the assumptions and values of different cultures affect members' preferences between those alternatives?

Information about how people in various cultures think about themselves, about God, and about life helps members to understand one another's points of view. Can they be sure exactly which assumptions and values their teammates from other cultures might demonstrate? No, because generalizations about cultural values don't tell us about how experiences—in life, in work, in relationships—have changed an individual's views. They don't tell us, either, how these values might be changing—even as we write—or how they might affect a person's decision as she or he contributes to a team. Nor do they tell us how subcultures of class or gender might influence people's assumptions and values even within the major culture. What they do tell us is that there are some deep value differences that may appear when members of different cultures start analyzing arguments and making decisions.

Some people think of gender as a subcultural variable, because within cultures there is evidence that women and men develop different value/ethical structures. Men appear to develop hierarchical, rule-oriented ethical systems; women appear to develop more global, intuitive systems. This seems consistent with the findings of Carol Gilligan and associates (1988). Their research supports the idea that women and men develop a "difference in moral voice and moral orientation" (p. ii).

Gilligan calls the two ethics "justice" and "care." "A justice perspective draws attention to problems of inequality and oppression and holds up an idea of reciprocity and equal respect. A care perspective draws attention to problems of detachment or abandonment and holds up an ideal of attention and response to need" (p. 73).

In a justice perspective, the mark of a person's moral maturity is an objective detachment from situations. In the care orientation, detachment "becomes *the* moral problem . . . the failure to attend to need. Conversely, attention to the particular needs and circumstances of individuals, the mark of mature moral judgment in the care perspective, becomes *the* moral problem in the justice perspective—failure to treat others fairly, as equals" (p. 82).

Studies indicate that both sexes can use both orientations, but men are more likely to focus on the justice orientation and women are more likely to focus on the care orientation. There are differences, too, in the values and ethics people have derived from experience, from education, from their professions, even from their characters and personalities (Gilligan, 1988).

What do you do with this information? Well, we hope you won't look at an individual Korean, say, and assume that she or he is not concerned with love, friendship, or health because one study, summarized by one researcher, found that one group of Koreans rated these as low values. We hope you won't assume that a woman can't apply an ethic of justice or a man can't apply an ethic of care.

There are some real differences among cultures, subcultures, and genders in the values their members bring to a group or team experience. Don't assume that anyone has *x, y,* or *z* values—but do recognize that their values may be radically different from yours, and that these differences may need to be examined, probed, and understood before decisions can proceed smoothly.

With some understanding of the reasoning process, of common fallacies, and of human assumptions and values, you now have a foundation for analyzing the information and ideas your team has so creatively generated.

Summary

Once a team has collected information, its job is to analyze it, cooperatively and critically. Toward that end, a team needs to set norms that will enable it to collaborate objectively. To analyze evidence, a team needs shared criteria and skills for weighing the credibility of sources and the quality of data. Basic assumptions are that the purpose of critical analysis is to make good decisions and that human beings are capable of the rationality necessary to make those decisions.

Making rational choices involves examining the inferential connections between data and conclusions. A useful way of visualizing these connections is to map them, showing the warrant (the reason that justifies connecting the data to the claim) and qualifiers that indicate the degree of certainty.

Problems in reasoning include overgeneralization in inductive reasoning; improper deductive reasoning from a general statement to a specific instance; unjustified inferences of causation in cause-and-effect reasoning; and fallacies in connecting data, warrants, and claims.

Problems also arise because people bring assumptions and values—often influenced by culture, gender, and other individual variables—to their analyses without stating or, sometimes, even being aware of them.

Exercises

1. Using Form 6.1, rate the way you think with a group of people. What do you do well? What do you want to improve? How could your leadership help your team with critical analysis?

2. Be a critic. Record a serious discussion among several people, perhaps in class or from TV. Using Form 6.2, tally the statements each member of the group makes about data or analysis. Then discuss:
a. To what extent did members work together to think critically?
b. How thorough was the group in analyzing reasoning?
c. How well did the group analyze the data?
d. How objective were interactions in regard to data and reasoning?
e. How rational were the group's conclusions?

3. Find an editorial or short article that argues for a position. Map the relationships among data, warrant, and conclusions. (The data and/or warrant may not be clearly stated; you may have to infer them from what the author does say.)

Did the writer analyze background leading to the warrant? Were conclusions qualified or stated absolutely? How complete, rational, and ethical was his or her communication? Based upon this analysis, would you or would you not use that editorial as a data source for a group project? If so, why and how? If not, why not?

4. Cooperatively analyze reasoning. As a team, look over these questions and use them to analyze the statements that follow:
▌ What assumptions might the speaker be making? What assumptions might other team members make about the statement?
▌ What differing values might various members of a team bring to their analysis of the statement?
▌ What reasoning (inductive, deductive, cause-and-effect) does the statement imply?
▌ What fallacies does the statement reflect?
Here are the statements:
a. Abortion is a question of right to choose or right to life.
b. Only the United States can ensure world peace.
c. Educational excellence is declining because of television.
d. People who smoke infringe on other people's rights.
e. If executions were televised, crimes would decrease.
f. When pornography is available, people buy it because it's available.

FORM 6.1 ▌ SELF-ANALYSIS OF LOGICAL AND CRITICAL THINKING

Think about how you analyze information, reasoning, and conclusions when you're in a task group. Then rate the degree to which you think you are effective on each area.

When I'm working with a group, I:	GOOD	SO-SO	COULD BE BETTER
1. Examine source credibility.	☐	☐	☐
2. Show where reasoning doesn't make sense.	☐	☐	☐
3. Analyze causes and effects.	☐	☐	☐
4. Catch overgeneralizations and try to correct them.	☐	☐	☐
5. Suggest alternative choice options besides either-or.	☐	☐	☐
6. Examine connections among data, reasons, and conclusions.	☐	☐	☐
7. Stay objective in analyzing data and reasoning.	☐	☐	☐
8. Listen carefully to others' analyses.	☐	☐	☐
9. Examine assumptions behind reasoning and conclusions.	☐	☐	☐
10. Examine values in reasoning and conclusions.	☐	☐	☐
11. Evaluate ethical issues in uses of data and reasoning.	☐	☐	☐
12. Evaluate the ethics of decisions.	☐	☐	☐
13. Point out fallacies.	☐	☐	☐

F O R M   6.2   ▮   O B S E R V A T I O N   O F   L O G I C A L   A N D   C R I T I C A L   T E A M W O R K

NAME OF GROUP: _____

TOPIC: _____

Enter members' names in the diagonal spaces. When one speaks, tally the type of contribution she or he makes in the appropriate category or categories.

MEMBERS:									
Analyzes data									
Analyzes inference									
Tests reasoning									
Adds to analysis									
Qualifies conclusions									
Confuses issues									
Uses fallacies									

Comments:

The best contributions to analysis were:

The worst effect on analysis was:

The group used reasoning that was:

The group reached a conclusion that was:

I wanted someone to say:

Innovative and Creative Thinking:
Generating New Ideas

"But I'm just not creative . . . I never was any good in art or music."
"Where's an idea when I need one?"

Getting and applying good ideas are creative processes.

Your team has been charged by your advertising agency with preparing a "pitch" for a very valuable account. The present campaign is getting stale, and you think the advertiser may be ready to listen to new ideas. The team has met off and on for weeks, and the concepts you've come up with are as dry as the ads now running. It's frustrating. You're not making any progress. You begin to wish you were not a member of this group.

Most of us have spent time in sessions like that. They seem endless; maybe you could make an appointment for a root canal when the next meeting is scheduled.

The team needs a fresh approach—some creative ideas to get it out of its rut. But how do you get them?

Ideas, solutions, decisions, projects—they all have to come from somewhere. This is such a critical need today that major business schools offer creativity courses, and one-fourth of all organizations with 100 or more employees provide creativity training (Solomon, 1990, p. 66). These experiences are designed to improve people's problem-solving skills.

To make the rigorous journey from recognizing a problem or receiving an assignment to making and implementing decisions, your teammembers need well-exercised minds. An effective mind uses not only the critical thinking skills discussed in Chapter 6, but creative skills that lead to innovative ideas.

That's what this chapter is

about. We're going to examine some of the issues and processes involved in innovative and creative thinking. We look first at how thinking processes work and ways in which you can use that information to improve teamwork. The remainder of the chapter explores approaches to facilitate and improve creativity and details some methods for tapping the team's creative talents. This information will help you:

1. Become more aware of how you and others think when you process information.

2. Develop your creative abilities by using approaches to open up your thinking.

3. Use specific team techniques for increasing the number and quality of ideas.

Thinking Critically and Creatively

Thinking is both logical and creative, analytical and artistic. It takes an abundance of all kinds of thinking to work through information, ideate, analyze, and make decisions.

Immediately we can hear some students saying, "Forget it. I'm just not logical at all. I always lose arguments." Other students have the opposite reaction: "Creative? Me? No way. I can't draw a straight line." Who says logical means winning arguments? Who says a straight line measures creativity? Logical and creative are not ways that people "are" or "aren't." People often close themselves off from one type of thinking or the other because they have some narrow concepts of logic, of creativity, or—above all—of themselves. Davis (1983) describes the **creative process** as *combining or perceiving relationships of previously unrelated ideas* (p. 6). Many times the people who say, "I'm not logical," turn out to be extremely bright and analytical; and very often those who say, "I'm just not creative," come up with fresh ideas and innovative relationships. When they recognize what they've done, their barriers begin to crumble.

People can develop both their critical and their creative thinking and improve their contributions to team problem solving. The Frito-Lay corporation provided three-day workshops in creative problem solving for more than 7,000 of its employees, from vice-presidents to hourly workers. They estimate that by applying what they learned, the employees saved the company more than $500,000 (Solomon, 1990, p. 68).

Improving your critical and creative thinking abilities depends, in part, on understanding how the two of them work.

Understanding Brain Processes

It's generally accepted that the left side of the human brain does the **critical thinking**. It processes information in a logical, linear, rational, mathematical, serial, and organized set of patterns. It controls, to some extent, the use of speech, language, writing, arithmetic, and reasoning. The right side of the brain, it is thought, does the **creative thinking**—the nonverbal, synthetic, artistic, innovative, global, universal kinds of processes. It involves spatial, motor, musical, and touch abilities; it is the part of the brain that is visionary, intuitive, imaginative (Edwards, 1979).

Yet—and here's a mystery just beginning to yield to scientific investigation—the right brain also has some control over language; research indicates that a few language processes are dispersed across both sides of the brain. In some instances a second language may shift to the right side of the brain, while the primary language remains on the left. In fact, different kinds of words (such as nouns and verbs) and different concepts may be controlled in different parts of the brain (Blakeslee, 1991, p. C1).

Here's another teaser about how your brain works. There is evidence that a person's left and right brain functions, called "hemisphericity," may be deter-

THE IDEA BUSINESS

New ideas. They have the power to change the world, to change us. As Victor Hugo said, "An invasion of Armies can be resisted, but not an idea whose time has come."

But what role should original ideas and creativity play in the day-to-day workings of the business world—and the daily life of employees? For business, creativity is, in fact, a survival tool.

Yet unleashing creativity in the workplace is not a simple task. . . . Individuals need a certain degree of freedom to be creative, which must be reconciled with organizational objectives—specifically, the objec-

tive of operating profitably. The challenge, especially in large organizations, is to balance the need for a certain amount of structure with the desire to have a creative workplace.

Management must create a culture that encourages reasoned risk-taking. Employees must know that it is okay to fail. Failure is inherent in the creative process, as evidenced by Thomas Edison's more than 1,000 patents—most for inventions that have been forgotten and were probably not particularly useful from the beginning.

At United we . . . put an employee suggestion program in place in 1988. Our employees, working both in teams and individually, have submitted ideas worth more than $150 million to the company in either cost savings or revenue improvements. . . .

Just as important as the dollar savings is the way the program has encouraged and rewarded employees for their initiative and imaginative solutions. Those solutions represent the most important factor in the growth of business and the economy: human creativity.

An excerpt from "Editorial Opinion," by Stephen M. Wolf, United Airlines Chairman, President, and Chief Executive Officer, *VIS à VIS*, February 1991, p. 12. Used with permission.

mined by the way that individual has been conditioned by his or her culture and first language. Some research indicates, for example, that the left hemisphere of the Japanese brain processes "nonverbal human sounds, animal sounds, and Japanese instrumental music, while the right hemisphere processes Western instrumental music" (Lieberman, 1991, pp. 230–231). Lieberman points out that "previous research claimed all nonverbal sounds (human, animal, and musical) were processed in the right hemisphere" (p. 231).

So what does all of this tell us? Some tentative conclusions are:

1. Each of us is capable of thinking both critically and creatively.
2. Thinking processes may be very individual, possibly cultural.
3. The brain hemisphere we use more often may be influenced strongly by the languages we speak and the cultural or subcultural shaping we have experienced.

It's true that some people are more inclined to use one side of the brain than the other, and that one side predominates at any given time over the other. But look what happens when you work through a problem. You're analytical and rational for a while: you sift through your information; you seek out causes. Then, perhaps, you go off on a flight of fancy, imagining ideal, unrealistic solutions. Then you come back to thinking about what will really work—and go back to one of your fantasies and say, "Wait a minute. There *is* something there I can use. . . ."

When you do that, you use your left brain and right brain capacities in such quick succession that it might as well be concurrent. Our personal experiences as individuals and as teachers show us that as people become *aware* of their capacity for thinking in both modes, they develop the ability to switch back and forth at will.

What's the relevance of all of this in a group communication textbook? The more you know about the way human beings think, the better you can learn to think clearly, analytically, and creatively. The better you learn to do that, the more satisfying and effective will be your team experiences.

Critical *and* creative thinking are used at all stages of a team's work. In fact, it appears that the more diverse team members are, the more probable it is that at any one time different members will be thinking in different modes, or using opposite sides of their brains. That means two things to team members: It means that others' thinking may be operating differently from yours, so sometimes you'll have to work harder at understanding each other. But it also means you have a richer range of creative possibilities among team members.

Facilitating Creative Thinking

It can be difficult, at least for Western, left-brained, linear thinkers, to let go and let the creative processes work. Many people are task-oriented and feel uncomfortable when discussion gets too far from the goals. They may feel silly or, perhaps, inadequate at being creative and be blinded to relationships and applications that could lead to better solutions to problems.

Once the team breaks through those barriers, members discover imaginations they may have forgotten or never knew they had. Out of those imaginations come ideas that are innovative, original, perhaps daring. A major objective is to make it okay, acceptable, desirable, maybe even a norm, to be playful and imaginative. By allowing itself to "play," the team is planting a rich field of ideas from which later rational analysis will harvest good solutions.

To get the process going, teams must get rid of the blocks that inhibit innovation and be able to recognize the stages in creative thinking. We will also consider ways to reduce risks in order to create an innovative environment, and describe some methods for improving your own and your team's creativity.

Opening "Mind Locks"

Roger von Oech wrote an amusing, accurate, and successful little book on creative thinking that organizations all over the country have used to try to open up their employees' minds. In *A Whack on the Side of the Head* (1983), he lists ten "locks" that people keep on their minds. **Mind locks** are assumptions about how people should be—and they close off the ability to think creatively. Do you ever snap one of these closed on your mind?

1. "The right answer."
2. "That's not logical."
3. "Follow the rules."
4. "Be practical."

5. "Avoid ambiguity."
6. "To err is wrong."
7. "Play is frivolous."
8. "That's not my area."
9. "Don't be foolish."
10. "I'm not creative." (p. 9)

Each of these, you'll note, is a message we give to ourselves about ourselves. As children, people probably heard these scoldings at school or at home. These mind locks reflect three assumptions that people make about themselves:

1. "To be worthwhile, I must be expert, logical, practical, and serious." This sets up a tough set of self-requirements. You dare not be playful, adventurous, foolish, or creative. What stiff-necked stuffed shirts our society makes us, sometimes.

2. "I have to choose between two extremes." This keeps a person from considering more than one alternative at a time. The "right answer" and "avoid ambiguity" set yes-no, right-wrong limits on ideas and actions. Most things have many possibilities, but with these locks they are hidden behind the either-or doors.

3. "I have to do everything just right." You could rephrase this as "I can't color out of the lines." When a person must always "follow the rules," or fears to take a risk because "to err is wrong," then that person is blinded to the possibilities. What's worse, when an individual has this mind lock, it isn't just a question of following the rules that are there. She or he often assumes rules that have not been stated, and religiously follows them, too.

To be innovative and creative, team members need to turn some keys to these locks and open their minds. When you do, the interactions among you will increase the creative potential of each individual. This definitely is not a linear, 1–2–3 process. It's an interactive, multidimensional process that is not always definable. Scholars try, however, to get a picture of how it works.

Identifying Creative Stages

In *The Creative Brain* (1988), Hermann describes the creative process, identified years ago by Graham Wallas, as involving four stages:

1. *Preparation*—defining, motivating, gathering information, and setting up criteria for solving a problem.

2. *Incubation*—stepping back, allowing the mind to play with ideas, "contemplate, work it through. Like preparation, incubation can last minutes, weeks, even years."

3. *Illumination*—flashes of insight when "ideas arise from the mind . . . pieces of the whole or the whole itself. . . . Unlike the other stages, illumination is often very brief, involving a tremendous rush of insights within a few minutes or hours."

∎ STRENGTHEN YOUR INTUITIVE POWERS

To get in touch with your intuitive ability and develop it . . .

∎ Believe in your intuition. What we *believe* we can do is one of the most important factors in determining what we *can* do.

∎ Pay attention to your intuition. Very often, intuitive people are not even aware of their skill.

∎ Practice the skill. One way to do this is to keep an *intuition journal*, individually or as an organization, of insights, how and when they come, by what means (for example, dreams) and keep a record of their accuracy.

∎ Share your experiences with others. Form an *intuition club* where you can compare your skills with colleagues and record your successes and failures.

∎ Explore ideas without a specific goal in mind.

∎ Reserve judgment on ideas, rather than looking for immediate or simple solutions. Learn to tolerate ambiguity so you can study a problem from many perspectives.

∎ Stay receptive to unknowns. Avoid depending on rules, procedures, calculations and the status quo; this can inhibit flexibility.

∎ Think of unique solutions.

∎ Follow up on points that have no factual justification. Sometimes logical thinking prohibits the open-ended mental explorations that help to trigger fresh insights.

∎ Practice guided imagery by picturing a situation and considerng various possibilities. Or try hypnosis.

∎ Improve your concentration by meditating or focusing on a problem in a relaxed state. Relaxation can take you into your creative space where your mind can free flow with options and choices.

Condensed from "All about Intuition," an interview with Weston H. Agor, Director, The Global Intuition Network, University of Texas at El Paso, *Boardroom Reports*, December 15, 1991, pp. 13–14. Used with permission.

---

4. *Verification*—analysis of the idea, implementation, and assessment of its completion. (Hermann, 1988, pp. 187–188)

Others have added to Wallas's concepts. Fabun (1968) suggests you first have a desire or motivation; then, between preparation and incubation, you try out new arrangements; and just before illumination, you get good internal feelings that you're almost there. Haman (cited in Solomon, 1990, p. 67) adds an implementation stage, in which you transform ideas into reality.

Reading about these stages was a gigantic "Aha!" experience for us. Incubation and illumination describe exactly what happens to us, personally, when we have a problem to solve. Both of us—your authors—go through a sometimes long and painful hiatus while everything we've learned or thought about a problem incubates. We've now gotten to the point where we just look at each other and say, "Be patient, it's incubating." And then—suddenly—the idea is there, almost full-fledged and ready to fly. But it won't fly until we verify it, check it out, maybe alter it together to make sure its wings are ready. We also experience that good feeling described by Fabun just before the ideas emerge.

This process goes on, of course, in the individual's mind. Working in a team brings those individual processes together.

Scheidel and Crowell (1964) describe idea development in a group as a spiraling process. Members of a group tend to follow what they call a "reach-test cycle," in which someone suggests an idea (perhaps after incubation), some people agree, someone gives supporting examples of how the idea might work, and the group agrees or affirms the idea (verification, perhaps). There's a process of suggesting, agreeing, clarifying, affirming, and deciding, or "anchoring" the suggestion—before the group goes on to more ideas.

Reducing Risks

To unlock the mind, and to create the kind of transactional process that start a spiral of ideation, a team needs to develop the right atmosphere. This is one of the many areas in which leadership is important. Every member's leadership counts in helping every other member open up to creativity. Where there is a designated leader or where a team is responsible to a parent organization, the leader or the "boss" can help significantly by letting a team know that its creativity is highly prized and that it has the freedom, even the responsibility, to take risks and, sometimes, to fail.

Great ideas usually entail some risk—first to express the idea, then to make it happen. Some corporations expect a high percentage of their managers' ideas to fail; if all succeed, it suggests they are being too safe and not innovative enough. When a team is creating ideas, risk-taking is a positive value, so ideas are not cut off by anxiety. Later, you'll assess risks before you make decisions.

We suggest the following general guidelines for opening—and keeping open—the gates to creativity. It helps to discuss these as a team before you start working on creative issues.

Encourage playfulness. Make it "okay" to use the imagination, to play, to fantasize, to tease, to laugh. These are part of the energy and provide many of the stimuli to creativity.

Agree not to judge people or ideas. Let it roll. Sometimes a person comes up with the weirdest idea—and it turns out to be a treasure. But nothing turns off imagination like criticism or judgment. They have their place, but creative processing isn't it.

Look for different, even bizarre, idea relationships. Encourage each other to stretch, reach, deliberately match up concepts that you wouldn't normally put in the same ballroom.

Break down barriers. Don't "close" on ideas too fast; don't stereotype ideas or people; don't worry too much about "rules."

If you agree to these guidelines as a team, and if you set an interim goal of improving your team's creative problem-solving skills, you can increase both individual members' and the team's achievements.

Enhancing Creativity

Some team techniques can help to get thinking started. It may seem contradictory to talk about "techniques" and "creativity" in the same breath, but—remember the mind locks? This is one of those places where two seemingly opposite terms can be combined to create a new alternative.

FIGURE   7.1
What do you see?

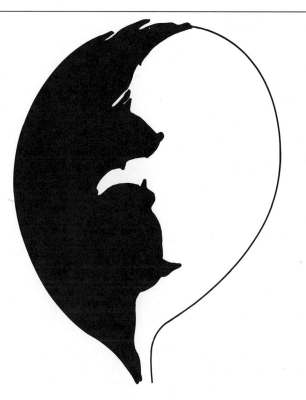

A multitude of activities, exercises, and problems have been created to help people open up their minds. They are designed to start you thinking of different ways of "seeing" or relating ideas. Four such approaches are: perception activities, open-mindedness exercises, role-playing, and team relaxation.

Perception   Perception exercises ask individuals to describe how they perceive a stimulus; members then compare their observations and discuss why and how their perceptions differed. For example, take a look at Figure 7.1. What do you see?

Do you see a demon? A man? They're both there. When you know they're both in the picture, can you see them both? Which one did you see first? What influenced your perception? Are you thinking about demons? About men? Did your eyes first hit the black area or the white one? How did the first thing you saw affect the way your mind organized the rest of the picture?

We know that a number of things influence the way we perceive things. What we want, need, or are interested in; how close to or similar to something else an object is; how much contrast it has to its background; what detail draws the eye as a center of interest—all of these will influence what you see or hear, or smell, or feel, or think about.

F I G U R E   7.2
Connect the dots by
drawing a *square* with-
out lifting the pencil
from the paper.

How does this relate to creativity? The more ways of perceiving any given object or idea you can handle, the more imagination you can bring to solving a problem.

Puzzles help people learn new strategies and approaches to thinking. Most puzzles have a fairly direct and simple solution, but often the foundation for that solution is outside of an individual's frame of perceptual experience. For example, Figure 7.2 contains four dots. Without lifting your pencil from the paper, and without rearranging them, connect the dots to make a square by drawing only four straight lines.

Was it easy? Was it difficult? Here's a hint if you need it: the instructions don't prevent you from going outside the arrangement of dots.

DeBono (1970) would call this "lateral" thinking, or thinking that goes outside one frame of reference to others. To do this, you have to be able to let go of standard operating procedures; to think randomly, provocatively; to look at things from above, from the side, from underneath. You need to go beyond your childhood connect-the-dots experiences. Then you begin to see solutions you wouldn't have seen before.

Open-Mindedness   Many exercises are intended to break down some of the mind locks we talked about earlier. Some of these exercises grew out Adorno's early personality research in authoritarianism, which found that children who grew up with punitive, harsh, dominant, and status-conscious parents often turned out to be rigid, conventional, hostile, obedient to authority, ethnocentric, prejudiced toward other groups, and unable to modify their behavior (Baum, Fisher, & Singer, 1985, p. 393). Although this is the extreme personality type that can develop from a rigid environment, research has revealed a milder, but still limiting, potential for individuals from such backgrounds to be closed-minded or dogmatic.

Exercises can help people break down some of these mind locks—get rid of the "rule" orientation, learn to be comfortable with ambiguity, not worry about logic or practicality, be unafraid to make a mistake or look foolish for a moment. At the end of this chapter, you'll find one of our favorite exercises, about "Joe Doodlebug." Try it out and see what you can do.

Exercises are especially helpful when a team works on them together, if they follow the guidelines we set out earlier for making it comfortable to take risks. Members can help one another discover strategies and approaches to solving their problems.

Role-Playing   Another way to loosen up your point of view is through **role-playing**. This can be useful if you want to get a sense of what someone else perceives or feels, or if you want to get a picture of how some idea might work.

To role-play, set up a situation with designated roles for individuals. Describe the outline of the situation and the characteristics of the individuals, but let the role-players work out the interaction as they go along.

Suppose your team is a cooperative task force between the school of education at your college and the local school system. Your task is to investigate the effectiveness of English as a Second Language programs and to make recommendations for new policies and programs. Although your team is multicultural, none of you attended ESL classes as children. To increase your sensitivity and awareness of what a child might experience, you set up a role-play situation. One team member is given the role of a child whose first language is—say—German. One member is given a description of the teacher to act out, and one member is given a description of a parent who speaks only limited English. The situation is a first meeting among teacher, parent, and child.

The role-players act out this situation as they think it would happen, while other members observe. Then they discuss how each person must have felt and what variables seemed to get in the way of, or facilitate, communication among the three people.

Role-playing is amazingly real for people. They don't have to be actors; simply as human beings, they feel some of what the persons they are playing might feel, and they act somewhat as those persons might act. Their audience begins to see some of the "truths" of the interaction in ways they would not comprehend from hard data or experts' opinions. This felt reality becomes the start for more thoughtful and creative solutions to problems.

Team Relaxation   As a group, go through a few relaxation or meditation exercises to free your minds. Here's one way of doing this.

Choose someone to be a "guide." Have everyone sit comfortably in a chair or on the floor. Everyone close your eyes, get comfortable.

Slowly and quietly, the guide takes you through the following script, pausing between ideas to give your mind time to create the scenes and the actions:

You're someplace that makes you feel relaxed and comfortable, someplace you always love to be. Maybe it's the beach, or the mountains. Wherever it is, you feel the peace and tranquillity of the place washing over you . . . soothing you . . . taking away the stress and pain. You're comfortable . . . you're relaxed . . . Look around you . . . see the things you love . . . touch them . . . feel the relaxation that comes from them. You have all the time in the world . . . enjoy the tiniest little shell . . . the smallest leaf . . . the delicate little breeze . . .

the sweetest scents. Now just explore your place for awhile, go a little deeper into it. . . . Feel it giving you energy . . . and strength . . . and imagination. Reach out to it . . . feel its peace and inspiration. . . . Think about what you will be able to do and accomplish with this peace and strength and creativity.

The guide allows the members of the team to meditate in their special places for a few minutes, and then says: "When you're ready, open your eyes and come back to our team and our meeting refreshed and ready to think together."

Then spend a few moments talking about where you've been, and use this sharing as a jumping-off point for generating ideas that pertain to the group's objectives. Sounds like hocus-pocus? It's not. It is a meditative way of shaking off the shackles of stress and tension; it opens up the mind so that you can work with greater energy and openness. This is a technique that anyone can use alone—and it's a helpful thing to do. When you do it as a team, it allows you to share some of your experiences, create a greater sense of syntality and synergy for the group, and move directly into generating ideas and solving problems that relate to the group's goals.

Generating Ideas

We've looked at how the creative mind works and at some ways to facilitate innovative thinking and develop your abilities. Now its time to put some of these ideas to work. Your team knows what its purpose is, has established its goals, has gathered and analyzed its information. You've loosened up your creative processes, and you're ready to go. How do you get some ideas to work with? We'll cover five approaches here: brainstorming, metaphorical thinking, fantasy chaining, synectics, and a couple of techniques to use with larger groups. You may use any one or a combination, depending on your needs and the time available.

Brainstorming

Brainstorming is something you may have done many times; at least, that's what you called it. Too often, though, people don't know how to make it work the way it should. It helps to have a facilitator to keep you from walking on each other and trampling the process, and you absolutely must have someone record and post (on a board or flip chart) the ideas as they emerge. The goal is to think of as many ideas as you can. The emphasis here is only on the number you can list, not on their quality—that comes later. Reach to the outer limits for wild and crazy thoughts. Energy usually is extremely high, and people are free to be humorous and weird.

When the inevitable periods of silence settle on the group, wait them out. Those painful quiets are incubation periods, and if everyone waits, someone will break through. When we conduct brainstorming sessions in corporations or classrooms, we unobtrusively mark the list at the point of quiet periods. People start

---

C A S E   A N A L Y S I S   7.1

The task force members developed this matrix and used it for brainstorming sessions to be sure they covered all possible waste-reduction approaches for all categories of packaging for the all business operations.

THE OPTIONS IDENTIFICATION MATRIX

MATERIAL, PRODUCT OR OPERATION	ELIMI- NATION	VOLUME/ WEIGHT REDUCTION	MATERIAL SHIFTS TO ENHANCE RECYCLING/ COMPOSTING	INCREASE RECYCLED CONTENT	REDUCE ENVIRONMENTAL IMPACTS IN PRODUCTION	REUSE	RECYCLING	COMPOSTING

Issues for Your Consideration

1. In what ways can such a matrix facilitate brainstorming? In what ways could it hinder the process?
2. Identify one item you might find at a McDonald's restaurant and use the categories to brainstorm possible approaches in each category.

---

getting edgy and want to move on. After we've completed the session we go back and ask the group to remember how they felt at that time. Then the group looks at the ideas that emerged after everyone thought they should be quitting. Most times, the more useful ideas came after the quiet periods. If we had quit then, we would have missed them.

When you and your team put brainstorming on your agenda, it's helpful to review the following guidelines:

1. Someone facilitate. Remind people not to stop to talk about the ideas; keep it moving fast.
2. Generate and post ideas as quickly as possible.
3. Do not "own" ideas, good or bad.
4. "Piggyback" or "hitchhike" ideas onto previous thoughts.
5. Do not evaluate any idea; bizarre or ridiculous is fine.
6. Sweat out the silences and plateaus until someone comes up with something.
7. After many ideas are on the list, discuss them and winnow them down.
8. Start serious analysis of the remaining possibilities.

Metaphorical Thinking

Metaphorical thinking is a part of creativity—often, indeed, its foundation—at any stage. Metaphors are powerful because they phrase comparisons between two things as if one thing were the other. Metaphors, some people believe, are the bridges with which people think and learn new ideas. Seeing similarities between two things makes you consider other similarities or differences. In your mind, you may suddenly "see" connections and relationships that you never saw before.

Suppose your team is having trouble working together, and someone says, "We're so discordant—we're all off key." Someone else picks up the musical metaphor and says, "No—we're just all playing a different place on the score." Someone else says, "Problem is, there's no conductor. . . ." Suddenly, the team sees what it needs—it needs some leadership. Ta da! Now you might ask some metaphorical questions: How does an orchestra get a conductor? What criteria should the conductor meet? How would your "orchestra" work with a conductor? Who should be your conductor? You're on your way to a solution—not there yet—but on your way.

Normally, metaphors just happen; sometimes, they don't. You may just get clichés—once juicy metaphors that have dried up from too much air. You can use metaphorical thinking in two ways. One is simply to be alert to the opportunities, exercising your leadership to get the process started and guide it along. The other is to use metaphorical thinking consciously as a creative strategy. If your team wants to try it, the following guidelines may help:

1. State the objectives of thinking in metaphors: to see comparisons between two ideas, and to gain new insights from comparisons.
2. Brainstorm possible metaphors for some aspects of the problem.
3. "Piggyback" on metaphors; build on them.
4. Choose the best metaphor to carry further.
5. Examine all imaginable areas of comparison in the metaphor.
6. Ask questions the metaphor might answer.
7. Look for insights into causes, effects, and solutions for your problem.

Fantasy Chaining

Fantasy chaining is an imaginative, creative process group members often start spontaneously. Bormann (1990, pp. 101–120) describes it as a series of ideas that members link together like a play.

Remember when you were a kid and you made up plays? "I'm the mother and you're the father and Tommy's the baby and Woof is the monster." "Yeah, and the monster comes in. . . ." "It's the middle of the night . . ." "Yeah, and there's a full moon . . ." "Yeah, and. . . ."

You may be able to think of a time in your adult life that you and your friends or family did something similar. Someone starts off an idea—perhaps a metaphor, a comparison, a pun, a joke—and from there the members create a series of fantasized events that chain out like a play or a story. As in a drama, the chain involves heroes, villains, plot, action, settings, scenes.

Fantasy chaining serves several purposes for team members. It releases tension and, like metaphorical thinking, can trigger insights and possibilities that do not show up in any other way. Perhaps most important, as the fantasy chain develops

THE KNOWLEDGE-CREATING COMPANY

In 1978, top management at Honda inaugurated the development of a new-concept car with the slogan, "Let's gamble." . . .

The business decision that followed from the "Let's gamble" slogan was to form a new-product development team of young engineers and designers. . . . Top management charged the team with two—and only two—instructions: first, to come up with a product concept fundamentally different from anything the company had ever done before; and second, to make a car that was inexpensive but not cheap.

This mission might sound vague, but in fact it provided the team an extremely clear sense of direction. For instance, in the early days of the project, some team members proposed designing a smaller and cheaper version of the Honda Civic—a safe and technologically feasible option. But the team quickly decided this approach contradicted the entire rationale of its mission. The only alternative was to invent something totally new. . . .

Project team leader Hiroo Watanabe coined another slogan to express his sense of the team's ambitious challenge: Theory of Automobile Evolution. . . . In effect it posed the question: If the automobile were an organism, how should it evolve? As team members argued and discussed what Watanabe's slogan might possibly mean, they came up with an answer in the form of yet another slogan: "Man-maximum, machine-minimum." This captured the team's belief that the ideal car should somehow transcend the traditional human-machine relationship. . . .

The "evolutionary" trend the team articulated eventually came to be embodied in the image of a sphere—a car simultaneously "short" (in length) and "tall" (in height). Such a car, they reasoned, would be lighter and cheaper, but also more comfortable and more solid than traditional cars. . . . This gave birth to a product concept the team called "Tall Boy," which eventually led to the Honda City, the company's distinctive urban car.

The Tall Boy concept totally contradicted the conventional wisdom about automobile design at the time, which emphasized long, low sedans. But the City's revolutionary styling and engineering were prophetic.

Reprinted by permission of *Harvard Business Review.* An excerpt from "The Knowledge-Creating Company," by Ikujiro Nonaka, November/December, 1991. Copyright © 1991 by the President and Fellows of Harvard College; all rights reserved.

it provides members with a mutually understood, shared set of symbols. People think and communicate in symbols. Sharing special symbols with members of the group creates closeness and makes communication easier.

A fantasy chain is a naturally occurring process. However, you can be alert to opportunities to build a chain when the team needs a sense of shared creativity, when it needs to expand its problem-solving possibilities, or even when it just needs to have some fun. When you want to exercise leadership in this way, keep the following guidelines in mind:

1. Someone's idea spontaneously starts an imaginative drama relating the problem to some event, story line, or plot. The catalyst may be a joke, a pun, a sarcastic remark, or characterizing a person in the problem as a "hero" or a "villain."

2. Someone else builds on the initial idea.

3. The group develops a chain of dramatic events. Someone becomes a villain, a hero, a supporting character; an imaginary plot develops; a pattern of action and reaction develops in the story.

4. The group develops a shared symbology and insights from developing the drama together.

5. Ideas and possible solutions are generated as part of the plot and action of the drama.

Synectics

You might be surprised how widely metaphor and fantasy are used. For example, a structured, applied use of metaphorical thinking and group fantasy is central to the process adapted by Gordon (1961) called **synectics** (from a Greek term for creating new concepts from previously unrelated ideas).

In synectics, often used in corporate groups, a person (acting as a client) presents a problem she or he needs to solve. A facilitator, who must be skilled in guiding groups, moves problem solving through several specific stages. Participants with expertise in the problem area may be drawn from anywhere within or outside the organization. They have one role: to generate ideas. To do that, they must have the skill and the expertise to question, probe, and understand the problem in depth. They also must be ready to move from critical thinking to creative thinking and back to critical thinking without mental blocks or self-consciousness.

After the client describes the problem, and the group probes the issues until they are well defined, the members use metaphors or fantasies to explore possible insights into the problem and its solution.

Napier and Gershenfeld (1985, pp. 340–343) describe an instance in which a synectics group focused on a manager's problem with the poor performance and low morale of a longtime employee. In brainstorming the attributes of morale, the members listed the concept "spirit"; spirit became a metaphor for morale. Members then brainstormed varieties of spirits, their qualities and effects.

When the group listed the qualities and effects of alcoholic spirits, this metaphor led to the fantasy of a supernatural spirit overlooking the department. When the group moved back to critical analysis and application of the concepts that had emerged from the fantasy, the members shifted their points of view to see the organization through the eyes of this supernatural spirit. That led them to think differently about morale and to address organizational problems from an entirely new perspective. The results not only addressed the difficulties of the specific employee, but also led to creation of a task force to recommend steps for humanizing the entire organization.

Throughout the process of synectics, a group, facilitator, and client build a tightly woven sense of trust and cooperation. Almost inevitably, the group develops mutually held symbols and humor that hold it together through difficult stages of critical analysis and application.

Group Techniques

Two other approaches for generating and evaluating ideas from groups of people are nominal group technique (NGT) and the Delphi technique. "When properly utilized and applied," according to Delbecq, Van de Ven, and Gustafson (1975), "both techniques are powerful tools for increasing a group's creative capacity to generate critical ideas and understand problems and the component parts of their solutions" (p. 1).

Both techniques ensure that individuals have opportunities to generate and evaluate ideas. The principal difference is that NGT takes place in face-to-face meetings, whereas Delphi is used without bringing the individuals together. Both are especially useful when groups are too large for all members to be highly involved all the time. They can also be used to draw ideas from those who are not on the team.

Nominal Group   In **nominal group technique (NGT),** each group member writes down ideas on cards. The facilitator has each person read an idea, one at a time, and writes them on a flip chart or board for all to see. Then the group works through the process of setting priorities and making decisions.

After discussing all the ideas, the group narrows down the ideas, much as it would in brainstorming, and settles on a few that might meet its goals. Then members multiple-rank the possibilities (we'll talk about that in Chapter 8) and, if a final decision is part of their task, take a final vote.

NGT is an orderly process for getting full participation, although it doesn't generate the variety or quantity of ideas that brainstorming can. If you want to use NGT, these guidelines will help you organize it:

1. Get each member to write ideas on cards.
2. Collect ideas round-robin, one at a time from each person.
3. Post them so that everyone can see them.
4. Discuss each idea in order.
5. Have individuals privately select and rank priority ideas.
6. Report and discuss the selections.
7. Take a final vote, possibly by individual rankings.

Delphi   Frequently, a team needs to involve a wide range of people, possibly from other groups or locations, who cannot get to meetings. **Delphi technique** can be used for this purpose at any or all stages of a decision-making or planning process. However, it does take time, effort, and, sometimes, money for printing and postage.

To be effective, the Delphi technique has to be carefully done. Participants must know, at every stage, what is going on. They have to feel that their participation counts, and they must be motivated to respond. Why? Because Delphi is conducted by repeated mailings, tallying, analysis, and reporting of questionnaires. When personal contact and transactions are limited or nonexistent, communication must be handled with extreme care.

Questionnaires must be written precisely and unambiguously to get exactly what the committee or team needs from the respondents. After receiving the initial responses, the committee redrafts the questionnaire to cover the next step of emerging ideas or issues, and distributes it again. As the process continues, it may be necessary to draft, send out, and tabulate several different questionnaires. Depending on what the respondents are being asked to do, the technique can be carried all the way from fact finding through ideation and problem solving to voting for decisions. Usually multiple ranking is used to narrow down the final decisions. It is essential that participants be kept fully informed all the way through implementation and review of any decision in which they were involved through the Delphi method.

If you want to use the Delphi technique, the following guidelines will help:

1. Identify the broad question areas, prepare an open-ended questionnaire, and send it to selected individuals.
2. Analyze the responses, redraft a more specific questionnaire, and send it to the same people.
3. Tally responses and narrow down the options.
4. Send out ballots, listing possible decisions, for multiple rankings. If the decision list is long, repeat this step until a decision is made.
5. Follow up with a report to all participants.

Summary

In this chapter, we contend that both critical and creative thinking are essential to effective team communication, and that everyone is capable of both. Although it is believed that the right brain controls creative processes and the left brain controls logical processes, some evidence now suggests that hemisphericity is not as absolute as once thought. It is influenced by culture and language and may adapt through experience or need.

People can expand their skills in either creative or critical thinking with practice. It helps to get rid of "mind locks" that limit people to thinking in terms of rules, either-or choices, or "logical" self-stereotypes. A team can open up creative thinking by making it comfortable to take risks, and develop members' abilities with exercises and activities. Then it can generate ideas creatively through techniques such as brainstorming, metaphorical thinking, fantasy chaining,

synectics, nominal group (NGT), and Delphi. These methods involve all team members in generating a large number of ideas and then analyzing them for quality and appropriateness.

Creative thinking can and should go on constantly in the team's life. These techniques can be used for defining problems, identifying questions, setting goals; for identifying resources and ways to use them; for thinking of solutions to problems or ideas for projects, finding ways to implement plans, discovering advantages and disadvantages; for finding ways to assess your team's processes or outcomes, and to overcome barriers or conflicts. The high energy and member involvement creative thinking demands not only increases the quantity and quality of innovative possibilities, but develops and intensifies individuals' effectiveness and team synergy.

Exercises

1. Your team has been called together to design an ad campaign for the Better Bricks Company. They make bricks—real, fake, big, little, all kinds and colors of bricks—which they sell to homebuilding companies as well as through retail outlets to do-it-yourself suburbanites. Using the techniques

of brainstorming, metaphorical thinking, and fantasy chaining, create a campaign concept. Use your critical thinking to refine it. Then present your campaign to the class and explain the processes you used to create it.

2. Use Form 7.1 to assess the group you worked with in the preceding exercise. How did you function on these variables? What did you do well? What could you improve, and how?

3. Using Form 7.2, rate yourself on each statement. What do you do that you've never thought of as creative? What else do you do, not listed on the form, that might be creative? How can you expand on those abilities?

4. As a team, figure this one out: Joe Doodlebug is a strange sort of imaginary bug that can and cannot do certain things.* He has been jumping all over the place getting some exercise when his master places a pile of food three inches directly west of him. As soon as he sees all this food, he stops in his tracks, facing north. He notes that the pile of food is a little larger than he is.

After all this exercise, Joe is very hungry and wants to get to the food as quickly as he can. He

*This exercise is based on a problem from Rokeach, M., *The Open and Closed Mind,* New York, Basic Books, 1960.

examines the situation and then says, "Darn it, I'll have to jump four times to get the food."

Joe is a smart bug, and he is dead right in his conclusion. Why do you suppose Joe Doodlebug has to take *four jumps* to reach the food?

The solution takes into account these five rules:
a. Joe can jump only in four directions: north, south, east, and west; he cannot jump diagonally (northeast, northwest, southeast, southwest).
b. Once Joe starts in any direction, he must jump four times in that same direction before he can change his direction.
c. Joe can only jump; he cannot crawl, fly, or walk.
d. Joe can jump very large distances or very small distances, but not less than one inch per jump.
e. Joe cannot turn; he always faces north.

5. With your team, create your own brain stretcher or puzzle. It can be in either written or visual form. The rules for designing your brain stretcher are: It should have a simple solution. It should not be deceptive, but it *should* require lateral thinking and breaking through mind locks to solve it.

As a group, present your puzzle to the class. Can they solve it? Teach the class what mind locks may have kept them from solving it and how creative thinking could have helped them.

FORM 7.1 ▪ OBSERVATION OF GROUP CREATIVE
                AND CRITICAL THINKING

Assess how well your own team—or a group you observe—does in using creative and critical thinking together:

IMPROVE	WELL	SO-SO	COULD BE BETTER
1. Members brainstorm many ideas.	☐	☐	☐
2. Members don't judge ideas as they brainstorm them—they wait until later.	☐	☐	☐
3. People have fun piggybacking ideas.	☐	☐	☐
4. People create metaphors and analogies.	☐	☐	☐
5. Humor helps the team to develop ideas.	☐	☐	☐
6. Members help each other break mind locks.	☐	☐	☐
7. It's a norm to fantasize and play with ideas and solutions.	☐	☐	☐
8. When it's time to analyze ideas, the members focus on it together.	☐	☐	☐
9. Members cooperate in analyzing the logic and reasoning of ideas, once they have some good ones in front of them.	☐	☐	☐
10. People appreciate one another's ideas and can be objective about their own.	☐	☐	☐
11. The team can be serious with analysis and have fun with ideas.	☐	☐	☐
12. The team values both creativity and critical analysis of data, reasoning, and conclusions.	☐	☐	☐

What could this group do to further stimulate its creativity and hone its critical analysis?

FORM 7.2 ■ SELF-ASSESSMENT OF CREATIVE THINKING

This assessment is a way to start thinking about your own creativity. Check off the extent to which you believe you do the following:

	A LOT	SOME	NOT MUCH
1. I think about what might explain people or events (I can imagine their stories).	☐	☐	☐
2. I enjoy playing mental games with an idea.	☐	☐	☐
3. If I can't find the right tool to do something, I can think of some other way to do it.	☐	☐	☐
4. I enjoy helping others find solutions to problems.	☐	☐	☐
5. I enjoy spinning a story to entertain others.	☐	☐	☐
6. I can find pictures in things like clouds or spilled paint.	☐	☐	☐
7. I enjoy connecting one idea to another to find a new concept.	☐	☐	☐
8. When I listen to others, read, or watch something, I get ideas that go beyond the message content.	☐	☐	☐
9. I tend to compare and relate ideas and think of analogies to explain them.	☐	☐	☐
10. I enjoy creating fantasies and stories.	☐	☐	☐

Think of other things you like to do, and things you do well, that require you to see things from a different angle; think of things that require you to separate or relate ideas so you see them differently. You're probably much more creative than you know.

CHAPTER 8

Problem Analysis and Decision Making:
Following Clear Systems

"Shall we flip a coin?"
Maybe not—50% of the time you lose!

You coach a Little League team and the kids' uniforms are in tatters. You call a meeting of the parents, kick the problem around for a while, and decide to accept the offer of a local food emporium to provide new uniforms. What you don't realize is that the company is going to splash its advertising all over the place—which might not be so terrible except that your kids will now be labeled with the name of the company: Lem's Supreme Hot Dogs. This is hardly the image you want the team to have. The decision, it seems, needed a bit more thought.

All decisions are made about unknown events; problem solvers and decision makers must try to predict them as accurately as they can. If answers were obvious, choices would be automatic and decision making unnecessary. Gut reactions and random choices may work out sometimes, but it's much better to steer a clear course to a decision.

In this chapter, we explore systems for steering through problem analysis and decision making. The first step is to identify and analyze problems, their causes and effects. Next comes the process of generating and analyzing solution options, using clear, mutually held criteria. Then we look at

some critical issues and methods involved in making decisions. Finally, you need to create a plan for implementing and assessing those decisions. Our goals for this chapter are to help you:

1. Make systematic analysis part of your team's work.

2. Identify and analyze problems.

3. Establish criteria for potential solutions.

4. Decide on the most appropriate action to take.

5. Develop plans to implement decisions.

6. Plan to assess the effectiveness of your choices.

Planning Approaches

All too frequently, groups do what the Little League parents did—they sit down and talk and make a decision. Sometimes the decision shows foresight; sometimes it shows no vision at all. Effective decision making, however, seems to have certain activities in common. Through the years, researchers have identified some of these activities, and their lists often serve as step-by-step agendas or work plans that guide a team's task processes. We're going to tell you about three of these: Simon's approach, which identifies broad categories of activities a decision-making team goes through; the **vigilant** decision-making approach, which provides a sense of the numerous small decisions that must be made throughout those activities; and Dewey's reflective thinking sequence, which provides a possible chronology of events.

You might remember that Chapter 5 mentioned Simon's four phases of decision making: intelligence, design, choice, and review. In intelligence, you gather and analyze the necessary data; in design, you create and select possible solutions; in choice, you make decisions; and in review, you assess the consequences of those decisions. These are broad descriptions of activities that distinguish effective decision making, and can be used as a guide to systematic processes.

The important activities, however, may be more specific. Several researchers have examined group decisions, good and bad, to see what makes the difference. They maintain that the quality of choices depends on how "vigilant" members are in their critical thinking and analysis in a series of smaller decisions at four stages: examining the problem, clarifying objectives, developing available choices, and examining potential consequences (see, for example, Gouran & Hirokawa, 1983; Hirokawa & Scheerhorn, 1986).

These group designs are similar to the now-classic **reflective thinking sequence** identified by John Dewey (1910) as the way individuals think through problems. As ancient as his approach is, it is still useful as a guide to problem solving, to setting agendas for meetings, and to establishing work plans for reaching team goals. According to Dewey's sequence, a group:

1. Feels something is wrong and recognizes a problem.
2. Defines the problem and its causes and effects.
3. Lists possible solutions.
4. Compares solutions' pros and cons.
5. Selects the best solution.
6. Implements the solution.
7. Reviews the effectiveness of the solution.

A team might well use this list to chart its work over an extended period of time. Frequently, a group will organize an agenda for a single meeting in terms of these, or some of these, steps. If one meeting is sufficient to resolve the problem, then such an agenda can work well as a guide to thinking and discussion.

Because problem solving is so detailed, however, and because thinking is often not so orderly as this outline, the agenda may be modified considerably as the meeting moves along. That's okay, too, if it serves to remind people to think things through.

Although all of these systems treat decision making as a series of stages, the reality is that people overlap, loop back, and jump forward in the real processes of task analysis and achievement. A knowledge of these systematic approaches, however, can be useful in three ways: (1) to provide strategies for team work plans; (2) to guide agenda designs; and (3) to remind members of essential elements so they don't miss something important in thinking through their tasks.

There are drawbacks to following a specific design for problem solving. Members may become so task oriented that they overlook the transactional processes that build emotional and social connections among people and allow the task processes to progress. There's also the risk of assuming that the systematic plan automatically guarantees clear thinking. It's not necessarily so. Sometimes groups proceed with no detectable system and make good decisions, while other groups meticulously follow a systematic plan and produce mediocre results (Janis & Mann, 1977). In short, these approaches to decision making remind people of the process and help keep them on track—but they don't guarantee thinking.

Analyzing Problems

Dewey (1910) tells us that people "feel difficulties" as the first step in problem exploration. They sense that something is wrong, but what? It's like the feeling students get when they lament registration or parking problems; sometimes there are as many explanations of just what the problem is as there are students lamenting.

The challenge is to move from intuitions about difficulties to isolating the nature and scope of specific problems. This step requires the team to apply all the skills developed in Chapter 5 on question asking and information gathering, Chapter 6 on analytical and critical thinking, and Chapter 7 on innovative and creative thinking. The main issues here are to avoid compounding problems through incrementalism, to identify what the real problems are, and to determine their causes and effects.

Incrementalism

Identifying problems can be extremely complex. Frequently they have been compounded by previous mistakes in problem solving. In a decision-making process called **incrementalism** (Braybrooke & Lindblom, 1963), decisions are made by bits and pieces, responding to pressures as they are applied. This is especially true, Barry (1991) notes, of policy-making teams which "are less likely to follow a clear sequence of team phases than project or problem-solving SMTs [self-managing teams]. They usually have multiple issues, events, and areas to consider simultaneously, and they tend to build up relevant policies and strategies in an incremental fashion" (p. 42).

The more complex and far-reaching the changes, and the more dispersed and extensive the possible information sources, the more likely it is that decisions will be made incrementally and with inadequate understanding or ability to predict the consequences. Such decisions create new problems and these spur new increments of change, which makes identifying new problems, causes, and effects even more difficult.

An example: A faculty/student team at your college has been charged with creating a new general education program. Its time limit is six months. The members have just begun getting information. Suddenly, the president requests a full list of problems in four days.

Increment 1   The team frenziedly whips up an intuitive list of problems and presents them.

Increment 2   The problems are not well identified, but the team now feels they are cast in stone, so it tries to work with that list.

Increment 3   Important problems are missed or misdiagnosed. The team makes some bad decisions, which are implemented, and new problems arise.

Ideally, teams should not have to make their decisions incrementally. All teams need to develop fully the processes of identifying the problems they're attempting to solve and analyzing their causes and effects.

Problem Identification

Identifying problems is not as easy as it sounds. It begins with "feeling the difficulty," then moves to scanning the general area of concern for trouble spots. Then it starts isolating problems by tracking them through the processes in which they appear, identifying how things are functioning, and comparing them against the ways things should work.

Etzioni (1968) used a military analogy to describe how people go through this process. Decision makers first try to get an overall picture of the situation, scanning the field for signs of danger. If there is a threat, they make decisions and take action immediately; if there is no obvious threat, they follow up with a more detailed examination.

Let's put this in the context of a college task force, of which you are a member, charged with improving registration procedures. First, your team gets as broad a picture as possible of how registration works. Then you identify the more glaring issues and get to work on finer analyses of those issues. You put aside issues that are not important and focus on those you see as most critical to the problems.

Your analysis might begin by seeking answers to some of these questions:

1. What difficulties are people feeling? What harms are being done?
2. What is the scope or extent of the problem? How serious is it?
3. What preestablished conditions or criteria relate to the difficulties? (Are there organizational policies, procedures, objectives, criteria? Laws or rules?)
4. In what ways do the difficulties/harms relate to these?

FIGURE 8.1

Flowchart of a college student's registration process

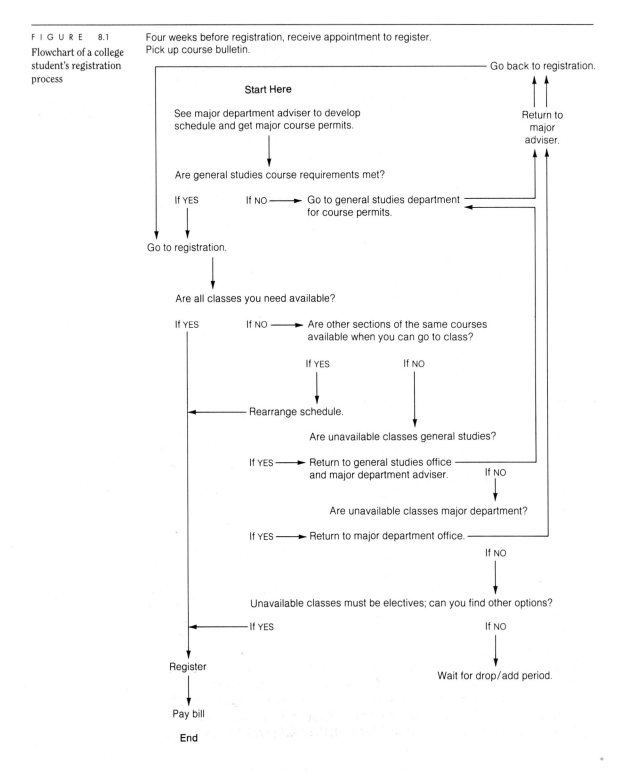

Four weeks before registration, receive appointment to register. Pick up course bulletin.

Go back to registration.

Start Here

See major department adviser to develop schedule and get major course permits.

Return to major adviser.

Are general studies course requirements met?

If YES   If NO ──▶ Go to general studies department for course permits.

Go to registration.

Are all classes you need available?

If YES   If NO ──▶ Are other sections of the same courses available when you can go to class?

If YES   If NO

Rearrange schedule.

Are unavailable classes general studies?

If YES ──▶ Return to general studies office and major department adviser.   If NO

Are unavailable classes major department?

If YES ──▶ Return to major department office.   If NO

Unavailable classes must be electives; can you find other options?

If YES   If NO

Register   Wait for drop/add period.

Pay bill

End

As you start to analyze the difficulties, you detect some specific patterns. One difficulty may be a lack of sufficient classes at the times students want them. The harms are fairly obvious: students can't get classes, or must take classes at inconvenient times; possibly they have trouble completing requirements or fulfilling prerequisites for future courses as a result. To analyze the problem, however, you also need to understand two other issues: the scope (how many students are affected?) and the conditions (college limitations, registration policies and procedures, departmental issues).

To analyze the problem, the team needs to trace through these issues and visualize them. We suggest a **flowchart**. Creating a flowchart of the registration process helps clarify the team's thinking; the completed chart helps identify the problems. A flowchart can be used at any stage of information sharing or problem solving, but it is particularly useful for explaining processes. It can be simple or complex, hand-created or computer-generated.

The flowchart in Figure 8.1 illustrates the registration process as it is experienced by students at the college in our example. A comparison of this flowchart with the procedures intended by the college would show exactly where and how the problems occur. Problems are usually found where there are deviations from expectations.

Causes and Effects

As you track the problems, you begin to see some of the reasons for them. Analysis of causes and effects can make or break problem analysis. If you make decisions that correct the wrong cause, you're not going to solve the problem—and you may create new ones. It can be difficult to determine whether one factor causes a problem or simply happens to be associated with the effect or with some other cause. Chapter 6 develops guidelines for logical cause-and-effect reasoning, and those principles must be applied to problem analysis.

A way of tracking and visualizing cause-and-effect relationships is the **fishbone diagram** suggested by Ishikawa (1982), which shows multiple causes and effects. As with the flowchart, the process of constructing it is almost as helpful to the team as the finished product, because it helps members think and see relationships among ideas. It's a good idea to do this together on a flip chart or large board, with all members contributing input.

To construct a fishbone, you draw a long line—vertical or horizontal—that represents the problem on which you're working. Then draw diagonals into the line, labeled with the issues that the team identifies as related to the problem. Ishikawa, working in an industrial setting, proposed that all problem analyses have at least four main "bones" to the "fish": people, machines, materials, and methods. Your college registration fishbone might have students, departments, resources, and procedures. From the diagonals you draw shorter lines, parallel to the "problem" line, that you label with subordinate issues or categories that affect the larger problems. The fishbone diagram in Figure 8.2 maps causes and effects your task force might find to be associated with the college registration problem.

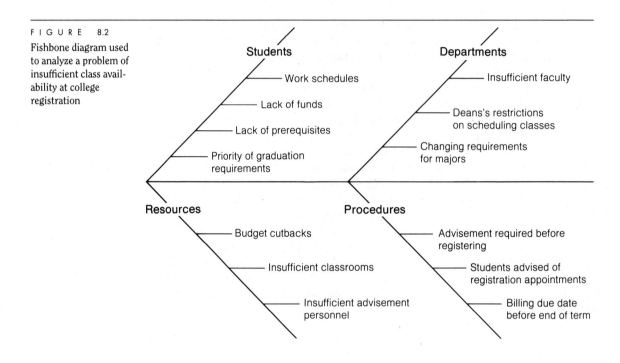

FIGURE 8.2
Fishbone diagram used to analyze a problem of insufficient class availability at college registration

Now you have a diagram for seeing and analyzing the issues that pertain to the problem. It doesn't solve it, and it doesn't even prove the causes, but it makes it all visible so you can work with it.

Generating and Analyzing Solutions

After carefully documenting a problem's causes, describing its effects, and noting the seriousness of their impact on people and operations, it's time to begin considering what actions to take. The main tasks at this stage are identifying options and setting criteria for analyzing them.

Generating Possible Solutions

Identifying a range of possible solutions takes time, energy, and dedication. The team needs real teamwork and the full creative thinking of all members, because the best decisions result when all possibilities have been considered.

At this stage, you want to get every imaginable solution out in the open. It's a time to use one or more of the idea-generating approaches discussed in the previous chapter, such as brainstorming, nominal group technique, synectics, or fantasy chaining. As always with these techniques, hold off judgment and criticism until you get the ideas on the table, and don't be afraid to get silly. For now, you want quantity of options; later you'll evaluate them for quality.

Establishing Criteria

Deriving quality decisions from a multitude of decision options depends on knowing what you require of the solution. You can't assume you'll "know it when you see it." You might not. Setting up clear criteria is extremely important to your success.

Brainstorm a list of what conditions would be like if you achieved the perfect solution or plan. If your task is to create a project for a class, for example, your criteria will include some that meet the objectives of the assignment, others that meet members' objectives for learning and grades, and still others that meet conditions that you, as a team, have decided to include in your project.

For example, suppose you're on a creative team for a video production class. Your list of "ideal" criteria might specify that the project:

1. Be original and unique.
2. Involve each team member in a specific role.
3. Deal with a controversial or timely topic.
4. Demonstrate skill in each area listed on the syllabus.
5. Have a well-written script.
6. Use graphics effectively.
7. Be cut and edited smoothly.
8. Achieve demonstration quality for each member's portfolio.
9. Serve as a foundation for next semester's project.
10. Be fun to do.
11. Earn an "A" for each team member.

Some of these criteria are dictated by the assignment; others are the product of the team's thinking about what will make a good project. The team may well add other criteria, and delete some of these, as it compares this list to specific project possibilities.

After you've drafted your criteria, try to *visualize* what the achieved solution will be like according to those criteria. We've talked before about the power of visualization in helping teams achieve their goals. All members need to understand the team vision, the projected consequence of your work; make sure everyone on the team has a mental picture of what that final result will be like, how it will feel, what it will provide. This process is important for two reasons. First, as you visualize and discuss the ideal solution together, you clarify any misunderstandings or assumptions that could cause problems later. Second, the vision you hold in common motivates members to achieve it.

▮ G E T T I N G   T H E   P I C T U R E   R I G H T   L E A D S   T O   B E T T E R   D E C I S I O N S ▮

The fact that we think in pictures or images rather than words is the basis of a new theory of decision making, known as image theory.

"The central notion is that people have an idea or image about how things ought to be," said Lee Roy Beach, a professor of management and policy at the University of Arizona, who devised the theory with Terence Mitchell, professor of psychology at the University of Washington. "This image is often heavily covered by people's morals or beliefs about what's proper—their value systems. People also have an image about where they see themselves going, not unlike the notion of strategic goal-setting in management. They also have an

image of how they're going to get there. But these images are rather vague."

According to the theory, three kinds of images are used to make decisions:

Principle images . . . our morals, beliefs, ethics or guiding values. . . .

Goal images . . . an idealized method of making principle images a reality.

Strategic images . . . plans or tactics to carry out goals. . . .

Traditional decision theory says that, in making decisions, people essentially make a cost-benefit analysis of options and then select

the best one. Image theory says that before people ever get to a cost-benefit analysis, they compare their options with these principles, goals and strategic plans. If the options don't fit those images, either the images have to be changed or the options are rejected. . . .

"The trend in decision research is to try to make people more and more analytic, rational and cold," Beach said. "But that isn't the way people think. People are much more pictorial or quasi-pictorial than we think. There's a mixture of words, pictures, and emotions in their heads which image theory takes into account."

An excerpt from Michelle Laque Johnson, "Executive Update," *Investor's Daily*, November 7, 1990, p. 8. Used with permission.

Finally—this is very important—*record the criteria*. Write out the criteria clearly and unambiguously, and make copies available to everyone on the team. As you go through the decision process, keep the criteria in front of you—possibly in big print on a flip chart—and check all possible "winning" ideas against them.

Making Decisions

At this point, your team has a list of possible solutions and a list of criteria they should meet. Decision making is intense, concentrated work. You can make it easier and more accurate by using visual charting methods to decide how each proposal weighs on each of your criteria. When you have completed this process, you're ready to choose and use one of several methods for making the final decision.

A little pragmatic planning will help the process along. Have a large-print chart of the solution options you've identified, and another of your criteria, right in front of the team as you work. You'll also find it helpful to chart your analysis—on flip charts, blackboard, or taped-up butcher's paper—as you go along.

PROS	CONS
Would meet increasing needs for care for the elderly	Would take priority over needs for infant and child care
Can get partial funding through grants	Construction would disrupt hospital procedures and patient care
Land is available on west end of present facility	Grants would require matching funds
Would improve community relations	Wealthy sponsor is pushing for a new burn unit instead
Wealthy patrons have promised gifts of equipment	Would require large additions of geriatric specialists on staff
Local media are critical of Care Memorial's attention to elderly—new wing would appease them	National media attention is on inadequate care for children in this country

FIGURE 8.3

T-chart of pros and cons relating to a proposal for a new geriatric wing at Care Memorial Hospital

Analysis Techniques

We suggest two approaches to charting your solution analysis: the T-chart for comparing the pros and cons of a given plan, and a decision matrix for making comparisons among several plans.

A **T-chart** is a simple and effective way of making sure that everyone stays focused on the comparison and that nothing is missed. It's called that because a large sheet or board is divided into a "T," with the two sides labeled "Pros" and "Cons." As members make their observations, you simply write each point in favor of or against a given proposal on the appropriate side. The resulting chart (see Figure 8.3) makes it easy to see, compare, and weigh the alternatives.

A **decision matrix** is a grid, also made large and roomy, that allows you to compare the merits of different plans. It lays out the comparisons visually and jogs members' memories when they are trying to process enormous amounts of information.

Across the top of the grid, you label each column with one of your criteria for the ideal solution. Down the left side, you label each row with a solution option. Working together, the team fills in the cells with notes as to how each plan meets each criterion. When you've completed the grid, you have a concise, easily comprehended set of comparisons among the proposals at hand. The information planning grid in Chapter 5 (Figure 5.5, p. 123) provides an example of this type of display.

Critical Issues

Having established and clearly visualized your criteria for the ideal solution, your team needs to consider four critical issues: the applicability, practicality, advantageousness, and desirability of any proposed decision or solution.

Applicability   Does a given idea or proposal meet your criteria for solving the problem or meeting some need? The extent to which it does so is its **applicability.** Questions to consider are:

1. Will the proposed step solve the entire problem?
2. If it solves only part, how significant is it?
3. What would have to be sacrificed to use this idea?
4. How does the idea compare to others on goal achievement?

Suppose you're on a church committee to raise $10,000 in matching funds for the purpose of sending the gospel choir to a music festival in Europe. On your brainstorming list is the ubiquitous "bake sale." Either somebody will have to bake a lot of cookies or you'd better have some more lucrative possibilities on that brainstorm list. Some proposals are clearly inadequate and eliminated, or combined with other possibilities, at this point. For the ones that remain, practicality becomes the issue.

Practicality   Every possible solution can raise sticky issues of **practicality**—that is, the feasibility of implementing it. Depending on the kind of team you're working with, who sponsors it, and what its purpose is, such issues might include:

1. How much time will be required?
2. How much money will be necessary?
3. What kinds of support from others (teams, agencies, parent organizations, individuals) will be necessary?
4. To what extent will each of these resources be available?
5. What kinds of barriers will have to be overcome?
6. Will it be possible to sell the idea to the organization or sponsoring group?

Practical drawbacks can kill an idea promptly. If money, time, or support are significantly short, or if there's going to be insurmountable opposition from a parent organization, then the idea won't do. Sometimes, however, you see ways to adapt a proposal to solve practical issues. Then weigh the adapted proposal with questions like these:

1. Does overcoming the impracticality weaken the effectiveness of the plan or solution?
2. Once adaptations are made to counter the impractical aspects of the plan, will it still be superior to other plans?

If a proposal is applicable and practical—if you think you can make it fly—then the next considerations are advantages, disadvantages, and risks that might be incurred by adopting it.

Advantages, Disadvantages, and Risks   Aside from simply meeting the criteria, implementing a proposed solution may bring with it extra advantages, disadvantages, or risks.

Consider what is likely to occur if the project is implemented. It may solve the immediate problem, but are there potential side effects, either beneficial (**advantages**) or harmful (**disadvantages**)? Some questions to think about are:

1. What effects would the implemented proposal have on individuals or groups other than those it is intended to affect?
2. What tangential effects would the proposal have on resources such as time, money, and supporting services?
3. Would the advantages flow automatically from implementing the idea, or require some other action?
4. Would the disadvantages be unavoidable, or would some minor modification eliminate them?
5. Are the advantages or disadvantages exclusive to this idea, or would the same ones result from other actions?
6. How do the advantages and disadvantages weigh against each other?
7. How do the advantages and disadvantages weigh against those of other proposed solutions?

These questions clarify the advantages and disadvantages. They also may unearth some previously unconsidered risks in the proposal. A **risk** is the chance a team takes in going ahead with an idea that might fail or produce serious, extensive, costly, and/or damaging results.

Any idea that is innovative and potentially successful involves some risk. By definition, a new idea isn't proven by long experience, so it carries the possibility of failure. Without risk taking, there would be nothing new, no progress, no exciting possibilities. But the reality is that people have to weigh their risks and hedge their bets. A team needs to take a hard look at the risks before making its choices.

One format for estimating risks is Maier's (1963) Risk Technique. It involves working with a facilitator who takes the team through the following sequence:

1. Review the proposal with the team.
2. Explain that the facilitator is there not to evaluate, just to keep the process moving.
3. Explain the procedures.
4. Brainstorm all possible risks. Follow the rules for brainstorming: don't allow evaluation; sweat out the silences. Post every concern on a flip chart or board.
5. Allow people to think about the risks between this meeting and the next. Send a copy of the brainstormed risk list to everyone.
6. Meet again; reconsider and add risks that have occurred to people.
7. Discuss each risk. Is it serious? How can it be handled?
8. Cross off risks that the team agrees are not serious.
9. Set up an agenda to discuss the remaining risks after members have had time to do research and think about them. (pp. 171–177)

As in brainstorming, the group owns each concern; it does not belong to any one member. This eases apprehension about looking foolish or overanxious.

CASE ANALYSIS 8.1

The task force established criteria for evaluating possible options generated in its decision-making process. Here is a condensation of the standards used:

1. Consistency with the priority order of the waste management hierarchy: first, reduce use; second, reuse; third, recycle; fourth, incinerate/dispose.

2. Magnitude of environmental impacts: consider both the size and the importance a given action might have.

3. Public health and safety: no option should risk the health and safety of employees, customers, or the communities.

4. Practicality: options must be feasibly applied in stores throughout the system with consideration for franchise holders and customers.

5. Economic costs and benefits: the expenses and returns involved for an option.

The task force expanded these criteria to include a set of "Guiding Principles" to evaluate possible proposals.

1. Consistency with the "Preferred Packaging Guidelines" previously adopted by the Coalition of Northeastern Governors' Source Reduction Council.

2. Accounting for "lifecycle" impacts to consider other positive and negative effects in the production, storage, shipping, and disposal of products.

3. Accounting for Tradeoffs Among Solid Waste Reduction Options considered that there are sometimes item-by-item exceptions to the waste management hierarchy.

4. The Goal of Maximum Reduction in Materials Use and Waste means that all items and operations must be examined to create a comprehensive plan providing the greatest reduction possible within the criteria.

5. Consistency with Existing Regulations means they must consider all applicable codes and laws—local, state, federal, etc.

Issues for Your Consideration

1. In what ways would the criteria and principles help evaluate options in the decision stage?

2. Compare these criteria to the task force goals (see Chapter 3, page 67). In what ways do these criteria help the team evaluate the achievement of its goals by being sure proposed solutions addressed the problems?

3. On what ethical foundations are the criteria and principles based? What values do they reflect? In what ways do the criteria help the team handle ethical issues and ethical dilemmas?

You might adapt this format to one or two meetings if your team is on a short deadline or if your risks are few. If your team must make major, far-reaching decisions with potentially serious risks, then this process may take several meetings to identify those risks and arrive at better decisions.

Desirability   No matter how perfect a proposed solution may appear to be in terms of the previous issues, it may rise or fall on desirability issues. **Desirability** judgments are based on the character of the proposal and the value systems of the members. That is, you examine the relative worth of probable outcomes and the values and ethical choices that impinge on the decision. Two questions may start the process of examination:

1. Does the proposal meet all other criteria well enough to make it worth doing?
2. Is the goal so valuable that any possibility of achieving it is worth the effort?

Here, values and goals really come into play, as the decision makers debate how desirable, how valuable, how worthwhile the goals are in terms of what it takes to implement a given plan.

We remember the shock, a few years back, when it came out that an automobile manufacturer had considered, and rejected, a proposal to recall cars because the number of people *killed* as a result of a safety defect was not enough to justify the expense of recalling the cars. The management team had weighed numbers of human lives against the cost of recall, and human life lost in the balance. How many lives, America wondered, would have made it worthwhile to recall those cars? And how could that management team have been so unethical and so stupid? In Chapter 13, we discuss groupthink—the analytical paralysis that allowed the decision makers to do this.

Meanwhile, as your team looks at its proposals, you might do better than that company by asking some of these questions:

1. How desirable are the probable effects of the proposal?
2. Will the implemented proposal serve the vision of the team?
3. Will the proposal serve the best interests of people who will be affected by it?
4. Will the proposal harm anyone spiritually, psychologically, physically, economically, and/or socially?
5. Is the proposal consistent with the personal value systems of the individual members of the team?
6. Is anyone uncomfortable with the ethics of the proposal?
7. Does the proposal violate any code of ethics to which the team is bound?
8. Does the proposal fulfill the spirit of any code of ethics to which the team is bound?

Even better than using this list, your team can brainstorm and refine a list of ethical criteria for itself. As you discuss ethical questions, you will find that some answers are easy. "No, that's against our values." "Yes, that's ethically defensible." Some questions, however, are not simple at all; they represent a dilemma between two choices.

FIGURE 8.4
Characteristics of ethi-
cal issues and ethical
dilemmas. From Bar-
bara Ley Toffler, *Tough
Choices: Managers
Talk Ethics*, 1986,
pp. 21–22. Copyright
© 1986 by John Wiley
& Sons, Inc. Reprinted
by permission of John
Wiley & Sons, Inc.

ISSUE	DILEMMA
1. Is easy to name	1. Is hard to name
2. Is acontextual: stands outside specific setting	2. Is embedded in a specific context
3. Agreement that the issue is ethical	3. Disagreement as to whether or not the case in point is ethical
4. Addresses the claims of a single stakeholder.*	4. Addresses the claims of multiple, often competing, stakeholders
5. Addresses the right and wrong of one value	5. Addresses multiple, often competing values
6. Assumes that individuals can do the "right thing" if they want to	6. Assumes that individuals want to do the "right thing" but (a) do not know what it is, or (b) do not have the capacity to do it.

*Individual or group who has a "stake" in what happens.

Barbara Toffler's work, discussed in Chapter 2, provides excellent guidance on this point. In her book *Tough Choices* (1986), she makes a clear distinction between ethical issues and ethical dilemmas. Figure 8.4 identifies the characteristics of each.

According to Toffler, an ethical issue is easy to identify as such, is not clouded by context, concerns only one person or group, addresses "right" or "wrong" on only one value, and assumes that individuals can do the "right thing." An ethical dilemma arises when any of these descriptors is complicated by numbers of competing people or values; when it is clouded by interpretations of whether it is an ethical question or not; or when it assumes that people can't identify or are unable to do the right thing, despite their willingness.

Let's take an example. Someone you know offers to sell you a stolen VCR. The issue is easy to recognize; the context is simple; it affects only you and the would-be seller; it's either right or wrong; you can choose to do the right thing. This is clearly a yes/no ethical issue.

Now suppose that your team believes the success of its project presentation depends on having a VCR, and a teammate offers a "hot" VCR purchased for the occasion. Now the responsibility for actually buying stolen merchandise is one person removed, and the issue is not so easy to name. The context—the team, the project, the goals—is much more complicated and cloudy. More people are affected in more ways, and some members who want to do the right thing may be prevented from making that choice. The battle lines are drawn when one member says, "So what? C'mon, this has nothing to do with ethics. It's just a practical matter," and another teammate says, "How can you say that? It's not right to buy and use stolen property!" Now you know you have an ethical dilemma.

What do you do with an ethical dilemma? First, the team must recognize it as a dilemma. Having recognized it, you talk it out. Sometimes this means getting a more objective outsider to facilitate; sometimes the team can do it alone with shared leadership. Jaksa and Pritchard (1988) point out that "seeking exact points of difference can help solve disagreements by eliminating false distinctions and evasions" (p. 9).

Take time to reflect on the issues, to examine what moral perspectives each person brings to the dilemma. Consider in what ways alternative responses to the dilemma can be justified, and examine each set of reasons in the context of individual and social codes of ethics. Above all, don't brush the dilemma off with "'Everyone's entitled to an opinion,' . . . or 'Value judgments are subjective.' Such statements tend to bring discussion quickly to an end. Although these statements seem to express an attitude of tolerance, they also suggest that we do not have much to learn from one another" (Jaksa & Pritchard, 1988, p. 9).

In working through ethical dilemmas, your team can learn to understand one another's points of view and to resolve the hard issues together. You're reaching for ethical choices that everyone can live with. That may mean taking more time and a higher road than some would prefer. But strive to achieve consensus on the issue as a team, and work out a decision with which each team member can live.

Decision Modes

The analysis of alternatives could go on indefinitely, but at some point the group needs to make decisions. Take time to be sure everyone is clear on the merits and characteristics of each proposal and to clarify questions. This lets you get second thoughts out in the open and check everyone's agreement. Then use an agreed-upon method of deciding.

All too often, groups fall into making "twofer" decisions: two people speak for a decision, and the silence of other members is interpreted as consent. It may look okay at the moment, but twofer decisions lead to disgruntlement and lack of commitment.

The team's method of deciding affects the fairness of the decision and members' satisfaction with it, so consider your choice of methods carefully. Possible methods include decision by consensus, majority vote, two-thirds vote, multiple rankings, and decision by authority.

Consensus   Consensus decisions are ideal; theoretically, they represent the full agreement of every member. Actually, consensus represents some degree of agreement by all members, and it may be achieved through intensive discussion and negotiation. Striving for consensus is worth the effort, even if the final decision has to be made by another method.

As we've noted before, a team that achieves a high degree of consensus develops stronger commitment to its decisions and is more likely to follow through than a

JAPAN AND AMERICA: CULTURE COUNTS

To understand the Japanese way of doing things, you must understand the meaning of *ningen kankej*, or social relationships. . . .

The need to maintain group harmony is a Japanese preoccupation. The business world achieves it through absolute consensus; before any idea or plan goes forth, it must have everyone's approval. In an American corporation, the opposite is generally true—decision making is centralized and responsibility dispersed.

When someone in a Japanese company initiates a proposal—*ringi*—it is passed up and down the corporate ladder. At each level

it must receive a stamp of approval, a *han*. A proposal may have dozens of hans before the plan is activated. That procedure is incredibly frustrating to Western business executives, who perceive the Japanese as hopelessly slow-moving. In fact, a lot is going on behind the scenes, and much of it is intangible.

The process allows Japanese executives, for example, to spend time developing strong relationships with people throughout the company. They place great value on completing human transactions, and are not bound to the fixed meeting schedules that plague their Western counterparts.

The constant nurturing of positive human relationships means that once the corporation as a whole comes to a final decision, the plan has everyone's total support. After a slow-moving beginning, action becomes swift and precise—further questions are unnecessary.

With information moving freely and openly, it is no wonder that some of the best proposals emerge from the middle and lower echelons of a company. . . . Management is accustomed to listening to employees and striving to achieve consensus.

Condensed from Barry D. Cooney, "Japan and America: Culture Counts," *Training and Development Journal*, August 1989, pp. 58–61. Published by the American Society for Training and Development. Used with permission.

team that does not. Individualistic North Americans are trying hard to learn the consensus techniques of the Japanese, because they clearly work so well. Japanese groups typically hammer out decisions in round-the-clock, patient, persuasive, exhaustive discussion until everyone agrees. This is a harrowing process, but once consensus is achieved, implementation proceeds swiftly with the full support of all concerned.

Voting   Most North Americans are accustomed to a **majority vote**—over 50 percent—as the quick and easy method of deciding between alternatives. If discussion has been thorough, and everyone has had his or her say, most people are willing to accept a majority decision. That's a big "if." Much too frequently, majority vote is a cop-out—a lazy way of pushing to a conclusion without vigilant and vigorous problem analysis. It's quicker, but it leaves more people dissatisfied and gets less cooperation than a consensus decision.

Majority vote may be a requirement if your group is part of a larger organization bound by a constitution, bylaws, and parliamentary procedures. You may be required to have a quorum of the membership in attendance—a minimum number specified in your bylaws—and to hold a formal vote on any decision. If so, the group still needs to work hard at developing mutual understanding and agreement on the decision.

In some instances, the bylaws of a group require a **two-thirds vote**: at least twice the number votes for a proposal as against it. This voting requirement applies to major issues, such as changing the bylaws, and to any proposal that interferes in some way with the rights of any member to discuss an issue fully, such as a motion to limit debate or change the agenda.

Multiple Rankings   **Multiple ranking** works well when there are several choices; it is often used with a long list of possibilities, in conjunction with the Delphi or nominal group technique. This method is time-consuming and bulky, because it can require several ballots.

Multiple ranking may involve recommendations, ideas, criteria, or people. Suppose you're on a nomination committee with a list of ten possible candidates and your group wants to recommend a slate of three for the larger organization's vote. You can winnow those ten down to three in a fair way using multiple rankings, as follows:

1. The members discuss the merits of each possibility.
2. Each member ranks his or her first ten choices from 1 to 10.
3. Tally the ballots.
4. Each possibility receives a sum of his or her rankings: for example, if candidate A received rankings 1, 5, 3, 3, 2, 1, 5, 5, 4, 1, then the total for that candidate is 30.
5. The three lowest totals represent the top three candidates. All other candidates are now eliminated from the list of possibilities.

Multiple ranking is a slow process, but it provides something close to consensus while efficiently working through a large number of possibilities to find the "best."

Decision by Authority   A **decision by authority** means that the team's decisions are only recommendations, not actions. Someone with higher status than the team members—perhaps a manager, an executive committee, or the president of an organization—has the final word. In some cases, the hierarchy is very clear: the team's function is to conduct the inquiry, do the critical and creative thinking, make recommendations, and wait for a decision.

One management consultant (Yanes, 1990) argues that an authority decision is better than consensus. In his view, consensus is a mediocrity trap that can cause members to opt for the middle of the road; instead, teams should "fight it out," with final decisions being left up to the manager or leader. Certainly an open process of analysis, including sometimes fighting it out, is essential to solving problems. We would argue, however, that leaving decisions up to the "boss" without striving for consensus is also a mediocrity trap. It's easy to shrug your shoulders with, "Oh, well. It's the boss's problem now."

This approach fails to build a real team. Often the team's job continues with implementing the decision after it is made and assessing the results. This phase is likely to be more successful if the team has worked out its disagreements together.

Creating an Implementation Plan

In our experience, it is at the implementation stage that teams often go astray. They may have really superb ideas, but when it comes to putting them into action, something slips. They miss some of the details that would have made it work. Successful implementation of an idea, or a change, requires close attention to designing methods for implementing the proposal and assessing the results.

Design

Implementing a proposal starts back with the original goals and vision for the team's work. What will the final product look like? Keep this idea in front of you at every stage of planning implementation, so the end does not get lost in the means for getting there. We suggest brainstorming, categorizing, timing, and visualizing the steps necessary to reach your goal.

1. *Brainstorm a checklist.* Include everything that must be done to implement this proposal. Ask yourselves, "Who does what, when, where, how, and from what resources?"

2. *Divide the list into categories,* such as:

∎ Resources needed—money; information; technological support; permissions and cooperation required from authorities, agencies, organizations.
∎ Actions that must be taken to get the proposal underway—contacts that must be made; communication needs; materials to be obtained; applications to be made for permissions, licenses; arrangements to be made for space, guests, equipment, etc.
∎ Steps to achieve each action.
∎ People responsible for each action.
∎ Time required for each step.

3. *Decide precisely who is responsible* for completing each step. Be specific. Make sure each person commits to his or her responsibilities. Put the list in print, and make sure everyone has a copy. When you have implementation meetings, go over the list to see if things are being done, and if revisions have to be made. Human beings have a touching faith in their memories; unfortunately, it is unjustified. No matter how many previous times a flight crew has flown a Boeing 747, they are expected to use the checklist each time. History records a few fateful times when they did not.

4. *Create a flowchart with time factors.* Assuming that you have carefully considered the practicality issues of your plan, you may already have a clear idea of just how long you have to accomplish the final goal. Now you need to establish exactly when you must have each step accomplished. That's when reality sets in.

Map out on a flowchart each step of the process, marking the time allotted and the person responsible for doing each. In some cases, steps will be concurrent or overlapping; in other cases, one step must be completed before another can begin. In mapping them out, you develop a strategy, or work plan, for the entire process.

CASE ANALYSIS 8.2

After deciding on options to recommend, the task force created an action strategy to serve as a "master plan" that would incorporate ongoing changes. It identifies the status of the idea, when it should be accomplished, and the departments responsible for assessing the implementation.

IMMEDIATE CHANGE/ EXISTING INITIATIVE	UPCOMING PILOT TESTS	LONG TERM RESEARCH & DEVELOPMENT	EXPECTED COMPLETION DATE	AREA RESPONSIBLE

Issues for Your Consideration

1. Does the form seem to be complete? Can you think of other items to be included?

2. In what ways could this form be useful in follow-up assessment of the plan? Would any changes make it more useful for assessment?

On your flowchart, build in contingency planning. "What happens if . . . ?" Indicate alternative paths on your plan, so that if one step is delayed or changed you know where to go. The flowchart should be complete, idiot-proof, and worked through step by step. The process of building it helps the team anticipate possible forks in the road, and the final product provides a map of your terrain. Figure 8.1 (see p. 170) shows a flowchart developed for analyzing the sources of a problem; the same approach can be used to display a working plan, which is then used to monitor the implementation process.

Assessment

Whether your task was small or enormous, you want to know how well you accomplished it. In Chapter 3 we talked about ways of assessing your team's processes; here we're interested in getting feedback on how well your team's decision works after it's implemented.

First, look at your goals and draft questions about their achievement. If your goal was to involve more freshmen in student activities, you will need to find out how many actually participate in specific events. But intermediate questions might be: "How many freshmen know where the Student Activities Office is?" "How many activities do freshmen know about?" The clearer and more specific your questions, the more directly you can answer them.

Next, devise ways of finding answers to these questions. Possible approaches include:

▌ Questionnaires or surveys aimed at the people affected by your project.
▌ Benchmark numbers of participants.
▌ Pre- and post-project tests or surveys.
▌ Observations and assessments by objective sources.

Each of these methods can give you useful information about the effectiveness of your decision or action. But assessment cannot be haphazard; it needs to be a regular part of the process. These guidelines will help you develop an assessment plan that works:

1. Everyone involved in the plan should also be involved in assessing it. Where possible, assessment data should be user-generated.

2. Assessment should be planned ahead of time. Methods should address the goals, instrumental objectives, and vision of the final task. When it is not pre-planned, people suspect the motives.

3. Assessment should be continuous. Feedback should occur on a regular basis, beginning early in the implementation period, so you can use the information to make changes quickly if things don't go as expected.

Summary

Systematic processes of analysis enable teams to arrive at good solutions. Dewey's reflective thinking sequence is a traditional approach, but teams vary the order according to need. Some systematic approach—scanning the difficulties, isolating primary issues, flow-charting processes—helps in identifying problems.

After analyzing causes and effects, with the help of fishbone diagrams, the team generates a range of possible solutions and sets criteria for the best solution. Making decisions by increments often leads to new problems, so a systematic examination of critical issues is in order. Critical issues include the proposed solution's applicability to the problem; its practicality; its possible advantages and disadvantages, as well as the risks it might entail; and the desirability of its im-

plementation. Assessing ethical issues and dilemmas is critical to this process.

Decisions may be made by consensus, majority vote, two-thirds vote, multiple rankings, or decision by authority, depending on the context, the system, and the purpose of the group. Consensus provides the best foundation for team commitment and follow-through on decisions.

Once a decision is made, the team may continue with implementation plans, flowcharted to show who is responsible for which steps when. The plan should include contingency adjustments and, finally, approaches to assessing and adjusting the implemented solution.

Exercises

1. Your team is a quality circle in a large corporation. Your attention has been called to the following set of facts:

   (1) ∎ The plant is in a rural industrial park.
   (2) ∎ The closest town is ten miles away.
   (3) ∎ Sometimes employees who have families seem distracted.
   (4) ∎ The town has one small day-care center.
   (5) ∎ Two churches have preschools that operate until five o'clock.
   (6) ∎ The company has no maternity/paternity leave benefits.
   (7) ∎ Many employees live twenty or more miles away.
   (8) ∎ Parents of small children are frequently late or absent.
   (9) ∎ Parents of older children miss many school holidays.
   (10) ∎ Some personnel have left the company when they started families.
   (11) ∎ Recent productivity declines are primarily among people ages twenty-five to forty-five, normally a productive age group.
   (12) ∎ Morale in the company is low.

   Using this information, identify the problem(s) these facts suggest and analyze and diagram their causes and effects.

2. Using the cause-and-effect diagram you created for the previous exercise, set goals your quality circle would like to achieve and set criteria for considering your solution to be satisfactory. Then generate possible solutions to the problems and create an implementation and assessment plan.

3. Observe a group or team as the members try to solve a problem. Using Form 8.1 as a guide, analyze the team's processes. What worked well? What didn't? Where did members seem to conform to what you've learned in this chapter? Where did they not? What could they do to improve their processes?

4. Recall a time that you've been in a group (school, work, family, community) that had a problem to analyze and a decision to make. Using what you've learned in this chapter, reflect on how your experience relates to effective processes of analyzing problems, generating and analyzing solutions, making decisions, and implementing and assessing decisions.

FORM 8.1 ▮ OBSERVATION OF A GROUP'S PROBLEM ANALYSIS AND DECISION MAKING

Observe a group as it solves a problem. On the form, mark each time someone in the group contributes to a function (listed on the left) during each period of the discussion (listed on the right)—early, midpoint, or late in the discussion. If no one contributes to a particular function, then check "never" when the discussion is over.

	EARLY	MID	LATE	NEVER
1. Suggests a system for problem analysis				
2. Defines a problem				
3. Identifies goals				
4. Analyzes causes and effects				
5. Identifies criteria for solutions				
6. Generates possible solutions				
7. Analyzes solutions				
8. Suggests decision mode				
9. Guides final decision process				
10. Designs implementation				
11. Designs assessment				

On the basis of your observations, consider:

Was the process systematic? What worked well? What functions needed more attention? What would a diagram or flowchart of the team's process look like?

Which critical issues—applicability, practicality, advantages/disadvantages/risks, desirability—did the team consider?

Did the team consider ethical issues or dilemmas? How did the members work through these?

How satisfied with the outcome did the team appear to be? How committed do you think the members were to their decision? Why?

Leadership through Transactional Processes

Team Communication and Climates: Connecting through Language

"If I say what I really think, everybody will get mad at me."
Maybe not—not if you know how to make the transactional processes work.

You're in a team meeting, loaded with reams of great information, thinking on eight cylinders, eager to get started on some probing analysis. Suddenly you realize that something has gone badly awry. Instead of working through the task cooperatively, the team has degenerated into hostility and resistance.

Chances are, something happened in the team's communication to throw a wrench in the transactional processes. If those aren't working well, the best intentions in the world won't make the task processes work.

Communication, according to Gouran and Hirokawa (1983), is the "means by which group members attempt to meet the requisites for successful group decision-making" (p. 170). The more complex the task, the in-formation, or the goals of a group, the more important communication processes are to its success (Hirokawa, 1990).

This chapter focuses on how members create connections and negotiate mutual meanings through communication. This process involves an awareness of language issues of power, choice, and dialogue, and contributes to the development of assertive leadership. These factors, in turn, enhance transactional processes and help create a supportive team climate in which to work.

Communication takes many forms. In this chapter, we focus primarily on verbal communication; in the next two, we look at nonverbal communication and then at listening and questioning. Because these activities are so closely interrelated, you need to bring all these ideas together to gain a fuller perspective on communication and leadership.

Our goals in this chapter are for you to:

1. Understand how language influences transactional processes.

2. Learn how to make language choices that are appropriate, clear, and vivid.

3. See your language choices as part of dialogical ethics, responsibility, and supportive climates.

4. Understand the role of assertiveness in transactional processes.

5. See what positive and negative communication climates are like.

6. Know how communication climates affect transactional processes.

Connecting Team Members

Communication connects individuals with one another. In a team, communication creates the transactional and task processes that provide the basis for success or failure in their efforts. The better members understand how communication functions in team settings, and the more effectively they put those principles into practice, the more likely it is that their team transactions will be satisfying and productive.

We will begin by looking at three aspects of how language works to connect individuals: its role in negotiating shared meanings; the power of language and its effects on people's perceptions; and the effects of dialogical choices on team transactions.

Negotiated Team Meanings

In Chapter 1, we defined communication as "the process of using verbal and non-verbal cues to negotiate a mutually acceptable meaning between two or more people within a particular context and environment." **Meaning** is whatever a person believes it is, depending on his or her experiences, motivations, values, and beliefs. Each person's reality is in the meanings she or he attaches to things. Those meanings are determined, in great part, by the words and symbols an individual knows to describe a concept. You may think creatively with images and associations, but even in your mind, you use words to frame what you mean by an idea. To share ideas among teammates, you use words to negotiate your individual images into concrete ideas that all can share. The thoughts you can communicate are limited by the language, or languages, you speak and by the perceptions they represent.

"Now, let's put our heads together and see if we can get a clear picture."

The ways in which individuals negotiate—reveal, trade, alter, and adapt—their individual perceptions create team meanings and team realities. The language with which they negotiate is symbolic, and most words carry as many meanings as there are people to interpret them. Words are abstract; they are not the same as solid objects. They are in the minds and hearts of the people who use them, and their meaning is shaped by the experiences of those human beings.

What, for example, does "freedom" mean to you? Independence? Slavery? Education? These words represent extremes of meaning among subcultures of English-speakers. Think of a team comprised of a person from a wealthy, privileged, North American family; a U.S.–raised child of a Cuban refugee family; the grandchild, raised in the inner city, of a slave couple; a battered wife who has just returned to school.

How would each of these people feel those words? How would each of them hear those words? And when they speak them, what would each of them mean by those words? They have some denotative meaning in common, of course. Denotative meanings are in dictionaries. But what about connotative meanings? Connotations are the emotional, psychological, cultural, experiential meanings of symbols to each individual. In the team we just hypothesized, words such as "freedom" and "slavery" are very different for each member.

To arrive at a mutual understanding of such individual connotations, the team goes through a process like that illustrated in Figure 9.1. As members offer their own interpretations, listen, and adapt to one another's understandings of words, they negotiate a team meaning with which they can work.

The more abstract the term, the more difficult communication among people becomes. And the more difficult, important, and far-reaching a team's job is, the more it may have to talk about abstract ideas. The team has to work at finding ways to bring the various meanings into closer alliance.

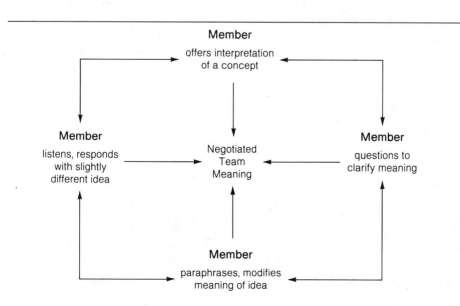

F I G U R E   9.1

Process of negotiating meaning among members

Language and Power

The way members negotiate meanings depends, in part, on how they interpret one another's power and status; and these are conveyed through language style. Power and influence pervade all of communication; they are critical variables in the way people interact in groups.

People use language to influence one another. Some people have higher status or more power than others, and that position is reflected in the language they use. Conversely, powerful language contributes to the attainment and maintenance of more power. From a team point of view, understanding what makes language powerful or powerless enables you to listen more perceptively and to help others increase their power, enhancing their potential contributions and increasing the team's overall impact. Your awareness of the power in your own use of language can also make you more effective in leadership.

Powerful and Powerless Language   Societies generally have both **powerful** and **powerless languages** that emerge from and reflect an individual's status, position, gender, education, and success.

On a medical team for example, doctors, high-status and powerful, say things like, "The patient's blood count is up; discharge him." Other team members speak more tentatively, as in: "Yes, Doctor. Did you see on the chart . . . I think his temperature was 102?" "Well, uh, I just wonder . . . I think there's no one at home to care for him." "Maybe . . . perhaps he should have a chest X-ray first?" These team members know perfectly well the patient isn't ready for discharge, but they have to be very careful to say it in a way that defers to the doctor's power.

What has been called the "female register," or the way many females talk, is closely similar to powerless language; the "masculine register," or the way many males talk, is synonymous with powerful language in most societies. In the medical team example, the doctor is using a "male register," and team members a "female register," whatever their genders. In a few societies, powerful/male language and powerless/female language are reversed in their characteristics. Males, who hold the power, use language that is accommodating, polite, and tentative, whereas females, outside the power structure, use language that is dominant, argumentative, and confrontational (De Klerk, 1991). Either way, those within and outside the power structure use their respective powerful and powerless languages.

Kramarae (1981) talks about "muted groups"—those who haven't had a chance to learn how to communicate at a high power level in their society, with the result that their communication style keeps them from being heard at those levels. Typically, muted groups are women, minorities, subcultural or lower-caste groups, and the poor.

The differences between powerful and powerless language have been investigated in women's as compared to men's communication (Pearson, Turner, & Todd-Mancillas, 1991) and in the communication of people of higher status compared to those of lower status. Powerless language is more tentative, more polite and proper, more deferential. The speaker uses tag questions (it's true, don't you think?), fillers (you know, and . . .), hesitations (well, that is . . .), hedges (I'd like to, if you would), qualifiers (I believe, I think), and intensifiers (it was just the most beautiful . . .). Powerless language uses fewer expletives and profanity, but it tends to be more "colorful," more concerned with aesthetics, and to have a richer vocabulary of expression.

Powerful language is more self-confident and commanding. The speaker is more colloquial, casual, less precise and correct, and may use more expletives and profanity. The speaker of powerful language tends to confront and work toward a goal, to be direct, declarative, and fluent. Tag questions are used differently: whereas powerless language leaves the question open for affirmation from the other person, powerful language demands an affirmative response ("So that's it. *Right?*"). The powerful language speaker is less accommodating, presents more opinions, suggestions, and orientations, talks more, interrupts more, and overlaps others more (Pearson et al., 1991, pp. 104–127).

When you consider that culture, gender, and status may affect how people speak and how credible they are perceived to be, you can see how important powerful or powerless language may be in group interaction.

Language Power Effects on Teams   Powerful and powerless language affects members' participation and credibility. Teams must be alert to the dangers of stereotyping: A woman may not be thought credible, for example, partly because she uses powerless language and partly because she's a woman. A man using powerful language may be considered credible, even if he isn't. A man *or* woman who uses powerless language, as a residue of his or her social status, may be stereotyped and disregarded. A foreign speaker may speak English very politely and correctly; she or he may feel too unsure of the language to do otherwise. That may be perceived as powerless talk and, therefore, be less influential than that of other members of the group.

Powerful language, however, can go amiss in a team. An adolescent may use expletives and profanity to establish his or her power (De Klerk, 1991) and offend less aggressive members of the group. A person accustomed to authority and power may seem dominant and confrontational simply because she or he has learned powerful language as part of a career or a profession. That individual may have no intention of flexing muscles; command may be a habit hard to break.

Language Choices

Your language choices affect other members' abilities to listen, to judge ideas, and to make decisions. This implies that you should phrase ideas in a way that facilitates transactions within the team. In making choices about language, you need to consider the degree to which it is both appropriate and clear.

Appropriateness   Using appropriate language means fitting it to three criteria: team members, yourself, and the team context. That requires some analysis and understanding of all three.

▮ W H E N   W O R D S   R E C R E A T E   R O L E S

One of the biggest challenges in implementing self-directed work teams is that it involves the transformation of roles of both managers and employees. "We eliminated the terms *supervisors* and *employees* and replaced them with *coaches* and *players*," says Diane Pewitt of Northern Telecom's Santa Clara plant, which produces Meridian telephone equipment.

Under team direction, managers go from bosses/dictators to coaches/facilitators. Facilitators help guide, direct, and support the team, but they don't control it. . . .

An excerpt from Jana Schilder, "Work Teams Boost Productivity," *Personnel Journal*, February 1991, p. 69. Used with permission.

Making language appropriate to your *team members* depends on interpersonal sensitivity to two things: how people react to ideas, behaviors, and styles of other team members; and how you use communication to keep transactional and task processes open and supportive.

Sensitivity requires both heart and mind: the mind contributes the analysis, and the heart contributes the response. What is appropriate to your listeners is dictated by their backgrounds, culture, values, attitudes, beliefs, needs, gender, and expectations. If you want to, you can find out about those influences on their responses. Seek to understand more about their experiences and backgrounds. Watch for, listen to, and seek clarification of their reactions to ways you express your ideas. If you don't feel sure of how someone sees things, if you're concerned about how someone interprets what you've said, ask.

At the same time, your language should be appropriate to *yourself*. The way you talk reflects a lot of things, including your self-image and self-esteem. Choosing words and fitting them to the team and the situation may involve difficult choices. To make them, you have to start with who you are.

We know one young woman who breaks all the powerless stereotypes of women's talk because her own self-image is strong and aggressive. So is her language. That's fine, as long as her listeners are not intimidated by her, or as long as they don't find it inappropriate to them or to the situation. But sometimes she has to adapt to her listeners.

Should you gauge the appropriateness of your language in terms of your listeners to the extent that it is inappropriate to yourself? No, but those are extreme alternatives. There almost always is a middle ground. Our strong friend might intimidate a team whose members are shy, soft-spoken, perhaps from a "muted group," and accustomed to allowing powerful-speaking people to run right over them. If she does, the team may become defensive. If she moderates her language, and adopts a more tentative, open, supportive style, she won't lose her strength; in fact, she'll be using it to empower the others in the team.

Once in a while, a student says to us, "But isn't adapting the same thing as hypocrisy?" We'll give you the distinctions that we believe are important here.

Hypocrisy would be lying or distorting what you believe, how you feel, or who you are; adapting is finding ways to communicate that allow others to receive your message openly. Hypocrisy keeps up interpersonal barriers and deceives others into believing those blockades are not there; adapting in response to what you know about another opens channels and breaks down barriers to open communication.

An example: You're a highly educated member of a team that includes some minimally educated people. One of the minimally educated people seems defensive about his or her lack of academic preparation, and makes snide remarks about people from "ivory towers." You're proud of your education. If you say, in order to achieve some identification with this person, "Ah, education means nothing. It's worth zilch. I wasted a lot of years," that's hypocritical. You don't mean it, and you're reinforcing a barrier as you pretend to knock it down. If you adapt to that person by avoiding academic jargon, and by looking for things you *do* have in common with him or her, then we'd call that an honest, and probably effective, way to break down a few barriers and open up communication.

As you consider language choices, you also need to be aware of the *context* in which your team is working. The purposes of the team, its goals, the system within which it operates, and the surrounding variables of the situation can affect what's appropriate. If, for example, you're in a religious group, profanity is probably inappropriate to the context, even if it wouldn't offend the other people or you in some other situation. If you're working on a campus task force with an easygoing bunch of folks, swearing might be perfectly all right (although it still might be inappropriate to you or to some of the members).

To take another example of appropriateness to context, compare two corporate teams. Team A, a management team, is under the gun to produce a budget within a brief time limit. Members need to keep their language task-oriented, highly focused, and very specific. Team B's purpose is to explore a wide range of alternatives for developing a supportive organizational culture. Its task requires creativity and imagination. This team needs language that is exploratory, feeling-oriented, and metaphorical.

Appropriateness of language isn't just being nice, or following rules. It's using language that enables people to interact freely, without unnecessary barriers to communication.

Clarity   Effective language is not only appropriate to the person, the group, and the context. It also must say what you want it to say. Clear communication breaks down barriers to understanding content. If you want your ideas to be clear, you need to eliminate ambiguities in your language, use the most concrete terms possible, and use vivid images and examples.

Can an expression be taken two or more ways? If so, it's ambiguous. *Eliminating ambiguities* means examining your language, your phrases and sentences, and your intent.

Here are some kinds of ambiguities that can crop up in your language:

Terms. If your team proposes to survey college "personnel," does that mean faculty? Custodial staff? Support staff? Student aides?

Phrases. "The committee will take it under consideration" may mean "We take your idea seriously and it's at the top of our agenda," or "Not in this lifetime will we consider this."

Syntax. The arrangement of a sentence can imply more than one meaning. "The team seeks to solve this campus problem with militancy." Is the team intending to be militant, or is militancy the problem?

Qualifiers. "I think it's a really good idea, probably, but I'm concerned that the effect might be confusing, unless, of course . . ."

Ambiguity may result when people are not sure of their thoughts. Sometimes, though, it's deliberate. Ambiguity can give you a chance to think through a response, to defuse a situation, or to pull back and let others think out an idea. Deliberate ambiguities, however, can make people very defensive. Even if they can't quite figure out where and why the ambiguity lies, they sense it and they may resent it. It's better to avoid ambiguity and say, "I'm just not ready for that," or "Let me think that through," or "Let's take a time-out and come back to that later," or even "What do the rest of you think?"

You already know that language is abstract and symbolic; you can't get away from that completely. But it helps if you keep your language as *concrete* as possible and if you find ways to make even the abstractions clearer. Here are some suggestions:

Define your abstractions. If you know members are unfamiliar with a term, you can offer specific, supported definitions.

Qualify your terms. If you're not sure whether people know a term, you don't have to insult them by waving a dictionary at them. Build definitions in with clarifying phrases or examples. "It seems to me this problem is entropic—it's just so random and disorganized—I'm having trouble . . ." You defined entropic in the context of your sentence; you didn't say, "Let me define this term for you."

Use comparisons and contrasts. This is what it is; this is what it is not. "Teamwork is mutual, cooperative effort toward a goal; teamwork is not competition among members."

Use analogies. Show the similarities between a more familiar concept and the one you want to clarify. "Leading a team can be like conducting an orchestra."

To keep your team's attention and help members understand you, use language strong enough and *vivid* enough to overcome distractions or indifference. Active, colorful, personal words, as well as humor, metaphors, analogies, and supporting examples, serve to clarify ideas and to hold people's attention. These, of course, need to meet the "appropriateness" criteria. If you use a vivid example, a funny line, an insightful analogy or metaphor, you may get attention and make your message clear. But if you use too many examples, if you extend them too long, or use a joke that's inappropriate or offensive, you'll obscure your message instead.

Dialogical Choices

Dialogue assumes mutual respect and caring between or among individuals; in a team, it also assumes a mutual concern for the processes and outcomes of the team. Communication in the team's transactional processes depends on language that advances, rather than impedes, dialogue.

In the dialogical perspective on team ethics, we suggested that transactional and task processes must be conducted in such a way as to support and encourage an authentic, inclusive, mutual sharing and negotiation of ideas and members' perspectives. In a dialogical climate, members help each other think and communicate. They understand one another's needs for help in clarifying thoughts and ideas, and they take responsibility for the dialogue needed to provide that assistance. Language choices enhance the quality of the team's interactions and respect and uplift its members.

We suggest the following guidelines as a partial list for measuring the dialogical ethics of your team's language:

- Does it advance the goals of the group?
- Does it break down barriers?
- Does it open up understanding?
- Does it encourage people to think?
- Does it confirm and support people?
- Does it encourage ethical analysis and choice?
- Does it respect everyone in the group?
- Does it avoid profanity—words derived from bodily functions, or that belittle religious beliefs?
- Does it avoid sexism—belittling one sex or the other, or implying stereotyped characteristics of males, females, or homosexuals?
- Does it avoid racism—diminishing or stereotyping any race or ethnic group?
- Does it avoid handicapism—belittling or stereotyping people who are disabled?
- Does it avoid classism—stereotyping or implying superiority of one class of people over another?
- Does it encourage others to express ethical or religious beliefs?
- Does it include people regardless of their political beliefs?
- Does it avoid stereotyping the individual who is using it? Does it help his or her listeners keep an open mind?

Fostering Effective Leadership

Your communication abilities and approaches enable you to exert your leadership and contribute effectively to your team. Your leadership is enhanced by the assertiveness and responsibility with which you express your thoughts and by your ability to enhance transactional processes in your team. Let's look at those factors next.

Assertive Communication

Assertiveness is communicating openly, with awareness of yourself and concern for others, what you need or want them to know. It is important to understand what assertiveness is, and what it is not.

Assertiveness is self-disclosing, speaking openly about your own ideas or feelings; it is *not* "spilling your guts," or unloading inappropriately on others. Assertiveness is stating your position honestly, *not* communicating aggressively. Assertiveness is taking care of your own rights, *not* disregarding the rights of others. Assertiveness is being sensitive to and concerned about other people, *not* becoming a martyr to placate or protect others. Assertiveness is being responsible for your own communication, *not* allowing someone else to control your feelings and your communication.

Assertiveness requires the sensitivity and the ability to know what you want, to cope with risk in communication, to state a position responsibly and openly, and to understand and care about how your communication might affect others. Figure 9.2 gives an overview of assertiveness in relation to other behaviors.

The assertive person (upper left quadrant) is self-disclosing, seeks to influence others, and has high concern for the rights of others. That's the ideal.

When people can't manage assertiveness, they adopt strategies to deal with moments when they feel threatened or angry. The resulting behaviors appear in the other three cells of the grid.

The person who is self-disclosing and seeks to influence others, but has *low* concern for their rights (lower left), tends to exhibit **aggressiveness.** Communication is openly "me first," based on low regard for the rights or feelings of others, and seeks to control others' responses. It may be a verbal (or nonverbal) "punch in the nose," or it may simply be vigorously pushing others to do what the aggressor wants, regardless of their own feelings.

	Self-disclosing Influencing others	Self-protective Influenced by others
High concern for rights of others	Assertive Open climate	Passive Closed climate
Low concern for rights of others	Aggressive Hostile climate	Passive-aggressive Anxious/hostile climate

F I G U R E 9.2
The communication climate/assertiveness grid

Genuine assertiveness is a better tool for communicating effectively, even in highly persuasive situations, than is aggressiveness. Assertiveness considers the impact on others; aggressiveness does not.

The self-protective person who is highly influenced by others and also highly concerned about them (upper right) tends to show **passivity**. This person closes communication with silence or false agreement, and doesn't express feelings or ideas. This behavior appeases others and subordinates the individual's rights in deference to those of others or in fear of possible consequences.

The person who is self-protective and readily influenced but *not* concerned for the rights of others (lower right), may behave with **passive-aggression**. This person finds some obscured or indirect way to block other people, halt progress, or hurt someone without being caught at it. Passive-aggressiveness conceals anger and hostility for the person who feels controlled by others and resents it. This person seeks to protect himself or herself and still "get" the others.

Individuals can move around on this grid; they don't always stay in one place. People are constantly developing, changing, responding—often as a result of the team's interactions.

What Affects Assertiveness   What makes team members passive or aggressive? A person may need to express an idea, facts, feelings—and be afraid to do it. There is some element of risk or threat in expressing oneself. Threat is anything, no matter how small, that people might interpret as infringing on their rights; as making a situation ambiguous and uncertain; or as requiring some kind of defense. That's a broad scope, open to individual interpretation. What is challenging, or even fun, to you may be threatening to a teammate.

Team members may also fail to be assertive because of their own needs. Some people need to have control and, threatened by loss of it, react aggressively. Others need love and belongingness so badly that they will passively agree to anything to get other members' approval.

Some people misunderstand assertiveness and use it as an excuse for bad behavior. A teammate—eyes blazing, chin out—may say, "I'm an assertive person. I just say what's on my mind. If anybody doesn't like it, tough." The subtext to that statement is, "Y'wanna make somethin' of it?" This individual has rationalized aggressive behavior as assertiveness.

How Nonassertiveness Affects Teams   If a member of your team stops participating, starts staring out the window, and mutters "whatever you guys want to do," you've lost that individual's potential for helping the team. It's possible the person is distracted by some outside issue, but it's also possible the passive response is to something that's happening within the team. Perhaps your teammate is angry, but is afraid to express it.

An angry member may quietly torpedo another's work or "forget" a responsibility—a classic case of passive-aggression. Suppose, for example, that Sam is to bring background theory on a topic the team is investigating, and Harold is to get applied examples of the theory. At the meeting, Sam brings excellent material.

▮ CHUTZPAH

Alan Dershowitz' reputation as chutzpah champion of the American legal system has been spread by his spirited defenses in famous cases. . . . We asked Dershowitz, author of the best-selling book *Chutzpah,* to share his expertise. . . .

What is chutzpah?

A polite word for it would be *nerve*. It's an acquired characteristic. . . . Its goal is to level the playing field—when you are confronting someone who is more powerful than you in a situation.

Where does the word come from?

Nobody knows for sure. It's neither Yiddish nor Hebrew in origin, but is probably Aramaic, going back thousands of years. Today, its Yiddish and Hebrew meanings are different. In Yiddish it's more positive—a kind of assertiveness, a boldness, an aggressiveness. In Hebrew the meaning is more negative—arrogance and pushiness. . . . I use it in the positive sense.

What is the value of chutzpah?

Chutzpah helps underdogs fight against bullies—people who have more power. It should never be used in a bullying way. . . .

I believe that the reason chutzpah is considered a Jewish quality is that Jews, for centuries, have always been on the bottom, trying to fight their way up.

Is chutzpah just for Jews?

Absolutely not! You don't have to be Jewish to have chutzpah. In fact, today, in America, chutzpah is needed, and used, by several less-advantaged groups. . . .

You mean that any American can aspire to have chutzpah?

I have the sense that chutzpah is now the quintessential American characteristic. . . .

How do I develop chutzpah if I haven't got it?

The first rule . . . is to constructively challenge authority. You have to think of yourself as equal to anybody else. . . .

Also important: Understanding that everybody has different talents, techniques and weapons in this contest of life . . . and knowing where your special strengths lie. The next time someone looks at you with an aloof, smug look—because he's a foot taller than you, a million dollars richer than you, etc.—you can break through that veneer using your superior talent. That's chutzpah. That's what you have to practice. . . ."

Can chutzpah be misused?

Definitely. It's often misused . . . it should never, *ever* be used in your personal life. . . .

Can you be shy and still develop chutzpah?

Absolutely. . . . I'm very shy at parties . . . but I am very successful using my chutzpah in my professional life.

Where did you learn chutzpah?

From my mother. But I never, never use it *in relation* to my mother. . . .

Condensed from "Chutzpah Lessons from Alan Dershowitz," *Bottom Line/Personal,* December 15, 1991, pp. 7–8. Published by Boardroom Reports, Inc. Used with permission.

Harold mutters, "Well, I decided to do something else. Sam got all the good stuff out of the library."

Many things could be going on. Harold may be mad because Sam got to the library ahead of him, even though he knows that other resources could have given him what he needed. By not doing his own job, Harold may be punishing Sam and the team as well. Sometimes people "defend" themselves by punishing others in ways they think will not be detected as aggression by others who might think less of them or, perhaps, retaliate.

If Harold were to be outright aggressive, he might shout, "Listen, you people aren't doing anything, I'm sick of this stuff, and I want to change the topic!" Harold may have something on his side, but he won't have for long with that approach.

Enhancing Transactional Processes

Effective leadership depends on communicating clearly in ways that facilitate your team's transactional processes. Skillful, sensitive communication involves taking responsibility for your own ideas and feelings and confirming those expressed by others. This type of communication helps your team develop the dialogical perspective discussed earlier in this chapter.

Responsibility Statements Language provides ways for people to take full responsibility for their communication behavior—responsibility for their own ideas, for expressing them well, and for the impact they have on group members.

We draw from a simple, but invaluable, list of guidelines that family therapist Virginia Satir (1990) found helpful in facilitating communication within families. Her approach fosters the types of transactional processes that also make team communication effective. Use these suggestions to guide you in expressing ideas with sensitivity:

1. Use words that take responsibility for your position or feelings; avoid words that blame, judge, or ascribe something to others. Make "I" statements, such as "I think," "I feel." These allow other members to have their own feelings and opinions without having to defend themselves against yours. Be careful with "you"; it can imply a judgment of the other. If I say, for example, "I'm frustrated by our lack of progress," I leave room open to discuss the problem. If I say, "You people aren't doing anything," I put the entire team on the defensive.

2. Use language that allows room for degrees of probability; avoid language that is absolute and know-it-all. "I believe" or "probably" leaves room for people to disagree and still communicate. "Always," "never," and "impossible!" cut off negotiation of ideas.

3. Use specific language; avoid language that obscures issues. If you mean "yes," say it; if you mean "no," say it. People often fog over affirmatives and negatives out of politeness or dread of dealing with issues. "I'm sorry, but I won't do that" is clear; "I am very hesitant to take such an action" is ambiguous. Which one would you take for "no"?

4. Use definite pronouns; avoid indefinite ones. Two culprits are "it" and "they." "It seems to be a problem." What does? "They said we had to." Who did?

5. Use words of choice; avoid language of guilt. Avoid "ought" and "should"; they imply guilt and induce resistance. Substitute "can," "want," "will," "might"; or "won't," "don't," "refuse to," or even "can't."

Confirming and Disconfirming Responses When one person speaks, others respond. Their responses may reflect that they heard and cared about what the speaker said; or they may ignore the speaker (no response is also a response); or they may put the speaker down by indicating that the comment was wrong, stupid, or insignificant. These three response types are called confirming, rejecting, and disconfirming (Watzlawick, Beavin, & Jackson, 1967). Confirming responses build communication bonds; rejection and disconfirmation dissolve them.

A *confirming* response indicates understanding. It may take the form of acknowledgment ("that's a good idea"), support ("you've earned the right"), clarification ("do you mean?"), or a positive expression ("you said that so well").

In a *rejecting* response, the person may walk away without a word, or interrupt you in midsentence. Sometimes you get a pseudoconfirmation ("that's great, now let's eat") or an irrelevant statement that has nothing to do with what you said.

A *disconfirming* response may be impersonal ("that's not my problem"), incoherent ("it's, like, you know, that's . . . well"), or an incongruous response in which the words say one thing but the tone and other nonverbal communication contradict it.

People whose statements are confirmed tend to continue contributing to the team. Rejection and disconfirmation lead to defensive, self-protective behaviors. This damages the climate in which the team works.

Creating Team Climates

The metaphor of "climate" is often used to describe how organizations, groups, or individuals are influenced by conditions around them. Figure 9.3 illustrates the relationship between team processes and team climate.

This model shows transactional and task processes flowing in concurrent, interacting streams and suggests that transactions among people may focus on one or more of three areas: the task, the individuals, and the team. Even though the subject of conversation may be only one of these, transactions involving the others are always present, because the three occur simultaneously in verbal and nonverbal interactions.

The model also suggests a mutual interaction between the climate and the communication processes. The nature of the team's transactions influences the climate in which the transactions take place—and the climate influences the nature of the team's transactions. They are interdependent and mutually influential.

For example, a team member may say, "This team couldn't have gotten this far without your help, Trish." This is an interpersonal message, focusing on an individual. When Trish responds, "Thanks, Dan!" and other members respond by saying, "Right!" or "Uh-huh," we have three transactions: one acknowledges a person, the second relates to the task, and the third relates to the team as a developing whole. If Dan conveys an honest appreciation for Trish's contributions, then the transaction is positive. If he's perceived as sarcastic, in order to get a wandering Trish back on the subject, then there's a negative force to the transaction. Whichever it is, the three transactional elements impact on one another: Trish feels appreciated or rejected; the team feels closer or more divided; synergy for the task is strengthened or weakened.

The qualities of these transactions, then, affect the climate in which the team operates. That affects the next set of transactions, which in turn will further influence the team's climate.

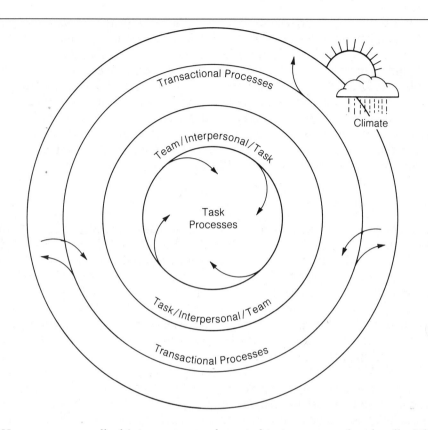

FIGURE   9.3

Model showing relationships among transactional and task processes and team climate

Have you ever walked into a room and wanted to turn around and walk right back out, because you could "feel" the tension? Or walked into a room and never wanted to leave, because you could "feel" the acceptance? It's almost tangible, isn't it? How was your own communication affected by each of those atmospheres? The communication climate is so important because it affects a team's ability to do its job.

Positive Climates

Kinlaw (1991) reports that "hundreds of statements" in his research reveal that members of outstanding work teams have strong feelings of inclusion, commitment, loyalty, pride, and trust in their teams. Members commented that "nobody was left out," "we respected each other," "if [other people] said they were going to do something, they did it," "it felt like a family," "people went out of their way to make somebody else look good," and if someone needed help, "we all jumped in" (pp. 48–50).

These feelings are nurtured by a climate that is open, supportive, inclusive, challenging, and rewarding. Such a climate encourages diverse and different ideas, expressions of disagreement as well as of agreement, change and growth. It supports people's rights to express themselves, their feelings and opinions, their work, and the risks they take in looking for better ways to achieve their goals. Every member is a part of the whole. All are concerned for one another and rewarded in emotional as well as material results for their teamwork.

A climate like this is productive. Remember the ideal superteam we described in Chapter 4? That team can exist only in a positive climate. Such a team has a strong syntality, a group personality distinguished by flexibility, commitment, and strength. It seeks new and interesting tasks or goals. It develops healthy cohesiveness and vigorous synergy. These characteristics are reflected in one team member's comment: "It felt so important to get the job done that you sometimes forgot about anything else" (Kinlaw, 1991, p. 48).

Negative Climates

As you might suspect, a negative climate is closed, defensive, blaming, alienating, discouraging, risky, and punishing. It is closed to ideas, challenges, feelings, innovation. It is defensive because people feel threatened and under attack: constantly expecting the worst, they withdraw or play manipulative games. It is blaming and alienating because the norm is to look for somebody to be at fault. Members feel no connection or inclusion—they are all out for themselves—yet the climate fosters conformity through pressure and fear. It is discouraging for all these reasons, and because it offers slim promise of reward and satisfaction. Why should an individual or a team bother when the work will not be appreciated? In fact, it is punishing; even the best-intentioned actions, in this climate, may elicit such defensive, angry responses that individuals feel punished.

People trying to work in a negative climate feel alienated, defensive, angry, and distrustful. They spend their energy either distancing themselves from the team and its work, or fighting unseen dragons. The result is a weak, manipulative, sick team syntality. Like an individual, a team can't withstand that kind of negative pressure. Its synergy is unstable and unpredictable, and when it is able to sustain itself in such a climate, its goal achievement is usually below standard.

Worst of all, a negative climate is destructive to the team members, because the stress of such an experience goes beyond the team into their personal lives. The effects permeate the boundaries of subsystems so that families and other groups, too, feel the negative influence.

Influences on Team Climates

What creates a team's climate, positive or negative? Some influences come from outside the team: the political situation, context, or culture of a parent organization and related systems can permeate the climate in which a team works, for good or for ill. The style or personality of a leader or, in an organization, a manager can profoundly affect the climate.

We heard of a new president who went to a meeting of managers and said, "What can I do to motivate you people?" Eight little words, and that individual had created a climate of apprehension and dismay. This person had talked down to the managers, implying that they had to be controlled from the top, that they were unmotivated and not doing their jobs. To make it worse, with "you people," the president had lumped them together in a way bound to create an adversarial relationship.

Within the team itself, transactional processes create a climate just as surely as if the members were working under a sunlamp or a fog machine. In the remainder of this chapter, we'll focus on what you, as a team member, can do to influence your team's climate. We'll examine the types of transactions that affect it positively or negatively and those that make you a more effective team member.

Communication and Climates

Jack Gibb (1961) observed groups and charted how communication acts and emotional responses led to defensive or supportive climates. "**Defensive behavior**," he says, "occurs when an individual perceives threat or anticipates threat in the group" (p. 141). The person reacts with hostility, which absorbs much of the individual's energy and feeds into a circular, progressively more defensive set of interactions.

Supportive behavior has the opposite effect. "As defenses are reduced," Gibb notes, "receivers become better able to concentrate upon the structure, the content, and the cognitive meanings of the message" (p. 141). Johannesen (1990, p. 69) observes that supportive communication is essential to a dialogical ethic of group communication; only in this positive climate can people maintain their own ethics, dialogue openly, and make ethically acceptable decisions.

Gibb identified six pairs of communication behaviors that either increase defensiveness or develop supportiveness between and among people:

1. *Evaluation versus description.* Blaming or judgmental statements tend to make others defensive. Simply describing situations or feelings, without judgment, increases supportiveness.

2. *Control versus problem orientation.* Pushing or manipulating others' actions or responses may draw a defensive reaction. Focusing objectively on an issue, with a mutual interest in solving the problem, enhances supportiveness.

3. *Strategy versus spontaneity.* Communicating with preconceived plans to set people up or with ambiguous intent arouses others' suspicion and defensiveness. Being open, honest, and direct elicits trust and support.

4. *Neutrality versus empathy.* Conveying lack of concern or not caring produces defensiveness. Concern, caring, and seeking to understand make others feel supported.

5. *Superiority versus equality.* Conveying a sense of greater importance and value—whether from status, power, or personal characteristics—puts others down and creates defensiveness. Conveying equality by valuing others and their ideas allows them to feel supported and comfortable.

6. *Certainty versus provisionalism.* Communicating absolute sureness about ideas and conclusions, leaving no room for questions, fosters defensiveness. Qualifying statements and recognizing other points of view support others and allow them to consider more possibilities.

In Figure 9.4, we've sketched the alternative routes that defensive versus supportive transactions can take in developing and perpetuating a team's climate.

As you can see, defensive individual transactions short-circuit task and team transactions. Defensiveness escalates. The escalation may reach the explosion point, or people may simply withdraw. The alternatives are to terminate activities or to alter the climate.

The supportive climate also escalates, building openness, trust, and empathy. These three elements are interdependent; each contributes to and reinforces the others. When one increases, the others grow; losing one destroys the others. They are so critical to creating a positive climate that we'd like to talk a little more about each of them.

Openness Openness implies much about group communication. Members are *open-minded*—not quick to prejudge or stereotype, interested in learning, motivated to see things from others' points of view. They may also be *open-hearted*—willing to understand and to forbear. Finally, they may be *open-selved*—willing to take risks, generous in sharing themselves, eager to grow, capable of change.

Openness can be difficult. In a group of several people, you are risking more than you would be in a one-on-one dialogue. You have to judge how much openness you can risk until you develop a climate of trust.

Trust No two people, let alone a team of people, can go far without trust. In a team, you trust one another to be honest, to be ethical, to be committed, to give your best to the team. Trust is built by increments and negotiation. One person takes a tiny risk by disclosing some small thing. The team is supportive; the climate is comfortable; the risk is justified. Someone else takes a small risk, and that's supported, too. With each transaction, members take slightly greater risks. A bit at a time, they make it safe to trust and to be trustworthy, and they open the climate further.

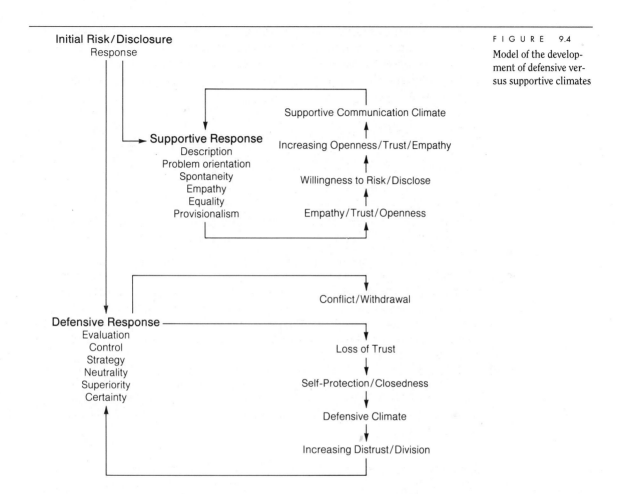

F I G U R E   9.4

Model of the development of defensive versus supportive climates

Trust is faith in someone's goodwill and good character; it's a willingness to count on another's ability to support, perhaps protect, one's confidence.

Empathy   Empathy has been described as walking in another person's moccasins, or feeling what another person feels. Broome (1991, p. 239) suggests that empathy is learning to understand "the other's values, meanings, symbols, intentions, etc."

Empathy does not mean sympathy. Empathy suggests understanding what another is thinking and feeling; sympathy is an emotional response of your own, possibly pity or sorrow. Nor does empathy necessarily mean approval of the other's behavior. A teammate may be drinking excessively and falling down on the job. You can understand the person's distress empathically; you may have sympathy for him or her under the circumstances; but you can still disapprove of the drinking.

Some team members may be more empathic than others. It appears that people in helping, caring, or artistic fields are more empathic than people in more structured or competitive careers. Perhaps those who empathize learned it in their training; perhaps they chose their careers because they had strong empathy; perhaps the two interact.

Similarly, Gilligan's (1982) research, which indicates that socialization produces a male ethic of justice and a female ethic of care, could support the idea that it's easier for a woman to be empathic than for a man. Women are expected to think more in terms of relationships than men are, and they're socialized in that direction. Women's traditional roles and "characteristics" are to nurture and develop relationships, men's to compete and survive.

All this implies that empathy is not simply an innate talent, skill, or personality trait; it can be developed. Broome (1991) suggests that to empathize with people who are culturally different from yourself, you need to understand three things:

1. Empathy is incomplete, changing, and provisional as we try to learn about the other.
2. Context affects all meaning for all people; to empathize, we must understand how the context colors and shapes another's thinking and feeling.
3. Empathy does not mean giving up one's own identity; it means extending understanding to share some of the other person's perspective (pp. 240–243).

With supportive transactions—communication that is descriptive, problem-oriented, spontaneous, empathic, equal, and provisional—you develop an ongoing climate that encourages team members. Your team develops a spiral of openness, trust, and empathy that reinforces and perpetuates a healthy atmosphere.

Summary

Communication creates teams. Knowing and applying sound communication principles makes you effective in creating supportive climates and achieving personal and team goals.

Members connect with one another when they recognize that meanings are within individuals and work to negotiate interpretations together. Language choice is vital to achieving understanding across the barriers of differing cultures and powerful versus powerless language styles. Language should be appropriate to the speaker, to teammates, and to the situation, and it should encourage the team's dialogical analysis.

Assertiveness contributes to effective leadership, whereas passivity, passive-aggression, or aggression undermine the team's processes. Taking responsibility for the impact of your communication and confirming, rather than rejecting or disconfirming, others' responses are ways of using assertive communication to foster a positive team climate.

For good or ill, a team's climate creates, and is created by, the quality of its transactional processes. Transactional processes move communication about tasks, team, and interpersonal relationships concurrently, interacting constantly with the climate. A positive climate is supportive, allowing people to communicate safely and effectively. It depends upon openness, trust, and empathy. A negative climate is defensive; it closes off communication and feeds problems and conflicts. With sensitivity, awareness, and skill, team communication can achieve a supportive climate in which transactional processes among members enhance effective task processes.

F O R M 9.2 ▮ A S S E R T I V E N E S S   A S S E S S M E N T

When you're working with a group of people, how assertive are you? Think about the following questions:

1. If I think my rights are in conflict with others' rights, do I
   a. Worry a lot about what they might do if I confront them?
   b. Worry more about how they will feel than how I feel?
   c. Feel too much empathy with their positions to argue?
   d. Feel empathy with their positions yet know I have a right to my own?

2. If somebody does something that makes me angry, do I
   a. Keep it to myself?
   b. Describe the problem without attacking the person?
   c. Keep quiet but look for a way to "get back"?
   d. Attack the other person verbally?
   e. Attack the other person physically?

3. If I want something to happen, do I
   a. Express my preferences but allow others to have theirs, too?
   b. Look for ways to get others to do what I want without having to ask?
   c. Keep quiet, go along with others, and figure it doesn't matter?
   d. Keep quiet, go along with others, and seethe?
   e. Seethe quietly until I blow up?

4. If I must confront a difference or issue, do I
   a. Use language that blames or manipulates others?
   b. Use language that takes blame on myself?
   c. Use language that is direct, responsible, and problem-focused?

   If you can feel empathy with others' positions and still know you have a right to your own, if you can describe the problem without attacking the person, and if you can express your preferences but allow others to have theirs, too, then you're on your way to being assertive. If you also can confront issues with language that is direct, responsible, and problem-focused—you are assertive.

Nonverbal Cues and Meanings: Enhancing Team Messages

"Tom definitely supported me—I could tell by his eyes. But Katrina didn't. She *said* she had, after the meeting, but . . ."

Actions *do* speak louder than words.

This incident actually took place. The head of a new corporate program was asked to represent her department on a committee. She told us this:

Actually, Tom may have been the only member of that committee on my side. They'd asked me to come to explain how our program related to theirs. And I wanted to do it . . . I wanted cooperation. But I felt the tension when I walked in. They sat me at the side of the table and I felt surrounded. They had a video camera pointed at me—they didn't even ask me if that would be okay! The chairperson didn't even smile, didn't acknowledge me at all. Lois and Eduardo wouldn't look at me; they just looked down at their papers the whole time. Darrin sat with his arms crossed and glared at me. And Redonna . . . brrr! She looked straight at me, like ice, not even blinking. When she finally spoke, her jaw was so tight you could have cracked a walnut between her teeth.

This individual experienced a defensive, hostile climate communicated entirely *without words*. This particular incident did conclude well: through careful verbal and nonverbal communication, questioning, listening, and climate change, the program head turned the responses around and gained the committee's support. But she knew she faced a challenge the moment she walked in—just from the nonverbal cues.

Nonverbal communication can create or destroy the climate in which a team works; it can determine the meanings teammates get from one another's messages. This chapter examines the impact of nonverbal communication in defining roles and perceptions of team members. It examines ways in which people communicate nonverbally and the impact of environmen-

tal and technological factors on a team's climate and transactions. Finally, it looks at leadership in terms of understanding and using nonverbal communication effectively. Our goals are for you to:

1. Understand nonverbal communication and its importance to teams.

2. See how nonverbal communication patterns and perceptions affect relationships among team members.

3. Become aware of the many ways individuals send nonverbal cues to team members.

4. See how environmental and technological factors communicate in team settings.

5. Use leadership to improve nonverbal communication on your team.

Teams and Nonverbal Communication

In the example we just gave you, nonverbal cues affected the climate and the messages among team members as well as between them and their guest. Even the baleful eye of the videocamera had an impact.

In looking more closely at nonverbal communication, we'll begin with its importance to teams, its influence on roles and relationships, and its relation to individual differences and perceptions.

Importance to Teams

"You can't not communicate." It's true—mainly because people constantly bombard one another with nonverbal cues. Even silence can be filled with meaning.

Nonverbal communication occurs through cues accompanying language or separate from language that people may interpret as having meaning. It carries, supplements, enriches, diminishes, or substitutes for verbal communication. People communicate nonverbally with their eyes, bodies and faces, voices and speech patterns, touching, and the ways they use personal territories.

Any given nonverbal behavior may be conscious or unconscious and can be interpreted in multiple ways; negotiating meaning from them can be tough even for one person. The problems steadily increase as the team increases in size because:

1. Nonverbal cues, even from a single individual, *outnumber* verbal cues. Every verbal statement comes with multiple nonverbal cues.

2. Nonverbal cues may *confirm* or *contradict* a verbal message. If a person says "I agree," maintains an open posture, smiles, and nods, the message is confirmed. If the person says "I agree," but withdraws into a closed posture, frowns, perhaps rubs his or her face, the verbal message is contradicted.

3. Nonverbal cues are *believed*. When nonverbal cues contradict verbal messages, people believe the nonverbal. In some contexts, nonverbal cues account for more than 90 percent of the interpretations of feelings Americans communicate; less than 10 percent comes from the words (Mehrabian, 1971).

4. Nonverbal cues are *difficult to interpret*. Ekman observes, "The great majority of us are easily misled. It's very difficult, and most people just don't know what cues to rely on" (quoted in Goleman, 1991, p. C1). People unjustifiably trust their ability to read nonverbal cues, and their mistakes misguide team transactions.

5. Nonverbal cues are *multiple in groups*. Interactions bombard each member with nonverbal cues from all participants at all times, even though verbal messages may come from one member at a time.

6. Nonverbal cues also come from the *environment*. Team members are affected not only by one another's nonverbal cues, but also by the surroundings in which they meet.

Team Role Relationships

Building relationships and communication patterns in a team is something like creating a three-tiered, multidirectional system of freeways. Each road is interconnected, in some way, with the others. The interchange system and structures then affect the way the entire entity functions. If the pieces are connected properly, strength is distributed appropriately, and traffic flow is regulated effectively, then the system works.

Something has to build and regulate those relational processes and traffic patterns. In a team, nonverbal communication "regulates" the team's processes for several purposes, including establishing role relationships and dominance, appropriate levels of intimacy, and emotional tone, as well as timing and synchronizing communication (Heslin & Patterson, 1982, p. 91).

The relationships among team members reveal the ways in which those purposes are achieved. Mehrabian (1971) identifies three important relational dimensions that nonverbal cues reveal between and among people:

1. *Liking* reflects the degree to which a person wants to be close to or avoid another.
2. *Status* reflects the degree of power, authority, or dominance a person feels in relationship to others.
3. *Responsiveness* reflects the degree to which a person reacts positively or negatively to another, to the environment, or to the climate of a situation.

Team transactions demonstrate these nonverbal dimensions. One person shows liking, status, and/or responsiveness to others; this is perceived and elicits responses from them. With time, that individual's nonverbal action combines with the reactions of others and a multitude of other interactions to build a structure of relationships among the members of the team.

Take status as an example. Suppose Ali comes into the first meeting of her group with nonverbal cues that communicate her belief that she has higher status than others. Some members may respond submissively: okay, they think, she *does* have higher status. Others may react defensively: no way, they think, is she going to run the show. As these and other transactions take place, a structure of relationships and patterns of behavior emerges. There may be a struggle for control; communication patterns between members become clear. Finally, these interactive influences on relationships regulate the processes of the team—for better or for worse.

What happens between and among members involves a web of influences and counterinfluences; as a team member, you are affected by each of those intricate relationships in everything the team does.

Individual Differences and Perceptions

To team members, an individual's nonverbal behavior may reveal his or her character, credibility, and acceptability as a teammate. They could be wrong, however;

a person's cues may be influenced by many factors. How one sees an action may be very different from what it means to another. Some influences on these individual behaviors, and others' interpretations of them, are:

Personality. People may conclude that someone is aloof, gregarious, or submissive on the basis of that person's nonverbal cues, and they could be right: these characteristics do seem to be connected to nonverbal behavior (Goleman, 1991). Often, however, a nonverbally cued impression of another's personality is wrong.

Gender. Many nonverbal cues are attributed to an individual's sex or psychological gender, primarily through socialization (Borisoff & Merrill, 1992). She takes up a lot of space; he takes less (p. 46). She shows what she's feeling; he hides it (p. 51). Many stereotypes are culture-bound, however, so it's best not to use expectations of how a woman or a man uses nonverbal communication as measures of a person's sexuality or character.

Background. People learn nonverbal norms from their backgrounds—their families, cultures, experiences. One touches, another doesn't; one talks loudly, another softly; one stares, another drops the eyes. When people from one background interpret the norms of another, they may make wrong inferences. "Those Italians," a German may say, "they're too emotional!" "Those Germans," an Italian may say, "they're so cold!" Neither is necessarily true. It helps to be aware of how your own background has shaped your nonverbal behavior and to understand that others' socialization also has affected theirs—but to avoid stereotyping at all costs.

Special Groups. Teammates' other groups—professional groups, teams, friends, and/or subcultures—also may condition them to use distinct nonverbal cues that affect group images and norms, as in dress, hairstyles, seating postures, and amount of eye contact.

People may draw conclusions about themselves and about others based on how they see nonverbal communication. Beware of overgeneralizing. Often, in this book, we cite examples of differences among people based on gender or culture. Such examples come from research that frequently focuses on small subgroups. The findings exemplify how actions and interpretations vary across cultures and genders, but they provide no absolutes about how a given group of people "is." If, for example, we cite what "Latin Americans" do, remember there are many different cultures and subcultures in Latin America, as in every other part of the world, and they vary widely among themselves according to status, gender, personality, and experience.

The point is that people are socialized and influenced by their backgrounds; this affects both their nonverbal communication and how they interpret others' cues. In diverse teams, the differences can lead to misunderstanding. It is necessary to refrain from judgment and explore messages and meanings together, so please be careful about making broad generalizations that lead to stereotyping.

STEREOTYPES AND ASSUMPTIONS

Some experts say stereotypes are not necessarily bad—it's what we do with them. I disagree. . . .

Stereotypes hurt individuals when invalid conclusions are reached about them and when those conclusions remain untested and unchanged. Take this scenario: A white male manager walks through the office, passing two black men talking at the water cooler. He is slightly irritated.

Why are they standing there wasting time? A moment later he passes two women coming out of the ladies room talking. He wonders what they are gossiping about and hopes they get back to work quickly. He comes upon two white men leaning on the walls of a cubicle, also talking. He thinks nothing of it.

What are his assumptions? The women and minorities are "goof-

ing off," but the white men are talking business. Since he hasn't really listened to the conversations, he doesn't realize that the women and the black men were talking business while the white men happened to be talking about their children. Instead, his misinterpretation of what he saw will only strengthen his bias that women and minorities don't work hard enough.

An excerpt from Lennie Copeland, "Learning to Manage a Multicultural Work Force." Reprinted with permission from the May 1988 issue of *Training* magazine. Copyright 1988, Lakewood Publications Inc., Minneapolis, MN, (612) 333–0471. All rights reserved.

Please note, too, that there is great variation in the nonverbal cues any individual transmits. It's important to look for patterns and deviations. In a team, you get to know one another's communication habits, you see many nonverbal cues along with verbal ones, and you become aware of patterns and changes in nonverbal communication. For example, if you normally have straight, open posture, but you slump and turn your head away during the team's discussion, this might tell your teammates that something's making you uncomfortable. Perhaps a teammate said something that hurt you, or perhaps you have a headache or are worried about an exam. A team that picks up nonverbal cues can respond and help both the individual and the team's transactional processes.

Individuals' Nonverbal Messages

People derive their ideas about others, in large part, from something they do nonverbally—but what? A lot of things. One person sends many nonverbal messages, using his or her eyes, face, body, touch, and personal space and territory.

Eyes

Poets have spun thousands of words about them: "Her eyes are like limpid pools," "Drink to me only with thine eyes. . . ." Cultures enforce many rules about how their members may use their eyes: "Don't look at me in that tone of voice, young lady!" "She cut her eyes at me!" "Look at me, I'm your elder!" "Don't stare at your elders, it's disrespectful!"

People communicate through eye contact and eye movements (or lack of them) for many purposes:

Understanding. In a group situation, where you can't get verbal cues from everyone at once, you rely on nonverbal cues. Listeners look at a speaker more steadily than speakers look at listeners, presumably to help them understand the message (Argyle & Ingham, 1972). Rightly or wrongly, people watch others' eye movements to understand their responses. For example, your teammate widens her eyes. How do you interpret that? It depends. If she's a North American Anglo, it might mean surprise. A Chinese might be angry; a Frenchperson, disbelieving; a Hispanic, confused; an African-American, feeling innocent or intending to persuade (Condon, 1976). Or any of these people might have a different meaning behind the widened eyes, depending on subcultural variations, experiences, and situations.

Relationships. Eye contact indicates liking and responsiveness; it may suggest intimacy or sexual interest; and it can establish dominance or status. Observers see a speaker who maintains strong eye contact as dominant, but listeners who do the same as submissive (Dovidio & Ellyson, 1982). You might think that women are more responsive, because they use eye contact more than men do and value it more highly. Sometimes they avert their eyes (a submissive or embarrassed response) more than men do, whereas men stare more frequently (Pearson, Turner, & Todd-Mancillas, 1991, p. 135). The stare may be to communicate aggression, to make the other person anxious, or to say "I'm interested."

Regulation. People use their eyes to cue stops and starts in discussion. You might look at someone else as a cue that its his or her turn to speak; you might drop your eyes if you don't want to be called upon. These cues, too, are influenced by culture. Eye rolling, winking, eyebrow raising, eyelid lowering, all carry meanings that have cultural interpretations. You may be speaking to your team and think someone's eyes are saying "Shut up, you're being a jerk" when, in fact, they mean "Wow—tell me more!"

Body and Face

People figure out most of what others feel from their faces, and infer how intensely they feel it from their bodies (Ekman & Friesen, 1967). The study of body and face communication is called **kinesics**. If a teammate's face is scrunched, and his or her body looks tense, you might infer that the person is very tense, or responding to an internal anxiety.

The body is a constant communication satellite of its own: it communicates within itself, about itself; and it communicates to others through kinesics. Every nerve and muscle responds to signals from the brain, which is responding to signals from everywhere. The results are complex nonverbal messages conveyed by facial expressions, body postures, and gestures.

Facial Expressions   Although many expressions are well-nigh impossible to decipher, Matsumoto (1991) points out that they "convey discrete emotions, making them the most specific and precise nonverbal signal system" (p. 128). People everywhere seem to understand at least ten types of emotional expressions, also called "affect displays": happiness, surprise, fear, anger, sadness, disgust, contempt, and interest (Ekman, Friesen, & Ellsworth, 1972), plus bewilderment and determination (Leathers, 1976).

Both facial expressions and others' interpretations of them are complex. If, for example, your feelings are mixed, your cues will be, too; your face may be difficult to decode. Then, too, facial cues are "simultaneously universal and culturally-specific" (Matsumoto, 1991, p. 128). Your upbringing and culture may have allowed you to express your emotions easily, whereas another person may have been taught not to show feelings openly.

Your ability to decode others' facial cues is also influenced by a number of factors. Women on your team, for example, may be better at showing and interpreting facial expressions than the men are (Buck, 1975), perhaps because women in this society are allowed more freedom to share emotions, and are expected to empathize more with others' emotions, than men are. Although some expressions are universal, you may not understand your teammates' facial cues because of a variety of influences on how they reflect feelings and how you interpret them.

Body Postures   Your teammates' postures can say a lot about how they feel at any given moment. Postures and hand positions of group members change over time, apparently indicating how members come to feel about the group and one another (Mabry, 1989). People communicate four things through the way they stand, sit, or lean: immediacy (degree of accessibility to others); responsiveness; agreement (coorientation with others); and power or status (Leathers, 1976).

These are very similar to Mehrabian's concepts of liking, responsiveness, and status. You might think that someone whose body is arranged similarly to another's agrees with or is responsive to the other person. You might interpret a forward-leaning, relaxed posture as indicating openness, liking, and interest, or see a person who leans over another as having status or seeking power and control.

Once again, however, socialization, group norms, clothing styles, all might affect posture. Power and status, for example, might be seen in the way men sit—more relaxed, open, and leaning backward more than women, who tend to be more closed and rigid. Women could be thought to be more responsive because they adapt their positions more to others and make the respondent more comfortable than men do (Pearson, Turner, & Todd-Mancillas, 1991, p. 140).

Gestures   Gestures, another form of kinesics, provide much of our nonverbal communication. Some are clearly understood symbols, shared within a culture, but most gestures are unconscious, created spontaneously by the gesturer for many reasons (Ekman & Friesen, 1969). In team communication, the important purposes are to give specific information, to illustrate a statement, or to regulate communication flow.

Gestures with specific meanings are *emblems*. They work especially well when other means of communication are unavailable. Signs used by coaches, pitchers, and catchers at a baseball game are examples; the gesture used by an irate motorist who has just been cut off on the roadway is another.

TELLTALE SIGNS

Watch for body-language cues that flash "trouble ahead."

Stress   Signs of stress include:

A blank expression or phony smile.

Tight posture, with arms held stiffly at the person's sides.

Abrupt motions . . . sudden shifts of eyes, head, leg.

Sudden mood shifts in speech: toneless, soft to animated, loud.

A tense brow or fidgeting fingers.

Observation: Postpone discussions; ask thoughtful questions to find the problem; and proceed only after you have done so.

Incomprehension.   When you encounter silence or a lack of questions, look for signs of doubt or uncertainty. Examples:

Knitted brows.

A deadpan expression.

Tentative, weak nodding or smiling.

One slightly raised eyebrow.

"Yes" or "I see" in a strained voice.

An "I understand" accompanied by looking away.

Observation: Restate, solicit questions, keep explaining. . . .

Hesitation.   Spot reluctance to speak on sensitive topics by:

A slight raising of the head and eyebrows.

Unconsciously lifting one finger.

Licking the lips.

Deep breathing with eye contact.

Observation: Sit back, smile, relax and display your own body language signs that say "It's safe to talk."

Disagreement.   You can spot hostile submission by watching for:

Downward movement of body and/or eyes.

Closed eyes and a hand put over the nose.

Observation: Counter this one head-on. Ask the individual to tell you his (or her) objections, concerns or questions.

An excerpt from "Telltale Signs: Watch for Body Language Clues That Flash 'Trouble Ahead,' " *Executive Strategies*, June 5, 1990, p. 8. Published by National Institute of Business Management, Inc. Used with permission.

Although members of a given culture or subculture know exactly what a specific emblem means, that gesture may convey a radically different meaning to someone else. In the United States, a palms-out gesture means "Stop!" In Greece, it's an insult. In the United States, a raised hand, palm turned toward the sender, and fingers wagging means "Come here." In Italy, it means "Good-bye."

As you can imagine, emblems can cause some amusing—or not so amusing—intercultural incidents. They are, however, important in many ways. Used well, they help clarify communication enormously. Emblems compose much of American Sign Language used by many hearing-impaired people, who also receive communication through other emblems, signed words, lipreading, and sensitivity to a wealth of other nonverbal cues. If your team includes hearing-impaired individuals, it's one of many reasons to keep your emblems clear and your communication visible to your listeners.

Illustrators are gestures that reinforce the verbal message by nonverbally demonstrating what it means. Illustrators help to make a point clear and vivid. You're describing teamwork, for example, and you say, "It's interdependent, interwoven, cooperative." As you say this, you weave your fingers together to help the team visualize the concept.

Regulators are nonverbal cues that control turn-taking, or who speaks next, so they are especially important in group communication. Nodding at points a team-mate has made encourages talking, as do smiling, looking agreeable, giving a thumbs-up sign, and saying "um-hum, yeah, hmm."

People stop other people from talking by frowning, shaking their heads, nodding their heads rapidly (meaning, "Yeah, yeah, it's my turn"), dropping their eyes (or staring intensely), cutting off supportive noises, looking at their watches, fiddling with extraneous objects, moving their bodies into closed-off positions, or, perhaps, moving as if to leave.

Voice and Speech

"It's not what you say, it's how you say it" refers not only to the words you use, but also to your voice and speech. Called **paralanguage**, this nonverbal communication is in the pitch, tone, volume, range, and quality of your voice; in the pronunciation, articulation, and rate of your speech; and in vocalizations such as groaning, sighing, and "uhmming."

Your voice and speech have great relevance to your message content. They determine how well you're understood, and how your credibility is perceived. Have you ever missed half of what someone said because she or he mumbled, turned away, droned, or talked at ninety miles an hour? It made it hard to pay attention. Similarly, the clarity of your speech and meaning communicated by your voice can make the difference in other people's understanding you.

Paralanguage cues are especially important for members of a team who are visually impaired. The person who cannot see you clearly must get all the meaning from hearing you; other nonverbal cues aren't available. Only your voice and speech regulate the communication, emphasize important concepts, provide enough variety to maintain interest, and communicate your feelings and your information. Only your volume and pitch, your pausing, pacing, rate of speech, articulation, and inflection can make these clear.

Using good paralanguage does more than help the other person understand you. It also influences how people perceive your credibility and believability (O'Sullivan, Ekman, Friesen, & Scherer, 1985). Sadly, it is the trigger for a lot of stereotyping. People make inferences about your personality, character, mood, race, age, and even body type on the basis of your voice. Listeners often stereotype a speaker with characteristics believed to belong to a given group or subculture based on his or her dialect or vocal qualifiers, or assume that a man is more credible than a woman because his deeper, firmer, louder speech links to this society's associations with power and authority.

Touch

Touch plays an essential role in human interactions. People need to touch and be touched. In this way, they establish their feelings of liking, responsiveness, and status toward others. The manner and extent of touching, however, is controlled by widely varying cultural norms and rules.

"Well, good old slap-'em-on-the-back Harry just lost that contract for us!"

In this society, for example, women put a higher value on touching and make a clearer distinction between affiliative touching (for warmth and affection) and sexual touching than men do. Men often see touching others as either needful, childish behavior or sexually motivated (Pearson, Turner, & Todd-Mancillas, 1991, p. 142). Fortunately, some of these cultural norms and restrictions are changing, and males are being allowed, even encouraged, to engage in more touching with family, friends, co-workers, and subordinates.

Often, as a team develops, so do close relationships. For some teams, touching or hugging become norms that express mutual support and caring; for others, a professional distance seems more acceptable. A team's norms for touching emerge as the team develops, and it is essential for them to be congruent with the values and beliefs that each member brings to the team.

Because teams so often work within organizations, it's important to recognize how volatile the issue can be. If a person believes a touch is sexual in its intent, she or he has a right to complain and, perhaps, to charge sexual harassment. People working on teams must be sensitive to how much and what kind of touching they do. A good rule of thumb is to be sure it's appropriate to the context; give

---

▌ N O   " P A T "   A N S W E R   ▌

One well-meaning North American manager's experience went like this: After learning that a friendly pat on the arm or back would make workers feel good and motivated, a manager took every chance to pat his subordinates. His Asian employees, who hated being touched, avoided him like the plague. Several asked for transfers. (If he had treated female employees this way, he could have had other problems on his hands.)

priority to what the other person is comfortable with; and be supportive, not exploitative. If you're in doubt on any of those issues, don't touch.

Time

The way a person uses time says something about him or her to others. Expressions such as "time is money" reflect cultural values and cultural rules: "don't be late," or "don't waste time." People often judge others as irresponsible if they are late for appointments or deadlines. They may see it as indicating another person's inferiority, incompetence, rebellion, hostility, or effort to take control. We're tough on time in this country.

This is, however, another variable radically affected by culture. Some languages don't even have words for "time" in the sense that English does. In many cultures people don't look at things to do in terms of starting and stopping points along a line. Events are understood in terms of processes.

This difference in how people understand and use time can create misunderstanding and conflicts. In a task team, time elements can be critically important; teams need to use their time well. Members unaccustomed to this norm may think it's ridiculous to emphasize being on time for meetings and accomplishing work when it is due. For members accustomed to having time to play an important role in their lives and relationships, others' failure to meet time requirements can be frustrating. It helps if members recognize that individuals may have different understandings of time, and work at finding mutually acceptable norms and ways of observing them.

Territory

People are funny about their territory. They use all kinds of ways to define it, mark it, defend it. Territory is the space around each person that she or he feels is for personal use only. Territory is part of **proxemics**—the way people use and react to space between and among people and/or objects. We'll look at space again in the context of environmental cues. For now, think of the space around you.

Spatial Boundaries   Each person in a group moves inside a psychological, inviolable "bubble" (Sommer, 1959). The size and importance of this bubble depends on a person's background, culture, and gender. If team members don't understand the ways people define and protect their territories, they can tread on one another's spaces.

Hall (1966) identified four boundaries that define distances that people put between themselves and others: intimate, personal, social, and public. In North American society, the definitions seem to be approximately as follows:

1. *Intimate distance* ranges from zero to about eighteen inches; it's acceptable for comforting, loving, intimacy, and contact sports. Others should not enter without invitation.

2. *Personal distance* (normal for team discussions) runs from about eighteen inches to four feet. It's a comfortable conversational distance for most westerners. Closer, you invade the intimate area; farther, you create an urge to close the gap.

3. *Social distance* is from four to twelve feet. That's about the right distance for interacting with strangers or for business contacts or shopping. Often it's set by the presence of a desk, a counter, or some other barrier that says "this close, no closer."

4. *Public distance*, from twelve to twenty-five feet, is for addressing groups or alerting someone from a distance. It's too far away for much confidentiality, and far enough away to include a number of people. When the size of a group or a meeting table puts some members this far apart from one another, it's hard to keep focus and build the team as a cohesive unit.

How intimately a person shares space, and with whom, is one of the ways she or he expresses liking, status, and responsiveness. For example, an individual may express his or her status or power in a group by standing when others are sitting. It appears that people judge another's dominance by his or her elevation more than any other factor (Schwartz, Tesser, & Powell, 1982). Similarly, distance signals a person's desire for power or control. An executive may deliberately sit at a distance from committee members to make them feel subordinated. Conversely, a person of high status and power may intentionally take a more accessible position to make others feel more equal and comfortable in expressing themselves.

Boundary Variations   Individual bubbles set up boundaries, but members of a group vary these distances widely. Choices about boundaries are made according to the type of activity, the relationship of the people, and the homogeneity or heterogeneity of race or culture within a given group (Dolphin, 1988, p. 322). How close an individual wants to be to someone whose background and culture, or subculture, are the same may be quite different from how close she or he wants to be to a stranger.

People of various cultures negotiate their boundaries differently. Hall (1966), for example, observed that Arabs keep much less distance from one another than do Westerners. Latin Americans also speak within a closer distance than do North Americans. To many other cultures, North Americans seem cold and unfriendly with their "arm's length" conversation (Dodd, 1991). Men and women also differ in how they use proxemics. Stewart, Stewart, Friedley, and Cooper (1990) report: "Women are perceived to be more social, more affiliative, and of lower status; as a result, space surrounding women is considered more public and accessible than space surrounding men" (p. 90).

This takes us back to questions of status and power: whoever has the greater power, in a given culture or situation, is allowed (and usually takes) the greater amount of space. The individual's socialization prepares him or her to protect the allotted territory with whatever tools the culture or subculture allows.

Observing the proxemics in a team, and becoming more aware of your own territoriality, is fascinating and informative—especially in the context of all the other forms that nonverbal communication can take.

Environmental Nonverbal Messages

When people meet as a group, the climate and their transactional and task processes are influenced—sometimes dramatically—by the aesthetic environment of the room, by the ways arrangements permit visibility and interaction, and by the technology used to facilitate or even to conduct the meeting. We turn now to a consideration of these nonverbal influences from the environment.

Meeting Space

Team interactions are affected by a room's environment. Think about these environmental conditions, and how they affect members' interactions in a space:

Aesthetics. Ugly rooms make people hostile; beautiful rooms make them comfortable and motivated to stay. The appearance of a room even affects the way people perceive others' communication (Mintz, 1956).

Color. Color can calm aggressive people or incite passive people. Legendary football coach Knute Rockne, we're told, gave his teams pep talks in rooms painted a vivid red, but housed visiting teams in rooms painted a soothing blue.

Light. The amount of light affects interactions. Gergen, Gergen, and Barton (1973) found that people in a well-lighted room chatted for an hour at comfortable conversational distances. People in a poorly lighted room huddled together uncomfortably, touched a lot, and finally stopped talking.

Sound. Music creates moods, and noises can be distracting. Acoustics can make or break a meeting. We recently taught most of a semester in rooms adjacent to a large, noisy generator. Talking and listening above the constant roar exhausted the students and us, making teaching and learning extremely difficult.

Temperature. If it's too hot, people feel sluggish; if it's too cold, people need to move around and can't focus on discussion. It's frequently difficult to find comfortable levels to meet individual needs; comfort for one member may be intolerable for another.

Air quality. Anything that affects breathing can distract people, too. Nonsmokers' suffering from others' smoke, smokers' lungs begging for a "hit," stale air, or humidity too high or too low—all can make people irritable or depressed, affecting a team's transactions.

Smell. An odor can drive you out of a room if it's bad enough, or encourage you to linger if it's inviting enough. Even subtle aromas affect moods and motivation. Companies now market a wide variety of scents (cypress for relaxation, lavender and peppermint to increase efficiency) to pipe into office buildings and hotels (DeVito, 1990, p. 208).

Seating Arrangements

Even when all other elements are perfect, the seating arrangement of a room can determine who participates, to what extent, and with what impact. This is obvious in classroom arrangements. In one classroom, seating is arranged in rigid rows, with all students facing the podium at the front of the room; in another, chairs are arranged in a circle, enabling each student to see all the others. Which of these makes it more comfortable for you to make comments or ask questions?

When your team is trying to create open, dialogical communication and a positive climate, you want to look at ways to maximize those possibilities. Some issues to consider in arranging a meeting room are how visibility and physical position affect participation and the roles people take. People communicate more freely when they can see each other. They tend to talk more to people across from them than to their immediate neighbors, although sometimes, where a leader is very strong, people talk to those on either side of them (Shaw, 1971, p. 133). King Arthur had a solution—the round table.

Leadership Positions

Frequently, where an individual sits influences others' perceptions of him or her as a leader. In western societies, there is a clear relationship between the "head" of the table and dominance or leadership. A person at the head of a table is judged

Look over the seating arrangements, postures, gestures, eyes, and facial expressions of people in this group. What do they imply about issues of status, liking, and responsiveness? Who is the leader? Who is second in command? What implications are apparent for issues of gender and diversity? How might the microphone affect the interactions? What communication climate would you infer from this photo? (Photograph © 1990 Rhoda Sidney/Stock, Boston.)

to be the leader (Strodtbeck & Hook, 1961; Russo, 1967); the individual at the foot of the table is often seen as second in command.

Visibility and space seem to influence emergent leadership, too. When there's no designated leader, someone emerges as leader most frequently from a seat with high visibility. Even at a rectangular table, if there are three people on one side and two on the other, the person most likely to become leader is one of those on the two-person side (Baker, 1984).

In our classes, we've found that when people are asked to take the "leader's seat," they choose that position according to their backgrounds. Those inculcated into the dominant culture often sit at the head of the table; people from other cultures often do not. When we discuss this with the group, we find that those who grew up in the dominant culture "just know" where the dominant person sits, whereas those who developed in a different culture often do not. It just isn't in their frame of reference.

For your amusement and amazement, try watching a group convening for the first time or a group that has experienced a power struggle. See who makes a conscious choice for the head of the table and who avoids it. Then watch the roles people take, the interaction, and the efforts to guide or dominate the discussion. You'll quickly see how status, power, and dominance issues emerge.

A person who understands this dynamic, and who is more concerned for the team than for his or her position, may choose a seat according to what she or he thinks the team needs. We've heard someone say, "I'm going to take the head of the table; this group is foundering and I can get it back on track." On other occasions, we've heard a high-status person say something like, "It's crucial for so-and-so to get a chance to state her position. I'm going to get her to sit at the head of the table so people will focus on her."

In cases like these, the individual is selecting the position and the space most appropriate to his or her objectives, to the situation, and to the group or team. Understanding and wisdom make the difference.

Technology

A powerful nonverbal force in a meeting comes from the technology used to supplement or conduct it. Even a tape recorder or a videocamera can have a psychological effect on members' participation in a meeting. The implications of today's technology, however, go far beyond that.

Williams (1987) notes that accelerating technology is creating an entirely new environment for communication. He describes it as "a *grid*, an omnipresent availability of communication links and services," resulting in "a quantum increase in what we might call *connectivity* in our modern communication age" (p. 7).

Connectivity and Team Interaction   At any time a team may find itself on that grid, and that connectivity will influence, perhaps structure, the team's communication. At a minimum, members may use an electronic aid, such as an overhead projector or a computer to access information from a database. It's possible, however, for the meeting to be *conducted* through electronic media.

Team members may "meet" electronically, by **teleconference**. In teleconferencing, you may be sitting alone in an office, talking on a telephone with several other people, possibly using fax machines to send visual information. You may be in a conference room, linked by video and audio to people in distant conference rooms. You can share information, diagrams, or notes by such technological wonders as electronic blackboards, telewriting, or remote slides—all electronic methods by which you can reproduce a message on a board or screen at a site far removed from your own.

Issues with Electronic Media   The use of electronic media raises a storm of communication, social, and ethical issues. Does it dehumanize group processes? Does it shortcut thinking and analysis? Does it remove people from concrete, real, or ethical considerations by its distant and abstract nature? Does it put too much power in the hands of those who know how to use it, or of those who can afford it?

As telecommunications become progressively more involved in our interpersonal transactions as well as in our team tasks, these issues will become increasingly important:

The use of electronic media affects the quantity and kind of nonverbal communication. Computer communication eliminates nonverbal cues. With purely audio communication, you have only your voice to provide cues to the meaning of your words. Even with video communication, distance and the electronic nature of the images limit what you send and receive.

Individuals' levels of competence and comfort in using electronic media affect the quality of transactional and task processes. If people are unskilled in using a computer terminal, or uncomfortable in speaking to others through an electronic medium, their transactional and task competencies and openness will suffer.

The appropriateness of a medium to the team's task affects the members' ability to use it effectively. If, for example, a team's purpose is to plan a project that requires the use of flowcharts, timelines, and diagrams, an audioconference alone will be frustrating and ineffective.

The expense and complexity of the medium affects its accessibility and the way it is used. Although the situation is improving, telecommunications are very expensive, and some require complicated arrangements and technology. That makes accessibility impossible for some and limited for others. Out of sheer necessity, people using electronic media tend to keep the emphasis primarily on the task, which may mean sacrificing important interpersonal issues and feedback.

The Medium as a "Member"   Every team member adds a different dimension to the team's transactional and task processes. A telecommunications medium becomes, in a sense, a "member" with specialized functions. Its effects are felt not only in the actual use of the particular technology, but also in the ways that team

How does the setting in this teleconference room affect transactions with others in the meeting? In what ways do the multiple screens enhance communication? In what ways would a face-to-face meeting be different? More effective? Less effective? (Photograph © 1991 Matthew Borkoski/Stock, Boston.)

members interact face to face. Their awareness of, and focus on, the added entity permeates all aspects of their work.

Four people connected from distant points through the most sophisticated audiovisual telecommunications technology do not have the same session as those individuals would have meeting together in the same room. It is not that an evil robot has entered the bliss of perfect team interaction, but a team needs to be aware of how deeply it is affected by the nonverbal presence of a medium that gives and demands so much. It gives the ability to bridge distances and bring together sources and ideas that previously would have been unattainable. At the same time, it demands verbal skills, limits or eliminates the contributions of nonverbal cues, and requires technical competence for its usefulness.

This doesn't mean that face-to-face meetings are inherently better; that depends on many other variables, including the time and cost involved in getting together. It is important to understand, however, that the medium does become part of the transactions and that technologically mediated meetings are different. A team needs to adapt to its medium "member" and make it a valuable contributor, but not a dominating force, in the team's processes.

C A S E   A N A L Y S I S   10.1

The task force held more than thirty meetings, each lasting a day or two. To balance the expenses for the organizations, the meeting locations varied; most sessions were held at various McDonald's or EDF sites in New York, Washington, and Oak Brook, Illinois. At times the team met at supplier locations to study products, and some meetings were conducted by conference calls.

Issues for Your Consideration

1. What nonverbal messages are communicated by changing the locations? What effect should changing meeting sites have on issues of territoriality?
2. Would you suggest that the first meeting of the group be by telephone conference? In what ways are telephone conferences different for members who have met previously than for those who have never met?

Leadership and Nonverbal Communication

Sometimes a team's climate is full of nonverbal storm warnings, but nobody sees them. Your awareness of nonverbal communication is an important way in which you can use your leadership to enhance your team's transactions. It can enable you to recognize problems, clarify interpretations of nonverbal behavior, and improve your own communication effectiveness.

Recognizing Problem Signs

Nonverbal cues can alert you to many problems in team interactions. Because they are so plentiful and frequently unconscious, they are often the first sign of potential trouble. Some things you can look for are individual differences, power struggles, and confusion.

Individual Differences   Unless a team is in total agreement, or split right down the middle, any issue will generally have a "minority view." In addition, team members are likely to be of different cultures and genders, and to have differing political, religious, and social points of view. On all these dimensions, some people are in the majority, others in the minority. Whoever is in the minority is at risk of being separated, stereotyped, or simply overlooked by members of the majority.

An important leadership function is being sensitive to the nonverbal behaviors that say "I feel segregated/dominated/inferior/uncomfortable." These may be communicated through any combination of nonverbal cues. Someone has to see the problem and help people in the minority be as fully participative as those in the majority.

Issues of Power   Conversely, you may see someone in the group use body position, space, gestures, or voice to take or exert power over other people. Sometimes this is unconscious—it may be natural to someone who has always had power and privilege—but it often inhibits the participation of less dominant people. It also can trigger power struggles in the group. Someone who sees such moves and carefully steps in can ensure better participation and equality in the group.

Suppose for example, that Angela interrupts, stands over people, and uses heavy gestures that dominate others. You notice that Carl becomes progressively more quiet and shrinks away from her. You might position yourself next to Carl, find opportunities to listen to him, and find out what he'd like to say. You might ask Angela to let Carl get a word in, or you might interrupt her yourself, if necessary, and ask Carl to speak to his point.

Confusion   Watch for extreme nonverbal reactions, or signs of confusion, in the group. That's your cue to speak to the issue. Comment on the fact that there seems to be a climate of confusion, and you're wondering about the reasons. Get people to talk through the issues, and support them with your own nonverbal behavior.

Clarifying Interpretations

People often interpret nonverbal behavior incorrectly, but it's possible to improve your batting average. Here are some things to work on if you want to improve your ability to read another's nonverbal communication:

1. *Be tentative.* Don't jump to conclusions and/or stereotype people. Formulate hypotheses carefully; wait and watch people's nonverbal behavior to see if they seem to be supported. ("Maybe she's tense about this assignment. Maybe she's angry at someone. Wait and see.")

2. *Observe people over time.* A nonverbal cue on one occasion won't tell you too much; patterns give you a sense of how an individual uses nonverbal cues.

3. *Look for consistency among an individual's cues.* What nonverbal cues are consistent with each other, and which are consistent with a person's verbal communication?

4. *Look for inconsistency among an individual's cues.* What cues contradict each other; which contradict verbal communication?

5. *Look for interactions in the group.* What kinds of transactions might have triggered an individual's nonverbal behavior?

6. *Be aware of multiple causes.* A person's nonverbal behavior may reflect internal thoughts and feelings or may be in response to multiple cues from members of the group.

7. *Ask for clarification.* If verbal cues and nonverbal cues are contradictory, or if you are puzzled by a nonverbal response, ask for clarification. ("You say you're

okay with this decision, but I hear something unhappy in your voice. Is there something here you're *not* okay with?")

Improving Personal Effectiveness

Improving your communication is a lifelong job, and nonverbal communication is especially demanding. It's hard to identify, and harder to control—but possible. Here are some approaches that can help:

1. *Seek congruity within your messages*. The information and feelings you want to communicate should be consistent with the verbal and nonverbal messages you use to express them. Accurate, assertive communication works when these are all aligned.

2. *Ask friends and family*. Have people observe you and give you feedback about your nonverbal communication. Ask about your habits, what you do, how consistent you are, and how well your nonverbal cues support your verbal messages.

3. *Watch others' responses*. Look for positive, negative, or comprehending responses from others. Ask how they perceived your message.

4. *Use videotaping*. There's no substitute for observing yourself. Look for what you do well; note where your nonverbal messages are clear and consistent; listen to your voice when it provides effective emphasis and tonal qualities. Watch your listening behavior; see if you communicate interest and provide feedback for the speaker. Look for inconsistencies, contradictions, or bad habits as a speaker and a listener.

5. *Decide what to change*. Identify specific things you want to do differently. Ask yourself, "What should I be doing if I stop doing what I want to change?" Practice the new behaviors.

Through these efforts, you can command the effective use of nonverbal communication—from which, you may recall, people derive more than 90 percent of their interpretation of your message.

Summary

We've explored the difficult, culture-bound, gender-influenced, complicated, multichanneled nature of nonverbal communication. Nonverbal cues influence every message and are difficult to decode because they outnumber verbal cues, especially in a group. They may contradict or confirm the words people speak. They are hard to interpret, but they constitute more than 90 percent of a message's meaning to the re-

ceiver. People believe nonverbal cues more than the words people speak, and they often stereotype and judge others on the basis of their nonverbal behavior.

Nonverbal cues come from multiple sources, including the context and the individual's personality, culture, gender, and experiences. Nonverbal communication relates to liking, responsiveness, and power/status issues in team relationships, and much nonverbal communication relates to establishing dominance and submissiveness. These relationships contribute to team patterns, structures, and regulation of communication transactions.

People communicate nonverbally through eyes, body, face, gestures, voice, speech, touch, time, space, and territory. Environments communicate nonverbally through conditions such as aesthetics, temperature, color, sound, light, smell, and technology. Technology affects communication through electronic media and teleconferencing.

Developing the ability to send and receive consistent, reliable nonverbal messages that encourage participation and equality is important to individuals and the team. It can be done by using feedback, becoming aware of the various aspects of nonverbal communication, and developing skills in encoding, decoding, and facilitating understanding of members' nonverbal communication.

Exercises

1. Observe—preferably, videotape—a group of three or four members. Using Form 10.1, chart nonverbal transactions among group members. What patterns did you observe? What did you think specific nonverbal cues revealed about members' feelings/ thoughts? In what ways did you think others' nonverbal or verbal responses showed their interpretations of teammates' nonverbal cues? Which types of nonverbal cues (body, face, gestures, voice, touch, space/territory) had the strongest effects on others' responses?

2. Set up a conference call with two or three teammates. Agree to discuss a topic—it could be class assignments—that requires you to share information and ideas. Talk for at least fifteen minutes. Then get together to discuss the following questions:
   a. Knowing what you know now, what would you do differently to prepare for the conference call?
   b. What advantages and disadvantages, if any, were there in being on the phone instead of talking in person?
   c. How did the lack of visibility affect your understanding of others' messages?

   d. How did your environment during the call affect your communication? Your feelings? Your concentration?

3. You're watching a team of six people interact. Alice, Mary, and Tom sit close together, using eye contact, smiling, and touching one another. Alex remains detached, looks over others' heads when he speaks, and leans or stands over their space. Tanya watches Alex, avoids conversations with other members, ducks her head and drops her eyes when Alex looks at her. Renée tries to force eye contact with Alex, always arrives early and takes the chair with greatest visibility, talks loudly, and leans forward and gestures broadly into the group.

   What's happening? What structure of status, liking, and responsiveness is emerging? Which cues tell you that?

4. Think about your own nonverbal behavior and responses to nonverbal cues in a group. How and to what extent do you think you use nonverbal cues to protect your territory or express liking, responsiveness, or status? In teammates' nonverbal behavior, what makes you comfortable, what makes you uncomfortable, and how do you respond?

FORM   10.1   ▮   OBSERVATION   OF   NONVERBAL   BEHAVIOR   IN   A   GROUP

As you observe a group, chart your observations of individual members' nonverbal behaviors and the way you see others reacting to them. Write the names of members down the side and across the top. When a member provides a nonverbal cue that gets an observable reaction from another member, go to the cell that the two members share: note what the cue was in the top of the cell, and what the reaction was in the bottom of the cell. (You may want to copy this form onto a larger sheet of paper for ease of recording.)

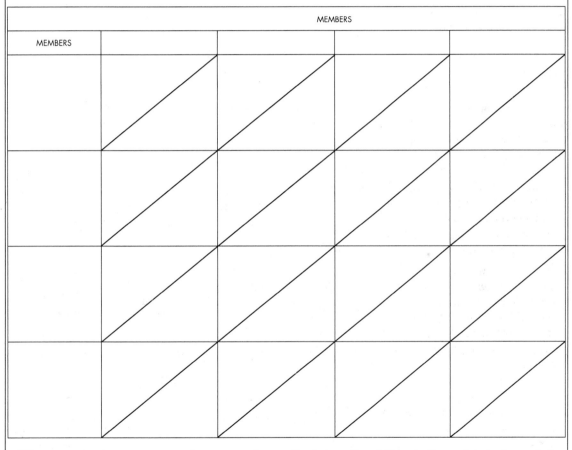

What patterns do you see emerging as you observe the interactions? How do they relate to the verbal interactions that accompanied the nonverbal?

Listening and Questioning: Developing Team Dialogue

"Yes, of *course* I heard you . . . what'd you say?"
Teamwork really goes awry when everybody talks and *nobody's*
listening and questioning.

A meeting that's all talking and no listening can give you a headache. Reflect on this example of a college program committee's deliberations. The members are considering a proposal to allow two radically opposed groups to argue their positions in a debate on campus.

Brenda: I just don't think those people should be allowed on this campus!

Cassie: Oh, there you go again, Brenda. Just because you hate . . .

Tim: How about freedom of speech?

Deirdre: Did you hear about that guy in the student center?

Brian: Yeah. He really went nuts . . .

John: Right, Tim. We've got to let them debate, because . . .

Brenda: Why? They're stupid and people would just come to watch . . .

Deirdre: I guess he was mad because he didn't get to . . .

Brenda: Anyway! They'd just come to watch them be stupid, not to learn anything, and besides, why should groups like that be given attention?

Larry: What? Have we started? I'm sorry, I was reading . . .

Cassie: Well, Brenda, if you feel that way, maybe you should go live in China!

Brenda: That's not fair! I'm just saying . . .

John: Hey, if Brenda feels that strongly about it . . .

Tim: How about freedom of speech? Can we deny them access?

Larry: What did she say?

John: Oh, shut up, Tim. Brenda's got a point . . .

What's happening here? Is anybody really listening? Poor Tim can't get people to think about his issue—no cooperative analysis is going on here—nobody's dealing with Deirdre's side trip (it might relate to the issue, who would know?). John's more interested in soothing Brenda than in resolving the problem; Cassie's more interested in personal attacks on Brenda; we don't know what Brian's interested in; and Larry's lost. Certainly, this committee isn't functioning well.

These people obviously need help. They certainly don't understand how to question and listen to one another to arrive at good decisions, or how to become a team that functions in a positive communication climate and succeeds in its job.

Listening and questioning are extraordinarily important aspects of a team's verbal and nonverbal communication. In this chapter, we explore how they contribute to dialogue

among members and a positive communication climate. As a foundation for listening and questioning, we identify some of the barriers that people build against them and suggest appropriate team norms. The heart of this chapter offers guidelines for active, interactive, empathic, and dialogical approaches to listening and questioning. Through listening and questioning—and listening and questioning some more—members engage in the kind of cooperative analysis and argument that produces clear, valid decisions. We close with a view of how your leadership can guide a team to use these interac-

tions effectively. Our goals are for you to:

1. Understand how listening and questioning are essential to a team's dialogue, climate, cooperative analysis, and success.

2. Know how to build foundations for good listening and questioning.

3. Understand how to use active, interactive, empathic, and dialogical listening and questioning.

4. Know how your leadership can facilitate listening and questioning transactions for your team.

Listening and Questioning in Teams

Listening and questioning are two interdependent communication skills that facilitate the team's transactional and task processes. Through listening and questioning, members actively engage themselves and one another in finding out what each person means, thinks, and feels.

Verbal communication and nonverbal cues convey messages; only listening and questioning provide the ongoing feedback to negotiate what they mean. These processes create the dialogue, climate, and cooperative analysis for individual and team success.

Creating Dialogue

The concept of dialogue underlies good communication in groups and teams. It's the only way group members can cooperatively engage in the analysis and argumentation that guide their way to a good decision. Effective dialogue relies on good listening and questioning.

Dialogue means more than taking turns speaking. It has qualities that bring out the best in people as they develop meanings and insights together. It involves sharing ideas, listening, paraphrasing, questioning, adding on, changing—until common meaning emerges.

Sometimes people think of dialogue as involving only two people. Certainly it's easier to develop a give-and-take of authentic, open communication in private exchanges between two people. But Johannesen (1990) notes that philosophers such as Buber, Howe, Jaspers, and Rogers believe that dialogue happens in many arenas, including groups that meet over time (pp. 68–69). We think it's essential to view team communication in this way, but it takes members' conscientious effort and commitment.

Much of what we have to say about listening and questioning relates to what Stewart and Thomas (1990) call **dialogic listening**. In dialogic listening, the participants immerse themselves in creating and developing ideas *together*. It is "listening that values and builds mutuality, requires active involvement, is genuine, and grows out of a belief in and commitment to synergy—the idea that the whole actually can be more than the sum of its parts" (p. 193).

It is no accident that we talk about creating dialogue, dialogical ethics, and dialogic listening in this book. These closely related concepts stem from philosophers who assume that people are capable of respecting each other and themselves, of seeking truth and justice together, of caring about what they do and how they do it. Those assumptions underlie dialogical ethics, which provide a way of examining the attitudes and behaviors of a team in action, and dialogic listening, which provides a way of developing dialogue to create new meanings among people.

That philosophy underlies everything we'll talk about in this chapter. Later, we'll talk about approaches to listening and questioning, including suggestions Stewart and Thomas make for dialogic listening, but first let's examine how listening and questioning influence a team's communication climate.

Creating Climates

We described supportive climates and defensive climates in Chapter 9. Good listening and questioning help develop the former; bad listening and questioning virtually ensure the latter. Supportive climates occur, in part, because people listen and question in ways that develop trust, that confirm each member's worth, and that commit members to finding shared meanings.

When you know your teammates really listen to you, when they ask you questions supportively—questions that enable you to make yourself understood and to think clearly—you feel you can trust them. That trustworthiness reduces the amount of risk you must take to communicate and encourages you to share what you know openly. When they listen and ask questions that indicate your ideas are worth thinking about, then that confirms you as a person. Maybe Carl Rogers (1990) speaks for all of us when he says, "When somebody really listens to me, it feels damned good" (p. 439).

■ SUSPEND JUDGMENT

Managers are called on daily to evaluate product lines, markets, numbers, and, of course, people. And in turn, they are evaluated on how well they do. The danger, then, is that this bias for judging will subvert a manager's inclination to listen carefully and, in doing so, sabotage his or her ability to make accurate business and people judgments.

Managers may be tempted to resolve this paradox as an either/or. And for good reason: rarely in their training have the two mind-sets been reconciled. Business schools, for the most part, still reinforce evaluative listening; they teach students to defend their own positions while scoring points against others'. And those behavioral experts who do focus on nonevalu-

ative listening tend to focus almost exclusively on the importance of empathy. But if one thing has made itself clear in the past 40 years, it is that managers must have the capacity to do both. They must recognize that to make judgments, you must suspend judgment.

Reprinted by permission of *Harvard Business Review*. An excerpt from "Retrospective Commentary," by John J. Gabarro, UPS Foundation Professor of Management at the Harvard Business School, in "Barriers and Gateways to Communication," by Carl R. Rogers and F. J. Roethlisberger, November/December 1991. Copyright © 1991 by the President and Fellows of Harvard College; all rights reserved.

Effective listening and questioning develop a climate in which people are committed to developing shared meanings. When you listen to one another, you make a commitment—a commitment to make the effort required to understand one another. Stewart and Thomas (1990) say that in "the most fruitful and satisfying conversations, our listening is focused less on *re*producing what's 'inside' the other person and more on co-producing, with the other person, mutual meanings *between* us" (p. 193). This mutuality enriches the communication climate and makes it healthy.

Listening and questioning are almost absent in defensive climates. Sometimes they're abused, becoming tools to compete with others for attention, to win points, or to express hostility and judgment of others. When members can neither listen nor question, the defensive climate escalates because information is not clarified, meanings are not shared, and problems are not solved.

When these conditions afflict a team, it ignores members' ideas. Members withdraw, feeling they are not welcome, and the team loses their input. The team listens to no one, questions no one, and soon not one member cares to bring in ideas or information. They feel the team isn't worth their effort. The team that shows these signs is operating in a poor climate; it's a team whose members are blocked from listening—and don't dare to question.

In a climate that bad, you're not going to find clear thinking or cooperative analysis.

Creating Cooperative Analysis

As a team, you are working toward a set of goals; you have a vision; you have a task. You're trying to be vigilant. Vigilance, as you remember from Chapter 8, suggests that a group must exercise watchfulness in all of its task processes. It emphasizes the quality of your interactions as you set goals and criteria, analyze your information and problems, generate solutions, and make decisions (Gouran & Hirokawa, 1983; Hirokawa & Scheerhorn, 1986; Janis, 1989a). Quality interactions involve **cooperative analysis,** a process of listening and questioning that make it possible for team members to think together—critically, creatively, analytically—and to test the logic and validity of their arguments.

A team's advantage is its variety of viewpoints, experiences, backgrounds, and ways of seeing. But that is no advantage at all if members cannot probe others' meanings to arrive at new or better understandings. Excellent listening and perceptive, analytical questioning accomplish that goal.

Creating Success

For a team, success is creating a positive climate, developing strong transactional processes, and achieving its goals effectively. For the individual team member, success is all of those things, plus achieving his or her own personal goals.

Listening and questioning skills help to achieve all those objectives. As an individual, you should know that students who are good listeners are more successful than those who are not. They actually succeed beyond the level their standardized IQ tests would predict (Legge, 1971).

There's no question that listening is essential to success in the workplace. It has been identified as one of the more important skills for entry-level positions, for managerial competence, for job success, for career competence—and for corporate excellence (Wolvin & Coakley, 1991, p. 153). As organizations focus increasingly on teams and teamwork, they become progressively more convinced of the importance of listening skills. In one survey of the 500 largest U.S. corporations, more than 50 percent of those responding reported that they provide listening training for their employees (Wolvin & Coakley, 1991).

Foundations for Listening and Questioning

Good listening and questioning are very difficult in teams. Members attend to and process a number of messages concurrently. Several people may speak at once, or overlap or interrupt one another. Each message has a variety of possible interpretations, and individual members bring a multitude of differing motivations, perceptions, and objectives to the situation. Finally, any group situation has multiple distractions. All of these factors make it difficult to concentrate and to comprehend another's ideas.

Barriers to Listening and Questioning

Individuals and teams put up a variety of barriers that can prevent cooperative listening and questioning. Recognizing them is the first step to tearing them down.

Individual Barriers   A basic barrier to finding out what another means may be that a person simply doesn't know how to listen and question well. Rarely have people been taught these skills, and, like any other skills, they need to be learned.

Another problem is that people are often taught *not* to listen. Bolton (1979) suggests that

most of us receive a very rigorous early training in nonlistening . . . parents say things like:

"We don't listen to those things in our family."

"Don't pay any attention to him."

"Pretend you don't notice."

"Don't take it so seriously."

"He didn't mean what he said."

"Don't give them the satisfaction of knowing that you heard them." (p. 176)

This type of advice is meant to protect individuals from discomfort; or perhaps from an attack on one's sense of self; or from information that might cause psychological conflict among values, beliefs, and behaviors. But all that self-protection reinforces bad listening habits.

People have other bad habits that block listening. See if any of these barriers are in your head:

Zeroing in on one idea that you want to rebut or support. People tend to start mentally rehearsing their responses and miss everything else the speaker says.

Stereotyping or labeling the speaker or the subject. When you label according to preconceived ideas, or by some sign that you associate with a negative idea, you block out what you might be able to learn.

Judging the speaker rather than trying to understand the message. Focusing on an individual's presentation, teamwork, or personal attributes that aren't relevant to the task interferes with understanding the ideas being expressed.

Reacting to loaded words. Every person has a knee-jerk reaction to some specific words. You won't see the rest of the picture if you push your mind's pause button and stay focused on the loaded word.

Being disinterested in the topic, attended by mental comments such as "boring" or "I couldn't care less." This ensures you won't find anything of interest and won't engage with anything the speaker says.

Being distracted. If you think about what you're having for dinner, what's on the test next period, or how cute the person is who just walked by the door, you won't hear what your teammate says.

Distracting others. Making comments or carrying on side conversations not only keeps you from getting the message, it ensures that others don't either.

Assuming interpretations or details about the speaker's information. It's easy to fill in what the person didn't say, and the fillers may be wrong. Don't assume—ask.

Fake listening, also known as the "wide-asleep listener." You nod brightly, look directly at the speaker, and dream on into oblivion. You also gain no information.

Bad habits aside, the sheer volume of demands on you as a listener can be a barrier in itself. Think about a day when you must listen to, question, analyze, and organize material from three reports to your team; material from two lectures; and information for three exams. Students suffer this "information overload" frequently.

Information overload and the need to organize so many ideas get in the way of processing and retaining what you hear (Beatty, 1981; Benoit & Benoit, 1991). Anxiety or apprehension about the situation, about the message, or about other things in your life can also interfere (Preiss & Wheeless, 1989; Fitch-Hauser, Barker, & Hughes, 1990).

Listening and questioning responsively take intellectual, emotional, and physical effort. As a student, you probably spend most of your classroom time listening. At work, North American employees typically spend about 60 percent of their communication time listening to others (Brown, 1982), and the amount of time a person spends listening increases with his or her responsibility. Asking questions to clarify information and understanding helps you overcome some of those barriers and arrive at mutual meanings.

Team Barriers   Teams build barriers against good listening and questioning in a number of ways; not surprisingly, they're the same ways teams build negative communication climates.

A negative team climate produces norms against dialogue. Members constantly interrupt one another. They use questions that aren't really questions—they're bullying, discounting, or ignoring statements with question marks at the end. Humor is sarcastic and cutting. Support is weak. People listen only for material with which to put someone else down. In a group where norms are poor, you frequently see people working against one another.

Defensive norms often arise from competition among members. People become motivated to score points against others, and the team can't seem to establish a norm for cooperation and mutual support. As long as that continues, a team will not develop a positive climate—nor will anybody be able to listen to anybody.

Norms for Listening and Questioning

With effort and open discussion, a team can develop norms for good listening—a few clearly understood standards that the team observes in its transactions. These norms might include:

1. Take turns in speaking; pay attention to nonverbal cues indicating that others want to speak.
2. Listen openly and supportively; don't cut others off, put them down, or interrupt.

SPINNING   PEOPLE   MAGIC   AT   MILLIKEN

Ten years ago Milliken & Co., a major textile manufacturer long recognized for quality products and its use of state-of-the-art technology, asked itself why some Japanese competitors achieved higher quality, less waste, greater productivity, and fewer customer complaints while using technology less advanced than Milliken's. The reasons, company executives found, lay in management approaches and in personnel practices that, along with technology, drive improvements in quality and efficiency.

"I remember a meeting in which a manager looked at me and said, 'There are only five managers in this room who know how to listen' (and there were over 400 people in the room)," recalls Roger Milliken, chairman and CEO. "That was a disturbing eyeopener, and I believed him. At the end of the conference and after some practice, I jumped up on one of those little banquet chairs and, raising my right arm, asked them to raise theirs and repeat after me: 'I will listen; I will not shoot the messen-

ger; I recognize that management is the problem.' It was a breakthrough moment."

[Milliken has flattened its management structure, turned over work to self-managed teams, and learned to listen to its employees. The company increased productivity by 42%, increased sales significantly, and was awarded the Malcolm Baldridge National Quality Award in 1989.]

An excerpt from J. G. Bowles, "The Human Side of Quality." Reprinted by permission from a paid advertising section in *Fortune* magazine, September 24, 1990.

3. Help others get the floor. Ask for attention to others; ask others to speak; ask the team to listen when someone is being ignored.
4. Ask questions that help others clarify ideas and information.
5. Use questions supportively. Focus on content, ideas, analysis—not on the person.

By observing these standards, you help create a positive communication climate. As a team member, you are encouraged to share your ideas and your feelings because you know that others really are listening to you, that they want to negotiate a shared meaning with you. Fortunately, these norms—and the necessary skills to make them work—can be developed by individuals and by teams.

Approaches to Listening and Questioning

Every team—and every team member—experiences times when listening and questioning to understand another is hard work. Some writers advise people to ask, "What's in it for me?" when they are about to listen to someone else. That's good advice, but we'd expand it. Find what's in it for you, for the person to whom you're listening, for the relationship between you, and for the team as a whole. All four can motivate your listening concurrently.

A member of your team may be reporting information that she or he worked hard to get. You listen intently and question probingly because (a) you need to understand the information, (b) you want that person to know that his or her work is appreciated, (c) you want to build stronger bonds with your teammate, and (d) your listening, as part of the team's transactional processes, contributes to the communication climate and synergy needed for the task.

To accomplish those purposes, you will at times listen and question silently, but actively; at other times, you will listen and question interactively, empathically, and dialogically. We're going to talk about developing each of those skills.

Active Listening

Active listening refers to the processing that goes on in your head. In active listening you are engaging with the speaker at an intellectual level. You're not asking the speaker questions—but you're analyzing and asking questions of yourself. You're "tuning in."

Active listening involves capitalizing on your thought speed to process information. There's a band of available time between the rate at which people speak (about 100 to 150 words per minute) and the rate at which listeners can process information (500 to 600 words per minute). That differential is a window of opportunity for distractions and daydreaming, or for information processing and analysis. Active listening commits the time to a number of deliberate behaviors:

Get set physically for listening. Place yourself where you can see and respond to the teammate who is speaking. Use nonverbal cues such as leaning forward, maintaining eye contact, and nodding at appropriate times; these help your teammate, and also help you to concentrate.

Screen out distractions. Adopt a mind set that says, "Person at work. Do not disturb." If your mind does wander, pull it back quickly. If the thought is compelling, jot it down for future consideration. This frees you to get back to full listening. Take control of your listening environment. Close doors or turn down stereos when they distract.

Focus your listening to get main points and concepts. Don't get stuck on small details. If a detail worries you, make a quick note to clarify it later, then get away from it.

Organize and key the information while you're listening. Connect thoughts logically, synthesize concepts, use key words, and make associations with ideas so they make sense to you. Even if your teammate has provided you with excellent organization and explanations, connect the ideas in your mind so you can work with and remember them. Create analogies and metaphors, or connect ideas with familiar examples.

Analyze the information mentally. Sort through what you're hearing. Ask yourself questions about the material; note discrepancies for future analysis; look for the evidence, the values, the assumptions, and the arguments the speaker makes.

Each of these suggestions involves a very active mind and physically attentive body; what they don't involve is direct verbal interaction with the speaker. In a group situation, you often need to listen silently—but actively—as another member makes a report or develops an idea. Active listening then leads to interacting with the speaker and with other team members.

Interactive Questioning

Interactive questioning focuses discussion on clarifying, probing, analyzing, and following up information your teammate has expressed. It means applying your analytical and critical thinking skills—not, we remind you, critical of people, but critical in your investigation of problems, causes and effects, information and evidence, proposals and projects.

By asking questions of a teammate who has presented information or opinions, you can help to develop a positive climate and work toward your goals. But questioning goes much further than that. As you think about the discussion and the processes of the team, you'll want to address questions to the team as a whole. These questions have several purposes:

1. To clarify information that is not clear. ("Can we go over that point again, please; it's not clear to me.")
2. To expand information that is incomplete. ("Does anybody have information on this?" "How can we find this out?")
3. To get people to think critically about information or ideas. ("Anybody have any thoughts about this?" "How does this line up with our criteria?" "What is the logic—rationale, evidence, support, justification—behind this?")
4. To improve task processes. ("How should we approach this job?" "Anybody see a way to move ahead faster?" "How do we get around this roadblock?")
5. To improve transactional processes. ("What can we do to improve our morale?" "How can we be sure that everyone's involved here?" "Any ideas on how to manage this conflict?" "How do you feel about this issue?" "What are the ethical implications?" "Is everybody comfortable with this?")

Questioning the team in this way will help all of you to keep on target, to examine information and ideas, and to ensure that your transactional processes are working well. Here are some basic guidelines to keep you on track in your questioning:

Test the reasoning and the evidence. With your questions, test the connections among fact, inference, and judgment. Look for the fallacies and correct them, but be sure you keep the focus on the issues and not on the people.

Ask the questions that provide analysis. Phrase questions that get to cause and effect, tests of good solutions, criteria. Focus them in such a way that the issues can be discussed without putting the speaker on the defensive.

Ask the hard questions, but ask them the easy way. Ask about underlying assumptions and values, about ethical issues, about the reliability, validity, and credibility of sources—but ask them by relating issues to criteria, goals, and values the team has established and not to individuals or personal motives.

Know what you want to ask. Be clear about what you're looking for. If you're not sure, say so and ask for clarification.

Be as specific as possible. Be clear in your terms; ask just what you need to know. If you must precede the question with an example, observation, or hypothesis, keep it clear, objective, and concise. Don't make speeches that pretend to be questions. If you have a point to make, make it in discussion—don't tack a question mark on it.

Ask one question at a time. If you have a two-part question, preview it: "I have a two-part question. Part one is. . . . Part two is. . . ." This helps the speaker to answer, and keeps issues clear.

Confirm information with feedback questions. If you think you understand, but you want to be sure, state what you believe the speaker said and ask if it's correct.

Ask in ways that help the speaker answer. "Could you please clarify that?" requires the speaker to grope around for a way to meet your request. Good ways to help a speaker clarify a point include asking for examples; asking for definitions; paraphrasing what you think the speaker said and asking if you're correct; giving your own examples or analogies and asking if they represent what she or he said.

Probe for further information. Ask (tactfully) for supporting evidence for a statement; probe for assumptions of facts or values that the speaker may have made; ask about ethical issues or dilemmas. All of these can be done with minimal defensiveness if asked in a supportive spirit of finding out rather than in an argumentative spirit of winning.

Listen to questions others ask. Someone else may ask your questions. The goal is to analyze ideas and reach shared understanding of messages, not to conduct your own personal interrogation. Be sure to listen to those answers.

The entire nation saw horrible examples of questioning in the infamous U.S. Senate hearings on Clarence Thomas's appointment to the Supreme Court in 1991. Senators violated every rule of good questioning. They made nineteen-minute speeches and then, in the last minute of their allotted twenty-minute period, asked the respondent a question that forced him or her to agree with everything the senator had just said. It was so embarrassing that afterward some senators apologized to the nation for the behavior. The worst of it is, this kind of questioning does not arrive at understanding, clarity, or truth. It subverts the process.

Active listening and interactive questioning require special skills that need thought and practice. Listening to the answers and responding to the nonverbal cues require empathy.

Empathic Listening and Questioning

Some definitions of empathic listening focus on it exclusively as something you do to help another person by hearing and reflecting back what is behind his or her words. That puts empathic listening very much in the emotional helping category—something you do in a support group, or as a professional counselor with a client, or as a dear friend.

If, however, you think of using empathic skills in listening and questioning to assure that the transactional processes are meeting individual as well as team needs; if you think of **empathic listening** as a way of helping you identify personal or interpersonal issues *as they impact on the team or the task*, then empathic listening and questioning are essential to team processes.

Empathy is understanding the ideas and feelings of another. Teams need to understand each member well, and all need to understand the negotiated meanings resulting from the team's processes.

At the same time you're exercising active and interactive skills, you're listening and questioning empathically. It's a matter of picking up what a teammate is feeling while you're processing the information in his or her message. This enriches your understanding and enables you to support and question the speaker in ways that facilitate the development of mutual meanings.

A few guidelines can help you to listen empathically and interactively at the same time:

Tune in to the speaker. Watch your teammate's nonverbal and verbal cues. Be aware of body, face, gestures, and voice as they convey emotion. Be sensitive to the ways she or he phrases ideas, or to cues that indicate defensiveness, threat, or some emotional response to a subject.

Be sensitive to "ism" issues—sexism, racism, classism, handicapism. It may not even occur to other members that a teammate might be bothered by a racist joke, a sexist assumption, a cultural slur, a power play, or an offhand comment that reflects on his or her particular style, affiliation, or even disability. People often don't recognize these abrasive events unless they happen to hit their own, personal, raw nerve. An empathic listener will be alert, however, to others' responses to unintentional or intentional insults.

Be tentative with your empathy. Recognize that you never know exactly how someone feels. Your caring, empathy, sensitivity, and intelligence give you an awareness that a person is feeling something and, possibly, an ability to share some part of that feeling.

Be careful in communicating your empathy nonverbally. Emotional responses are complex, personal, and private. Even when you feel intensely with teammates, you have to respect their privacy. Use nonverbal communication—eye contact, body posture, face, voice—to communicate that you are "with" them, but don't push, and do be sensitive to their preferences. Let others establish their own distances and degrees of contact.

Be careful in establishing your empathy verbally. Avoid saying "I know how you feel," or "I had the exact same experience," then using it as a transition for your own ten-minute story. Reflect carefully what you think a teammate has said—"You sound as though that made you pretty angry" or "That must make you feel pretty good"—but don't project your interpretations beyond the speak-

What types of listening and questioning are occurring in this group? What is going on that leads you to those conclusions? (Photograph © 1989 Jeffry W. Myers/Stock, Boston)

er's own statements. Bolton (1990) suggests four types of door openers for further understanding:

1. A description of the other's body language ("You look bright and happy today!")
2. An invitation to talk or to continue talking ("Please go on . . ." "Care to talk about it?")
3. Silence—giving the other time to consider whether and how she or he wants to talk.
4. Attending—eye contact, posture demonstrating your interest. (p. 185)

Question carefully to develop empathy. With open, supportive questions, you can develop a shared base for mutual empathy among members of the group. This includes paraphrasing what you think a teammate is saying, and asking for confirmation to correct your impression. You also can ask for examples, or explanations, of the other person's feelings or ideas. In the proper context, you can share your own experiences to help bring together a shared empathy.

These approaches help clarify issues clouded by personal feelings or interpersonal differences. That can be important to team syntality and to achieving the team's goals.

Finally, active, interactive, and empathic listening and questioning are at their best when they are part of listening dialogically.

Dialogic Listening and Questioning

Dialogic listening is a process of "sculpting" ideas, as if two or more people had an uncut piece of marble and, together, they chipped and shaped away at it until they created a three-dimensional sculpture of meaning. It involves listening, questioning, paraphrasing, building on one another's ideas (Stewart & Thomas, 1990). Dialogic listening brings all of the skills we've talked about into one framework that is particularly valid for team communication.

Stewart and Thomas identify four distinct features of dialogic listening:

1. It focuses on *ours*. The entire process is mutual—not my interests and your interests, but *our* meaning.
2. It is *open-ended and playful*. Remember how creativity and eliminating mind blocks rely on a group's ability to open up and play? So does dialogic listening.
3. It centers ideas and issues *in front of* the participants, not on what's behind their responses. It is not, in other words, psychotherapy in the small group.
4. It deals in *presentness*, rather than in the past or in the future.

In a team, as members work together to build insights, the creative and analytical potential is enormous. In sculpting meaning, Stewart and Thomas suggest that listeners and talkers apply these conversational strategies:

"Say more." Encourage the other person to develop thoughts and suggestions, think deeper, identify more possibilities, clarify and expand ideas.

Run with the metaphor. This may remind you of the creative thinking strategies we talked about earlier. Grab a metaphor and develop it, play with it, use it for deeper analysis.

Paraphrase plus. Put another's statement in your own words, but develop the ideas. Then ask for a paraphrase of what you have said. As you do this, you begin to discover ideas that each of you may have had but didn't recognize. Participants truly create a meaning together.

Build context. Explain your frame of reference for what you have to say, and get others to explain their contexts. Help the team understand the variables that shape each individual's meanings, so you can shape mutual meanings out of them.

These approaches to "sculpting" meaning take time and commitment. Members have to learn how to do them together; otherwise, some people will think others are nuts ("What do you mean, 'Say more'?" "Run where with my metaphor?") and members may get impatient with the process. Dialogic listening is a skill that members learn, develop, and use together because they are motivated to search for more complete, more mutual interpretations and because they want to build a team that analyzes issues effectively.

You can see the way active listening leads to interactive questioning, and how these skills can be expanded into emphatic listening and dialogic listening in Figure 11.1. When you use these approaches to listening and questioning well, the

FIGURE 11.1

Relationships among types of listening and questioning

Active Listening ⟶ **Interactive Questioning** ⟶

Active Listening
Focus on gaining and analyzing information given by a speaker

Silent, asking questions mentally, responding nonverbally but not orally

Interactive Questioning
Focus on helping the speaker to give clear, accurate information and analysis

Asking questions for clarification, explanation, detail

Empathic Listening and Questioning
Focus on the speaker's feelings and experience
Reflecting the speaker's feelings
Supporting verbally/nonverbally
Asking questions to understand what the speaker feels
Paraphrasing for understanding and/or clarification

Dialogical Listening and Questioning
Focus on mutual negotiation of meaning in the present
Encouraging each other to develop ideas, use metaphorical thinking
Questioning to clarify or extend ideas
Paraphrasing ideas and developing them further

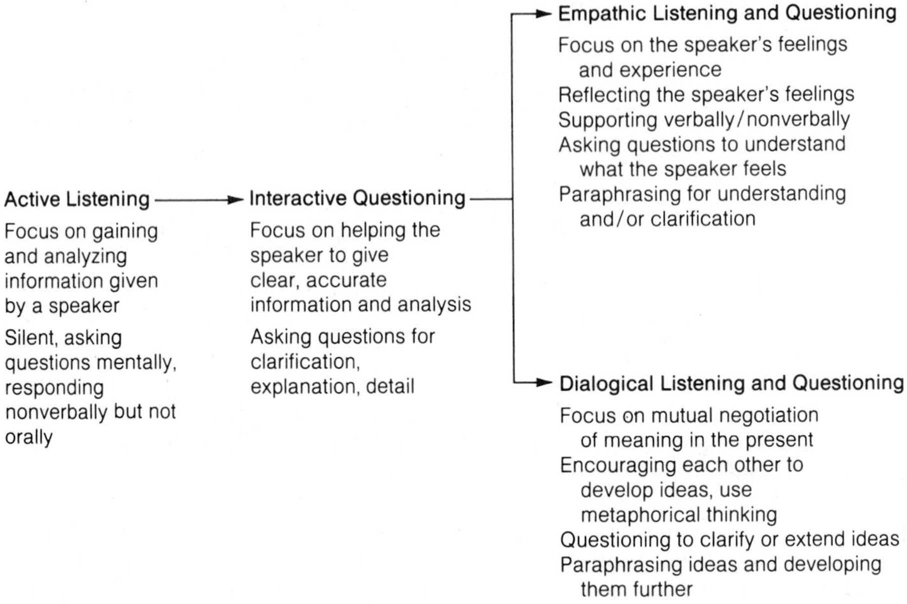

transactional processes produce interpersonal understanding and team cohesiveness, understanding and analysis, creativity and ideation. They help to build a team and reach its goals.

Leadership in Listening and Questioning

One of your leadership functions is to help team members listen to one another. You can use your thought speed to observe the members of the group at the same time you're listening. Your objective is to help members listen and speakers communicate to ensure their full participation and responsibility.

Facilitate Turn-Taking

People take turns talking in groups. In Chapter 10, we mentioned some of the nonverbal cues that are used to signal a change in turns. Each member has to be alert to those cues and be sure they work.

Generally, in this society, you signal that you've finished speaking by dropping your voice, pausing, and either dropping your eyes or, if you want to pass the turn to a specific person, making direct eye contact with him or her.

If you don't want to pick up the turn, you drop your eyes or look elsewhere. If you want to get a word in edgewise, you lean forward, open your mouth, perhaps reach out with a gesture, maybe make some vocal sounds. You may be driven to say, "Excuse me, please . . ." "I've simply got to say this . . ." or "Let me get this thought in here, please. . . ."

Turn-Taking Blinders   Unfortunately, a number of things can put blinders on people when it comes to giving and taking turns in conversation. People who are vision- or hearing-impaired can miss the cues. Or a person's background or culture may have given him or her a different approach to turn-taking. Men in this culture overlap and interrupt much more than women do, for example. A person from an Asian culture may have been brought up to wait—forever, if necessary—for a long pause and a signal from a person of higher status before speaking up. Another person may have been raised with a norm for interrupting loudly whenever the spirit moves. To others in the group, the first person may seem passive and disinterested, and the second may seem rude and unfeeling. The fact is that neither one understands the norms and cues for turn-taking in the predominant culture.

It may be that the speaker, for similar reasons, is unaware of the signals that others want a turn to speak. Sometimes, a speaker would love to turn the floor over to someone else but goes on and on, desperately waiting for someone to interrupt, because he or she doesn't know how to stop. These are times, Elgin (1989) suggests, to "help the helpless" (p. 215).

Ways to Facilitate Listening and Turn-Taking   Keep an eye on people's nonverbal as well as their verbal behavior. If others seem confused or frustrated, it's a good time for you to help. You can ask a clarifying question or help another person get the floor to do so. It's not hard to do this with tact. Suppose Joe looks confused. You can make a statement such as, "I'm not sure I'm clear on this," then turn to Joe and say, "Have you got it, or are you confused, too?" This allows Joe to express his doubts without looking like a fool. If Joe has got it, or pretends he has, that's okay. You've opened the floor to questions, and nobody loses.

If a speaker flounders and can't shut up, that's a good time to interrupt politely, "Excuse me, Shirley—would you mind if I added something here?" or "Just a second, Marty—if you don't mind, let's hear what other people think about this . . ."

If you see another person trying to say something, and being cut off repeatedly, you can interrupt (still politely) and turn the floor over to her or him. If it's appropriate, a little humor can work. "Hey, Toni, time out! I think Elyse has tried about ten times to say something—c'mon, Elyse, what have you got to say?"

Usually, interrupting is considered rude, thoughtless, and disruptive—but not always. Sometimes interruptions are brief supportive statements ("Yeah, right, I absolutely agree with you!") or quick supplements ("Sure—remember what happened in class the other day?") from which the first speaker continues his or her contribution.

Other times, interrupting serves a turn-taking purpose. Hawkins (1991) found that if you interrupt a speaker unsuccessfully—that is, you disrupt his or her talk, but the person picks up and continues—then you are likely to be the next speaker in the discussion. Perhaps your interruption somehow establishes in the minds of other members your right to be next. Whatever the reason, a careful interruption can sometimes get you in when the speaker does stop. Then you can either speak yourself, or turn the floor over to someone who has not been able to get a turn.

Interrupting should be used carefully, as a way of facilitating turn-taking when other means won't work. Used excessively, interrupting is a self-centered exercise in disruption, and it reduces your credibility with the team.

Distractions and Constant Interruptions   If the system is breaking down—if members interrupt each other, don't let a person finish his or her thought, go off on tangents, or otherwise distract each other from listening—you can help bring attention back to the subject and the member who was speaking.

One way of doing this is to ask the speaker a question that focuses attention back on the content. You might say something like, "We've talked about so many things here, I need to find out where we are. Let me summarize what you've said, John . . ." You follow this with a very brief paraphrase of what the speaker has said—which serves to get the group back in focus—and add, "Is that about right? Okay, thanks—then please go on. . . ."

If the discussion is completely out of hand, and nobody's listening to anybody, it's time to ask for a time-out to talk about the team's transactional processes. You can make descriptive observations of the norms that seem to be operating, and try to set a new norm for turn-taking and listening. Again, it takes tact—you have to describe the problem without blaming people—but it can be done, and somebody's got to do it if a team's going to work together. That's leadership.

All of these concerns about sharing, listening, and sculpting meanings together are part of what we talked about, in Chapter 2, as an ethic of team process. Another leadership function any member can fill is assessing how well the team is fulfilling that ethic.

Test the Ethics of Team Processes

At every juncture of a team's work, questions of ethics arise. Because ethical issues are related to individuals' values and beliefs, they strike right to the core of who a person believes himself or herself to be. That's why a team needs to be especially sensitive to those kinds of questions.

An ethical process is one in which a team shows respect to every member, listens to every member, enhances members' self-worth, and is concerned for all who might be affected by its decisions. To conduct its transactional processes in a way that reflects such a dialogical perspective, members must use their questioning and listening skills to explore issues responsibly and to arrive at ethical decisions.

Summary

Listening to one another and supporting one another are critical to a team's climate, dialogue, cooperative analysis, and success. We've examined the foundations of good listening and questioning, as well as barriers that both individuals and teams put up. We've suggested that teams set norms for listening and questioning, and that members develop the abilities to listen and question.

Active, interactive, empathic, and dialogic listening and questioning work together in a team. Active listening involves the concentration, commitment, and intense involvement of the listener with the speaker's content. Interactive questioning confirms, clarifies, probes, and analyzes information, and empathic listening seeks to understand and confirm teammates' feelings. Dialogic listening involves all these skills in a mutual, creative process of sculpting meanings through talking, listening, and questioning.

You can exercise leadership by facilitating turn-taking and discussion so that listening, questioning, and talking can be fully participative. Your leadership is important, too, in assessing the ethics of the group's transactional and task processes.

Exercises

1. Either with a group of which you are now a member outside of class, or with a class team, do the following:

    Using Form 11.1, have each member evaluate the group's listening and questioning behavior. Then discuss the evaluations.

    Where do members agree? Disagree? What accounts for the disagreements? How do listening and questioning relate to the climate in the group? To the dialogical ethics of the group's processes and decision making? What's good, what's bad, what should be improved? How?

2. Observe and evaluate a televised, taped, or live group discussion in terms of barriers to good listening and questioning. Use Form 11.2 to record the barriers you detect, as well as the barrier-reducing processes. What suggestions can you offer to improve this group's listening and questioning?

3. Practice dialogic listening and questioning. Meet with three or four other people, and select one of these topics for discussion:

    What should be the U.S. government's role in citizens' health care?

    What should be the policy of the United States on pornography?

    What should be the trade relationship between the United States and other countries?

    Now discuss the question, following these rules and procedures:

    a. One person explains her or his views on the question.

    b. Another person *paraphrases* the speaker's statement—not repeating it, but summarizing the meaning. Others may also paraphrase if they think something needs clarification, or they may ask the original speaker if the paraphrase is correct.

    c. Any member now adds to the speaker's thoughts ("paraphrase plus"), and/or creates a metaphor to take the idea further ("run with the metaphor"), or asks the first speaker to keep talking ("say more").

    d. Once another full statement is made by anyone in the group, someone must paraphrase and start the process again.

    Keep working at this process until everyone has acquired new insights into ideas, feelings, and/or the process itself. Then discuss:

    What did you learn from the discussion?

    How, when, and to what effect did assumptions and values surface?

    Which points raised questions of ethical choices or dilemmas?

    When and how did new insights emerge?

    What got in the way?

    What barriers to thinking broke down, when, and why?

F O R M 11.1 ▮ L I S T E N I N G A N D Q U E S T I O N I N G I N T E A M S A S S E S S M E N T

Individually, check off the extent to which each statement describes your team's communication. Then compare and discuss your responses.

The members of the team:

	ALWAYS	SOMETIMES	NEVER
1. Listen and question cooperatively for critical analysis of issues.	☐	☐	☐
2. Negotiate meanings by openly sharing values and assumptions.	☐	☐	☐
3. Convey empathy and trust with sensitivity and care.	☐	☐	☐
4. Play with ideas and metaphors to find meanings together.	☐	☐	☐
5. Monitor turn-taking, making sure everyone gets to be heard.	☐	☐	☐
6. Break down ambiguity with clear language and questioning.	☐	☐	☐
7. Test the ethics of team processes by questioning and listening.	☐	☐	☐
8. Help one another to clarify and elaborate ideas.	☐	☐	☐
9. Use listening and questioning to help less dominant members be heard.	☐	☐	☐
10. Listen to people of minority cultures and both genders.	☐	☐	☐

What this team does well in listening and questioning is:

What this team needs to work on in listening and questioning is:

FORM 11.2 ■ OBSERVATION OF GROUP LISTENING AND QUESTIONING	

As you watch a meeting, record each time you observe each of these barriers and barrier-reducing processes:

BARRIERS

1. Making sarcastic, "put-down" remarks	
2. Interrupting abruptly	
3. Ignoring a person's turn to speak	
4. Asking loaded questions	
5. Stereotyping and judging a speaker	
6. Criticizing a person (rather than a problem)	
7. Creating distractions	
8. Reacting to loaded words	
9. Rebutting instead of listening	
10. Focusing on details, missing concepts	

DIALOGICAL PROCESSES THAT BREAK DOWN BARRIERS

11. Helping a member get the floor	
12. Asking questions that show empathy	
13. Giving a speaker nonverbal support	
14. Paraphrasing and confirming	
15. Asking clarifying questions	
16. Asking questions that test reasoning and evidence without attacking people	
17. Asking probing questions for information	
18. Asking questions about a speaker's context	
19. Supporting a speaker with self-disclosure	
20. Testing ethics of the team's processes	

Challenges to Leaders and Leadership

Teams and Designated Leaders: Fulfilling Role Expectations

"What this team needs is a real leader!"
Okay, what is a *real* leader, and what does a real leader *do*?

Ever try to identify a "real" leader? Where do you look? In politics or government? In business or at work? In sports, perhaps? Maybe in your family? When we ask our students to think about this, they find examples from all of these areas, but they can't agree on anyone who meets their criteria of a national leader.

It's popular, at every level of human interaction, to grouse about the deficit of leadership or about the crying need for "a real leader." This seems to indicate that people want someone to tell them what to do, to inspire them, to motivate them, to solve problems for them, or to provide them with a direction in which to go.

Are those the things that leaders do? Maybe identifying a leader is like defining pornography: it's hard to define, but you know it when you see it. In this chapter, we look at leaders—who they are, how they got their jobs, and what is expected of them. We explore their sources of power, the ways in which they lead, their responsibilities, and how you can develop the skills to be an effective leader. This chapter will help you:

1. Know some basic concepts about leaders and leadership.

2. Understand how leaders get their positions.

3. Recognize how expectations affect a leader's success.

4. Perceive how leaders use and abuse sources of power.

5. Identify styles and approaches to leading.

6. Discern a leader's tasks and responsibilities.

7. Learn ways to increase your effectiveness as a leader.

259

Leaders and Leadership

In Chapter 2, we talked about leadership as the responsibility of every member in the group. We defined leadership as "verbal and nonverbal communication behavior that influences a team's transactional and task processes in achieving members' and the team's needs and goals." Although every member should serve the many functions of leadership, groups often have one or more designated leaders charged with specific expectations and responsibilities.

A leader, according to Hosking (1988), provides organization and structure in a process by which "social order is negotiated, sometimes tacitly and sometimes explicitly" (p. 154). "In many modern situations," suggest Manz and Sims (1991) "the most appropriate leader is one who can lead others to lead themselves" (p. 18). Both are on target; both describe the activities and objectives of a good leader.

Sometimes ordinary mortals cannot imagine themselves as leaders. We look at leaders who have changed the way we view the world—Mahatma Gandhi, Martin Luther King, Jr.—and we are awestruck; we look at leaders who have ravaged human souls—Hitler, Jim Jones, Stalin—and we are horror-struck. Whether for good or evil, a few people become leaders in some incredible, powerful, overwhelming ways that move others and change some aspect of human life.

We can learn much about leadership from the great leaders of history, and much to avoid from the despots. Leading, however, goes on at far more ordinary levels than these. Much current analysis of leadership centers not on the leaders of history, but on the leaders of contemporary organizations—executives, managers, and team leaders trying to do a job and learn to lead at the same time. Kinlaw (1991) observes that managers' jobs are shifting "from managing by control to managing by commitment; from focusing on individual motivation and output to focusing on team motivation and output; and from traditional functions of planning, organizing, staffing, evaluating to the functions of coaching and facilitating" (p. xix).

How Team Leaders Get the Job

A number of factors may affect who becomes leader. Whether a leader is appointed, is chosen by the group at the outset, or emerges over time, the choice is influenced by the situation and by the personal qualities and qualifications of the individual.

Situation

Situational influences within an organizational culture, though they might have little to do with a person's qualifications, can make the difference in who becomes the leader. These influences may include seniority, politics, and/or conditions that allow a leader to emerge as the team develops.

In some organizations, particularly those involving unions or guilds, seniority is used as a criterion of fairness in many decisions. Even if seniority is not stated as a basis for choosing a leader, it may have a strong influence. A person who has been in the organization longer than others may well be viewed as the right choice for leader. In some cultures or subcultures, too, those who have accrued more years and experience are thought to have greater wisdom and to deserve greater respect. Among the Japanese, for example, age seniority is the primary criterion for selecting a negotiation team leader (Hellweg, Samovar, & Skow, 1991, p. 189).

Organizational politics can have an impact, too. A person who is seen as having some political advantage may well become the team leader, or an individual may be assigned the position of leader as a reward for doing favors for someone else. Sometimes a person who has connections with influential people will be elected because of his or her potential for using those connections to get resources or support for the team. The implications of political factors are endless, and they may well affect who is appointed or elected as leader in addition to, or in spite of, his or her personal qualities and qualifications.

Sometimes an organization and/or a team decides to wait for a leader to emerge. Over time, an **emergent leader**—or leaders—is recognized by other group members. The way this occurs in groups can vary widely, but some researchers have recognized patterns.

Bormann (1990) reports that the process takes place by "residues" (p. 205). Members are eliminated one by one until the remaining person assumes the leader role. Groups, he finds, sometimes discover it is easier to decide who should *not* be the leader than who should take the responsibilities. Schultz, on the other hand, has found that the ways individuals communicate predict how probable it is that they will emerge as leaders. In one study (1986), she had group members evaluate one another's communication behaviors after their first meetings; on the basis of those ratings, she predicted correctly the emergent leaders in eight of nine groups. What did those people do? Their teammates rated them highly on goal-directedness, direction giving, summarizing, and self-assurance (p. 64).

Those who emerged as leaders in Schultz's study, then, tended to demonstrate qualities that contribute to positive task and transactional processes in a group. Let's examine some other personal qualities and qualifications that encourage people to choose an individual as leader.

Personal Qualities and Qualifications

Many assertions (and reams of research) address what personal qualities, traits, or attributes make a person a "good" or a "bad" leader. Historically, leaders have been characterized as naturally endowed with greatness; as being in the right place at the right time; or as possessing a set of sterling traits or skills.

All of these may be true. However, most explanations are inconclusive, moderated by the situation, or just plain wrong. There's an old cliché that describes the business leader as a "40 long," referring to suit size—a definition that effectively

"What leadership's all about is bringing into being something that wasn't there before. That'll *always* radically change the chemistry of a situation."

"Truth, like electricity, is all around us, but we have very few conduits for it. What you do is plug the people into your socket, they give you that electricity, and you give them heat and light. Lots of people say, you know, 'He's a great speaker.' Well, speaking is a result of feeling, of *thinking*—you *thought* of what to say. . . ."

"You got to be moving toward the heart of the matter, got to burn people's souls. You got to get *inside* of people. That's where it all is. And you can't get inside of them unless you open *yourself* to be got inside of. . . . The key to other people's hearts is finding the key to yours. Got to give to receive, got to open up yourself to get inside somebody else."

"From alderman up to governor up to senator, they have territory on *paper* as their domain. . . . But at some point the real mandate and power and initiatives have to come from a relationship with people, not with official structures."

Excerpts from Marshall Frady, "Outsider: Part I—The Gift," in Profiles, *The New Yorker,* February 3, 1992. Reprinted by permission; © 1992 Marshall Frady. Originally in *The New Yorker.*

excludes most men, all women, and many ethnic groups. Yet all can be very effective leaders when given the opportunity.

A number of leader qualifications do emerge across various research studies, however, that are in tune with common sense: preparation for the task, credibility, adaptability, ethical principles, personal involvement, and communication skills. Let's look more closely at each of these.

Preparation for the Task   The degree to which an individual is seen as prepared for the job may determine whether she or he becomes a leader. Preparation, obviously, covers a large territory. It may mean having experience, training, and proven effectiveness in leading others; or it may mean simply talent or proven skill in doing a job, not necessarily in leading a team. You're superb at creating training films, so you're made assistant manager of the human resources and training department. Maybe you have the preparation for this job, and maybe you don't. You may need training to lead others so they can do the job as well as you can.

Often, however, preparation means nothing more than doing your homework. You're a member of corporate task force; you come to the meeting well organized, supplied with the information the group needs, and ready to talk about it. You are perceived as the leader because you're the one who's ready for the task.

Credibility   Credibility, discussed at some length in Chapter 2, is the way others perceive a person to be. It is the extent to which one person sees another as competent, objective, trustworthy, cooriented, and—with greater or lesser degrees of importance—dynamic.

An individual's culture, gender, or background may strongly affect how she or he interprets these factors. Status, rank, age, sex, and/or influence make a big difference to some, and not to others.

Hellweg, Samovar, and Skow (1991) investigated the bases on which countries selected their negotiation teams and found some revealing differences. Status is important to French, British, Chinese, Japanese, and Saudi Arabian teams, but not to North Americans, who base team selection more on technical expertise. French teams also are based on "social, professional, and family ties" and on interpersonal similarity among the team members, whereas British negotiators don't put much stock in interpersonal similarity. In addition to status, Japanese teams value knowledge; but they set age as a top priority. Mexican negotiation teams are most influenced by personal attributes and *palanca* (leverage, connections, clout), which may or may not be connected with formal status (pp. 189–190).

It's also true that one culture's interpretation of competence or expertise may be different from another's. In Western societies a person is seen as an opinion leader only in a specialized area of expertise. In many other, more traditional, societies people "perceive expertise across many topics residing in only one person" (Dodd, 1991, p. 260). Thus, in the United States, a person of great technical expertise in one field might be regarded as inconsequential in other areas; that person would not be considered for leading a team not immediately related to his or her field of competence. In Africa, conversely, an opinion leader respected across a wide range of topics might be a credible choice for leading a group unrelated to any specific expertise.

Adaptability   As teams have become increasingly important, their memberships more diverse, and their purposes more complex and varied, leading them has become more demanding. Julia Wood (1977) suggests "that successful leading would be characterized by a leader's ability to adapt . . . methods of behavior to . . . goals and to the values, idiosyncracies, and expectations of a given membership that exists in a particular situation" (p. 152). She found, in fact, that not only did good leaders adapt to situations, but they remained leaders only if they did adapt.

Studies of leaders strongly indicate that three abilities—to monitor yourself, to understand others, and to focus communication on others—can enable you to emerge, to adapt, and to lead effectively.

Self-Monitoring   People who are **self-monitoring** really monitor others' cues as well as their own behavior. Because they are "sensitive to and accurate in diagnosing social cues in each situation" (Anderson, 1990, p. 149), they know how and when to adapt to those cues. High self-monitors are, according to Dobbins, Long, Dedrick, and Clemons (1990):

1. Concerned about the appropriateness of social behavior.
2. Attentive to social comparison information.
3. Relatively adept at acting.
4. Able and willing to control behavior and optimize self-presentations, even if this means portraying themselves very differently across various contexts. (p. 610)

Self-monitoring appears to be more important in some situations than in others. In New Zealand, highly self-monitoring team leaders were most effective with their mixed-culture groups of Polynesians, Asians, and white New Zealanders. With homogeneous groups, leaders who were low self-monitors seemed more effective (Anderson, 1990, p. 151). That seems odd, but then adaptation isn't as important when people in a group are "all alike."

Coorientational Accuracy　How clearly and accurately a leader can assess team members' perceptions obviously affects how well she or he can adapt to them. As you recall, people perceive another's credibility, in part, by how cooriented they think that person is with them—how closely she or he shares their values, beliefs, positions.

Coorientational accuracy gauges the correctness of an individual's understanding of another's position. If you can't imagine what other people's perceptions are, it's pretty hard to identify yourself with them. If you can judge those perceptions accurately, then you can establish a sense of coorientation between yourself and others.

It seems that women tend to be more coorientationally accurate than men (Natalle & Papa, 1990), possibly because women hear more of what is said and because "women's ability to more accurately decode nonverbal cues and meta-messages gives them more information about their interaction partners" (p. 40). It may be that other subordinate groups also tend to be more coorientationally accurate than dominant groups, simply because they have to read the messages of those to whom they answer.

Person-Centered Messages　A leader who is self-monitoring, coorientationally accurate, and adaptable must be able to use these characteristics to communicate effectively. This shows up in a leader's ability to use **person-centered messages** "that imply a recognition of the other as a unique person, and a sensitivity to the other's unique qualities, goals, feelings, and concerns" (Zorn, 1991, p. 183).

Dialogic listening and questioning, climate building, transactional processes—all of these require a leader to think about other members of the team and about his or her own behaviors. Such a leader expresses messages that are centered on others because she or he understands the importance of those persons to dialogue and to the team.

Principle　Adaptability, with all its components, raises an interesting ethical question: Self-monitoring, looking for coorientational accuracy, constructing messages so they'll be acceptable to other people—isn't all of this rather hypocritical?

Our personal answer is a firm "yes and no." "Yes," it's hypocritical, if these skills are used without principle; "no," if they're the skills of a **principled leader.** That's why an important qualification for leading is being a person of principle. A principled leader has internal ethical standards that guide his or her choices.

What principles would apply? One might be not manipulating others to do something that violates their personal standards and values; another, not to take advantage of or injure another. A principled leader might ask of every message choice: "Is this fair? Is it honest? Will it foster the team's efforts in the best, the healthiest, the most ethical directions?" These suggestions are only a start. What would you add to the list?

What does a principled leader accomplish? Such a leader maintains a dialogical ethic of group process, and that provides the team with a sense of equity and procedural justice. Even when the team does not have the final decision, if a leader has objectively and openly encouraged members to have their say, they consider their leader to be just. They then are willing to endorse him or her as leader (Tyler, Rasinski, & Spodick, 1985).

Leaders who reason with principle apparently influence their teams to do the same. And the influence seems to be a lasting one: after working with such a team, members continue to use more principled reasoning for themselves (Dukerich, Nichols, Elm, & Vollrath, 1990).

Personal Involvement   Personal involvement is essential to being a leader. We see involvement in terms of two broad categories: the first is the "three Cs" of leadership—confidence, commitment, and concentration; the second is pro-activity.

Confidence, Commitment, and Concentration   Becoming a leader, or maintaining leadership, requires all three. This is not to say that successful leaders are brazenly self-assured and arrogant; in fact, one of the elements that Larson and LaFasto (1989) identified in top leaders was a *lack* of egocentrism and arrogance. "The most effective leaders . . . were those who subjugated their ego needs in favor of the team's goal" (p. 128). You can be confident, committed, and concentrated on the team and its goals without ego getting in the way.

According to Warren Bennis (1989), one of the most influential writers on leadership today, "Leaders know themselves; they know their strengths and nurture them" (p. 22). He recounts the story of Karl Wallenda, head of the Flying Wallendas, a world-famous family of aerialists and tightrope walkers. The secret to Karl's continued success—and existence—was total concentration and commitment to what he was doing. One day, for the first time ever, he personally supervised the installation of the lines stretched between two buildings in Puerto Rico. That day he fell to his death. Later his wife said it was the only time, in all those years, that he "had been concentrating on falling, instead of on walking the tightrope" before his performance (p. 22).

As long as he was fully confident in his skills, concentrated on his performance, and committed to its outcome, Karl Wallenda was invincible; when he lost that, he died. Leadership, though not generally a matter of life and death, is the same: a leader must be confident in his or her skills, fully concentrated on the team's processes, and committed to the vision and goals of the team.

Proactivity   **Proactivity** means reaching beyond the moment and creating opportunities. Compare it to *re*activity. The reactive person waits for something to happen or someone to say something about a problem, then knee-jerks in response. Even if the knee jerk is appropriate, it's a reaction that excludes analysis and decisions to take innovative, affirmative steps forward. The proactive person anticipates, thinks of possibilities and contingencies, plans ahead, and acts. It's important for a leader to be able to take risks and move beyond the reactive point of view.

Proactivity shows in preparation, in coming to meetings with information and ideas, in caring about and enjoying people and processes, in being able to play with ideas, in seeing the humor in situations. Proactivity is taking the first step forward; it is *participating*.

Communication Skills   We won't belabor this point, since this entire book is about communicating effectively in groups. In the previous three chapters, we've focused on specific skills that all members need. Your ability to build communication climates, to use verbal and nonverbal communication, to listen and question dialogically—it is all these skills that enable you to be an adaptable, principled, proactive leader.

Expectations of Leaders

When you take on the job of leader, what do people expect? Expectations are preconceived ideas about how people are, what their legitimate roles are, and how they should behave. These preconceptions may be related to an individual's socioeconomic status, education, class, race, culture, age, gender, special abilities or disabilities.

What people expect ranges from leadership functions—how a leader should be, how a leader should act—to personal qualities. Expectations may start with stereotypes and extend into assumptions about the individual's values, beliefs, intelligence, and behaviors. They may be very positive expectations, or negative ones.

You may have heard some version of these comments made about a candidate for leader of a group:

"Make him chairperson. He went to Yale." (People with high-powered educations must make better leaders.)

"Don't make him leader—he'll always be late." (People from *his* culture don't value time the way *we* do.)

"She must be voting for him because he's a hunk." (Women think with their hormones.)

"She can't be chairperson—she'll be biased." (She might select people from her ethnic group instead of sticking entirely with mine.)

Are these stereotypes old-fashioned, passé, obsolete? Yes, but they're still with us. For example, even when people are given *identical performance information* about male and female leaders, many think they would like female leaders less and would prefer not to work for them (Nye & Forsyth, 1991, p. 376). "Men are expected to lead well while women are expected to be better followers" (Stewart, Stewart, Friedley, & Cooper, 1990, p. 219). The same types of expectation problems afflict anyone who belongs to a group or subgroup that doesn't fit a dominant group's expectations of what a leader is like.

What if you become a leader in the face of expectations such as these? What if people expect you to fall on your face? What happens if, contrary to expectations, you turn out to be very competent indeed? In this case, it seems that people tend to rationalize that you are the exception to the rule. When expectations are violated by a *better* performance than expected, a group may evaluate a person *more* highly and treat her or him with greater respect, or less hostility, than it would another for whom it had higher initial expectations (Bradley, 1980). That allows them to cling to previous expectations about people like you, while at the same time enjoying the benefits of your effective leadership.

The message is obvious. If you fit the going stereotype for "leader," then you need to be clear on what you and others expect. If you can meet those expectations, that's great. If you can't—or won't, because they violate your sense of who you are or your principles—you need to negotiate those expectations. If you don't fit the current stereotype, you simply have to be better than those who do. Then people will be so startled at having their expectations refuted they will think you're wonderful.

While you're being good or better, keep in mind your own expectations. For a person who isn't too experienced in leadership, these can be the heaviest burden of all. After you've exercised leadership for a while—either as a very involved member of a group or as the designated leader—you begin to give up some of your definitions and to formulate others. You find out what you can reasonably expect of yourself, and how to adapt your leadership to members and situations.

It helps to understand that expectations can, and probably will, clash. Suppose your personal role definition is that of a nurturing, supportive person—and you're in a leader's role that requires you to be tough and assertive. You might have to negotiate those roles within yourself and learn how to live with a more complicated self-concept than you had previously. That's very much a part of learning to be an effective leader.

You can't meet all expectations, and you shouldn't even try. Some expectations, in fact, are unrealistic or defeating or against your principles. Sometimes, therefore, you must violate others' expectations; that may require some careful discussion and negotiation of what you expect and what others expect. For example, the founder of your team may expect you to lead it to a specific goal and produce results rapidly. Perhaps your expectation for yourself is to empower team members, to lead them to lead themselves; that takes more time. One reasonable expectation of you, as a leader, is that you will manage these conflicting role expec-

In what ways are each of these people leaders? How do they affect the lives of others? What aspects do they have in common? How do they differ as leaders?

Consider the personal qualities and qualifications of leaders developed in this chapter—preparation for task, credibility, adaptability, personal involvement, principles, and communication skills. Which of these characteristics stand out as most significant for each of these people? (Photographs © UPI/Bettmann Newsphotos) tations with communication and compromise. It isn't always easy, but it's what you have to do.

Power and Authority

We've commented before that issues of control run through human needs and relationships. A designated leader normally has some authority to make decisions; usually, she or he also has some power—or ability to influence others—on which to draw. Next, we look at the sources of power leaders have available, and ways in which that power can be used and abused.

Sources of Power

The type of power and authority a leader has influences his or her effectiveness. French and Raven (1959) have identified five sources of power in groups, organizations, or among individuals; we have added a sixth, information, to the list:

1. **Coercive power** derives from the ability to punish. If a person can fire you, demote you, reduce your salary, inflict emotional or physical pain upon you, that's coercive power.

2. **Reward power** is the reverse of coercive power, although they often go together. If a person can hire you, promote you, raise your salary, give you physical or emotional pleasure or relief, help you meet your goals, fulfill your needs, or achieve your desires, that's reward power.

3. **Legitimate power** is inherent in the person's position or office. A police officer, your boss, your teacher, all have degrees of legitimate power.

4. **Expert power** flows from an individual's expertise, academic credentials and/or certification, experience, research, and competence in a given area.

5. **Referent power** is the influence inherent in the respect and admiration others have for an individual. A person who is perceived as credible, as having wisdom, as having goodwill has the power to change others as a role model, a counselor, a guru.

6. **Information power** lies in a person's possession of data that could allow others to make decisions or to understand issues and processes. It differs from expert power in that all experts may have information, but a person may have information without the other attributes of expertise. A secretary may have no other significant power, but he or she can make or break events in an organization because of information about the history, personnel, and informal networks of the organization.

Uses and Abuses of Power

We suppose it's all too obvious that power can be abused to manipulate others or to promote individual interests above team interests. Pettit, Vaught, and Pulley

---

WE HAVE LOTS OF MANAGERS . . . WE NEED LEADERS

Drop your stereotypes! A few years ago, the United States Marine Corps Combat Correspondents Association gave a top award to an article titled "Leadership and Love." It proposed that leadership is a subset of love and that if a person was not capable of loving and being loved, then most likely he or she was not capable of being a good leader either.

While it will offend some and puzzle others to look to the military for lessons in leadership, it is well worth ignoring the stereotypes. The United States Marine Corps, *Guidebook for Marines* lists eleven leadership principles.

Take responsibility . . . for your actions as well as subordinates.

Know yourself. Be honest. Constantly seek self-improvement.

Set an example. Your conduct influences others.

Develop your subordinates. Guide but be confident in them.

Be available . . . but don't take away others' initiative.

Look after the welfare of your employees. Help but don't pry.

Keep everyone well informed. Stop rumors, provide the truth.

Set achievable goals. Successes will be more easily reached.

Make sound and timely decisions; have courage to change bad ones.

Know your job. Stay abreast, learn, adjust to new ways.

Build teamwork. Assign projects to your entire staff. Train employees so they understand contributions that each makes to the entire effort. Insist that everyone pull his or her share of the load. When you do something well, celebrate it.

Condensed from Patrick L. Townsend and Joan E. Gebhardt, "We Have Lots of Managers . . . We Need Leaders," *Journal for Quality and Participation,* September 1989, pp. 18–19. Published by the Association for Quality and Participation. Used with permission.

(1990), writing about ethics in organizations, note that "humans are primarily directed in ethical areas by their sense of morality and inner conscience. However, they may at times, in response to organizational authority and power, be asked to violate that personal code of conduct" (p. 241). Rewards, coercion, a sense of loyalty, compulsion to obey—all these may induce an individual to behave unethically in response to the pressure of a leader's power.

A principled leader must recognize the sources, uses, and potential abuses of power. Ideally, a leader empowers the entire team by sharing all possible information, choices, and decisions. Some self-managing teams make decisions about schedules, employment, assignments, promotion, pay increases, and most aspects of their tasks. Much power resides in such a team.

But team power, authority, and structure vary widely, according to the type of organization, the team's stage of development, and the training of the members. In some cases, neither the leader nor the members have authority to reward, to punish, or even to make decisions; these may belong to outside group leaders or managers while the team develops. Even so, the leader and team members have information, expert, and referent power. Often, these sources of power can overcome enormous hurdles—if leaders and members know how to use them.

A student of ours used these three sources in a personal campaign to induce his college to reinstate the discontinued ice hockey team. He had no legitimate, reward, or coercive power. Instead, he used expert power (he knew his game), information power (he did a lot of research to back up his proposals), referent power (he was respected by students and teachers)—and grit. He got the team reinstated against seemingly insurmountable odds by those who had all the *other* forms of power at their command and didn't really want to bother with ice hockey. It was gratifying to see.

Styles and Approaches to Leading

The way one individual leads others is a constant source of amazement to scholars of group communication. We will look first at three basic leadership styles and then at some more contemporary approaches.

Classic Styles of Leading

Some realities don't change much. The three classic styles of leading identified by White and Lippett back in 1960 (p. 12) are still very much in evidence.

Laissez-faire leadership refers to a kind of neutral, kick-back-and-let-the-folks-do-whatever-they-choose style. You must already be designated as "the leader" to be laissez-faire, because being this laid-back rarely gets you the position. This style works just fine for a team of real experts who want to share the leadership and charge ahead. Otherwise, productivity, quality, involvement, and satisfaction suffer.

Authoritarian leadership is just what it sounds like. The authoritarian leader keeps tight control, runs meetings by the book, sets schedules, and may use coercive or reward power. Authoritarian leadership often increases productivity in the short term, but it also increases aggression and turnover rates among members. Some people equate authoritarianism with leadership, however, and their expectations are met by an authoritarian leader.

Democratic leadership fits the Western ideal. The democratic leader makes sure everyone is heard, guides and facilitates discussion and decision making, and shares power. This style of leadership lowers absenteeism and turnover, and increases members' satisfaction, participation, innovation, and commitment to decisions.

Contemporary Approaches to Leading

Although you certainly will see each of the classic styles applied in a variety of group settings, you will also observe modifications based on these complicating factors:

1. A given style may be more appropriate to one group's set of expectations or specific task than to another.
2. The needs of a team may change as it develops, and appropriate styles may change, too.

3. None of these styles seems to address fully the idea of "empowering" a team to move forward; they seem to involve guiding or controlling a group more than building a team.

As a result, contemporary approaches to leading are likely to consider situations and contingencies, life cycles, and empowerment of teams.

Situational-Contingency Leadership   **Situational-contingency** approaches recognize that situations, tasks, purposes, members, and leaders vary, and that a leader's approach may need to vary accordingly. This is basic common sense, and it underscores the importance of adaptability as a qualification. Hollander (1978) describes the bases for deciding how to lead in terms of three overlapping circles, or areas of concern:

1. Situation—task, resources, social structure, rules, setting, background.
2. Leader—power source, motivation, personality, competence.
3. Members—expectations, motivations, personalities, competencies.

Suppose, for example, that you head an executive committee of capable, confident people. The team makes most of its own decisions. The members like it that way. You like it that way. One day, information comes to you about a serious, life-threatening crisis in the plant. It must be resolved immediately. Can you call a meeting and work out a decision? No, somebody might die before action is taken. For this situation, you adopt an authoritarian mode, make a decision, issue orders—and then tell the committee about it. The situational contingencies dictate your style for that moment.

Life-Cycle Leadership   In their **life-cycle theory** of leadership, Hersey and Blanchard (1977) suggest that a leader's style is determined by the maturity of the followers. Maturity, in this sense, is "the ability and willingness of individuals or groups to take responsibility for directing their own behavior in a particular area" (Hersey, Blanchard, & Natemeyer, 1979, p. 420). They suggest that leaders adapt their communication according to the degree of maturity that members exhibit, moving from telling, to selling, to participating, to delegating.

Telling communication is directive, nonnegotiable task ordering for teams with low maturity; it uses coercive and some, but not too much, reward power.

Selling communication is more supportive, rewarding persuasion for teams with low to medium degrees of maturity. Power and direction are still centered in the leader; the focus is still on task, not transaction.

Participating communication, for teams with moderate to high maturity, brings the members into the process as partners; it supports, encourages, and builds leader-member transactions and relationships.

Delegating communication is appropriate to highly mature teams; it involves little direction and permits teams to make their own decisions.

In short, the leader changes his or her style, becoming less authoritarian and more democratic, as the team matures enough to take responsibility for its own development and actions. Concepts of group maturity, uses of power, communication styles, and roles provide useful insights into adapting to situational contingencies. They suggest how a leader contributes to transforming a team through various stages of growth and achievement.

Empowering Leadership   A leader who knows how to adapt to situational contingencies, and who understands her or his role in helping a team develop maturity, is a leader who can empower a team to develop and use its own power effectively. Bass (1990) talks about the differences between transactional leading, which exchanges rewards for performance, and **transformational** leading, which elevates, motivates, inspires, and develops the team. It thus meets members' goals and needs *and* fulfills the vision and goals of the team and the organization. According to Bass, transformational leaders demonstrate:

1. Charisma . . . provide vision and a sense of mission, instill pride, gain respect and trust.
2. Inspiration . . . communicate high expectations, use symbols to focus efforts, express important purposes in simple ways.
3. Intellectual stimulation . . . promote intelligence, rationality, and careful problem solving.
4. Individualized consideration . . . give personal attention, treat people individually, coach, advise. (p. 22)

Bass compared leaders in organizations and found that transformational leaders had better relationships with their own supervisors than transactional leaders did; furthermore, people worked harder for transformational leaders than for transactional leaders. He concluded that "transformational leaders make the difference between success and failure" (p. 24).

Similarly, Warren Bennis (1989) has observed that outstanding leaders are skilled at four things:

Management of attention. They draw others to them, focus their attention on a vision, gain their commitment.

Management of meaning. They communicate their vision; they use symbols, metaphors, images to make the meaning mutual.

Management of trust. They are reliable, constant, consistent; people know what to expect of them.

Management of self. Leaders know their skills, deploy them effectively, see their mistakes as steps to successes. (pp. 22–21)

Such leaders, Bennis says, empower others by making them feel significant, helping them feel their learning and competence are important, making them feel a part of a community, and instilling in them a sense of excitement about their work.

F I G U R E 12.1	STYLE OR APPROACH TO LEADING	SOURCE OF POWER	CONTROL OF TEAM	SUPPORT OF TEAM	TEAM'S AUTONOMY	EFFECT ON TEAM
Characteristics of styles and approaches to leading	Laissez-faire (White & Lippett, 1960)	Legitimate	None	Little	Complete	Demoralizing
	Authoritarian (Ibid.)	Coercive and reward	Strong	Variable	Little or none	May increase productivity but also increases hostility and turnover
	Democratic (Ibid.)	Possibly all except coercive	Loose	Strong	Extensive	Openness and ability to work together
	Situational-Contingency (Hollander, 1978)	Varies	Varies by situation, leader, and members	Strong	Depends on situation, leader, and members	Enables team to meet situational needs
	Life-Cycle (Hersey & Blanchard, 1977)	Legitimate, and other sources as appropriate	Adapted to maturity of members—telling, selling, participating, or delegating	Adapted to maturity of members	Adapted to maturity of members	Members develop through stages of ability to guide themselves
	Transactional (Bass, 1990)	Legitimate and reward	Control through negotiation	Strong	Moderate	Positive but less productive and committed than with the empowering leader
	Empowering and Transformational (Bass, 1990)	Legitimate, referent, expert, "charisma"	Coaching, inspiring, intellectually stimulating, individual	Strong	Encourages freedom and responsibility; relinquishes control as much as possible	Empowering; developing personal leadership in team members

We have given you quite a dose of theory—sources of power, styles of leadership, contemporary approaches. To give you a clearer idea of how it all fits together, Figure 12.1 relates each of the styles and approaches we've discussed to questions of power, control, support, autonomy, and overall effect on the team.

Responsibilities of the Leader

Theory is all well and good, but when it comes to actually leading your team or group, you probably want to know some specific things to do that will fulfill expectations and help you develop the team as well as achieve the tasks.

The first responsibility of the leader is nicely summarized in a job description seen at McDonnell Douglas: "Teamplayer: Unites others toward a shared destiny through sharing information and ideas, empowering others and developing trust" (Kinlaw, 1991, p. xvi). That's certainly the foundation. We'll build on that by examining a range of functions that leaders frequently—but not always, or in all ways—should fill. These fall into broad categories of linking and buffering; motivating and coaching; and managing and moving the team.

Linking and Buffering

No team works in a vacuum; the group and its leader must deal with a parent organization and other systems and subsystems. The organization has its needs, and so does the team. It's the leader who links the team to the organization and buffers it from interference.

Linking involves satisfying the needs of both the team and the organization. A leader's responsibilities in this area include:

1. Promote the organization's vision, culture, and goals.
2. Motivate, encourage, inspire, and supervise the team.
3. Consult with and report to the parent organization.
4. Coordinate with related teams, subsystems, and departments.
5. Guide methods of assessment and quality control.
6. Manage personnel issues, including expertise, affirmative action, gender, power, and control questions within the team.
7. Manage public relations issues (related to the team's activities) within and outside the organization.

What these mean, at the bottom line, is that an organization expects team leaders to demonstrate loyalty, perceptiveness, commitment, intelligence, and innovativeness, as well as skill in managing and talent in inspiring people. Nothing much.

There's a symbiotic relationship between the organization and the team: they're interdependent, and each fills needs of the other. The leadership functions that contemporary observers and consultants stress unanimously are:

Buffering the team. Creative and research teams, especially, need autonomy to function effectively. The leader works between the team and the outside—consulting, representing, feeding back, moderating.

Securing resources. The leader seeks time, money, materials, information—as expediently as possible, but without sacrificing the integrity of the team. (Ancona, 1990)

In a real sense, a leader's job is "public relations oriented" (Kolb, 1991, p. 4). Kolb found that successful research team leaders spoke and acted as representatives of their groups; maintained cordial relations and influence with superiors; and kept the group in good standing with higher authority. This protected members from interference and provided them with the support and autonomy they needed for their research. Combined with giving their teams meaningful levels of responsibility, these leaders' contributions empowered their teams to do their work (p. 9).

Motivating and Coaching

Most people really do expect a leader to inspire them, to motivate them, to help them transcend their ordinary selves. It's a big order, but not impossible. Here are some suggestions:

Envisioning. Listen carefully to the team; help to articulate its goals in clear, symbolic terms. Help members to see themselves as a cohesive whole and to see the goals by finding images that work for them.

Developing others' self-leadership. Identify members' strengths; suggest areas in which they can take special responsibility; encourage their leadership; appreciate their successes.

Setting standards. People often look to a leader to set standards for both the work and the ethics of the team. Help the team to brainstorm and set standards for its processes. Express high standards of your own, and manage your own behavior to provide a model for others.

Guiding ongoing assessment. It's often up to a leader to make self-evaluation a desirable, shared, helpful process. With the team, develop methods and criteria for assessing processes and outcomes.

Coaching. Understand the processes; explain, encourage, and help people assume responsibility for themselves. Become expert yourself, then coach members in how to go out and do it. When a project is to be presented, not only help to organize it, but coach members in their roles and encourage their success.

Managing and Moving

Members sometimes are shockingly grateful when a leader simply manages and moves the task. Yet these are probably the easiest skills to learn and to provide for a team. They include planning and following through, and assuring task and transactional processes.

Planning and Following Through   *Somebody's* got to take care of the details but, if you haven't noticed, all too often nobody does. Where there's no designated leader, a team must pay extra attention to delegating these tasks. Where there is a designated leader, it's generally expected that she or he will perform them or delegate them specifically to other members. A checklist can help:

1. Plan meeting times, places, and arrangements.
2. Make sure information and resources are available.
3. Plan agendas (with the team or delegated members).
4. Communicate plans by publishing and distributing notices and agendas in plenty of time.
5. Contact, set up, confirm experts, consultants, or guests for meetings.
6. Be sure follow-up mail, memos, and acknowledgments are written and mailed.

That's the detail work; all it takes is being organized and doing it.

Assuring Process   Transactional and task processes have been discussed at length in previous chapters; the leader's responsibility is to make sure those processes work. A good set of standards to keep in mind is that suggested by Larson and LaFasto (1989):

1. Avoid compromising the team's objective with political issues.
2. Exhibit personal commitment to the team's goal.
3. Do not dilute the team's efforts with too many priorities.
4. Be fair and impartial toward all team members.
5. Be willing to confront and resolve issues associated with inadequate performance by team members.
6. Be open to new ideas and information from team members. (p. 123)

To achieve these objectives, according to Barge (1991), the most important functions and skills in a leader's task competence are:

Facilitate participation. Encourage, motivate, and get members to participate. Ask for and give information on the problem, solution generation, evaluation, and implementation.

Define roles. Regulate participation and structure role expectations for ensuing meetings. Make sure everyone gets a chance; keep people from dominating; consider differences and needs of members.

Keep discussion coherent. Make connections among ideas. Refer back, when appropriate, to previous information or to related information from other experiences. Help to synthesize concepts, identify relationships, or find new interpretations or applications of ideas within the discussion topic.

C A S E   A N A L Y S I S   12.1

Review the task force members' backgrounds, described in Chapter 4 (see page 90).

Issues for Your Consideration

1. Speculate about the leadership in the group. Who do you think was the designated leader? Would there be more than one designated leader? Why do you think that person or those persons would have the position?

2. Considering the roles and status of the group members and the team's task, what type of leadership seems most appropriate? Why? What approaches to leadership would seem to be doomed to failure?

3. From the limited knowledge of backgrounds and expertise provided, in what ways do you speculate leadership might be shared or distributed among the members? Who is likely to take what roles?

Control discussion inhibitors. Try to keep people from sidetracking the discussion, withdrawing, criticizing negatively, or contributing to confusion in the group.

All of the information in this chapter is great in theory; in fact, we know from experience that it's great in practice. But when you get right down to it, it's the practice that makes it possible. It is possible to learn to lead; moreover, it's challenging, fun, fulfilling, and useful. We have a few suggestions for doing just that.

Learning to Lead

Learning to lead, like any other skill, is a matter of mapping out an approach and following it. We suggest these four steps:

1. Identify people you consider to be excellent leaders, coaches, mentors, teachers. Analyze what they *do* that makes them so effective, and use them as models for your own leading.

2. Identify your own strengths and build on them. Observe yourself on videotape; use the self-analysis instruments; ask for feedback. Think about your skills in terms of what you've learned here and what you've observed in your models. Practice your strengths, make them even better, and reward yourself for what you do well.

3. Identify what you'd like as new strengths. Write affirmations (remember Chapter 2?) that describe you, how you feel, and how you act when you're being the kind of leader you'd like to be. Visualize yourself that way. See yourself being an effective leader; imagine how it would feel, how people would respond.

4. Look for opportunities to practice leading. They can be small tasks: chair a committee, get a group together to take on a campus problem, teach a Sunday school class, coach a Little League team. Practice, evaluate how you did, and develop your skills.

Being a leader can be a big responsibility. Seeing your team develop its strengths, become a force to deal with, move forward to accomplish its goals— and knowing your leadership contributed to that—now there's a great feeling.

Summary

We've explored in this chapter the mundane to magical expectations, qualities, functions, and behaviors of leaders. Leaders influence transactional and task processes, effect change, and empower others to lead themselves.

People become leaders because of situations, seniority, politics, and/or personal qualities such as credibility, preparation, and adaptability. Adaptability requires self-monitoring, coorientational accuracy, and the ability to center messages on the interests of other persons. Leaders should be principled and involved—confident, committed, concentrated, and proactive.

Expectations—from self, the team, or the organization—affect how an individual is perceived as a leader. People's expectations of a leader may conflict with their expectations of a person as social stereotype, and this may affect how they perceive an individual's potential and performance as a leader.

Leaders draw upon six sources of power: coercive, reward, legitimate, expert, referent, and information. A good leader's objective is to empower the team, and uses of power may depend upon style, members, and situation. Classic styles of leadership are laissez-faire, authoritarian, and democratic. Contemporary approaches to leadership—situational-contingency, life-cycle, empowering—recognize that leaders must adapt their styles.

Leaders link the team to the parent organization and outside systems and buffer the team from interference. They motivate, coach, manage, and move the business of the team through transactional and task processes.

People can learn to lead by taking on responsibilities, using role models, feedback, visualization, and practice. Remember that leaders are not just people who do things right; they are people who do the right things (Bennis, 1989).

Exercises

1. As an individual, think of someone you consider a leader (living or dead, public figure, family member, friend, anyone). Make a list of what it is that person is or does that distinguishes her or him as a leader.

   Now, with a small group of other students, share your lists. What do your leaders have in common? Where do they vary in the qualities that each of you considered important? What accounts for those variations?

2. With the same group, consider your leaders in terms of styles of leadership—laissez-faire, authoritarian, democratic, situational-contingency, developmental, transactional, and transformational. Then:
   a. Decide which style(s) each person you've identified as a leader used.
   b. Examine if, why, and how the style(s) used by the particular leader was appropriate to his or her group and situation.

c. Decide which of the responsibilities of the leader, as we've discussed them in this chapter, each of your leaders fulfilled.

d. If a given leader fulfilled some and not others, why? And why was that person still a good leader? (An individual can be a good leader without meeting all criteria.)

3. Recall a time when you've been the designated leader of a group, or imagine yourself in that position. Using Form 12.1, identify what you can do that makes you potentially a good leader. What do you want to work on to develop your strengths?

4. With a group to which you now belong, whether or not it has a designated leader, evaluate its leadership using Form 12.2. As usual, do it first as individual members, then compare and discuss your responses as a team. Where do you agree? Disagree? Why? What can the team do to develop strong leadership? List what you intend to do, then reassess your leadership in a few meetings. Has the leadership developed further?

Team Pressures and Conflicts:
Meeting the Challenges

"Communicating in this team is like running
through a minefield—anybody got a detector?"

It's possible to prevent, detect, and dismantle group mines before they blow up.

Everything we discuss in this chapter concerns rocks, boulders, and mines in the path to a team's goal. Some of these are created by team pressures—the pressure deviant members put on a team, and the pressure teams put on the deviant to conform to its ways. Other land mines are found in the causes and consequences of groupthink, hidden agendas, competitive communication, and conflict.

If you consider problems as boulders or mines along a team's path, you'll understand why some theorists view group interaction in terms of a *path-goal* model. Every activity moves, overcomes barriers, or deflects the team in its effort to reach the goal. If you think of it that way, every member's leadership helps the team along the path.

Dennis Gouran (1982) has developed a theory of "counteractive leadership" as "acts directed toward coping with obstructions in a group's goal-path. . . . Leadership functions to counteract those influences acting on a group which, if left unattended, would prevent the members from achieving their goals" (p. 150). A designated leader may or may not guide a team effectively. When the team comes up against problems, members' combined efforts are essential to get the team back on the path.

Your leadership can help your team hurdle its barriers or avoid building them. To those ends, this chapter seeks to help you:

1. Understand the pressures groups put on individuals.

2. Know the causes and consequences of "groupthink," and ways of preventing it.

3. Detect and manage individual hidden agendas that block progress.

4. Recognize and manage competitive communication strategies.

5. Understand and manage conflicts in your team's processes.

Team Pressure

Pressures on the team and its members come from many sources. In this book we have examined many of these in one form or another. Here, we're concerned with a kind of point and counterpoint set of pressures. Pressure on the team is created by individual members who deviate from what the team expects; pressure on individuals builds when other members try to get them to conform to their preferences.

Deviance

Deviance is lack of conformity to others' expectations. It's breaking the mold. An individual may or may not intend to break the mold, but it's easy to do. Is it always a bad thing? Not at all. Let's take a look at three ways in which a person might be deviant, and then at why deviance is both good news and bad news for a team.

Types of Deviance　People may be seen as deviant because of the way they play roles in the group, express opinions, or use innovation to extend and advocate those opinions (Putnam, 1986).

Members have many preconceived ideas about how people should fulfill their roles. A member who fails to conform to those ideas may be seen as deviant. These expectations may seem insignificant, or they may be critically important to the group. Some examples are:

1. Infractions of general group norms. "We dress casually, but he always wears a tie. The guy just isn't like us."
2. Violations of expected behaviors in specific roles. "A leader should be formal, she's relaxed. She can't be a leader."
3. Breaks in social stereotypes and role expectations of gender, class, race, status, or age. "Women should be nurturing—but she's tough!" "Men should be tough—but he's nurturing!" "Students should be submissive—he's assertive." Deviants, all.
4. Reversal of expectations developed over time. "Hey, you're our clown—you can't get serious on us!"

Opinion deviance is perceiving and expressing ideas differently from the way the group's majority sees them. The opinion deviant is the minority voice. Often, the deviant is the person with the guts to raise issues, to suggest alternatives, to unsettle a group's complacency. Because the majority tends to protect its decisions from minority opinion influence, members may take an irrationally strong stance against the opinion deviant.

Innovation deviance takes opinion deviance further; it amplifies, strengthens, and extends a position. Frequently, this person's ideas on the issues are too far out front of the rest of the group's thinking. The innovation deviant may identify implications of an idea the team hasn't considered, suggest alternative approaches, or advocate new points of view.

Bad News and Good News   Deviance creates the old bad news/good news dichotomy. Even more, it can be a prime cause of ethical dilemmas in team processes. On one side is a set of priorities for the team's goals—presumably worthwhile, valuable goals. The team wants to reach those goals expeditiously, and deviance may seem an impediment. Too much deviance leads to incessant arguing and random decision making. It's distracting, it's time-consuming, and it comes from people who are not "just one of the guys." There's plenty of motivation for silencing the deviant member.

On the other side of the deviance dilemma is the dialogical ethic—that every member be able to express opinions, feel free to participate, and be acknowledged as an individual important to the group. Silencing a member violates that ethic. Further, the majority, left to itself, tends to be unoriginal and closed. Dissenting or raising controversial issues "generates a variety of ideas, allows for contrast and comparison, and gives everyone the chance to evaluate the quality of opinions that might otherwise go untested" (Thameling & Andrews, 1991, p. 5).

Conformity

Because deviance puts pressure on the majority, people have an overwhelming urge to throw everyone in a pressure cooker and make them all come out the same. When people want conformity, they can really turn up the heat under the lone deviant in that pot.

Conformity is behaving in ways consistent with the group's norms and standards. Obviously, everybody complies with some rules and norms; if they didn't, people would all spin out into their own orbits and there would be no society. Conformity becomes a problem when people want others to conform to their preconceived ideas whether they make sense or not—no deviance allowed. It helps to understand people's motives, methods, and choices of strategy for pressuring others to conform, as well as how people under pressure respond to it.

Motives   Members may put pressure on others to conform for three reasons (Clark, 1979):

1. *Protection of ego, or self-image.* A challenge to a person's assumptions, values, beliefs, or stereotypes may also challenge his or her self-concept. One way to avoid dealing with that challenge is to label the other a deviant (or whatever term is in style for people who don't quite fit).

2. *Instrumental.* The deviant blocks progress to a goal. A team may pressure members to conform in order to remove barriers along the path toward their goals.

3. *Interpersonal.* People are uncomfortable with deviant behavior; they want the deviant to either change or go away.

Just say "NO"

Methods   Individuals and groups use a variety of communication strategies to get others to do what they want them to. These strategies cause—and are caused by—the kinds of climates in which people function. The following lists condense strategies from several sources into methods of applying pressure as they might appear in cooperative and supportive climates compared to those in competitive and defensive climates (Cody, Woelfel, & Jordan, 1983; Hunter & Boster, 1987; Kipnis & Schmidt, 1982).

Cooperative/Supportive Strategies for Gaining Compliance

1. *Direct, friendly strategies:* assertive requests or supportively phrased orders.
2. *Persuasive strategies:* focusing on the desired behavior by presenting reasoning and evidence; explanations of benefits, offers of reward; identifying the desired behavior with the relationship between the persuader and the nonconformer, with mutually held values, or with mutually respected others.
3. *Indirect, friendly strategies:* setting a supportive mood, hinting, using intermediaries to negotiate, saving face, offering favors or rewards without linking them directly to the desired behavior.

Competitive/Defensive Strategies for Gaining Compliance

1. *Direct, unfriendly strategies:* issuing ultimatums, giving aggressive orders, blaming, attacking, being hostile and/or sarcastic.
2. *Coercive strategies:* threatening, withholding rewards or encouragement, using double-bind messages, playing games.
3. *Indirect, unfriendly strategies:* implying guilt or aversive results, lying or misrepresenting, using intermediaries to imply threat or aversive consequences to noncompliance.

Most people prefer to use cooperative approaches. In one study, the majority of college students chose variations on cooperative messages—direct requests and simple statements, reasoning, and liking—as their methods of appeal (Levine & Wheeless, 1990). Even in difficult situations, only one-fifth of the students chose to threaten the deviant. Sullivan, Albrecht, and Taylor (1990) also found that supervisors usually choose direct, cooperative strategies of reasoning and friendliness to gain compliance from their subordinates.

It's also true, however, that groups can single out a deviant member. They start by focusing communication more on nonconformers than on others. At first, they're friendly, waiting for the person to become aware that she or he is out of line. They may move to gentle teasing and then to ridiculing and sarcasm if the deviant hasn't gotten the message. Then the members intensify persuasive efforts and finally, if she or he continues to dissent, they outright reject the nonconformer by discontinuing communication entirely (Bormann, 1990, pp. 187–188).

Groups are inconsistent about using these strategies. If a group expects a person to be incompetent—because of role expectations—it may exert pressure to conform when that person proves to be competent. Sometimes, however, such a deviant's competence seems to surprise the group and draw greater support than a nondeviant might. In one study, for example, groups treated competent female dissenters less cooperatively and more emotionally than it did male deviants who expressed the same ideas with the same language (Thameling & Andrews, 1991). Another study (Bradley, 1980) found that women who were not competent also antagonized the male majority with their deviance, but highly competent female deviants influenced their groups to shift opinions more than equally competent males or less competent females were able to do.

Choices   A number of factors influence an individual's choice of strategy to induce conformity, including the way he or she has been socialized in terms of gender or culture.

For example, it seems that men are more competitive and less trusting, whereas women are more cooperative, accommodative, open, trusting, and trustworthy. Women seem to use more friendly appeals to get others to conform, and to take a little longer than men do to become punitive. Men report that they shift from cooperative strategies to coercive strategies on the second try to get compliance,

ROLE EXPECTATIONS: OBSERVATIONS OF SURGICAL TEAMS' NORMS AND CONTROLS

At first we were surprised by the norms of emotional expression in the operating rooms. The first time we entered the room where a coronary bypass operation was being done, for example, we were surprised by the loud rock music blaring from the speakers, the smiles on the faces of the surgical team, and the constant joking. . . . One reason that Sutton almost passed out during a tonsillectomy was that he became very upset when the surgeon laughed, joked, and talked about "what was on the tube last night" while blood from an unconscious child splattered about. . . .

Nurses in this social region had to follow different norms of emotional expression than did the surgeons, and nurses had much less choice about which emotions they could express. . . .

As with all activities in the operating room, nurses who did not follow doctors' wishes about emotional behavior often would be sanctioned. For example, two nurses began talking very quietly between themselves after two of the surgeons started swapping stories about the Detroit Tigers. The head surgeon responded immediately by aiming a nasty glare in their direction and bellowing, "Come on people, let's keep it down in here!"

Excerpted from Daniel R. Denison and Richard I. Sutton, "Operating Room Nurses," in J. Richard Hackman (Ed.), *Groups That Work (and Those That Don't)*, Jossey-Bass, 1990, pp. 300–301. Used with permission.

whereas women don't get that aggressive until the third try. So far the stereotypic role expectations hold. But women also use more competitive strategies than men do in a wide variety of situations, and if placed in defensive positions, women apparently mirror others' competitive strategies and forgive violations of trust less easily than men do (Conrad, 1991).

You can also see marked differences between the ways Westerners and Asians approach conformity. Westerners generally prefer direct strategies, whereas East Asian societies take indirect, nonconfrontational approaches.

In Asian societies, conformity to the group is critically important to group cohesion, but pressures must protect personal face. "Face," according to Stella Ting-Toomey (1988), "is a projected image of one's self in a relational situation . . . conjointly defined by the participants" (p. 215). To confrontationally force a member to back down would humiliate that person, cause him or her to lose face, and damage the group—so more indirect methods are used.

Suppose, for example, you've taken a strong stand in opposition to the rest of your team. Your Western teammates might work together in a meeting, directly trying to persuade you to conform. Your Asian teammates might send a friend to talk to you privately about your friendship, your goals in common, and the importance of the team's success to all of you. The intermediary might indirectly suggest ways you could change your mind without seeming to do so. Either approach may or may not induce you to change, but each has its distinct strategy and sense of individual and group priorities.

Responses   Sometimes members' reasoning and explanation make sense, and an individual goes along because she or he is genuinely persuaded. Sometimes the

GRANFALLOONS

"Granfalloons," a term coined by the American novelist Kurt Vonnegut, are the "proud and meaningless associations of human beings."

British social psychologist Henri Tajfel assigned complete strangers to groups on the most trivial, inconsequential criteria imaginable. Despite the fact that they had never interacted with one another and never would, and that their actions were completely anonymous, they acted as if those who shared their meaningless label were their good friends or close kin. Subjects indicated they liked those who shared their labels, rated them as more likely to have a pleasant personality and to produce better output than out-group members, and allocated more money and rewards to them than to other groups.

What makes the granfalloon tick? First, knowledge that "I am in this group" is used to divide up and make sense of the world. Differences *between* groups are exaggerated, whereas similarity among members of the granfalloon are emphasized in the secure knowledge that "this is what our type does." Out-group members are dehumanized, represented by a simple, often derogatory label. It is a lot easier to abuse an abstraction.

Second, social groups are a source of self-esteem and pride. To obtain the self-esteem the group has to offer, members come to defend the group and adopt its symbols, rituals, and beliefs.

Condensed from Anthony Pratkanis and Elliot Aronson, *Age of Propaganda*, W. H. Freeman and Co., 1992, pp. 167–168. Used with permission.

individual just rolls over rather than fight the pressure. But usually it's a little more complicated than either of those alternatives.

Conformity research goes back a long way. It's been found that under some circumstances, people will change their attitudes, their beliefs, or even their perceptions of reality to conform to a group's norms or opinions, even if they are correct and the group is wrong.

Unfortunately, there's no guarantee that a group will be right. Groups sometimes appear to be "mindless": members lose their individual identities and exhibit "the tendency to become collectively fixated on a rigid frame of reference" (Elmes & Gemmill, 1990, p. 29). In many instances of apparently insane group behaviors, people forget their individual ethical principles, go along with the crowd, and do things they would never do if they had to take personal responsibility.

One explanation for this is the sense of anonymity a group can provide. "I had nothing to do with it. It was the committee's/the union's/the management's/the family's decision. The *group* did it, not I." Anonymity can protect individuals from detection and separate them from self-awareness and moral restraints. When that's gone, mindlessness can rule.

If you want examples of group mindlessness in history, look at the lynch mobs that murdered thousands of African-Americans in the nineteenth and twentieth centuries, at the atrocities of the Chinese Red Guard during the cultural revolution, at the insanity of the Nazi Youth Movement, or at neo-Nazi groups in the United States. They all relied on mindlessness; on group pressure for conformity; on norms and rules; on symbols such as uniforms, salutes, music, posters, and flags. All these can assuage individuals' confusion and need for order, deindividuate people, and enforce a mass mentality that leaves their personal ethical systems far behind.

Perhaps you think that's not a danger in a task team. Sure, it is. Your team's decisions can be important. And too much pressure on one lone voice can silence it, resulting in nobody's noticing that the emperor's stark naked and leading the parade.

But dissenting voices can be heard, and deviant members can influence groups. Conformity need not be mindless, but reasonable and sufficient for a group to be effective. It requires principled leadership and vigilance to achieve that ideal.

Groupthink

Without vigilance, the best of teams can slide into **groupthink**. Irving Janis (1982) coined the term to describe a set of behaviors consistently exhibited by high-power groups that made disastrous decisions. Groupthink, too, is a kind of mind-lessness, or perhaps, "single-mindedness." It keeps out everything but what the group assumes and wants to be true.

When the *Challenger* exploded, the nation was thunderstruck. No one understood how it could have happened. As the inquiry proceeded, it became painfully obvious that information had been available to prevent the tragedy, but it never reached the top levels of the hierarchy. The goal and lift-off date were set; the public relations value of the launch was critical to the administration; and NASA officials were closed off to, and protected from, the data that would have delayed the blast-off and allowed the fatal flaw to be corrected. These people were not stupid; they were both the perpetrators and the victims of groupthink.

Knowing how groupthink happens, what it does, and how to correct it is vital to any ongoing team that has decisions to make.

How Groupthink Happens

Some conditions are like a petri dish in which groupthink can—not necessarily must—grow. These "antecedent conditions" (Janis, 1989a) include group cohesiveness as well as the structure and situation in which the group functions.

Cohesiveness We talked about cohesiveness in Chapter 4 as a glue among team members that can contribute to productivity but can also give members illusions about their group's effectiveness. Even when problems loom, nobody wants to sacrifice the group's cohesiveness by introducing anything that might dissolve the glue, so problems are not discussed. An unwritten "group harmony rule" silences the members (Janis, 1989a, pp. 56–58). Harmony does *not* necessarily mean sweetness and light. Members who don't even like one another may maintain harmony against pressure or a common enemy. This helps them maintain cohesion, self-esteem, and focus. It also can block a group from dealing with issues.

Structure   Structural conditions that make it easy to develop groupthink include homogeneity, inadequate group processes, and insulation from the outside. With homogeneity, members who are alike and like-minded think in narrow channels. With inadequate processes, the group lacks norms for critical thinking and impartial, principled leadership that protect the team's openness to ideas and dissent. With insulation from the outside, members lack information and stimulation necessary to develop and to be effective.

Situation   Situational stress can pressurize a group into groupthink. In the face of a crisis, threat, or even competition with extremely high stakes, members are more likely to remain closed to new or different ideas. This is particularly true if the group's leader advocates a solution and the members see no viable alternative. The problem is worse if the team's self-esteem is low because of recent failures, or it's up against an impossible task, or it faces moral dilemmas for which no alternative meets members' ethical standards. A team in this depressed situation may accept alternatives that, as individuals or under other circumstances, the members might reject.

What Groupthink Does

Teams who experience some or all of the antecedent conditions do not necessarily fall into the groupthink trap, but if they do it shows up in their decision-making processes. Members aggrandize the qualities of the team, close off their minds, and pressure themselves and each other to be unanimous. Consequently, the team fails to survey alternatives, settles quickly on one, and ignores possible difficulties with it. As a result, the groupthinking team does not work out contingency plans for operationalizing its decision—in short, a recipe for disaster.

Here are things to watch out for:

Illusion of invulnerability. Members feel that the team is stronger than any counteracting forces. This leads them "to become over-optimistic and willing to take extraordinary risks. It also causes them to fail to respond to clear warnings of danger" (Janis, 1989b, p. 225).

Belief in inherent morality of the group. The group assumes it has the forces of "right" on its side; therefore, anyone who is in opposition must necessarily be with the forces of "wrong." This relates directly to the next two issues.

Stereotyping members of out groups. The feeling that the "in" group is especially strong and moral is facilitated by feeling that an "out" group is inferior. Groupthink often builds on a "we against them" mentality by stereotyping others as incompetent, inferior, or immoral.

Closed-mindedness and collective rationalizations. Groupthink closes off the group, and members cooperate to resist new ideas and information and to build rationalizations for their preconceived positions. They exclude or fail to get information from experts, outside groups, or resources that could increase their understanding. They also tend to pay attention only to those facts that support a position they favor and to ignore those that weaken it.

Self-censorship. Members of groupthink teams don't allow themselves to say, or sometimes even to think, something that counters the group's thought. Individuals rationalize their positions so they can believe in the unanimity of the group.

Pressure on dissenters. Members of the group exert pressure to conform on anyone who expresses a dissenting thought. Leaders may reinforce this pressure by ignoring, downplaying, or even ridiculing a dissenting view.

Mindguards. Members appoint themselves to keep the leader from hearing anything that might disturb or upset his or her point of view. They deflect messengers with bad news, filter, distort, and hide information that might disturb the illusions. In recent years, congressional hearings have revealed instance after instance of important data that officials allegedly have concealed or distorted in their reports to the president. "Don't bother the chief" means the chief makes groupthink decisions.

Illusion of unanimity. All of this leads to the team's illusion that they all agree, which comes around in a spiral to reinforce all of the behaviors which led to that illusion in the first place (Janis, 1982, 1989a, 1989b).

These behaviors certainly protect a team's sense of self-esteem, superiority, cohesiveness, and strength, but they also create a stranglehold on the group's ability to think rationally and critically. Scary, isn't it, when you consider that the Bay of Pigs, Watergate, Iran-Contra, the *Challenger* launch, and many other disastrous decisions were made under the influence of groupthink (Jaksa & Pritchard, 1988). Even as you read this, groupthink afflicts groups that make high-level decisions affecting your safety and well-being, and that of the entire nation.

It's also vastly irritating, at the least, when groupthink besets less earthshaking policies and actions. We remember a group of students who got together to study for an exam. Under stress but overconfident, they failed to research their topic, they ignored a professor's offer of help, and they relied upon one student's recollections about Plato and Aristotle. As they talked, they created a rubric of misconceptions that all members then used as the database to write their exams. Their professors were boggled at the extent of the inaccuracies—and the students were shocked that they did so poorly. Groupthink had convinced them they had the right information.

How to Reduce Groupthink

It is possible to avoid this blight on teamwork. We suggest that you practice these groupthink-busting methods:

Norm setting. Discuss and agree to norms for openness, protecting the right of dissent, principled leadership, and transactional and task processes.

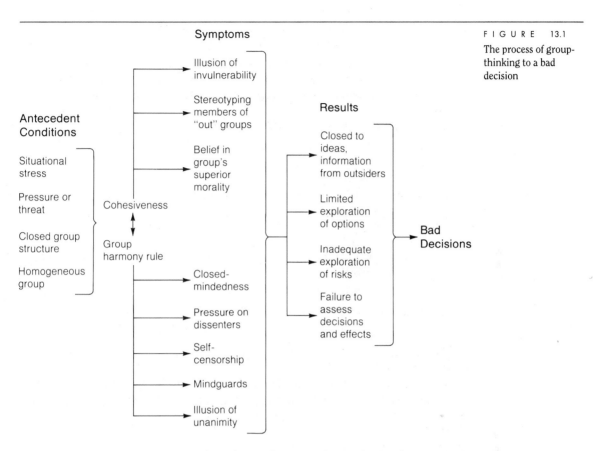

Symptoms

Illusion of
invulnerability

Stereotyping
members of
"out" groups

Results

Closed to
ideas,
information
from outsiders

Belief in
group's
superior
morality

Antecedent
Conditions

Situational
stress

Pressure or
threat

Cohesiveness

Limited
exploration
of options

Bad
Decisions

Closed group
structure

Group
harmony rule

Inadequate
exploration
of risks

Homogeneous
group

Closed-
mindedness

Failure to
assess
decisions
and effects

Pressure on
dissenters

Self-
censorship

Mindguards

Illusion of
unanimity

FIGURE   13.1
The process of group-
thinking to a bad
decision

Assumption testing. Examine discussions for assumptions about facts, values, or people. Look for illusions of invulnerability, moral superiority, or unanimity. Check for stereotyping of other groups and making assumptions about others' behaviors or values.

Information scouting. Aggressively seek outside resources, experts, and relevant information. Janis (1982) suggests inviting outside experts to each meeting and asking them to challenge team members' views. Make it a group expectation that each member will discuss ideas with his or her outside groups and bring the responses back to the team.

Challenging. Have all members take the role of critical evaluator, regularly challenging ideas, information, and suggestions. When considering policies, appoint someone to be devil's advocate, arguing as persuasively as possible for the "other side" (Janis, 1989a).

Structure shifting. Set up outside groups to work on the same issues, and compare deliberations. When considering policies, divide the team into subgroups and meet separately, then come back to the full team and hash out the results.

WHY GOOD MANAGERS APPROVE BAD IDEAS

A recent example [of groupthink] is the film *The Bonfire of the Vanities*. In *The Devil's Candy: The Bonfire of the Vanities Goes to Hollywood,* the new book chronicling the making of the $50 million box-office bomb, author Julie Salamon details how many of the people involved in the making of the movie privately doubted casting decisions and changes in the story line, but no one voiced these doubts to the director, Brian De Palma. De Palma had reservations as well, but because everyone seemed to be in agreement, he convinced himself that he had made the right decisions.

Excerpt from Aimee L. Stern, "Why Good Managers Approve Bad Ideas," *Working Woman,* May 1992, pp. 75, 104. Reprinted with permission from *Working Woman* magazine. Copyright © 1992 by Working Woman, Inc.

These strategies help break down problems of insulation and illusions of unanimity (Janis, 1989a).

Focus meetings. Set up special meetings to focus on single issues when policy decisions may involve serious risks (Janis, 1989a).

Reviewing. Hold "second chance" meetings for people to review decisions and to raise new ideas or concerns about them (Janis, 1982).

Processing. At every stage, review and assess transactional and task processes to be sure that everyone is heard, that pressures to conform are within bounds, and that the team is cohesive without using groupthink.

If your team is vigilant in avoiding the groupthink traps, you can develop a cohesive, productive team that investigates and analyzes its issues openly, clearly, and critically.

Hidden Agendas

You may have left a meeting muttering, "I don't know what he wanted—but I know he stopped us cold." The chances are, that person had a **hidden agenda.** Hidden agendas—individuals' unstated expectations and objectives—underlie many problems teams encounter, because they dictate a person's communication behavior in ways that divert or subvert the team's efforts.

Hidden agendas may be conscious or unconscious, benign or malignant. They stem from many sources and have many effects. We will look briefly at two basic types: egocentric agendas and other-group agendas.

An *egocentric hidden agenda* seeks to achieve objectives exclusive to the individual's personality, needs, wants, expectations, characteristics, and/or background. For example, John, who deeply needs to feel loved, hides an agenda to earn the team's affection. He buries conflicts; he's excessively nice; he may distract the team's attention with personal problems and appeals for sympathy. Sue's agenda is to increase her self-esteem; she acts authoritarian, superior, and concerned only for her own status, thereby creating a defensive climate in the group.

Then there's Tony, whose egocentric hidden agenda is to use the group only as a means to a promotion or to make contacts for business or social purposes. Tony overrides the best interests of the team or the team's goal in pursuit of that agenda.

Other-group hidden agendas are influenced, or even dictated, by members' associations with other groups. These may be reference groups—cultural, ethnic, religious, gender, social, academic, work—whose opinions or wants personally influence the team member; or they may be other groups or levels within the organization that use the individual to influence the team. Other-group hidden agendas pervade group communication at all levels.

A member of your class group, for example, keeps insisting on changing the group's research topic from "Contemporary Protest Music," with which everybody else is happy, to the "Electoral College." Then you find out that she has promised the Political Science Club your team's research for the club's scheduled debate on that topic. Or you discover that your congressperson has "buried in committee" a bill that would protect children from inflammable garments; his hidden agenda is to serve corporations whose products are in violation of the proposed legislation.

Most groups are affected by someone's hidden agenda, large or small. Often hidden agendas distort the flow of information and the processes of analysis. People speak ambiguously, or they create distractions, in order to promote their own agendas. Real issues and assumptions are buried beneath mixed motives, extraneous arguments, manipulation, and games.

Competitive Communication

"They are playing a game. They are playing at not playing a game. If I show them I see they are, I shall break the rules and they will punish me. I must play their game, of not seeing I see the game" (Laing, 1970, p. 1).

You've no doubt felt this way at some time in your life. When you were a child, did you ever go to a friend's house and see the parents deliberately baiting each other? "Too bad you didn't have time to fix dinner, darling." "Yes, dear, but if you'd remembered to fill the gas tank I could have gone to the store." "Right, my love, if I hadn't taken all day to repair that lock you broke." "Well, sweetheart, I wouldn't have broken the lock if you'd installed it the way my brother told you to in the first place." The children know the game; they've seen it played often enough. They pretend not to hear. As a guest, you wince each time one player scores, but you know you must pretend you don't notice. If you reveal your awareness, you know you'll be drawn in.

Like families and other social organizations, teams can get caught up in playing **games**. We're going to examine why people play games, how they play games, how games affect the communication transactions in a team, and how to manage games when they occur.

Why People Play Games

You may have noticed that some people think it's fun or smart to manipulate others with a game. You may also have noticed that some people seem to prefer game playing to direct communication. Why?

To understand why people play games with each other, think back to Chapter 4 where we discussed how people compare costs, benefits, and alternatives to choose an action that provides rewards. When a person manipulates others into playing a game, it is to gain some reward or "payoff." The payoff need not be positive; it's defined in terms of what the individual needs, wants, expects, and can handle emotionally. Those issues go back to infancy and early childhood.

Psychologist Eric Berne (1966) points out that babies start out with the need for contact, or intimacy, with others. Children who grow up in game-playing families may be torn between their need for interdependency and problems the interdependency creates. For example, a child reaches out for comfort when it's hurt; the parent blames the child for the injury and, later, taunts the child for his or her stupidity. The ridicule manipulates the child into doing something the parent wants. This little one has learned the rules of the parent's game. She or he now knows, too, that it's essential to find a way to get the comfort without the blame. The child must develop strategies to control interactions, and these methods carry on into adulthood.

How People Play Games

The game-playing adult has learned to manipulate others into playing out scripts that keep interdependency with others within the individual's survival range and that provide rewards that meet his or her needs.

There are several clues, besides your almost certain gut feeling, that somebody's playing a game. These include the gimmick, the repeated script, and the payoff.

Gimmick   The game player often starts with a particular approach or phrase that requires others to respond as the game player wants them to. Jan comes into your study group meeting, for example, and says, "I just don't get it—I guess I'm stupid or something—I studied for hours, and I just don't get it." This is a negative self-visualization, and unhealthy, but anyone might say it at some time. Jan, however, does it frequently. It's a gimmick when it's repeated and when it leads into a script.

Script   Although a script will not be repeated word for word every time an individual puts it into action, it has an observable general structure. As a script, it includes heroes and villains in some plot, action, and climax.

Back to Jan. If she wants to launch a game, she starts with her gimmick. At this meeting, you respond by saying, "Hey, no, really—it's easy. Just let me show you . . ." and Jan, flaring up as she has at almost every meeting, yells, "Don't patronize me, you jerk. Just because you think I'm an idiot doesn't give you the right to put me down." When this happens, you realize that you didn't want to get into this game again, but somehow you were trapped.

You'll know it's a repeated game if your mind goes back over it: "What am I supposed to say, for crying out loud? How can I make her see I don't think she's stupid?" As you phrase responses to meet her requirements, you're well into the script. Are you the villain? Is she the hero? The victim? What is the plot?

Payoff   As a script develops, a plot emerges—and the climax is the payoff. How can you tell what the payoff is? It may be something tangible; sometimes people set up scripts like these so they can blow up, walk out, and not be held accountable for the work. It may be more complicated, however. Does Jan need to be a victim? Does she need to feel stupid? Does she need to be angry, find a scapegoat, and not deal with learning what she needs to learn? Who knows? Perhaps figuring it out should be left to psychologists. It's enough to understand that strategic communication is going on and that there is *some* reason for it. Your concern, as a team member, is understanding how the game can affect your team's climate.

How Games Affect Climate

Game playing devastates communication climates. You can almost measure the barometric changes, humidity, temperature, and wind chill when a group gets trapped in a game. You remember that supportive climates are cooperative, open, trusting, and empathic; defensive climates are competitive, closed, and lacking in trust and empathy.

A key to how games affect climate is the difference between cooperative and competitive approaches to communication. Competitive approaches assume that if there's a winner, there also must be a loser. There are only two alternatives: *win or lose*. Under this assumption, no one can be trusted, and any risk one person takes is calculated for the purpose of defeating another. A competitive approach means anticipating what others might do, weighing the consequences, and choosing an offensive action or defensive counteraction. Competitive games are appropriate to sports, advocacy, debate, chess—any enterprise in which the objectives are to hone competitive skills and win a victory.

Cooperative approaches assume the opposite on all counts. They assume that it is possible for both—or all—parties to win: a *win-win* outcome. Cooperation relies on trust and taking risks to maximize gains for all. Obviously, cooperative approaches are appropriate to situations in which the objectives are to hone cooperative communication skills, develop relationships, and achieve the goals of all involved.

A person who takes a competitive approach to a situation that should be cooperative will manipulate others' responses to "win points." This leads to others' loss of trust and unwillingness to take cooperative risks. The result is often that no one wins—a *lose-lose* outcome—and the climate is seriously damaged. Yet people repeatedly find themselves in presumably cooperative situations in which others are playing competitive games.

How to Handle a Game

You'll note that we deliberately use the term "handle"; that's because you may or may not be able to stop it. You and the team may hate it, but the person or persons perpetuating the game have rehearsed the script for a long time; they're "one up" on you.

First, analyze the situation. You can start your analysis by answering these questions:

1. How seriously is the game affecting the team? Is it slowing down progress, alienating people, creating minor stress or extreme tension, or bringing work to a halt?

2. How reasonable is the game player? Is the person someone you think you can communicate with cooperatively? Is she or he so intense, so manipulative, or so involved in the game that every communication transaction is a move toward checkmate?

3. How clear is the source of the game? Is it between two people? Does one person regularly open the game and bring other members into his or her transactions?

4. How obvious is the payoff? Is it on someone's not-so-hidden agenda? Is it an identifiable, concrete outcome or an individual's unidentifiable personal need or want?

5. Is the payoff something the team can legitimately assist in providing? Is it an objective the game player can achieve with the team's cooperation? Or is it unrelated to the team or inconsistent with the team's goals?

Based on this assessment, decide whether, and if so how, to confront the issue. The decision can be guided by these general considerations:

Whether or not to intervene. If the game is not bothering the team much, if it's only a minor irritation or even a source of humor, then don't bother. It takes time and energy to end a game. If it's a real problem, then the team needs to consider how to confront it. This requires careful leadership and communication.

Getting to the game. If the game player or players are obvious, then you know where to start. If they are rational and capable of being cooperative, then you have reason to try. If you think the payoff can be identified by discussing the problem—if you think it's something the team can help with, something unrelated to the team, or something of which the team can at least be supportive—then you have a goal to work toward.

Under these sets of circumstances, you may want to confront the game. The criteria in Chapter 9 for cooperative communication climates, in particular the ways to use language, apply here. You have to be sensitive to how you phrase your concerns, because game players are likely to see anything as a move to control them, rather than a move to create a better climate. That's probably how they've learned to see the world.

Never say, "You're playing a game." It's direct, but it's blaming, judgmental, and it triggers yet another game. Own your feelings; use "I" statements; be descriptive; be problem-oriented. Say something like, "I feel uncomfortable, I feel that something's going on here under the surface . . ." or "I'm frustrated because I feel that when you say _____, then I have to say _____. That feels like a game to me, and I'm uncomfortable with it."

No matter how careful you are, a real game player will come back with, "I am *not* playing a game! How dare you accuse me . . ." because that, too, is a game. Then you have to reaffirm your position, gently, assertively. "I didn't say you were playing a game. I only know what *I* feel, and *I* feel our communication is scripted somehow . . ." And so on. Step by step, never casting blame, you work out an understanding of the underlying issues and a more direct way of communicating about them. Working a group's way out of a game can be very painstaking and difficult, but it's possible if all of the above conditions are met.

Conflict

Conflict often scares people. Some people like a good fight, and some greatly enjoy negotiation, but many would prefer not to have to deal with conflict at all. The bottom line, however, is that conflict is inevitable and, sometimes, cyclical. Conflict episodes tend to increase when groups reach the midpoint of their lives, when issues of power, conflict, and decision emerge (Kivlighan & Jauquet, 1990).

Good leadership frequently brings conflict to the fore—not for a fight, but to examine alternatives. Sometimes you have to see how ideas, information, and values clash in order to make reasoned decisions. To do that effectively, you need to understand the various types and sources of conflict and how different people approach conflicts. On those bases, you can learn ways to communicate in conflict and to manage it.

Types of Conflict

Conflicts occur when two or more people perceive that their individual goals are mutually exclusive; that is, accomplishing one's goal keeps another's from being achieved. Differences may be negotiated cooperatively, or transactional processes may degenerate into a dysfunctional clash. That is, it gets personal. Putnam (1986) notes that members may blame one another for disagreements rather than looking to the circumstances. "The tensions inherent in decision dilemmas are managed through power plays by dominant members who control decision rules, procedural directives, and topics of discussion" (p. 179).

It's clear that conflict may be productive or dysfunctional for the team. Witteman (1991) makes the distinction this way: "Productive conflict involves the critical evaluation of ideas. In dysfunctional conflict, members either completely suspend evaluation or focus it on the behavior and personality of other members" (p. 28).

FIGURE 13.2 Bipolar characteristics of conflict	PRODUCTIVE CONFLICT	DYSFUNCTIONAL CONFLICT
	Positive	Negative
	Depersonalized	Personalized
	Substantive	Affective
	Cooperative	Competitive

Take a look at Figure 13.2, in which we've lined up the bipolar characteristics of conflict. When conflict is productive, members depersonalize the process and focus cooperatively on substantive issues. Although competitive conflicts seem to be associated with personalized issues, groups can learn to differentiate types of conflict. Those that do form a mutual understanding of depersonalized conflict, both competitive and cooperative, are more able to reach consensus and cohesion as a group (Pace, 1990, p. 92).

Sources of Conflict

Conflict can arise from a number of sources. One key to understanding a conflict is to discover its source. Some sources are more emotionally laden, and some more easily dealt with, than others. Major sources of conflict are:

Information. If individuals have contradictory information, or differ on the way they interpret the same information or ideas, they may come into conflict.

Resources. When needed resources—time, money, materials, support—are insufficient to go around, people may conflict over who gets what or over how the group should go about getting what it needs.

Expectations. If members' expectations—of individuals' roles or stereotypes, of leadership, of structure or process, of goals—are not met, or if the expectations differ among group members, then pressure to conform and competitive behaviors may lead to conflict.

Needs. When individuals' personal needs, motivations, or agendas block or clash with those of the group or of other individuals, it can lead to pressures to conform, game playing, and/or conflict.

Power and control. Individuals who compete to achieve greater power, to control others' responses, and/or to control outcomes in the team often come into conflict.

Values, attitudes, and beliefs. When two or more individuals hold radically opposed attitudes, values, or beliefs, they may irritate or anger one another. The more deeply an individual holds a value or belief—the more central it is to his or her self-concept—the more threatening it is to have it challenged by another.

Ethics. If values clash over ethical choices, then people may conflict on both philosophical issues and on concrete decisions, because ethical choices often rest on deeply held concepts of self and society.

CONFLICT,   CULTURE,   AND   POWER

Some conflicts that supposedly reflect cultural differences are really power struggles. In one European consortium, the Italian representative succeeded in having a major project named after an Italian hero. One British observer thought this was because Italians are especially conscious of symbols; however, others suggested it was an example of a smaller partner seizing any opportunity to assert its will over larger, more important partners. Understanding Italian culture would not have helped in this situation as much as a grasp of power dynamics.

Personality. If individuals' personalities (which may be linked to any or all of the previous sources of conflict) irritate others, then affective conflict can compound even the most rational conflict over simple content issues.

Approaches to Conflict Management

Your team starts with the styles and approaches that individual members have already learned for dealing with conflict. We're going to look at some of those, and then at some ways your self-awareness and ability to adapt communication can help to manage conflicts.

Individual Styles   According to Katz and Lawyer (1985), "A person's conflict style is in fact determined by the amount of concern he or she has for the relationships and for the personal goals of the parties involved" (p. 95). See if you recognize your own responses to conflict in any of these:

Collaborator. This individual operates from a cooperative, win-win perspective. She or he brings everyone's interests and point of view into perspective and tries to ensure that each person's goals are achieved.

Compromiser. This person works from a cooperative point of view, but doesn't see everyone's winning as a possibility. His or her focus is on negotiating some gains for everyone.

Accommodator. The accomodator's assumption is that situations are competitive, but it's better to yield than to fight it out. The accommodator shifts positions to allow others to win.

Controller. This person has a competitive, defensive, win-lose orientation. Conflict management is a matter of making the right moves to win points and control the responses of others.

Avoider. This response to conflict assumes that all is competitive, win-lose, and that loss is inevitable. This person simply avoids conflict by any means possible.

These styles are related to what psychologists call *fight or flight* reactions to threat. Conflict arises, and adrenalin pumps. People can't often walk out or slug it out, so they adapt their responses to civilized alternatives. An individual who wants to run away may play the role of an avoider or, perhaps, an accommodator. A person whose urge is to fight may be a controller. Either one may moderate his or her urges by working as a collaborator or a compromiser.

Any team may have people who use any or all of these styles of conflict management. A good conflict manager can adapt to the situation; there are occasions when each response may be best. It's helpful to recognize these styles and to work on developing your own flexibility in using—and coping with others'—styles of conflict management.

Communication Adaptation To work with conflict situations, you need to be aware of your own strengths and limitations. It's essential to assess your strengths and build on them. It develops both self-confidence and skill.

By self-awareness we also mean awareness of your own feelings while you are communicating with others. In conflicts, you need to constantly test internal states as well as monitor external communication. You need to check in with your physiological and psychological condition. Is your heart beating too fast? Are you becoming angry, flushed? Do you have your adrenalin under control? Are you cool? Conflict management requires you to be as much in control of yourself as you can, and self-awareness helps you to recognize when you need to step in and work on your own responses. Telling yourself "I'm cool, I'm okay, I'm dealing with this" can help keep your own tendencies to fight or to flee in check as you work with others to manage a conflict.

Self-awareness is also a process of monitoring your verbal, listening, and nonverbal communication with others. It is never more important to be aware of the messages you send or of their possible impact on others than in a group conflict. Sometimes, particularly when the stress is high, people don't hear themselves at all.

Self-monitoring takes practice. Try to listen to what you say and how you say it; try to know what your nonverbal cues are. Watch and listen to others for feedback on what you are doing and how it is affecting them. Adapt and correct your communication to more accurately reflect what you want it to reflect. As you monitor your own communication in a group, you can learn to modify it. We've written at length about transactional and task processes, and about verbal, listening, and nonverbal communication in other chapters, so here we're just going to stress a few things that help to ensure your effective communication in conflict management:

> *Concern for individuals and the team.* Be sure that your coorientation comes through, that it's clear that you care about a win-win solution for everyone, that you can handle your own goals and feelings. At the same time, don't overlook or avoid your interests in the conflict. Just keep them in the broader framework of solutions that work for everyone.

> *Fairness and equity.* People can work through conflict when parties to it work for balance, justice, and fairness. They feel better about the process, they un-

derstand that an ethical framework has surrounded it, and they are able to adjust better to one another.

Good humor. Neale and Bazerman (1991) note the importance of a negotiator's good humor in influencing the generosity and helpfulness of others, enhancing liking and reducing hostility and aggressiveness, and developing creative solutions (p. 161). Good humor is an attitude, a willingness to cut others a little slack.

Sense of humor. Related, but not identical, is an ability to see the humor in a situation, to appreciate an irony, to alleviate stress with appropriate levity. As Napier and Gershenfeld (1985) have observed, "Humor is extremely difficult to quantify, a bit like describing the light emitted by a firefly" (p. 389). Humor can reduce anger and tension; it can point up foolishness and contradictoriness in a friendly way; it can bring people back to focusing on issues and away from personalities. It should be noted, of course, that joking around can also be used to avoid dealing with conflict. In that case, someone needs to identify the problem and get the team focused on managing the issues.

Processes of Conflict Management

You may have noticed that we talk about conflict "management," not conflict "resolution." There are several reasons for this. First, when conflicts are resolved, it's because the team managed a process to achieve that resolution. Second, conflict management may actually require finding a conflict—identifying issues, raising points of clash, and then analyzing them—in order to make good decisions. In that case, the point is not resolving a conflict but discovering and managing it. Third, resolving a conflict, once and for all, isn't always possible. When the sources of conflict remain, a single issue may be resolved, but the potential for conflict continues. A team needs, therefore, to develop skills and approaches to managing conflict through its transactional processes.

Here are some suggestions for starting the process of conflict management:

1. Assess its importance. Is the conflict one that can impede the team's progress, impair relationships, or impact on a decision? If it is, it's important.

2. Diagnose the conflict. What are the sources of the conflict? Where and how do goals conflict? What is the focus—substantive, content, task issues? Interpersonal, emotional clashes? Both?

3. Analyze people's interests. Do they have positions on a question, fact, information? Are they motivated by differing needs, attitudes, values, beliefs? What are their goals? What expectations do they have?

4. Analyze the way the team normally transacts individual, task, and team issues. Are there patterns or expectations that can form a basis for managing the conflict, or are there factors that have to be dealt with before the conflict can be managed?

The answers to these questions can help you select the strategy most appropriate to managing the problem. Among the possible strategies are ignoring it, approaching it indirectly, or confronting and negotiating it.

Sometimes ignoring a conflict does work; sometimes it doesn't. You just have to hedge your bets in making that decision.

Managing conflict indirectly is a choice based on the norms and expectations of individuals and the team. Normally it is called for if interpersonal or private issues are involved, and/or if individuals are not likely to respond positively to direct confrontation. Remember, for example, that Asian groups often use intermediaries. But unlike North Americans, who seek an objective, detached person as a conflict mediator, Asians seek intermediaries who are personally involved with the parties and have more "face," or status and respect, than the conflicting individuals have. This intermediary helps each person work out ways of saving face so she or he can accept a resolution to the problem (Ting-Toomey, 1988). Some ways of approaching a conflict indirectly are:

1. Use an intermediary to negotiate privately.
2. Restructure responsibilities or contacts to diminish interdependence between conflicting people.
3. Suggest new, more acceptable ways of interpreting the differences.
4. Confer with the conflicting parties and the leader, a member, or a consultant.

Confronting and negotiating the issue requires cooperative, win-win, full involvement of the members. If this is the best bet for your team, we suggest that you follow the diagnosis process with these steps:

1. Identify what each party to the conflict wants. Talk until it's clear and affirmed by each person.
2. Identify in what ways both parties can get what they want, and isolate the items that seem to be irreconcilable.
3. Assess the value of the achievable, mutual goals. Work for agreement that these outweigh the irreconcilable points.
4. Talk these points through. Eliminate unimportant differences, and isolate important ones.
5. Talk through important differences; find all points in common within each difference, and work out compromises.
6. Agree on the solution.
7. In a substantive conflict, move on.
8. In an affective/personal conflict, create an agreement or contract as to what each party will do to manage potential problems in the future. Make it positive and specific.

The last two may require some further explanation. If the conflict is substantive—say, over whether the team has enough money for a project—then a decision "yea" or "nay" allows you to go on to your planning. But if it's affective—if, for example, a personal conflict has arisen because I'm sarcastic and you're sensitive—then I need to agree to monitor my behavior, be aware of your feelings, and soften my communication. You probably need to agree to try to take me

---

CASE ANALYSIS 13.1

The diverse task force members' personalities "meshed" well. Conflicts focused on issues, not on individuals.

One way the team managed conflicts was to go back to common goals. Members focused on the similar things they wanted to achieve rather than on differences among them. Early in the life of the group, EDF members brought in a proposal. After discussion, they found that McDonald's already had some action under way in each of the ten proposed areas. That provided common ground for subsequent work.

Some conflicts were resolved through hours and hours of discussing differences. The team worked through those by exploring basic assumptions and getting down to very specific levels of detail in terms of how things would work in the day-to-day McDonald's operations. Members from "both sides" altered their positions as they learned from one another.

Issues for Your Consideration

1. What principles of conflict management were present in the task force's handling of different positions?
2. What characteristics of this task force could have created serious, even insurmountable conflicts had the members not handled issues in the way they did?
3. In what ways did the membership and processes of this team help to avoid groupthink?

---

with a grain of salt, but also to tell me if you're upset before you get to the explosion point.

It's probably obvious that, at each stage of this process, it is vitally important to *listen empathically and interactively*, to *support and confirm each other*, to *communicate clearly and assertively*, and to *maintain a cooperative, open, nondefensive climate*.

Summary

In this chapter, we've called your attention to some challenges that teams face, including members' deviance from group expectations and pressures to conform. Conformity pressure can short-circuit ethics and good decision making by giving people anonymity within the group and by silencing important contributions. Principled leadership, support from others, and competence make it more likely that a dissenter will be heard.

Cohesiveness, necessary for group satisfaction and productivity, can also be a problem. Too much cohesiveness, along with structural problems and situational pressures, can lead to groupthink. Under the illusion that it is superior, moral, and invulnerable, the group screens out information and analysis. Groupthink decisions can be disastrous. Clear norms for vigilant information gathering and decision making help to avoid groupthink.

Hidden agendas distort group processes through individuals' egocentric or other-group goals and often result in game playing, or scripted and manipulative communication.

Games involve a starting gimmick, a predictable script that controls communication choices, and some payoff or reward for the game player. Stopping a game requires a cooperative, win-win, trusting, supportive climate in which to examine carefully the interpersonal dynamics of the game. Sometimes it requires a full conflict-management approach to get it under control.

Productive conflict is substantive, depersonalized, and cooperative; it can yield better analysis and decisions. Dysfunctional conflict is personalized and competitive, and can harm the group's cohesiveness, productivity, and satisfaction. Managing conflict requires diagnosing the types and sources of conflict. As a conflict manager, you need to be self-aware and adaptive; important qualities are concern for individuals and the team, fairness and equity, good humor, and a sense of humor. Appropriate management strategies range from ignoring a conflict to full-fledged confrontation.

Exercises

1. With a group in class, go back over the chapter and list ways a team can manage conflict. Starting with this list:
   a. Refine it into a list of the most important ideas.
   b. For each item, write a short, clear statement that describes the team or member behavior.
   c. From these items, create an assessment form that a team could use to evaluate how well it manages conflict.
   d. Test the form by administering it to another group.
   e. Revise the form, using feedback from the other group.

2. In a group, brainstorm a list of games you've seen people play in groups. Choose four or five games that you all have seen or experienced. For each game on your list:
   a. Give the game a name that describes it.
   b. Identify the "gimmick" that is used to start the game.
   c. Describe, briefly, how the "script" develops.
   d. Identify payoffs that might motivate a person to play the game.

   e. Suggest ways that a group can stop or manage the game.
   Share your game book with the class.

3. Think of a time when a group pressured you to conform to its opinions or norms. What was the situation? Who put on the pressure? How? How did you feel? What did you do?

   Was there ever a time that you put pressure on a deviant to conform to a group you were in? How did you do it? What was the effect? How do you feel about putting pressure on others?

4. With a small group of students, review the concepts of groupthink. Then create a skit that shows a decision-making group with all the symptoms of groupthink. In your skit, have the group arrive at an ill-considered groupthink decision. Act out your skit for the class. Ask your classmates to identify when and how groupthink was operating and what communication behaviors revealed the effects of groupthink. Then discuss how the group in the skit could have prevented or stopped itself from groupthink effects.

Team Problems and Participation: Managing the Obstacles

"Just tell us what to *do* with this . . . #@!+*!"
Sometimes a little gravel in the shoe can halt the proudest parade.

One of "Murphy's laws" says that if it's possible for something to go wrong, it will. Groups of people only multiply the potential for problems. To cope with this law, we suggest you anticipate what could go wrong and prevent it. But if that should fail, turn the something wrong into something right. Make it work to your advantage. That's leadership.

The previous chapter dealt with mines and boulders on the path to the goal. This one deals with petty, annoying problems that throw gravel in your shoes and stop the team in its tracks. The trick is to manage the gravel before it turns into boulders or—maybe—to turn the gravel into magic dust to speed you on your way. Because sometimes what seems a problem becomes an opportunity, and the opportunity can lead to a triumph.

Specifically, in this chapter we focus on the problems caused by individual members who are difficult and problems faced by new members. We also consider ways to bolster inadequate leaders and leaders in transition and point out methods for making meetings—frequently the most complained-about issue—

more effective. Finally, we take a look at organizational and system issues. Our goals for this chapter are to help you:

1. Identify and manage individual member problems.

2. Recognize and manage leader problems.

3. Know how to help the team improve its processes and development.

4. Know how to improve team meetings.

5. Understand and solve problems with the organization and systems.

Individual Member Problems

Throughout this book, we've extolled the virtues of diversity and individual characteristics in team members. With the advantages, however, come problems with members' idiosyncracies. People who seem "difficult" may trip up the team, and members who are new or different may be lost because they're unfamiliar with the road the team is traveling. Teams must know how to identify and cope effectively with these problems.

People Who Seem "Difficult"

Even the nicest people sometimes get nasty when irritated. This is particularly true when one annoying individual blocks progress by teammates who are very interdependent and concentrated on their task. That individual may dominate the others or do distracting things; she or he may withdraw from participation or be irresponsible about the work. Even worse, the difficult person may be reprehensible—manipulating, unethical, dishonest, mean. When you run into any of these behaviors, it's a temptation to knock the individual "upside the head." Since that's not allowed, it helps to prevent mayhem and create harmony if the team keeps these points in mind:

An individual problem is a team problem. When even one person fails to be a full member of the team, the entire team suffers—and so does the task.

Something allows or encourages an individual to be a problem. According to Scholtes (1988), about 85% of problems are in the system and only 15% are directly caused by individuals. He suggests, "Examine each problem in light of what the group does to encourage or allow the behavior and what the group can do differently to encourage more constructive behavior" (p. 6-32).

The team must avoid attribution and labeling. The infamous tendency to attribute motives and characteristics to others, and consequently to paste a label on them, is a serious mistake. First, the label may be wrong. Second, it diverts attention from the issue and puts it on the individual. It's the problem that needs to be corrected—not the person.

The team must care about the individual. Even if you don't really like a person, you can care about him or her, both as a member of the team and as a human being. If the team cares, it can deal with the problem. If it doesn't, the team only makes it worse.

With these perspectives in mind, let's examine some specific problems in terms of three questions:

1. *What does the person do?* Isolate the specific behaviors or actions causing the problem.
2. *Why does it happen?* Figure out why and how the team permits it. Resolve to correct the team's motivation and behaviors that allow or encourage the difficult person to create a problem.

3. *How can we change it?* Focus communication to change the specific behaviors, not to punish or isolate the individual.

A team can use these guidelines to understand and influence the behaviors of difficult people.

Dominating   A dominating individual demands attention, controls the discussion, keeps others from being heard, and prevents the team from concentrating on its task. Often this person creates resentment and power struggles in the team. However, she or he may care about the team and its goals, have something important to contribute, and bring energy and enthusiasm to the team process. What can be done to get the benefit of a dominator's participation without being overwhelmed by him or her? Using the guidelines suggested previously, try analyzing and changing the situation.

What the Person Does   Does she or he interrupt a lot? Make too many authoritative-sounding assertions? Bully others with verbal or nonverbal communication? Always bring the focus back to his or her interests? Speak loudly? State opinions aggressively? Try to analyze the behaviors specifically.

Why It Continues   Does the dominator's behavior provide an excuse for not dealing with important issues? Is the team afraid of confronting him or her because of power or status, fear of conflict, or concern for the person's feelings? Is dealing with the behavior too much work, so members just withdraw and let the dominator control them?

How to Change It   First, the team must want to reduce the dominating behavior. If it doesn't, then it probably doesn't stop other blocking behaviors, either. The team may have to examine why it doesn't and why it should. Willingness to change goes beyond one person's behavior. It goes to team motivation and process, and it can be discussed in that context rather than in relation to one person.

If the team wants to deal with the problem, then members may be able to confront the issues. Specific approaches should fit the person's behaviors. For example:

Interrupting. Every time the dominator interrupts, you can say, "Wait, please, I'm not finished." If she or he has interrupted someone else, step in with "Wait, please, I want to hear what so-and-so has to say."

Authoritarian statements. You can ask (courteously) for more information or support, or help to qualify his or her know-it-all statements: "Where could we get some data to support that?" "Then you'd say that it's probably—but not necessarily—true?" "So this is your opinion, but it isn't proven yet?"

Bullying and power grabbing. If the dominator uses strategies to control others, you may have to confront the problem. Using descriptive statements, say how you feel when this person dominates: "I am uncomfortable when you stand

"I guess when he joined this group, political *action wasn't the kind he had in mind!"*

over me like that." "I am frustrated because I feel you control our meetings too much." Be ready to provide specific examples of the behaviors; ask what the team can do to keep participation in better balance; help the team to negotiate its role in the transactions. Sometimes a dominating person just doesn't know how to stop, and the team can help.

Distracting   Some people dedicate themselves to distracting the team from its work. They may be playful distractors, like adorable puppies—or aggressive distractors, more like vicious attack dogs. One is more fun than the other, but both keep the team from the task.

What the Person Does   Does he or she play, joke around, tease, and act up constantly? Mug? Tell outrageous stories? Change the subject as soon as the team gets its teeth into an issue? Does he or she pick fights? Divert attention to outside frustrations and conflicts? Take offense? Pout? Specifically identify the ways this individual distracts others.

Why It Continues   We've all been in classrooms where students gratefully egged on a clown or an irrelevant-questioner who diverted the teacher's attention from a boring lecture. We've all been in groups where it was more fun to play around, watch a fight, or advise someone on the impending breakup of her or his love life than to do the job at hand. Comics, wrestlers, and soap operas often draw more attention than real life.

A team's motivation to allow distractions could be that the members like being distracted; like an excuse for not accomplishing much; or like to think of themselves as nice, supportive people who understand when a member diverts their attention. They may be uncertain or fearful about confronting the problem. In these instances, the team may encourage the distractions by *not* bringing the conversation back to the topic, by asking questions or giving responses that encourage the distractor to keep going, or by piggybacking other distractions on top of the ones the "difficult" person has provided.

How to Change It   The team needs to assess its transactional, as well as task, goals and processes. Then it needs to commit itself to limiting distractions in order to achieve its task goals. These are issues that can be raised as matters of process, not in connection with one individual.

Specific approaches to various forms of distraction are:

Playful distracting. Humor or gentle teasing may help to stop distracting behaviors. Or direct intervention, carefully, good-humoredly, and repeatedly used, can get the point across: "I think I heard a bell—recess must be over." "I'm having fun, but I know I'm going to hate myself later. We'd better get back to work." In desperation, you can simply ask the individual to change: "Susan, you're one of the funniest people I know, but I feel we aren't going to get this job done."

Aggressive distracting. If a member is constantly picking fights and exhibiting anger, something is wrong. He or she may have an abrasive personality and/or be angry about some personal issues or conflicts. These distractions can ruin a team's transactional processes and climate. They must be handled with careful confrontation, using conflict management strategies such as those discussed in Chapter 13.

Nonparticipating   People who consistently stare out the window, doodle, mutter monosyllabic responses to questions, and say "whatever" to any suggestions may not seem to constitute a major problem, but they certainly reflect and create one. They reflect a problem in that the team's processes obviously do not involve every member; they create one in that they fail to facilitate the team's development and task. Their reasons may be many: Perhaps they really don't care, and they're in the situation against their will. They may feel excluded because they are different in some way, or feel underprepared and unqualified, or shy. Perhaps they are deeply distracted by personal issues. Whatever the cause, the determined nonparticipant can become a resistant mountain to move.

What the Person Does   Watch carefully. Does the individual fail to make eye contact, close off with gestures and body position, show facial expressions that are angry, sad, distant? Does she or he do other reading or writing, or pay attention to other things, while the team is working? Do the person's gestures, body positions, or facial expressions react negatively to others' actions or statements? When the person does speak, is his or her voice and speech closed-off and noncommunicative? What kinds of messages does she or he give? Does this member contribute well sometimes and not others? How consistent is the nonparticipation? Is it connected in some way with the task, with transactional processes, with other members, with topics?

Why It Continues   Groups often ignore nonparticipants because it's easy to do. They're quiet, after all. It's also easier to ignore people than to find out what's going on. If the team finds out that the individual's nonparticipation is caused by a problem with the team, it could be sticky to resolve the issue, and people often prefer to avoid sticky issues. Finally, teams sometimes ignore nonparticipation because their efforts to involve people meet with rejection, or even resentment. Consequently, members encourage the behavior by ignoring the individual, occasionally throwing a meaningless question his or her way, and failing to develop connections with that person.

How to Change It   The team must recognize the importance of each person to the team's syntality and resolve to work to gain full participation. That means making up your mind to be aware, empathic, and inventive in meeting the needs of the individual and the team. You can use some of the following options:

Reach out in discussions. If the person is simply shy, or feels inadequate for some reason, gentle questioning may do it: "Jim, what do you think?" "Hey, Jim, we need you here." "Jim's had some experience with this subject . . . got any ideas, Jim?"

Make assignments. If a member feels useless or unqualified, it can help to be sure that she or he, along with other members, has specific work to do for the team. Reporting and discussing it can help that person develop confidence.

Connect outside of the team. Somebody on the team may need to connect with the nonparticipant on a human level. It requires getting to know that individual, caring, finding out what's happening, acting as a bridge between the person and the team. When members know the individual, then it may be easier to draw him or her into participating.

Manage team problems. If you observe, or discover through outside discussion, that the member has withdrawn because of a problem with someone on the team or the team itself, then members need to deal with the problem in the same careful, problem-oriented way we talked about in managing conflict. And they may need to change some of their own behaviors in accordance with what they've discovered.

Irresponsible   Here's the team tooth-grinder: people who don't show up, show up late, and/or don't do their share of the work. Handle those, and you handle many of the problems in teamwork—but these may be the toughest of all to manage. Sometimes irresponsible behavior is the consequence of other issues, so you might think about the irresponsibility of a member in terms of what we've said about nonparticipants who have legitimate problems.

What the Person Does   An irresponsible person may talk a good game about being at meetings and doing the work, but doesn't show up and doesn't produce. This person may make excuses, laugh it off, make a plea for sympathy, and/or distract the team with other issues. She or he may barrel into a meeting (albeit late) with such enthusiasm and so many ideas (albeit unsupported by research or thinking-through) that the team believes the problem is now solved and this person will be reliable in the future. Be not deceived.

Why It Continues   Over and over again, we've seen groups sabotaged by one or two members' irresponsibility because the team didn't find the motivation to deal with it before it became a major problem. The members thought they had plenty of time; they thought it would work out; maybe they even enjoyed a hang-loose kind of norm in the early stages of the team. Sometimes they liked the irresponsible one and covered for him or her, hoping that person would change behavior soon. Consequently, they encouraged others' lateness, absence, and lack of work. By the time members realized that their effectiveness was being damaged, it was too late.

How to Change It   The first thing is to not allow these behaviors to start. Team norms and expectations about each person's responsibility and reliability have to be set early, and people have to be serious about them. Once an individual shows a pattern of irresponsibility, the members must pay attention immediately. You have these choices:

Ignore it. This is not a real alternative. The point of being a team is to be a team, and the irresponsible person is not a teammate.

Approach it as a team problem. Take up the issue of group norms. Discuss them as a team process problem. Talk about changing and reinforcing the norms.

Talk to the individual privately. Have the leader or one member approach the individual. Use reasoning; explain the importance of his or her work to the team; try to find out if there are outside or team causes behind the person's behavior.

Confront the individual as a team. Talk about the importance of his or her work to the team; ask for the person's suggestions as to how the problem can be solved; try to negotiate a different behavior pattern.

Go to a higher authority. No one wants to do this, but sometimes intervention by the boss, teacher, or group leader is needed. This obviously is getting to tough measures.

Throw the bum out. Occasionally, the situation is so desperate that a team wants to evict a member. It's rarely either a viable or desirable alternative within a team's structure or place in an organization. If the work has been brought to a standstill by one member's irresponsibility, and the team has tried every possible way to get his or her cooperation, then the members may be able to tell the individual she or he is no longer welcome to work with the team.

Most of these alternatives are designed to induce a person to behave more responsibly toward the group. Before the team gets desperate, it should try these positive approaches. Make it clear that the team cares about this person and truly wants his or her full participation. But what if the situation does degenerate to the point of separation? The person can face the consequences from professors or managers for work not accomplished, but you must be ready to justify your actions with clear, accurate accounts of the irresponsible behaviors *and* of the team's efforts to work cooperatively until the situation became impossible.

More realistically, if these all fail, you need a contingency plan. To make one, think of these possibilities for working around the individual:

Restructure job assignments and responsibilities. Find ways that the person *can* contribute to reaching the goal, but make his or her portion sufficiently discrete so that the team can achieve its purposes without that contribution.

Redesign the project or restructure goals. That might mean eliminating some goals or methods you had originally planned. The team may need to eliminate the need for some particular talent or expertise this person had been expected to provide.

We have seen teams in classes and organizations take exactly these steps. When the teams pulled together tightly to overcome the problem, they thought of creative ways to work around the irresponsibility of one or two individuals, and their final projects came out better than they might have otherwise.

"Waitjustadamminute!" you say? "That isn't fair! The lazy, good-for-nothing will profit (share in the team's glory, the grade, the reward) from *our* work!"

You're right, of course; it isn't fair. We have two responses to that. First, your objective as a team is to reach your goal with the best possible effect. If you have to see someone "get" something they haven't fully earned, that may just be a price you have to pay.

Second, "what goes around comes around." Many Chinese believe that life is a rolling wheel: people come around through reincarnation to places they have been. You may have an unsettled debt to that person from a previous existence. None of us can see the present and future effects of another's behavior, even in this life. It is enough to pull together as a team and reach the goal. If you can bring every member into full participation, that's the ideal. If you can't, then you get as close to the ideal as you can—and you reach the goal anyway.

Reprehensible   By reprehensible, we mean consistently unethical, dishonest, conniving, sexist, racist, bigoted, nasty. We mean a person who enjoys making other people miserable, who has no conscience that you can see, who takes the immoral road by preference. This individual constantly twists conversation into a negative rope with which he or she tries to hang the team. We hope none of your teams ever has such a person on it, but once in a while, it happens.

What the Person Does   Does this person make snide comments about people? Stereotype and make belittling jokes about intellect, sex, race, disabilities, nationalities, socioeconomic classes? Does the reprehensible one falsify evidence, lie, connive, or suggest dishonest and unethical actions? Belittle others' concerns for values and issues of fairness or justice, twist ideas into sarcasm, goals into foregone failures? Does this individual convey, with verbal and nonverbal communication, his or her feelings of superiority and desire to manipulate others?

Why It Continues   A team may fail to cope with these behaviors because members can't really believe they're happening, because it's too painful, because it seems hopeless. They may sometimes encourage racist, sexist, bigoted behavior by laughing at unacceptable jokes or unethical proposals. Often people react this way because they don't know what else to do. They don't think of laughing, or ignoring such behavior, as encouraging it—but it does.

A team needs to see such behavior as truly harmful. It's harmful to the spirit of the group, to members whose self-concepts or values it attacks, and to the ethics and worth of the team's decisions. Once members see the harm, they can determine to stop allowing the reprehensible individual to undermine their team.

How to Change It   Look at these acts as conflict, because they strike deeply at people's values, self-concepts, roles, and ethics. Therefore, you may have to use a full conflict-management process to handle them. For starters, however, be very assertive in these ways:

Don't laugh at jokes that belittle individuals and groups. Courteously, but assertively, state an objection to them: "Could we please not have that kind of joke? I, personally, am really bothered by it."

Do not let an unethical statement, suggestion, or act go unchallenged. It's one thing to recognize that another's ethical code may well be different and deserve respect; it's another to tolerate behavior that's odious to your own. Silence *is* interpreted as consent.

Become an advocate for members whom the offending member attacks, belittles, or manipulates. Protect, defend, stand up for those people. This is no time to be shy.

Convert negativism into positivism. Assertively state your preference for looking at things from a constructive point of view. Object firmly to a norm of looking at things negatively. Explain that negative thinking poisons creativity and hurts people.

P R O D U C T   D E V E L O P M E N T   T E A M S   D E M A N D   G O O D   C O A C H I N G

It's not uncommon these days for product development teams to be comprised of people from all walks of corporate life—R&D, manufacturing, marketing, finance and, in the most progressive companies, customers and suppliers. . . . But . . . conflict is a natural by-product of cross-functional teams, and proper conflict management is critical to team success.

Agreement on Intentions

"When you are able to get absolute agreement of strategic intent . . . things happen," said Xerox Corp.'s vice president of research, Frank Squires.

Andersen Consulting partner Tom Harig recommends: Provide the team with an external focus so members concentrate more on what they have in common and less on their loyalties to specific functional areas. Develop cross-functional measuring standards . . . they "indicate whether the entire process is in sync." [And] create a different organizational structure—"a project structure vs. a functional organization, for instance."

Structuring Rewards

Squires says "Structure rewards in such a way that teams win or lose depending upon the team's performance rather than individual performance. . . ."

Special Management Skills

Team managers are facilitators. . . . "They are consensus-driven, they have a high tolerance for ambiguity, and they know how to lead," Harig explained. "They have firm opinions, but they leave them at home and let the team build solutions."

A manager's empathy with members is important, but it's probably more important that team members have empathy for one another . . . best achieved, said Harig, by having team members "try on the hats" of those in different functional areas.

But perhaps the best chance for quality teamwork lies in the careful selection of the participants. . . . "Put together people who appear to be willing to change," Harig recommended. . . . "The ones you're looking for may not be the best performers," he added. "But they can be excellent performers in a cross-functional team environment."

Condensed from William Bonnar Yanes, "Executive Update," *Investor's Daily*, Friday, November 9, 1990, p. 6. Used with permission.

Members Who Are New or Different

People who are similar to one another, and people who start out toward a goal together, develop similar maps of the territory they'll travel. Some members, however, may join the team en route; sometimes teams change membership on a fairly regular basis. Others, even though they start out with the team, may have a different view of the trip; their cultures or subcultures make them new to the experience. This is obvious if a person is a recent immigrant, but it's also a factor for anyone who tries to participate in a group different from his or her previous experiences. Such a team member may be a stranger in a strange land.

Teams need to be able to provide a map for the new person. To do that, they must understand about newness; know how to develop an intergroup ethic for communicating with team members who are new and different from the majority; and be able to design strategies for orienting new and not-so-new members.

Understand "Newness"   According to Gudykunst (1988), the new or different member brings to the team the communication expectations and socialization of a different group; communication between the team and that person is, in effect *intergroup* communication. The stranger, not understanding exactly how this new group functions, feels anxious and tries to be accepted somehow. Initial encounters are "a series of crises," as the outsider tries to become socialized to the new situation (p. 125). She or he functions at a constant state of awareness and uncertainty in the new situation. The more established the team is, or the more homogeneous the other members are, the more developed is the team's syntality, and the more difficult, uncertain, and anxiety-producing the experience may be for the stranger.

Develop an Intragroup Ethic   For the sake of the strangers in your team, and for the sake of the group itself, your team needs an ethic that provides room for all. If you recognize the differences among groups and cultures, you realize that even "treating others as I would have them treat me" assumes that others wish to be treated the way you would wish to be treated. The others' world views and social expectations may intervene. You may need to consider how they would wish to be treated as, possibly, a little different from how you would.

We, the authors, like to be treated directly, so we've both always tried to treat others that way. Then we realized that some people really hate direct communication. Perhaps we need to say to ourselves, "I would like others to consider how I feel, and then try to treat me accordingly; therefore, I will consider how *others* might feel, and then try to treat them accordingly."

Richard Johannesen (1990) asks whether it is possible and desirable to have an ethical code for intercultural communication. He notes Sitaram's and Cogdell's (1976) proposed 35-item code of ethics for intercultural communicators (pp. 217–219). This code rests, it seems to us, on two major principles: (1) that a communicator should *respect* other people's religions, world views, norms, expectations, and their rights to behave in accordance with those bases; and (2) that an individual should *adapt* to others' experiences and expectations so as to create an open and supportive bridge between the two frames of reference.

Communicators who understand and apply these principles do not put others down or assume the superiority of their own groups. They are considerate in verbal and nonverbal communication; they seek ways of understanding; they broaden their tolerance; they adapt their communication to make the other comfortable. These principles seem to us to be basic to good transactional processes among all people, but especially with people who are strangers in any way.

Orient Members   This seems obvious, but teams, committees, departments—any group you can name—forget it constantly. Never mind student or classroom groups; we've seen college departments come close to losing valuable teachers because they took it for granted that those new people could just "plug in" to the program and the department's way of doing things. Orienting people involves several critical aspects:

Make sure someone takes responsibility. A designated leader or a specific member might take this responsibility. Of course, the entire team should make it an ongoing norm to provide orientation and to connect with anyone who might need that help.

Welcome and connect members to the team. The team needs to reduce the anxiety and uncertainty a stranger feels. Make a special effort to be interested, to listen, to try to understand, and to share yourself. This, too, seems obvious, but somehow it often gets lost in the press of the task or of already established relationships.

Design activities. Even if it's only "going for coffee," some social activities are almost essential for people to get to know one another without the pressures of the task. It is often in outside interpersonal encounters that a newcomer can ask the questions about team norms that she or he can't ask in team meetings.

Help people to understand group norms and characteristics. Listen carefully to find out what confuses the stranger. Trade understandings; that's the only way you can know how to help. Think about norms of power and status, of leadership, of participation. Perhaps your team likes to argue, and does it without rancor. Explain that so that the first time it happens the new member doesn't feel under attack. If the group seems lazy and laid back, but isn't really, explain that.

Don't count on the team's self-perceptions. What you think is "true" may not be to someone else. People of other cultures often see North Americans as "seeming friendly," but not really being so. Perhaps to North Americans "friendly" is a way of relating to others, not necessarily of developing closeness. To some other cultures, friendliness is asking people to your home for dinner, inviting them to an event, extending help. Many new immigrants have felt confused and lonely because their expectations of friendly Americans were so different from the "let's do lunch" they found.

Introduce people to the substantive issues of your team. Tell them about the team's history, purposes and goals, plans, timelines, projects. Explain the structural factors of systems, hierarchy, leadership, responsibility, limitations, policies, and rules that affect the team. Encourage questions; provide supplementary printed material; allow plenty of time for the person to absorb the information; provide opportunities later for further questions and reinforcement. If there's a lot of information, a new person can't absorb it all at once.

Leader Problems

A fine leader can help a group develop into a superteam; a poor leader can frustrate it at every step of the way. Teams studied by Larson and LaFasto (1989) were most frustrated when their leaders could not or would not confront members whose performance was inadequate. The second most frustrating problem was the leader who "dilutes the team's effort with too many priorities" (p. 137). Leaders often overestimate the morale, effectiveness, and satisfaction of their teams, and may be unaware of the stress their shortcomings place on the team. Members, however, tend to believe the leader knows what the issues are but just won't correct them. They often believe that the leader's insensitivity to members' frustration is due to personal ambition and a willingness to use the team for his or her career purposes (pp. 137–138).

In most cases, it is not within the power of the team to replace an inadequate appointed leader. There are, however, ways to bolster the leader, to make him or her more effective and helpful to the team. Often, too, teams go through crises when one leader leaves and another takes over. Understanding how to ease the transition can help a team to move ahead with its task effectively.

Bolstering the Leader

It isn't hard to know *when* you and your teammates should use your leadership to help an inadequate leader. You should do it when the team cannot replace the leader because she or he was appointed by a higher authority or because of an elected term, and when his or her lack of skill or commitment is damaging your team's effectiveness or morale. If you must choose between living with frustration or making the situation better, it's usually preferable to do the latter. *Why* you should do it, then, is to relieve frustration, improve morale, and increase the effectiveness of your team. To bolster the leader for these purposes, your team needs to understand the reasons for his or her inadequacy and know some strategies for correcting it.

Reasons for Inadequacy   Often a leader's inadequacy comes down to qualifications for leading. When a worker is promoted to team leader because of outstanding job performance, the person may or may not know anything about leadership. A leader who got the job because of political or personal connections does not necessarily know how to lead, either. Even when a team chooses someone as leader because the members like that person, his or her abilities are not guaranteed.

Sometimes, too, the circumstances make leading difficult. Howell and his associates (1990) have pointed out that "circumstances often counteract the potential power of leadership, making it virtually impossible in some situations for leaders to have much impact regardless of their style or how good the fit is between leader and situation" (p. 22). The leader may be unable to obtain resources or have no authority to make decisions, or responsibilities may be too dispersed.

The leader's own frustrations and defensiveness may intensify the problems. A person who doesn't know how to do a job and is afraid to ask for help is not likely to correct inadequacies. As a result, a designated leader may be a leader in name only.

In this case, the team may find itself without resources, with meetings in a shambles, with members snapping at each other and transactional processes a sorry mess. It may find it has no idea what its goals are, let alone how to reach them. Communication with the organization may be poor or nonexistent; members may have inadequate information, fed by rumors and speculation. The leader isn't correcting the problem—what can the members do?

Strategies for Improving a Leader's Effectiveness Although some approaches to improving this situation are purely within the organization's realm, there are some things that teams can do for themselves by working on transactional and task processes. For example:

1. Devise ways to get feedback from the task itself instead of from the leader. Use assessment as you go along; discuss your progress; design adaptations as a team.
2. Find and affirm the value in the team's job; talk about what it means to the team to do it well; celebrate your successes as a team.
3. Create cohesiveness by focusing on high performance, traditions, and connections within the team and by relying on the team itself to resolve problems and provide mutual support (Howell et al., 1990).

These strategies rely upon shared leadership among team members and intensive effort in both transactional and task processes.

The team can do some specific things, too, to straighten out disorganization and move the task along. They require tact and involvement, but they'll work:

1. Open communication paths with the leader; make suggestions, requests, and proposals for team needs. If the leader is simply unaware of these needs, communication may be all it takes.
2. Delegate among yourselves, or volunteer for, specific procedural and systematic tasks. One can draft an agenda, someone else can bring in information, and so on. Voluntary efforts can make all the difference when a leader is simply overwhelmed by responsibilities or doesn't know how to fulfill them.
3. Develop a group norm for each member's guiding both transactional and task processes. Make sure that all ideas are discussed and considered and all tasks are assigned.
4. Volunteer to make outside connections the team might otherwise expect of the leader, but do so only with the knowledge and cooperation of the leader. If the team is a unit of an organization, it requires great care to get what you need without "going over the head" of a leader.

Easing Leaders' Transitions

Occasionally, a leader leaves and another one takes the role. Even when the change is desirable, it can be unsettling to the team. Members, uneasy and apprehensive, may speculate about what the new leader will be like, what changes she or he may make, and how this may affect their teamwork. In the case of an organizational team, they may fear for their jobs. All this provides a rich field for rumor and frustration.

A change of leaders also provides an opportunity for power shifts and political positioning. Teams or individual members may create coalitions to push their interests. This is not necessarily a bad thing—the changes may be good—but teams need to recognize that political strategies *will* affect members' relationships with one another, the team, other subsystems, and the organization.

Once the change of leader is decided, it's best to limit speculation, rumor, apprehension, and politics as much as possible. If you can make the transition smooth and keep the team together, then you may have more opportunities to deal with whatever moves are necessary to the team's success. Some ways to smooth the transition are:

Keep rumors in perspective. Members can test rumors for their source and their probability, and refuse to pass them on.

Reinforce the team's perception of itself and of how it works. Reaffirming the team's goals, reinforcing the vision, strengthening syntality, cementing relationships—all help the team feel it is still a team as it weathers the transition.

Close the old era gracefully. You can call attention to what the team has accomplished and suggest ways of "winding up" the era that is ending. People need some sense of closure when a period ends, even when they will go on immediately into a new one.

Open the new era affirmatively. You can initiate a new leader's experience by suggesting ways to orient him or her to the team; asking questions to learn how this new person works; summarizing the team's accomplishments and its goals and tasks for the future. You need to incorporate the new leader into the transactional process and, at the same time, ensure that everyone understands what the task is and how and why it should proceed.

Meeting Problems

Probably the most frequent complaint, by groups of all types, is: "Our meetings are terrible." Unsatisfactory meetings undermine group cohesiveness, limit effectiveness and productivity, and frustrate people. And there's no excuse for them. Running a good meeting is just a matter of doing it right.

Let's look at some of the main problem areas—deciding whether or not to meet, adapting to situations, planning and preparing, and keeping on track—and what to do about them.

To Meet or Not to Meet

Many meetings are necessary, of course. Members need to develop full communication, mutual understanding, information, and cohesiveness by being together. However, members must also do a lot of the work apart.

There are times when people don't need a meeting. The ritualistic, pro forma meeting can be a bore and a waste of time. Hackman and Johnson (1991, p. 129) list four reasons *not* to call a meeting:

1. When other means (phone, fax, memo, letter) can be as effective.
2. When there isn't time to prepare for the meeting.
3. When a key participant cannot be at the meeting.
4. When issues are personal and should be handled privately.

We suggest that you *do* call a meeting for these reasons:

1. When the team needs to share information and resources.
2. When the team needs to work over goals, norms, and approaches.
3. When the team needs to develop plans, timelines, work distribution, and assignments.
4. When the team needs some time for team building and connecting.
5. When the team needs to resolve problems with transactional and task processes, conflicts, and/or norms.

Obviously, a team needs to meet frequently in order to maintain a mutual understanding of all of these issues. But if specific work can be done better apart, do it that way. Then get back together to report, share, and refine what the team will do next.

Adapting to Situations

Teams may encounter situations with meeting places and/or people that make it difficult to meet effectively. Sometimes those disadvantages can be turned into opportunities, if the members are sufficiently adaptable and creative. Here are some possibilities:

An uncomfortable environment. If the meeting place is not conducive to the team's purposes, the obvious solution is to change it. Get the team to brainstorm alternative locations or changes in the existing environment. Team involvement in finding and adjusting to the meeting place can be a team-building exercise that helps create cohesiveness.

Membership dispersed over an area. When members are spread over a defined area, try trading meeting locations. All members do not have to travel every time, and they have a refreshing variety of places in which to meet.

Membership dispersed over great distances. If it's too expensive or troublesome for people to meet, consider an electronically mediated meeting. Many colleges and organizations already have the technology for conferencing by computer, telephone, or even video. You may need to look for organizations and corporations in your area that provide these services. Meeting electronically is getting easier and cheaper. The *New York Times* (Rifkin, 1991) reports that, as of 1991, "a one-hour video conference between Boston and Los Angeles cost $20 an hour, compared with $2,000 a few years ago." One company will shortly have available a "desktop system that incorporates video conferencing into personal computers" (p. D12).

Divergent interests. The meeting place can be extremely important when members represent divergent interests. A task force comprised of competitive interests, for example, may want to trade meeting places on a regular schedule so that no one group has the "home court advantage." Another approach, when you're trying to cooperate on issues that could easily become adversarial and competitive, is going to neutral territory. International summit meetings are often held in neutral or nonaligned countries for this reason.

Unavailable members. Anything from conflicting obligations to a broken leg can make it impossible for a member to attend. The team can arrange teleconferencing with that person and/or contact the absent member to report team information, ideas, and decisions. Be sure that the person's contributions of information and thinking are reported back to the team accurately. Major problems can occur when teams let this go-between function slip. "Where did Shel set up our retreat?" "Oh, I thought *you* were going to call Shel!" "Who was?" "Samantha?" "Well, where is *she*?" "Did she call her?" "Could somebody call Sam?" "She's out of town? Can we call Shel directly?" "Oh, she's in surgery." "But the retreat's next week!"

Planning and Preparing

Another cause of meeting snafus is inadequate preparation. There is usually enough blame to spread around: preparation is the responsibility of the individual members and—with the leader's guidance—the team as a whole.

Preparation certainly starts with the individual members. We can't say this strongly enough: whatever an individual's role, he or she must *set aside time beforehand to prepare for the meeting!* Successful meetings absolutely require that each member arrives fully prepared. That means both material preparation—information, resources, and assignments—and mental preparation for what is to be done.

Hastings, Bixby, and Chaudhry-Lawton (1986), write:

The leaders and members of Superteams have high expectations of each other when working apart. Before the team splits up to work apart, they will have a clear idea of what each person is mandated to do. Each team member acts with delegated authority. Team members see that their roles are central to others, and develop a greater sense of responsibility to do what they have said they will do. Each person is seen as a team ambassador and is entrusted with the responsibility to manage those outside the team that they come into contact with. (p. 119)

We couldn't say it better. We'll add, though, that all members should put preparation time for meetings on their calendars. Too frequently, the meeting time goes on the schedule, but the preparation period does not. It's a good idea to block out time before and after meetings to get the work done.

Experts stress that all good meeting leaders share one characteristic: preparation. A lack of preparation will spell certain failure in the meeting room.

"Usually people will just dive into a meeting without thinking," said Ann Rice, a senior vice president with The Forum Corporation, an international training and consulting firm in Boston.

"People have to figure out what is the purpose and objective of a meeting. What do we want people to walk out of a meeting with?" said Rice. "Too many times, a meeting strays off course and hours are wasted."

Good meeting leaders don't meet unless there's an absolute need; they decide what their goals are, and then go about reaching them in an efficient manner. . . .

Beyond the logistical rules, personal leadership styles are critical—and highly variable. . . .

"Good meeting leaders do not always put themselves into so-called power positions," said Rice. "Power has this connotation of ego, charisma and dominance. There are times when it's wise to turn over a part of an agenda to the group or to someone who can create more power in the group."

Condensed from Dean Chang, "The Makings of a Powerful Meeting Leader," Strategic Meetings, *Corporate Travel*, Winter 1991, p. 30. Used with permission.

Preparation is also a team and leader responsibility. Teams need to assess exactly what they need to do for a specific meeting and be sure it's done. For example:

1. Before one meeting is over, the team should plan the objectives and needed resources for the next meeting.
2. Someone must be designated to make sure the meeting arrangements and resources are set up and ready.
3. The leader and/or designated member should create an agenda that considers time, participants, issues, and order of consideration (see Chapter 3).
4. Someone must be designated to publish and distribute the agenda prior to the next meeting, together with relevant information members may need for preparation.
5. Someone must be designated to make sure that any consultant or visiting expert is contacted, briefed, met, and delivered to the meeting—on time, in the right place, and with the appropriate orientation to his or her task.

Keeping on Track

Even when everything is prepared and structured, a meeting still may go off the track. Getting back on may take all your transactional and task skills. You are already aware that you can help a group get back on the subject by summarizing points, calling attention to the agenda, and asking people for their opinions or information on agenda issues. These help a lot.

Beyond facilitating the task in these ways, a team needs to adapt to members' expectations in order to move the task without losing the people. Meetings of diverse members may go astray because individuals truly have differing orientations toward what they're supposed to do. In a multicultural task force with which we once worked, for example, some people expected to make decisions in two *hours* and others needed ten *meetings*. Some people, therefore, thought "nothing was happening." They were wrong. Something was happening: philosophical and political issues were probed, feelings were examined, and insights were gained into issues that had never been suspected by the two-hours-to-a-decision folks. When each culture stopped to listen to the other, they built a fine team and achieved their goals.

When a meeting seems disoriented because people bring different understandings, the best approach is:

1. Listen and observe carefully; figure out how others approach the task; keep an open mind.
2. Ask questions to find out how others want to approach the objectives, what assumptions they are making about the process, and how the team can adapt to them.
3. Negotiate a way to adapt the agenda, goals, and timelines so that you can reach the goal, even if it's from another angle and even if it takes more meetings.

These steps work if the transactional processes work well. Members must be sensitive to the interpersonal connections, mutual concern, and communication that enable the team to develop cohesiveness and to achieve its goals.

If your team finds that these processes are not working, then its meeting problems are tied into a bigger issue—the team's syntality, synergy, and cohesiveness. In this situation, a team needs to set some special meeting times to discuss its own growth and development. Here are some ideas that can help your team work through difficult times:

Take a long-term view. Look back a month, six months, or a year or two. Where was the team at that point? What progress has been made? Goals seem more attainable when you see how far you've traveled, but you have to look over the entire road. Looking from meeting to meeting rarely gives that perspective.

Play together. We'd go so far as to say that every time we've experienced or observed an excellent team, it's been a group of people who could have fun together. Teams like this work hard; they know what they're doing; they're committed to their goals. At the same time, they take time to kid around, to socialize, and to celebrate individual and team achievements. Some corporations engage consultants to teach management to "play" because they find it contributes to building working teams and to individual creativity.

Focus on the team's successes. Someone is always willing to remind you of your failures, so the team should remind itself of its *accomplishments*. Think of it this way: failures are just accomplishments waiting to happen. Successes are the foundation for the future. Keep in mind the poster that reads "Be patient, God isn't finished with me yet." It applies to teams as well as to individuals.

Problems with Organizations and Systems

A team may be stymied by outside conditions. The parent organization may not give it the support, resources, autonomy, and recognition it needs to move ahead. Sometimes the parent organization provides what it needs, but the team is stopped because the interests of other groups are in some way related to or in conflict with those of the team. It's possible, however, to turn these problems around.

When the parent organization falls short of its responsibilities, a designated leader may be critically important. He or she can represent the team, negotiate, and be the public relations advocate for the team to the organization. With or without a designated leader, however, every member can provide leadership on the inside by maximizing the effectiveness of the team processes—and on the outside by conveying the team image, making contacts, and publicizing team goals and successes. If there are problems with the organization, the team might consider these possibilities:

1. As much as possible, be innovative and creative and rely on the team.
2. Develop a chart of the hierarchy and communication network of the organization; identify with whom the team needs to interact to get what it needs.
3. Develop a strategy for establishing cooperation with those individuals and groups.
4. Look for other (external or related) systems or groups from whom you can get the support or cooperation the team needs.
5. Use the personal resources of the team to make connections and get cooperation from others.

Sometimes teams can't get as far as they would like with a problem because it's too big or it involves conflicting sides. A cooperative intergroup project may be the answer. We're not suggesting that a cooperative effort with other teams or organizations doesn't have its own problems. But it can be a creative, exciting, and challenging approach to meeting a team's goals.

An intergroup effort may join two or more units from within one larger organization, or it may bridge entirely different organizations. You've followed such a venture in the Environmental Defense Fund/McDonald's Corporation Task Force case studies in this book. Such a task force can be a rich experience in connecting different, even conflicting, organizational cultures to attain a mutual goal.

An intergroup effort requires demonstrating the credibility of individual members and the team. It demands intensive, focused, analytical communication between teams.

Cross-organization or intergroup task forces can bring together corporate interests with public interests to address issues faced by all of us, large and small. It's entirely possible that intergroup projects are the *only* way for humankind to solve some of its overwhelming problems.

We suggested once that problems, even in small teams, may be opportunities. By analyzing your team's problems and implementing some of the suggestions, you can make your team more cohesive, stronger, and more effective.

Summary

We've looked at some ways of dealing with problems and obstacles that can halt a team's progress. Problems with "difficult" people—dominating, distracting, nonparticipating, irresponsible, or reprehensible team members—can be resolved by identifying the problem behaviors, understanding why the team allows them to continue, and finding ways to change them. A team also needs to orient and help members who are new or different, who feel like strangers in your midst. Problems with leaders may be due to inadequacy or the stress of transitions. Members can assume, redistribute, and share responsibilities in ways that support the leader *and* the team.

Leaders and members can minimize meeting problems if they know when, why, and how to meet and can adapt to situations such as the place and people's abilities to attend. They need to prepare properly for meetings and adapt task and transactional processes to accomodate members' diverse expectations and still accomplish the task.

Problems with organizations need attention from designated leaders and members in representing the team, communicating, and finding ways for the team to gain support, resources, and autonomy. When other systems and subsystems have differing or conflicting goals and approaches, the solution may be a special collaborative effort, linking different groups within an organization or across organizations.

Exercises

1. With a group to which you belong, use Form 14.1 to evaluate your meetings. As usual, complete the form first as individual members, then compare and discuss your results. After analyzing your responses, design methods for enhancing the quality of your meetings.

2. Here's a situation: A nonprofit organization, called Help, Inc., uses teams of employees and volunteers. On one team, there are six community volunteers plus three full-time employees. Their team task is to design and implement community outreach programs. In three months of weekly meetings, a lot of good ideas have been recorded in the minutes, but nothing's been achieved.

    Some difficulties are:

    Meetings never have the same people at them. The paid members never know which volunteers are going to show up at which time.

    Members never know when a volunteer will drop out and a new volunteer will be put on the team.

    Only half the people attending know what's happened before and what the goals are.

    There is no sense of cohesiveness or team identity.

    The paid members are responsible for making this team effective. What are the problems, and what can they do about them?

3. Suppose the following people were on your team:

    Ray—designated leader, friend of the boss, nice guy; knows nothing about the task or the team.

    Lou—takes twenty minutes of every meeting bewailing her divorce troubles.

    Luke—funny, great comic, relieves tension; keeps the team from working.

    Sheryl—smart, bright, committed to doing as little as possible; distracts the team with irrelevant comments.

    Kiri—new to this country, speaks moderately good English, tries to prepare but says nothing during meetings.

    Irene—brings attention to her own expertise and power at every opportunity; silences others' opinions with sarcasm.

    What questions would you ask about their participation, and once you had answers, what would you do?

F O R M   14.1   ▌   T E A M   M E E T I N G S   A S S E S S M E N T

As individual members, check off the frequency with which you think each of the following statements is true of your meetings.

At our meetings:

		USUALLY	SOMETIMES	RARELY
1.	Purposes for meeting are clear.	☐	☐	☐
2.	Agendas are organized and clear.	☐	☐	☐
3.	Agendas are flexible.	☐	☐	☐
4.	Members are prepared.	☐	☐	☐
5.	Information needed prior to the meeting is received in time.	☐	☐	☐
6.	Members share leadership.	☐	☐	☐
7.	Resources and materials are ready.	☐	☐	☐
8.	New members are welcomed and oriented to the team, its goals, and its processes.	☐	☐	☐
9.	Someone brings members who were absent up to date.	☐	☐	☐
10.	Someone regularly summarizes and checks consensus among members.	☐	☐	☐
11.	Members cooperate in critical analysis.	☐	☐	☐
12.	Members work on team building.	☐	☐	☐
13.	Members are mutually supportive.	☐	☐	☐
14.	Members take responsibility for resolving task problems.	☐	☐	☐
15.	Members take responsibility for managing team problems.	☐	☐	☐

PART SIX

Team Projects and Reports

Group Formats and Approaches:
Planning Public Meetings

"This sounded like a good idea . . . what have we gotten ourselves into?"
If your project turns into a big, public deal, your team can handle it.

Someday—perhaps at this moment, as a student in this class—you'll be part of a team charged with creating and producing a meeting for another group. The project could be a conference, a workshop, a forum, a town hall meeting; it could be for 15 participants or 500. Teams or committees usually plan and implement these larger group activities, and the chances are you'll be involved in that planning someday.

In most fields, individuals serve on planning teams for professional conferences or on public meetings related to their work, whether that work is geological surveying or cosmetology. These days, communication majors also have full career opportunities in companies that specialize in conference and meeting plan-

ning and/or in human resources training and development. Many corporations, too, have specialized departments that train, develop, and coordinate teams or manage corporate conferences and small group sessions.

The knowledge and leadership skills you've developed in this course will contribute to your success when you, either as an individual or as part of a team, plan a large group meeting. For us, knowing how to organize such programs—which we first learned as undergraduates in courses such as yours—has opened doors to opportunities throughout our careers.

With the possibility that you have an immediate project to do that involves your class—and with the recognition that your future may

hold responsibility for planning public group meetings—this chapter provides an overview of various forms of public group meetings and the goals they can achieve. It goes on to explain types of conference and workshop sessions and methods for generating audience participation and learning. It winds up with a planning guide for all public group projects. Specifically, this chapter will help you:

1. Become familiar with a number of different public meeting formats.

2. Understand the goals and various types of conferences and workshops.

3. Know ways to involve audience members in large group meetings.

4. Plan with your team for public group sessions.

Public Group Meetings

By *public* we mean any audience other than your team—members of a class, a church, businesses, a community—that meets together for some purpose. Such group meetings come in all sizes, varieties, and combinations of formats, and meet a wide range of goals.

Public Meeting Formats

A public meeting can be boring or it can be stimulating, and the format can influence which one it is. Some standard formats, which we'll highlight here, are forums, lectures, symposia, panels, colloquies, debates, and mediated or live performances. When you know these, you can mix, match, and alter the formats to meet the objectives you have in mind.

Forum   A **forum** is an audience-participation session, guided by a moderator, in which people express and advocate ideas and opinions, ask questions, and seek information. A familiar forum is the radio or television talk show, in which a host introduces an issue and then invites people to express their opinions and ask questions.

Lecture   The **lecture** or report format is still used extensively at public group meetings. Students, of course, know the difference between a deadly lecture and a stimulating one. An excellent lecturer who maintains a high level of interaction with the audience still stimulates thinking and learning.

Often, lectures and forums are combined. There may be a presentation, after which the audience participates in a forum session. An audience-participation segment gives an otherwise straightforward presentation format the sense of a public group meeting. College faculty frequently use this format for sessions at their conventions to learn about current research, and students often adapt the format for making group presentations to their classes.

Symposium   A **symposium** presents several speakers on aspects of a topic. A moderator introduces the topic and the speakers, each of whom makes a presentation. After the speeches, the moderator usually opens up a forum period for members of the audience to question the presenters and express their own opinions.

Panel   On a **panel**, several individuals interact among themselves. A moderator introduces them, but they do not make speeches except for, occasionally, brief opening remarks prior to an open discussion among the panelists. The term *panel* is often used to describe any group of people appearing together, such as a panel of speakers. As a format, however, it describes a specific type of interaction that takes place among those involved.

Panel discussions need an adept moderator; clear focus on an issue or question; and a specific agenda to ensure the discussion moves along to some closure point. The audience typically does not get involved until a question or forum period is announced.

Colloquy   In a **colloquy**, two separate groups interact, with or without an audience present. The interaction focuses on a specific topic. One group is of experts; the other of nonexperts, or laypeople. The rationale is that together, the experts and the nonexperts can make sense of a complex issue. The experts bring knowledge; the nonexperts bring experience, common sense, and questions to help clarify the experts' talk.

Originally, the nonexperts, perhaps including an audience, discussed the topic and used the experts like a library, asking them for information as needed. This format only works if experts are willing to sit back and let amateurs delve into their territories. That's unlikely, so the colloquy is often adapted. Experts may give brief presentations or may simply be introduced by the moderator. Then a panel of laypeople directs questions to the experts. In a similar format, a group of journalists sometimes interviews a panel of topic experts. It's a good format when planners want audience participation but the group's size or available time prohibits an open forum.

Debate   In a **debate**, speakers take turns advocating opposite sides of an issue before a judge or an audience. Each has a specified time limit for speaking and a fixed time for rebuttal of the other's arguments. Some formats include time for cross-examination during which the speakers question each other before the rebuttals.

Public debates often merge into forum periods for audience involvement, and they may conclude with audience ballots. They can be intensely involving even without direct audience participation; every listener has strong opinions and knows exactly what she or he would have said if given the opportunity.

Parliamentary debate is an approach that allows a large number to get directly involved in the action. This form, which requires a strong chairperson to guide the process, follows a set of rules to ensure that all sides get a hearing and that individual rights are protected. At the end, the majority decision still rules (Robert & Evans, 1990).

Mediated or Live Performance   Many creative approaches to public group communication involve a performance to provide information and stimulate discussion. Film, video, plays, skits, music, dance, demonstrations of art forms—any of these provide excellent ways to help people focus their thinking. Performances can also combine with other formats. A theater professor occasionally sponsors an evening of play analysis in this way: she has the playwright read his or her play aloud and then opens a forum; the audience asks questions and gives the writer feedback and criticism. It's a nice way to spend the evening; it entertains and instructs the audience; and it provides feedback and coaching for the playwright.

Goals for Public Meetings

Your choice of formats depends, in part, on what you want the meeting to accomplish. The clearer the goals, the easier the choice is. Purposes may include learning, decision making, helping, social facilitating, entertaining, and publicizing—but keep in mind that many sessions have multiple goals. Think of how these goals might combine in a single meeting:

Learning. The goal may be to increase participants' knowledge, understanding of issues, and/or skills. Lectures, panels, other presentational formats, and experiential methods (which we'll discuss later) advance this goal.

Decision making. Large-group decision making most often takes place in representative bodies. New England town meetings are among the few survivors of public groups determining their own laws and policies. Many private organizations still use large groups, such as stockholders' meetings, to make decisions in public, although they usually diffuse influence by using proxy votes and elected representatives. In our teaching experience, however, we were once part of a faculty that met as a full body to make decisions. At other times, we have participated in groups of more than 300 to decide on general directions and priorities for our college. These were intensely involving, challenging, and effective processes. They do require leadership, however. Most deliberative groups, whether public or private, rely on some form of parliamentary procedure to make decisions in large meetings. Even then, they can become chaotic.

Helping. The purpose of many meetings is for people to help themselves and one another. Twelve-step programs, such as Alcoholics Anonymous, and many nondirective group therapy sessions fall in this category. The goal may be reached in small, informal group meetings, but often it involves large group events planned and implemented by members and/or by outside experts and facilitators.

Social facilitating. A meeting may be held simply to give people a chance to socialize and get to know one another, but this also can be a secondary goal combined with other objectives. We often select one specific approach over another for problem-solving meetings because it also gives people opportunities to socialize. We've emphasized throughout this book the need for a team to be aware of the system in which it works and to develop connectedness among its members. Opportunities to interact with individuals in that system in ways not directly related to work can establish bonds that enhance your potential to solve problems together.

Entertaining. A meeting, large or small, may be held primarily to entertain the participants. Mystery parties, for example, involve people in living the roles of detectives, victims, and plotters for entertainment purposes. At the same time, they can help participants learn a number of skills or facts. Entertainment may be the instrumental objective to reach another goal. In fact, individuals are entertained by that which involves them and satisfies some personal need. In that sense, all public sessions should serve this purpose.

Publicizing. Rarely is publicity the stated goal of a meeting, but it may be the prime motivation for the sponsoring individual or organization. The congressman for the district adjacent to ours champions regular meetings for older constituents—lectures, panels, workshops—covering a range of interests. He may be altruistic, but he also receives exceptionally high support from that population in every election. Similarly, corporations directly sponsor programs for community relations purposes. One major corporation regularly sponsors art shows, career days for children, and charity events—all coordinated, planned, and implemented by one of our former students, now one of their public affairs officers.

Conferences and Workshops

Conventions, conferences, and workshops bring together individuals with similar interests to achieve common goals. People attend for some combination of all the objectives we've discussed. A **conference** or **convention** tends to be large; people often register in advance by mail and come from widely separated locations of the same organization or field. Big meetings like these may have a theme or focus that draws people with a common interest.

Workshops are usually smaller groups that convene to learn and develop specific areas of understanding, skills, or creative processes. They focus on learning and development goals, usually with high involvement by the participants. A workshop may stand alone, as the entire thrust of a group meeting, or it may be one form of session within a convention or conference.

Conferences and workshops serve a wide variety of goals and employ a range of public meeting formats. Planning them demands energy and draws from a wide range of knowledge and skills. Although a single person may be responsible for the plan, that person usually needs a lot of assistance; more often, she or he works with a planning team. Regardless of who does the planning, the first steps are to identify goals and determine what types of sessions will best meet those purposes.

Goals

In addition to the general goals we've talked about for public meetings, workshops and conferences usually address specific goals. Identifying the goals and determining the priorities among them is a critical step. Large organizations may use extensive consumer research methods or focus groups to ensure that the planners know the participants' needs and expectations, but even a planning team with a smaller group audience and no budget has to do everything possible to establish its own goals and those of its audience.

A workshop often includes the following goals:

1. Increase participants' awareness of particular professional or interest-group issues.
2. Increase participants' knowledge and/or skills in specific areas.

"MEETING DOCTOR" CURES "SICK" AGENDAS

There are new players on the management team with a daunting list of goals. An executive retreat is in order—but the two-day agenda must be airtight. You need some expert advice.

Who you gonna call? How about a "meeting doctor"? Dr. Michael Freidman is one of a growing breed of psychologists specializing in the corporate psyche.

"I don't believe there is a *right* agenda," Freidman told *Strategic Meetings*. "A lot depends on the purpose of the meeting. If it's for long-range planning, for instance, I may do a number of exercises to help people talk about their dreams for the future. . . ."

In some cases, a group interview with top executives provides an initial springboard for ideas, generating a list of key issues or goals for the meeting. Issues are then ranked according to importance.

"With that information, I can go off with a designated person from the group and develop a set of strategies and an agenda for the actual meeting," Freidman explained.

If a corporation seems stagnant and is looking for fresh new ideas, perhaps the agenda should call for sub-groups to meet and brainstorm.

The make-up of these groups is critical. "There are times when we want like-minded people to be in a sub-group," said Freidman. "Other times, we look for a mix of personalities and experience. Maybe we'll combine someone who's more of a dreamer with someone who's more financial-minded."

Ideas generated by sub-groups are then brought to the larger group for discussion and consensus. And if there's no consensus? "If one person vehemently disagrees and just will not give in, I sometimes set up a 'mock-trial' situation. One person represents each side and presents a 'closing argument' to the rest of the group as a jury," he explained.

Or, opposing members of the group may have to represent the *other* side of the issue. They'll be given time to prepare for the "trial" and research the opposing view. Often, in preparation, they'll discover new points or subtleties they weren't previously aware of.

Condensed from Loren Ginsberg, "'Meeting Doctor' Cures 'Sick' Agendas," Strategic Meetings, *Corporate Travel*, Fall 1991, p. 35. Used with permission.

---

3. Draw the maximum number of people to the event.
4. Allow people to network and establish professional and personal relationships.
5. Stimulate participants through entertainment and variety.
6. Raise funds.

Conferences and conventions of organizations whose members are dispersed across a wide geographical area usually have all of the preceding goals, plus some others:

1. Learn new research or methods.
2. Be involved in deciding the organization's policies.
3. Pursue career advancement.
4. Meet old and make new friends.
5. Develop slates of officers and/or elect officers.
6. Plan events.
7. Decide organizational involvement in political or social issues relevant to its membership.

Every planning decision should relate to the goals of the event. Goals of maximizing attendance and/or making a profit, for example, affect the major choices of location and theme. The planners must find the motivations for people to attend and pay the fees. Any or all of these goals influence the entire structure of the event, including the session types and arrangements.

Types of Meeting Sessions

Large, public meetings can be exciting, dynamic events from which participants emerge enthusiastic, charged to go forth to use their new ideas. Or people can leave uttering the anthem of the 1990s: "boring, boring, boring." The difference is in the way the planners draw from and adapt their knowledge of group interaction to develop active, involving sessions. That takes creative, detailed, hard work.

A conference—large or small—is divided up into units, or sessions. Those sessions are planned in blocks of time and designed to meet the goals that have been identified. Planning them is like fitting a jigsaw puzzle together without using your fist: each piece must be selected so that all the purposes, or edges, fit together.

Types of session are influenced by goals, but also by conditions. The numbers of people attending affects the number and types of sessions that are possible, for example. Special interest groups and committees—what they are, how many there are, how many people are involved in them, and which ones involve the same members—require space and time. Room availability, sizes, and equipment affect what types of sessions are possible. Balancing needs to socialize, network,

What is happening in this large group session? In what ways could the session format be changed quickly to increase the audience's involvement? How might the variety enhance the participants' satisfaction with the session? (Photograph © John Coletti/Stock, Boston)

and meet organizational and professional goals affects the format and arrangement of sessions. When you're planning a conference or workshop, you need to keep all these factors in mind as you choose among plenary sessions and various kinds of "breakout" sessions.

Plenary Sessions   **Plenary sessions** are planned for all conferees to attend. Usually, no other meeting is scheduled at the same time. The topics are of general interest, often the conference's central theme or objective. Programs may involve speakers (someone who will be dazzlingly interesting to your audience), symposia, panels, or other formats. Naturally, the planners want to make these programs so compelling that those at the conference won't want to miss them.

Plenary sessions often begin a conference; sometimes they conclude it as well. Often they follow meetings of breakout groups to allow participants to share ideas they've generated in sessions with similar topics.

Breakout Sessions   **Breakout sessions** meet simultaneously, preferably in separate rooms. They may work concurrently on the same topic or issue. More often they have different programs with panelists, presentations centered on a topic, or participative workshops on special areas of interest. People usually have to select some sessions and miss others, although sessions may be repeated so that people have more than one chance to attend a specific program.

If you have a limited number of rooms, each of which holds a small number of people, it's possible to survey participants prior to the conference as to their first, second, and third choices of sessions. Then you can assign people to specific sessions and give them tickets to those events along with their registration materials. If you're using repeated sessions, you can arrange for everyone to experience every workshop or session.

When the goals include sharing information and ideas, breakout groups are used to generate ideas that participants later share in a plenary session. When you use breakout group reports, give participants clear instructions at the beginning of the session and a format for reporting. They may adapt the methods, but instructions give them a starting point and help them focus on the goals for the session. The instructions should include the purpose of the report, its format, time limits, and other expectations.

Reports from small groups are usually presented orally, but visuals enhance their effectiveness. Overhead projectors or flip-chart paper posted on walls or easels work well, depending on room size. Be sure each group has the materials (pens, slides, newsprint) to prepare its visuals.

Teleconference Sessions   With satellite technology, groups may be part of **teleconference sessions**. Programs can be developed and transmitted to any site capable of receiving the signal. For a fee, a conference location becomes a downlink in the network and provides access to the local audience.

So far, teleconference formats are like plenary sessions attended in person; in fact, they may serve as special plenary sessions at large conferences. Speakers or panels perform about the same as for live audiences, and telephone links may allow audiences to participate in a type of forum.

The change in medium certainly changes the message from that of a live presentation, but it has great advantages. Teleconferences save enormous amounts of time and money for participants compared with the costs of individual travel to a distant site to hear a similar presentation. This potentially increases the number who can participate. Internationally known speakers who could not otherwise attend a conference can transmit a presentation by satellite. Panelists can be linked from throughout the world, just as news anchors bring in guests from multiple locations every day on the news. The loss of face-to-face interaction nonetheless limits some of the personal and social goals of conferences, so the method must be balanced with other opportunities to meet those needs. Here, again, planners need to consider carefully the goals of the program and determine the best ways to accomplish them. The potential of a resource is as great as the imagination using it.

Audience Participation Generators

Here's a workshop or conference presenter's nightmare: you ask, "Are there any questions?" and no one says a word. Unfortunately, this can happen even when you are most confident the group will really get involved in the topic. When you schedule time for audience participation, wisdom dictates that you also plan ways to get people started. Some of the approaches to help structure and enhance involvement include a variety of paper-and-pencil methods and small group participation.

Paper-and-Pencil Instruments

One way to enhance participation is to focus the participants' attention on a specific topic in advance by means of **paper-and-pencil instruments**. Questionnaires or surveys of the group prior to a session—whatever the format—can increase involvement in several ways.

1. It stimulates thinking, focuses attention, and mentally prepares the audience for the presentation or activity to follow.
2. The results can be tallied immediately, put on overhead slides, or given to facilitators or speakers to report or discuss with the participants during the presentation or activity.
3. Pre- and postsession attitude or information forms can be distributed before and after a speaker, panel, or debate. An immediate tally indicates how the audience's opinions changed, or didn't change. When this information is announced, participants will be more than ready to contribute to a forum.

Forms can be created fairly easily. They should be:

Brief. Ask enough, but no more than necessary.

Concise. Keep questions or statements down to a few words.

Clear. Keep language simple and to the point.

Objective. Avoid emotionally loaded statements.

Easy to take and tally. Structure for brief, quick answers.

One useful format is the agree-disagree discussion guide (Andersen, 1959). It is simple to design, easy to complete, and speedy to tabulate and can be adapted to many situations. To use this method:

1. Write a list of short statements about information the audience should learn from the experience, or their attitudes, values, or beliefs about the topic.
2. By each statement, provide a space to check "Agree" or "Disagree." Having only two choices provides a clearer picture of participants' perspectives and permits quicker scoring. You can use more categories if you need more detailed information, but it complicates tallying.

This format works particularly well for conferences and workshops. Suppose, for example, your session is on the welfare system and you have a panel of experts to discuss the topic. Prior to the panel, you ask the audience to complete an agree-disagree guide that states both facts and myths about present welfare needs and systems. What do people *believe* is true, as opposed to what *is* true? As the panel presentation starts, two members of the team tally responses to each statement and put results on an overhead slide. The presenters can later guide discussion by referring to those responses. You get audience involvement, panel members can adapt to what the audience knows and doesn't know, and participants learn more than they might otherwise.

Small Group Activities

Small group activities are great for involving members and reaching goals for learning, attitude change, and entertainment. We're going to look at three approaches to small group activities: buzz groups, role-playing, and exercises.

Buzz Groups   Contrary to what you might suppose, small group activities can be used with very large audiences. You can divide the audience into small groups and have them work on specific questions for brief time periods. All groups can work on the same issue, or different questions can be assigned. This approach has earned the label of **buzz groups** because that's the sound and participant energy they generate.

One method of using buzz groups is called "Phillips 66," not after the oil company but for its originator, J. Donald Phillips (1948). The 66 refers to having groups of six people discuss a topic for six minutes. It works like this:

1. Divide the audience quickly by having people in alternating rows turn around so each set of three forms a group with the three immediately behind or in front of it.
2. Give each group a card with a question to consider and the format for reporting their ideas.
3. Allow the groups to discuss the topic for six minutes.
4. Ask a member of each group to report its major findings very briefly, or to write them on a visual for display.

The presenters then incorporate the groups' ideas into their presentations or go on to further exploration. If you're in a more flexible space than an auditorium, you can combine groups and have them share information before reporting out. It works.

Role-Playing   Role-playing puts participants in another's shoes. It may be as simple as asking them to respond to a problem or situation, either with oral responses or on a questionnaire, from another's point of view. This opens insights and discussion into new information or attitudes. We introduced role-playing in Chapter 7 as a way to gain different perspectives. Here we will outline more fully the steps you need to conduct a session.

Role-playing involves assigning individuals parts to play in a situation in front of the group. This takes careful planning. We do it this way:

1. Design specific role definitions for each part. These might include the person's age, sex, and occupation, as well as his or her values, motivations, and attitudes relating to the situation at hand. Give each role-player his or her definition to look over for a few minutes.

2. Give role-players a situation in which their interaction will demonstrate specific encounters and issues that focus on the goals for the session. Do not give role-players any more information than they would naturally have in the situation.

3. Instruct your role-players to act just the way they think the person whose description they've been given would act. Reassure them that they don't have to be actors. Most people role-play remarkably well, and usually they demonstrate the points you want to make in a very natural way.

4. Stop the play when it has demonstrated what you want it to show. Applaud and appreciate.

5. Debrief the experience. Question the audience about what they saw, ask the role-players how they felt in the roles, and be prepared to bring out the important points.

Suppose, for example, that your learning objective is for the participants to understand assertiveness. You might prepare roles for assertive, passive, and passive-aggressive persons and place each of them in a situation in which another role-player tramples on their rights. After your role-players demonstrate their respective responses, the audience should be able to detect in which mode each responded. The role-players should be able to report how, as their characters, they felt. From there your questions facilitate discovering the causes and effects of these response patterns in communication.

Exercises and Activities   Structured, experiential exercises enable people to have firsthand experiences and make them active participants in learning. Such exercises, however, require preparation and guidance. "Experiential learning should involve a degree of structuring: a point of view imposed on the process allows participants to generalize and recognize patterns and skills" (Pace & Faules, 1989, p. 294).

In a structured experience, participants are given a task to do, such as a problem, a game, a case study, a creative activity, or a simulation. They work as individuals, in dyads or triads, or in small groups. Leaders give them instructions and guide them through the exercise, and then through debriefing steps to help them gain insight and see possible relationships between the information and their lives.

Pace and Faules (1989) suggest setting up experiential learning sessions in a way that alternates stimuli and activities. That is, alternate periods of stimulation with time for reflection; of intense involvement with time for pulling back to a safe distance; of talking with practicing; and of individual tasks with group tasks (p. 314). This advice is consistent with our own experience. We find that alternating methods keeps energy high and learning opportunities strong.

It's the debriefing, or analyzing the activity, that provide the educational impact. "Experiential learning occurs when a person engages in some activity, looks back at the activity critically, abstracts some useful insight from the analysis, and puts the result to work" (Pfeiffer, 1985, p. 3). Jones and Pfeiffer (1973) outline five steps in this learning process:

1. *Experiencing.* The activity takes place; participants respond to the structured experience.
2. *Publishing.* Participants "share what they saw and/or how they felt during the event" (Pfeiffer, 1985, p. 5).
3. *Processing.* The group "talks through" the interaction dynamics; it discusses the tasks and processes people experienced, looking for commonalities and differences.
4. *Generalizing.* Participants analyze what they have learned in the previous steps to identify principles that may emerge from their collective experiences.
5. *Applying.* Participants seek to answer the question "Now what?" They look for ways members can use the information, and perhaps identify personal goals for change, by responding to items such as "The next time I am in this situation, I will . . ."

Guiding structured experiences and activities requires a facilitator, not a presenter. Rather than listen to a speaker dish out information, participants help

FORMAT	EXTENSIVE INFORMA- TION	AUDIENCE INVOLVE- MENT	EXPERIEN- TIAL LEARNING	ISSUES ANALYSIS	DECISION MAKING	LARGE AUDIENCE	SMALL AUDIENCE
Forum	X	X		X	X	X	X
Lecture	X					X	X
Symposium	X	X		X		X	X
Panel	X			X		X	X
Colloquy	X	X		X		X	X
Debate	X			X	X	X	X
Performance						X	X
Buzz Groups		X	X			X	
Role-Playing		X	X				X
Structured Activity	X	X	X		X		X

FIGURE 15.1
Strengths and weaknesses of public meeting formats and activities

themselves to their own ideas and conclusions. The leader needs to ask the right questions, interject theoretical perspectives, and ensure that the group stays on track.

The various public meeting formats and activities we have been describing all have their strengths and weaknesses, depending on your goals and your audience. We have tried to summarize these for you in Figure 15.1.

Preparation for Public Meetings and Conferences

Let's assume you have a meeting to plan—perhaps for your class, perhaps for your corporation. Let's go over some of the things you need to consider and decisions you need to make. These include identifying your goals and participants, planning your program, finding your resources, rehearsing and running through programs, publicizing your meeting, and—after it has indeed taken place—evaluating its effectiveness.

Goals and Participants

Goals for your sessions and the participants' needs and expectations are almost inseparable. You start with what you want your audience to think, know, and be able to do as a result of their participation in the meetings. To set these goals specifically, you also need to consider what participants already know and what attitudes, values, and beliefs they bring.

Are they willing or reluctant participants? Some people attend meetings or workshops because they want to; others attend because it gets them out of something or because someone else, usually their teacher or boss, thinks it would do them good. How much do they expect to participate? If your group expects to sit back and hear a lecture, stirring them up may take careful planning. A group expecting involvement, however, may get impatient with any formal presentations of information.

Your goals are affected, too, by the time you have available. Your objectives will differ if you are planning a 45-minute session for your class or if you have a three-day workshop to prepare on the same general topic. Be realistic in what you expect to accomplish.

Find out everything you can about your participants—who they are, what they know and feel, what they expect. Find out about time limits and conditions. And then get those goals articulated. Everything must come back to that.

Programs

It takes extensive work to develop a meeting plan. Before you're finished, you will have a detailed agenda; a grid that displays times, places, and responsibilities; and about three dozen checklists to be sure nothing slips up. You need to start early and make adaptations as you proceed, because there are always surprises. Here we will look at things to consider in the plan and how to create the program.

A myriad of factors influence the development of a full meeting plan. Some key issues are:

Presentation methods. Format decisions depend on goals, audience, time, and resources. Which formats will work best? Will written material be used for some information? Can you create innovative formats?

Participant involvement. When and how will you use surveys, questionnaires, and the like? How can you divide participants into small groups? What planning will this take? Do you need additional space or rooms?

Scheduling the time. How will the various formats fit together? Do they provide variety in the types of activity? If sessions are intense or last longer than one and a half hours, you'll need to plan for breaks. Are rooms distant, necessitating extra time between sessions? Will you have meal breaks? If so, are meals provided, so that you can control the time, or are people on their own, requiring longer meal periods?

Registering participants. How will you send necessary information ahead of time? How will people register? How will you distribute the schedule and other information? Will you assign people to sessions? What will be the fee?

Closing the session. This takes more than singing "Cum Ba Ya." How do you bring the ideas together? What sense of closure will the participants and the presenters need? What feedback or evaluation do you want from the participants? How fast will people need to get away?

A well-developed **meeting plan** addresses five variables: *who* will do *what, when, how,* and with what *resources.* As you figure out all of these issues, it helps to put them on a meeting planning chart to see the relationships among parts.

Preparing a plan that incorporates these considerations is like fitting a model together. You need to be sure all the pieces are there, then put them in the right places to create the vision you have for the program. That gives you a program plan.

Resources

Resources include personnel (who possesses the talent and skills necessary to do which tasks), facilities (space and equipment), and finance (money to pay the bills). You can't know specifically what resources you'll need until you have some idea of what will happen at the meeting. To resolve this dilemma, you need to work through the two aspects together. The resource plan needs to include, for each item, what you need and how will you get it.

Personnel   It takes many different abilities to make meetings effective. Because few individuals have all the necessary talents, a number of people need to be involved. As planning team members, you may decide to fill the roles, or you may recruit outside specialists or experts. Here are some of the abilities the meeting may require:

Planner. This person needs the organizational ability to see the overall goals and to sense how all the parts fit together to achieve them.

Educator. This individual understands the goals and the participants, and knows how to manage activities so that learning occurs.

Facilitator. This person—possibly the same as the educator—is able to guide people through a process without being dominant. An effective facilitator asks the right questions, sometimes makes suggestions, and leads (not pushes) people along an agenda toward their goals. A facilitator is a helper, and generally has more questions than answers.

Presenter. Nothing substitutes for excellent speaking skill, whether you're a sole lecturer, part of a symposium, or a panel member. You need the ability to organize, support, and deliver ideas effectively within restricted time limits. In meetings and on panels, listening and questioning skills are also essential to connect with other ideas expressed during the session.

Presider. This role may be designated master or mistress of ceremonies, but it may be more like traffic cop than MC. The presider directs activities, makes introductions, and provides transitions along the way. This requires skill and flexibility in thinking, speaking, listening, summarizing, and adapting to crises. When presiding over large group decision-making meetings, the presider needs facility with parliamentary procedure to guide the process in an orderly manner.

Leader. This role encompasses all the others. The leader plans, educates, facilitates, presents, presides—whatever needs doing at any point along the way to help move the group toward its goal.

The planning team has to weave together carefully the talents it has available to make the most effective use of each. If you are working only with team members, then assign responsibilities cautiously. Volunteers are not always the best solution; sometimes you need a person's specific abilities to fill a spot no one else can handle.

AGENDA FOR A TWO-DAY PLANNING RETREAT

Retreat Overview

Objective:
To develop the bases for a college's five-year plan.

Preliminary Work:
All participants receive background information on issues affecting the college, including demographic data on college populations in its region.

Each participant has been assigned to a "community," based on expressed preferences. These communities are: outcomes assessment; access, including targeted populations; retention and persistence; general education program; and integrating computers into the curriculum. Each community is divided into smaller groups of six to eight participants.

Retreat Structure:
Friday A.M.:	Plenary session—review goals and background material.
Friday P.M.:	Work in groups—establish topic area objectives by visualizing "what things should be like in five years."
Saturday A.M.:	Work in communities—create implementation plans for objectives, determining "How do we get to where we should be?"
Saturday P.M.:	Plenary session—reports from work groups.

Retreat Agenda

Friday Morning: Plenary session
8:30– 9:00	Registration, coffee and Danish
9:00– 9:45	Welcome and charge by the president
9:45–10:30	Demographic trends affecting the college
10:30–10:45	Break
10:45–12:00	Presentations on background for work areas
12:00–12:45	Lunch

Friday Afternoon: Work in communities and groups
12:45– 1:30　Debrief morning information in groups:
1. What are the implications of demographic trends for the college?
2. Identify what has worked well in the past.
3. Identify general areas of concern or omission.

1:30– 2:00　Brainstorming
1. Each small group creates a list of potential subjects within its topic area that could be pursued, refined, and developed. (15 minutes)
2. Each group selects the "best" six to eight topics from its list and writes them on newsprint to post for the entire community. (15 minutes)

2:00– 2:30　Entire community selects six to eight subjects to develop.
1. Each small group presents a brief explanation of its list. (10 minutes)
2. Entire community selects one topic per small work group. (Other topics are saved for future consideration.) (10 minutes)
3. Individuals choose one of the selected topics on which to work. Work groups are rearranged to reflect the choices. (10 minutes)

2:30– 2:45　Break—Refreshments served in each community room.

2:45– 3:15 "What should things be like in five years?"
   1. Each new group selects one aspect of its topic area and develops a description of how things should be, using the following criteria:
   —Describe it in the present tense.
   —A positive statement, not just eliminating something.
   —Use vivid, active terms.
   —Avoid comparisons.
   —Realistic, doable.
3:15– 3:45 Consult with other groups.
   1. Each work group divides into two subgroups. One subgroup stays at the table and one moves to another table. Each table now has representative of two groups.
   2. In turn, each subgroup presents its descriptive statement to the other subgroup, which serves as consultants to provide feedback. The consulting process should focus on how well the description meets the criteria.
3:45– 4:15 Refine descriptive statements.
   1. The "traveling subgroups" return to their original tables.
   2. The work group shares the contributions from their consulting groups (each will have had two consulting groups) and refines its description.
4:15– 4:30 Entire community meeting.
   1. Each group gives its description of how things will be in five years. (10 minutes)
   2. Each individual gets a list of the topic areas being developed in his or her community. The participants have the option to change work groups for the next day.

Saturday Morning: Work in communities and groups
8:45– 9:00 Continental breakfast.
9:00– 9:30 Work groups review "what things should be like" statements.
9:30– 9:45 Discrepancy analysis—Identify the differences between how things are now and how they should be.
9:45–11:00 Identify changes to be made.
   1. Specify ways in which people and organizational structures need to change to achieve the goal. (15 minutes)
   2. Identify potential barriers. Analyze structural and attitudinal obstacles that must be considered to achieve the goals. (15 minutes)
   3. Identify ways to assess the proposal by answering the question, "How will we know we have achieved the goal?" (15 minutes)
   4. Identify who or what office should have responsibility for implementing this goal. Estimate the personnel, physical, and fiscal resources to implement it. (15 minutes)
   5. Determine timelines and benchmarks for achieving the objective. (15 minutes)
11:00–11:15 Break
11:15–11:45 Specify training and development needs to facilitate implementing the goal.
11:45–12:15 Consulting process, using the same format as on the previous day.
12:15– 1:00 Groups consider consultants' suggestions and refine plans. Complete an Action Planning Form and identify someone to make a one-minute report about your goal (not the implementation plan).
1:00– 1:45 Lunch

Saturday Afternoon: Plenary session
1:45– 2:45 Each group reports briefly on its goal.
2:45– 3:00 Wrap-up, including evaluation forms by participants.
3:00– 3:30 Refreshments.

Facilities Few concerns outweigh facilities planning. It begins with selecting the location and continues until the last conferee departs. Items include room availability, room convenience, proper equipment in place and on time, comfortable room temperature, appropriate seating arrangements, and timely, convenient meal availability.

With multiple, simultaneous activities, the proximity of various rooms and the routes connecting them are critical. Whether you're dealing with a single room or an entire complex, get or create a map giving you the dimensions and capacities of each space. Keep in mind that capacity depends on how the room is arranged. You'll need to know if tables can be added or removed or if there is immobile auditorium seating. Space planning involves such questions as:

1. Will the front of the room accommodate a table, lectern, or other necessary equipment?
2. Can the participants see easily?
3. Are the acoustics conducive to your format? Will panelists be heard, or will small groups be so close they drown each other out?
4. Is the lighting appropriate? Can you control it for specific visuals or activities if necessary?
5. Do you have any choices about the space? Could you change rooms or facilities? If you have multiple rooms being used simultaneously, could you switch any around?
6. How can you make it work? Can you adapt creatively to make the best use of what you have available?

Equipment plans must also be carefully prepared. Someone must be assigned to ensure that all items are in the right place at the right time. The plan should be laid out on a grid, by time periods, and should include:

1. What is needed at that time.
2. Where it is needed.
3. Where it will come from (e.g., a previous session or storage).
4. Who will bring it and set it up.
5. Who will remove it when the session is over.

If possible, arrange to have sessions needing the same equipment follow one another in the same room. This minimizes movement of equipment and potential problems. Remember that somebody usually forgets something, so have a contingency plan for getting what you need at the last minute.

Finance You need to know where the funds are coming from and where they are going. Funding may come from sponsoring organizations, participants' fees, or some combination of these. If fees are a principal source, then the planning must involve careful market research to provide good estimates of attendance.

Potential expenses include speakers, transportation, equipment, space, printed materials, advertising, and refreshments. For a relatively simple class project, you may have visuals to prepare and handouts to reproduce. For a major conference, guest speakers can run into thousands of dollars (remember Ronald Reagan's million-dollar speaking trip to Japan), and a day's video equipment rental and set-up can cost hundreds of dollars.

Obviously, you need a detailed budget. It should include all aspects of the program and cost projections for each. Then keep good records of actual expenditures as you create and implement the program.

Rehearsals and Run-Throughs

Rarely do you have the luxury of fully rehearsing an all-day event, nor should you if you could. A run-through, otherwise known as a dry run, is something you can and should do. That means a step-by-step review of the entire meeting, including the following:

1. Individual presentations can and should be rehearsed (see Chapter 16).

2. Panel discussions can't be rehearsed; they lose their spontaneity. Members should review the agenda and time frames, and briefly share views or philosophies. If a panel member has written extensively about a topic, we recommend that others review those materials.

3. Moderators must be in tune with their information, their roles, and their agenda. They need to review the speakers and their backgrounds and the program order. They must be ready to move the group; to intervene when one person dominates; and to provide the audience with the introductions and transitions that make the whole thing work.

4. Small group activities can be tried out with a volunteer group. At the least, facilitators should talk through the procedures to be sure they understand each step in ways they can explain to the participants. This review also ensures that materials and equipment needed for the activity are identified.

5. The planning team should run through the schedule and review each person's responsibilities. Everyone needs to be comfortable that all team members know when and where they have tasks to perform.

Remember, audiences are unpredictable. In spite of all your planning, you will probably need to adapt as the session progresses. We recommend contingency plans: in case you have a quiet group, have extra exercises or material ready to fill in; in case you have a riotous group, know where to cut out material for the sake of time. All of this makes meeting planning and management a challenging responsibility that continues until the last guest has left.

Publicity and Public Relations

Conferences and workshops don't happen without participants, and participants don't show up if they don't know about it. Meeting planning should include ways to communicate with various audiences about the activity. You might use advertising, press releases, press coverage of special personalities or events, and direct contact with key people. Consider multiple media—newspaper, radio, TV, direct mail, fax, and telephones. Plan carefully, with your specific audiences in mind, what you will tell them, what methods you will use, the frequency (how many times each person gets a message), and the costs involved.

Evaluation

Evaluation should be an ongoing aspect of program planning. You want feedback from participants on their experiences and from team members on their processes.

Participants   Your approach to feedback and reporting will vary depending on the objectives you want to achieve. You may want all participants to be informed about the feedback from every session; you may want chairpersons or workshop facilitators to have feedback specifically about their sessions; or you may want only the planners to receive feedback.

Planning for these objectives includes creating and distributing assessment forms, assigning people to be sure they're collected, and deciding how the results will be distributed. In some instances, you'll want the information given out during the conference or workshop; in other instances, you may send out follow-up reports at a later date.

The participants are the best source of information about the success of the sessions. They had personal goals for attending, and they experienced the activities directly. Evaluating the meetings' successes and identifying possible improvements are essential.

Develop the questions you want answered. Consider issues such as:

What were participants' goals, and were they met?

What aspects of the program contributed most?

What aspects of the program contributed least?

What would the participants have changed?

Would they have participated, knowing what they know now?

You may create evaluation forms or use other systematic research methods, such as interviews and focus groups, to get the information. To paraphrase the classic warning of historians, if we don't study the problems in our program and planning, we may be doomed to repeat them.

The Team   As you plan an experience, the team should examine its processes as well as its success. The team's work processes can be examined by drawing from the suggestions and evaluation forms throughout this book. Good team process evaluation requires open introspection by all members.

Working with a team to plan a conference or a workshop can be stimulating, challenging, exhausting, and very rewarding. We believe that the experience—even if it's only planning a special workshop for a class or a floor in your dorm—is immeasurably valuable. It draws on every skill you've learned, every talent you've developed, in group communication and leadership.

When it's all over, you may be disappointed in some aspects of your team experience, and thrilled with others. That's just the way it is. You learn from the negatives *and* the positives. Once the workshop or the conference is over, though—once you've collected and analyzed your feedback, once you've finished the last bit of the job—celebrate your experiences as a team and congratulate yourselves for what you've learned and what you've done.

Summary

You may well be responsible, now or later, for planning anything from a small workshop to a large public meeting to a full conference. You may use meeting formats that include some combination of a forum, lecture, symposium, panel, colloquy, debate, and/or a mediated or live performance. The goals of these formats can be to enhance learning, make decisions, provide mutual help, make social connections, entertain, or gain publicity for individuals (such as politicians) or organizations.

Conferences (large group meetings of organizations) and workshops (usually smaller and more experiential) are held for a variety of organizational, disciplinary, learning, research, and skill-development purposes. They usually include both plenary sessions, or meetings of the entire group, and breakout sessions, or small groups that focus on the same or various topics; they may also employ teleconference sessions—mediated programs that generally function like a plenary session.

Audiences gain more from meetings in which they are highly involved. Good planning turns passive, speaker-centered sessions into active audience-centered events by using techniques such as paper-and-pencil instruments, buzz groups, role-playing, and structured activities to achieve greater interaction among the participants.

Planning responsibilities for large group meetings include identifying clearly the goals and audience motivations; developing session formats; making the best use of resources (people, space and equipment, and financial); providing for rehearsals and run-throughs; creating publicity for the event; and evaluating the effectiveness of the sessions and the planning processes. The complexities of meetings demand a detailed plan that specifies for each activity who will do what, when, how, and with what resources. As the planning progresses, as the sessions occur, and after the meeting is over, teams need to evaluate their own processes and get feedback from the participants on the effectiveness of the experience.

Exercises

1. Think about your experiences with public group meetings, conferences, workshops, classes, lectures, and/or training sessions. Select the best *and* the worst experience you have had. Make a list of the characteristics that made one successful, and another of the characteristics that made the other a failure. Compare your lists with those of other students. What characteristics emerge as important to creating a good public meeting?

2. Your team of communication trainers has been hired to conduct a two-hour training session for a corporate self-managing team (SMT). The eight members take turns running meetings and representing the team; other leader functions are distributed among the members.

   The goal of your session is to increase the team's skill in conducting effective meetings. You've been told that the training should cover solid information that the team can refer to later; that the experience should be "hands on"; and that you can have whatever electronic or print resources you need.

Using Form 15.1 (Parts 1, 2, and 3), plan a session that will fulfill these requirements.

3. Your team is planning a public forum on a proposal to build a waste incinerator in your community. About 500 people are expected. They will meet in a large auditorium with fixed seats.

   The schedule allows for 90 minutes. A speaker will take about 30 minutes; you want to involve the audience as much as possible for the remaining 60 minutes. You can have any materials and equipment you need.

   Design three ways you can involve that audience.

Write up an agenda for your meeting, and assign responsibilities to the members of the team to ensure that your plan works.

4. Assess a project—possibly one of those planned in the preceding exercises—using the following steps:
   a. Go over your goals and objectives for the project.
   b. Review your criteria for achieving your goals and objectives.
   c. Review each of your methods and what they are intended to accomplish.
   d. Design two assessment forms for evaluating the success of your project—one for the participants, and one for your team—to be completed at the conclusion of the meeting.

FORM 15.1 ∎ PUBLIC MEETING PLANNING GUIDE

Part 1. Analysis

In the left-hand column, fill out the conditions and limitations with which you will be working. In the next column, write in the overall goals of the meeting. In the third column, write the objectives that must be reached for each goal. Draw a line from each goal to each objective that must be reached for that goal. With this information, go to the next planning sheet.

CONDITIONS & LIMITATIONS	GOALS	OBJECTIVES
Number of Participants Expected _____		
Total Time Available _____hrs._____mins.		
Space _____bldg._____rm.		
Resources Available _____ _____ _____		
Personnel Available _____ _____ _____ _____		

Part 2. Activity Planning

Using the information from Part 1, plan your group's activities according to the following categories:

OBJECTIVE	ACTIVITY	RESOURCES NEEDED	TIME REQUIRED	PERSON(S) RESPONSIBLE

Part 3. Space Arrangement

In this space, draw a complete diagram of the space(s) you will be using. Include *dimensions, exits and access, table and chair arrangements, positioning of podium, chalkboards, flip charts, screens, projectors, electrical outlets.* This diagram will show you what you need to do to set up the meeting, what you need to obtain in equipment and resources, and how flexible you can be in your activities.

Written and Oral Reports: Presenting Team Findings

"Now that we found this great material and have such brilliant ideas, how do we tell the world?"

Most teams have to report their progress, their findings, and their recommendations to individuals or other groups in the larger system. The ultimate judgment on the quality of the team may be based on how well the members communicate their material. Planning, preparing, and presenting reports, therefore, becomes a key ingredient in the overall effectiveness of the team.

Preparing reports is not an "add-on" to the team's responsibilities; for most groups, it's the principal task. Some organization,

client, or supervisor is waiting for those reports. No matter how excellent and careful your team's work has been—no matter how thorough and intelligent your research, processing, analysis, creativity, and problem solving—all of it can be diminished if the report doesn't reflect the same quality of effort.

Reports may be written documents, oral presentations, or, frequently, written documents supplemented by an oral presentation. This chapter guides you through your report preparation tasks. It starts with the steps that written and

oral reports have in common: analyzing your goals and audience; gathering, selecting, and organizing information; and planning for visuals. Then it takes you through the specific processes of preparing and presenting both written and oral reports. The information in this chapter should increase your ability to:

1. Follow the preparation steps that oral and written reports have in common.

2. Prepare manuscripts for written reports.

3. Prepare and deliver effective oral presentations.

Common Preparation Steps

Although differences between oral and written reports are significant, in the early preparation stages you go through the same six steps:

1. Analyze the goals.
2. Analyze the audiences.
3. Gather research information.
4. Select the material to be included.
5. Organize ideas to achieve the goals.
6. Plan visuals to supplement the text.

From this point, the paths diverge. A written report next moves to a rough draft; for an oral presentation, you prepare speaker's notes. But first, we'll look at the steps they have in common.

Goals

You begin the process by establishing clearly what the report is intended to accomplish. The team's mission helps clarify your goals, but you also need to consider the specific impact you want the report to make.

Team Mission   For ongoing teams, reports are a routine part of doing business; their purposes and formats depend on their goals. Here are some typical teams and routine reports they may need to prepare:

Quality circle or self-managing team. Such teams may report on a weekly, monthly, or quarterly basis to keep management informed and to get resources the team needs. They often use informal oral reports accompanied by specific written data.

Creative teams. They periodically report progress, provide concept presentations, and follow up with revised concepts and further progress reports as they move through a project. They seek approval and support, and formats are adapted to each report's purpose.

Management teams. They prepare periodic reports to inform higher levels of management. These reports usually have established, unvarying formats that can be quickly recognized by their audience.

Time is always a critical variable in choosing a format: a written report may take more of the team's time than an oral report, but the audience spends less time reading the information than listening to it. Often teams are asked to do both—prepare a full written report and give a brief overview as an oral report. That way the team does most of the work and the appointing authority minimizes his or hers.

A team needs to determine *in advance* whether it will prepare interim reports while working on a project or will wait for a complete report. Longer projects usually need periodic progress reports, and a team is well-advised to plan and schedule the preparation of these reports. Sometimes management requests an unscheduled report on very short notice, thrusting the team into panic. Better to anticipate the unanticipated.

Besides routine reporting, ongoing teams periodically make additional reports. They may want special proposals approved or funded, or they may advocate significant policy and procedural changes. Regular reports should keep the same predictable format. When a team's reporting goals are different, however, the format should be altered to ensure that the audience perceives the contrast.

An ad hoc or special team may have no specified reporting format, or its charge may detail the form and content of its report. Team members need to determine the expectations of the group's originator and prepare reports that fulfill the charge. If the choice of format is left to the team, it should be based on the goals and audience. If the people receiving the report are a manageable number and in close proximity, an oral report may do the job; if they're spread all over the map, a written report may be essential.

Whether the work requires routine or special reports, the team's impact and its success are significantly affected by its reports. Marshall McLuhan's (1964) insight that "the medium is the message" applies: the report's format and appearance communicate to its audience about the quality and significance of the team's work. Creative ideas are enhanced by creative reports; bland reports may be interpreted as presenting dull ideas.

Specific Purpose   People often describe a writing or speaking task in terms of what they have to *do*: "I have a letter to write." "I have a report to prepare." "I have a speech to get ready." Such statements focus on the work to be done or on the product—a report or speech. A better approach is to focus on the *results* you expect to achieve, rather than the method for achieving them.

The critical issues are: *Why* do you have a report to prepare? What do you want the report to *accomplish*? The answer might be: to meet course requirements and to get an "A"; to impress the oversight committee and get our proposal approved; or to get management to understand the team's findings. The actual objective, then, is to effect some change in another person or group. That change may be to increase the amount of information audience members have and/or to get them to respond favorably to your ideas. Express your specific purpose in those terms. The work of preparing and presenting the report is only the means by which the objective will be achieved.

Increasing Audience Information   Teams frequently make reports for the purpose of providing information. Ongoing teams make them routinely. Special teams often are created purely as fact-finding bodies; their goal is to gather and analyze information on a specific topic and report their findings.

In an information-sharing report, you want to be sure the material is presented accurately, clearly, and in sufficient detail. You want the reader or listener to get a clear "mental picture" of the data and the ideas they support.

Sometimes reports appear to be information-sharing when the true purpose is simply to document the team's work. They may meet a legal or regulatory obligation and fall into the infamous management category of CYA (cover your . . .). The goal is to demonstrate that formal requirements have been fulfilled, and the report is simply filed. Under these circumstances, the presentation must document what the team has done—the steps it took and the procedures it followed—to be sure it complies with regulations. The requiring agency or department usually provides guidelines outlining the critical information, and the team's task is to develop each content area accurately to be sure it is "off the hook."

Effecting a Change   Many team reports advocate action or acceptance of a proposal. The purpose of these reports is persuasion—to effect changes in policies and behaviors. The team may need to convince its audience of three things: (1) there is a need to change established ways of doing things; (2) the team's proposals provide the most appropriate ways to satisfy that need; and (3) the proposed changes are consistent with the receivers' attitudes, values, and goals.

In these reports, the team can build and demonstrate its credibility by using sound evidence and reasoning, clear structure and development of arguments, and a report style and format that demand attention.

In planning a persuasive report, the team should consider the nature and extent of the proposed changes. A report calling for a minor deviation from present procedures that won't cost much to implement will differ from one that proposes a costly major transformation from present practices.

Audiences

Your team's objectives are achieved in the minds and by the actions of its audiences. You will want to consider both primary and secondary audiences, some characteristics of those who will act on your proposals, and their prior expectations for the report.

Primary and Secondary   Any report may have multiple audiences. You may prepare a report for your immediate supervisor or manager, but it may also be presented to other levels of management, regulatory agencies, your peers or subordinates, and, possibly, public audiences. A team of teachers, for example, may submit a report to the principal proposing specific changes in the curriculum. This report may be made available to other teachers, to the superintendent, the board of education, and to the public through a parents' group or an open board meeting. Although the primary audience is the principal, the potential secondary audiences are significant.

Characteristics   Although any audience may represent a wide range of demographic and psychographic characteristics, what you need to know about its members can be narrowed down to three areas:

1. How much do they know about the topic?
2. What are their present attitudes about the subject?
3. What values do they have that impact on the issues?

What the audience already knows helps you determine how much background you need to give them to establish a clear frame of reference for the report. Those well-informed and close to the team's work require less introductory material than those who know little about the topic and the project.

The audience's present attitudes affect a team's decisions about how directly to approach the proposal and how much support to develop for the ideas. If people already support its contents, then it requires less documentation and persuasion to reinforce their attitudes. If the team intends to "sell" a proposal to people who oppose it, however, then the presentation must change those attitudes with greater documentation and stronger persuasive appeals.

For a noncontroversial proposal, you can present your recommendations in the first part of the report, and follow with supporting arguments and evidence. If the proposal runs counter to the audience's present attitudes, however, you need to establish common ground, developing evidence and reasoning to show that the goals and values of the proposal are consistent with theirs, before presenting the specific plan.

People try to act in ways consistent with their values, and sometimes you have to show the audience the importance of the values on which the proposal is based. For example, if your team proposes that the college invest in a sports program, you might decide what appeals to use based on the audience's priorities. You might choose to link your proposal to the president's and board of trustee's value of maintaining leadership and prestige, and/or to the economic value of potential alumni contributions, and/or to public relations benefits that might accrue.

Find out as specifically as you can what your audience's attitudes and values are. In connection with the previous example, we think of two different college presidents we've known. One, a former college football player whose top priority clearly was students, would be sold on your team's proposal by an appeal to his belief that sports are good for students' growth and development. The other, whose top priority clearly was personal prestige, would see the benefit of the investment in terms of the image of the college and its president. The appeal has to fit the audience.

Reports, whether written or oral, should reflect sensitivity—both in the way ideas are developed and in the language used—to issues of gender and culture. We've seen well-meaning people destroy their presentations with thoughtless uses of jokes, cartoons, and examples. Sexist or racist language and material offensive to members of certain cultures or subcultures reduce the credibility of the team report and directly affect the audiences' responses to the content.

If you consider your choice of appeals and language in the context of dialogical ethics, it will help you avoid doing things that could be offensive to members of your audience. Remember Johannesen's (1990) six criteria for a dialogical ethic: authenticity, inclusion, confirmation, presentness, mutual equality, and supportive climate (pp. 62–63). This frame of reference ensures maintaining a high level of respect for your readers and listeners, and invites them into a discussion on the topic. This creates genuine audience involvement, making them partners with the team in the proposals, because it considers them first.

Expectations   People who establish teams usually have certain expectations for the groups' performances, including some conscious or unconscious general notion about what a particular team's report will be like. If the preconceived image is of a brief report and the team produces a weighty tome, the team may be viewed as making too much of an issue; if a long report was expected and a short one is produced, the team may be considered irresponsible. Either error reduces the team's credibility.

Because expectations are not always communicated clearly, you may have to explore specific expectations—or requirements—with whomever established your team. Sometimes you need to negotiate the requirements. The team's research findings may provide reasons to clarify and modify the founder's preconceived notions, creating the need to discuss the framework for a "doable," appropriate report.

Research

If your team has followed the guidelines in Part Three of this book (Leadership through Task Processes), you will have virtually completed the team's work in gathering and analyzing information. As you prepare the report, however, review your material to find any gaps in information or logic. Often, organizing the material shows you what you *don't* know and what you must obtain to support your conclusions.

Because team members have been intensely involved in the work from its inception, they may already know much more about the topic than their audience. As a result, you may underestimate the amount of explanation and support your audience will need to understand relationships that are obvious to the team. Though you don't want to insult the intelligence of your audience members, you don't want to overestimate their background, either.

Content Selection

All the information the team has gathered and all its deliberations can't possibly go into a report. Selectivity is the key. At this stage, you need to identify the critical issues, the absolute "musts," for the report. Your guidelines for making these choices go back to the first two steps in the report preparation process: what is essential to achieve the *goals* based on what you have identified about the *audience*? The answers to this question influence every team decision about the report's content.

Two key content issues for your team to decide are: (1) the main ideas and arguments to use, and (2) the type and amount of supporting material needed to develop these points. In addition, you will have to select introductory and concluding material.

Organization

The structure of a report radically affects its success. Clear organization helps audiences understand ideas; strategic organization leads to acceptance and approval.

You're familiar with the three major subdivisions of a report: the introduction, the body, and the conclusion. Contrary to the order in which they will ultimately appear in the final report, develop the body first. After its content is firmly in place and the main points clearly structured, then create an introduction to prepare the audience for what follows and a conclusion to provide a strong close. Finally, make sure that your transitions keep all the relationships clear.

Body   People can process only a limited amount of data without information overload. Miller (1956) found that the number of items a person can process at one time ranges from five to nine, with the "magic number" seven as an average. These findings provide useful guidelines for organizing messages.

To see what we're talking about, try reading this list, then cover it up and repeat it aloud: dog, red, four, two, blue, one, cat, horse, yellow, bird, green, three. Could you remember them all after one reading? It's a list of more than seven, so most people would not remember all items on the first try. Now look at them this way: dog, cat, bird, horse; red, blue, yellow, green; one, two, three, four. How much more easily would you remember those three chunks of information, each containing logically related concepts?

Because people can't process or remember many ideas at once, it helps to relate some ideas and separate them from others in this way:

1. "Chunk" the information. Organize the ideas in neat groups of related items so audiences can process them easily.
2. Be sure that no presentation has more than five major chunks.
3. Be sure that no major chunk has more than five subgroupings or items.
4. Be sure there's a clear, identifiable, and logical relationship or parallel *among* all major chunks.
5. Be sure there's a clear, identifiable, and logical relationship among all items *within* any major chunk.

Clearly structured ideas create order and show relationships among a large number of items. The chart in Figure 16.1 demonstrates a way to view these relationships. It is analogous to an outline in which the main ideas are designated by Roman numerals (I, II, etc.) and the subpoints by capital letters (A, B, C). Laying out your ideas in this way can help you visualize relationships more clearly as you organize the report.

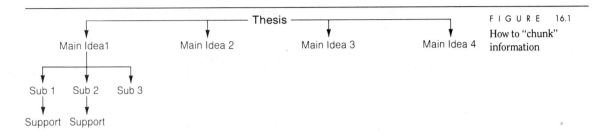

FIGURE 16.1
How to "chunk" information

Main Points   An organizational pattern describes the relationships among the ideas being structured. Various patterns have been given labels; you may be familiar with these from a composition or public speaking class. We will cover this material briefly here; for a more detailed review, you may want to refer to Verderber (1991, pp. 80–83) or Sprague and Stuart (1992, pp. 104–109).

In presenting your main points, you may lay them out in linear order; you may take a more conceptual approach, developing various parts to form a whole picture; or you may adopt a psychological strategy that moves the audience from where they are to where you want them to be.

A *linear* presentation may be chronological, taking ideas in order from past to present to future; or it may be developmental, detailing a process from the first to the last step. A conceptual, *parts-to-whole* approach might present the team's proposal by examining the political, the economic, and the environmental issues; or by looking at the students, the faculty, the administration, and the staff of a college community. A *logical/psychological* strategy might be to engage the audience in understanding the need, the solution, the ways in which the solution meets the need, and the advantages of the solution; or it might move from the audience's values, to how their values are being violated, to the proposed change, to how that change corrects the violation of those values.

Look again at Figure 16.1. All of the main ideas should reflect a clear and consistent relationship to one another. For example, you would not use Past, Present, Future, and Implications, because the first three chunks are linear and chronological, whereas the fourth (Implications) is a parts-to-whole category. Mixing these two patterns upsets the relationship and makes it harder for an audience to follow and comprehend.

Under each main heading, you may use different patterns without creating problems, but *within* each set of ideas there should be a consistent pattern. For example, in the subpoints under Past, you could use a parts-to-whole relational pattern, selecting from the standard journalistic formula of who, what, where, when, why, how. Under the second main point, you could use another pattern, such as spatial or geographic relationships (East, South, Midwest, West). Just remember the principle: all subdivisions of any section at any level of organization have clearly identifiable relationships.

Structures such as parts-to-whole, chronological, and spatial enhance understanding and are useful in reports to provide information, but they also aid the audience's understanding of the material in a persuasive report. Patterns such as problem-solution or motivated sequence work especially well in persuasive messages, but also provide clear divisions for many information-sharing messages.

Whether your report is written or oral, whether it's short and informal or long and formal, applying these organizational principles helps do two critically important things: clarify your own thinking, and assist your audience to comprehend, remember, and accept your message.

Introduction   The most common problem in preparing reports is getting started. People want to start at the beginning, with the introduction, but it's a difficult place to begin. Consider this scenario. It's the first class of a new semester, and you're seated next to a person you've never met before. Shortly after class begins, the professor asks you to introduce that person to the class. Wouldn't it be a lot easier if you had a chance to meet the person first and find out some things about him or her? That's precisely why the introduction should be prepared after the body of the report has been developed. At that point, you are more familiar with what you're trying to introduce.

An effective introduction has three basic goals:

Gain the audience's attention. You need to pull the focus away from whatever might be on their minds and get them involved immediately in your topic.

Motivate the audience to stay tuned. Some years ago, Borden (1935) proposed that presenters assume the audience response will always be "so what" or "who cares." Starting from that assumption you need to find ways to tell people "what's in it for them" and show how they will benefit from the information.

Preview the report. Whether the message is oral or written, follow the old advice to "tell them what you're going to tell them, then tell them, then tell them what you've told them." The introduction represents the first of these. It gives your audience an idea of where your presentation will take them.

Conclusion   The conclusion also has three main objectives—in some ways parallel to those of the introduction, but in reverse order:

Summarize the report. Identify key issues you want the audience to focus on in responding to the report.

Tell the audience what to do. Should they approve your proposal, or seek more information? Should they use your report as a basis for other plans? Should they lobby or contact legislators? Be specific. Your team has spent time developing the report, and that qualifies you to make recommendations.

Provide a strong finish. The first and last impressions are the most powerful, and you want the audience to remember your message.

Transitions   Transitions serve both as bridges between ideas and as road signs telling the audience when you are making turns or going in a different direction. To keep the audience's mind in the same place as your own, you need careful signposting at every turn or connection. The transition between two points, for example, might be: "We've seen that, morally, this proposal is the right thing to do. But pragmatically, is it something we can afford to do? Let's look at what it actually will cost us and how we can pay for it." The transition has reminded the audience of what it just heard, bridged the two "chunks," and previewed, or signposted, where the presentation is going.

Visuals

Both written and spoken words have greater impact when accompanied by visual messages. A study at the Wharton School of the University of Pennsylvania (1981) found that when messages were supplemented by visuals, receivers understood more of the content and, if asked to process the information to make decisions, arrived at better-quality decisions more quickly.

Good visuals arouse interest and hold attention by providing variety and aiding clarity of presentation. Readers or listeners get a quick, clear understanding of the written or spoken text with minimal effort.

In creating visuals for written reports, keep in mind the following criteria:

1. Use different, and appropriate, forms to accomplish your purpose. Consider graphs, tables, flowcharts, diagrams, models, checklists.
2. Keep them simple. Break complicated information into several different chunks.
3. Keep them clear. Round off numbers where possible; set up figures with plenty of room so that relationships can be seen vividly.
4. Be sure to include appropriate explanatory information (legends, symbols, specifics of data collection).

As important as visuals are for written reports, they are even more significant for oral messages. You can reread a report if you have to; you can't rerun the speaker. People process more messages received through their eyes than messages received through their ears. When the eyes are not required to look at the speaker and his or her visuals, they wander; when they wander, so does the mind. Oral presentations, especially, need ways to keep ears, eyes, and mind on the subject.

Although posters, flip charts, videotapes, and slides all provide effective ways to display visuals in oral reports, the Wharton School research concluded that visuals presented by overhead projectors achieved the most positive results. Assuming that they are done well, they have several specific advantages over most other visual aids used with oral reports:

1. They can be prepared ahead.
2. They are compact and easily transported. Some projectors even fold for easy carrying.
3. They can be created by computer software and with plain-paper photocopy machines.
4. They can be displayed with full room lighting.
5. The speaker can face the audience while also looking at the projector.

F I G U R E   16.2
Criteria for good over-
head slides

BIG

—Visible throughout room
—Check each before presentation

BOLD

—Make ideas vivid
—Use colors
—Use graphics

BRIEF

—Use key words/phrases

—Four-word maximum
—Avoid full text

—Five ideas per slide

—Use multiple slides
—Use overlays

When planning and creating visuals of any type for oral reports, be sure to make them:

Big. Be sure the visual can be seen without effort from any point in the room. Check in advance with the equipment you'll be using.

Bold. Give them life and interest. Computer programs can help you create slides with colors, graphics, appropriate humor, and interesting formats.

Brief. Use only key words or short phrases (up to four words). Limit each slide to no more than five key ideas. For complex ideas, use multiple slides, laying one over the other if necessary to bring the "chunks" together.

Figure 16.2 demonstrates brevity in its summary of these criteria.

As you plan the organization and content of your report, start planning the visuals. Final decisions, however, must wait until the report is closer to completion. The visuals should supplement the written or oral text, not substitute for it. Coordination of the two must be worked out carefully.

Preparation Differences

So far we have talked about steps that are common to both written and oral reports, but at this point the preparation paths diverge (see Figure 16.3). One path is designed to create a manuscript, the other to create a speech. You don't read and listen in exactly the same ways, and reports should not be written and spoken in exactly the same ways. Each has special requirements, and requires special handling when you're doing it as a team.

Written Reports

The first step in moving from the organized material to a manuscript is to prepare a first draft—a rough, maybe very rough, draft. The goal is to get something down on paper so you can work with it—rewrite, edit—to move toward final copy.

Writing is a creative process. It requires a free flow of thought coordinated with motor skills to get ideas out of your head and onto paper. The best advice we can

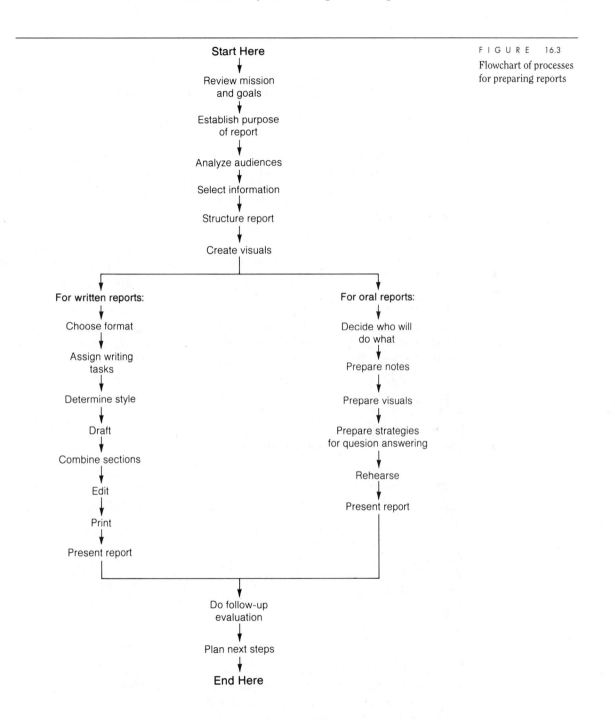

FIGURE   16.3
Flowchart of processes
for preparing reports

share is to write the first draft with a minimum of editing or criticism. Write or type as fast as your hands can move; don't stop to evaluate or make corrections. Evaluating and correcting are more analytical functions and tend to slow down the creative process of getting ideas out. You'll have opportunities to change and edit the text later.

When you come to places where you can't think of the right words or the correct spelling, leave a blank or spell the word the best you can and keep going. Every time you stop the creative process to turn on the analytical side, you have difficulty getting the flow back again. The more writing experience you have, the more easily you can make the transition from one process to another. If you're not an experienced writer, you can develop your abilities by focusing on one part of the process at a time.

The next step is to rework the draft, or turn it over to a teammate to rework. Rewrite sentences, paragraphs, or entire sections. Work to make the ideas clear, concise, and alive. Be conscious of the tone of the report: Is it too formal or too casual? Is the vocabulary level appropriate to the audience's knowledge and background? Does it reflect the importance of the content? Integrate the visuals with the message to maximize the impact and clarity.

The rewriting and editing cycle may take you through several drafts. The goal is to prepare a report that achieves the team's objectives and purposes: to convey a clear understanding of the information, to obtain favorable responses to the proposals, and to enhance the team's credibility with the audience. To ensure its effectiveness, consider the format you will use, how the team will work together to complete it, and how and to whom it will be delivered.

Format

A written report can range from a brief memo to an extensive, multipage document, depending on its goals and the scope of information you need to include. Regardless of its length, it should contain the critical information the team wishes to convey.

Most written reports include nine categories or sections. Usually they follow a prescribed order, except—and this can be important—for the placement of the recommendations. Recommendations may be early or last in the report, depending on the purposes and complexity of the information. The categories may be combined or labeled differently, but all issues need to be considered for inclusion, and should be structured using the principles of organization discussed earlier in this chapter.

If the report is only a short memo, the cover-page information is included in the headings, and the table of contents is omitted.

Cover page. This sheet contains the title, who prepared the report (name of the team and members' names), to whom it is submitted, and the date.

Executive summary. This section, the first in the report, should provide the reader with enough information to make a preliminary decision about what to do with the report. Assume that the person to whom the report is addressed will not read any further before determining whether the report needs further discussion or in-depth reading, should be passed to a subordinate for more detailed review and recommendations, should be filed without further attention, or should be presented orally to another body.

An executive summary is approximately 5 percent of the total report and includes a brief overview of the major categories in this list. Report recommendations should get clear focus here, and frequently begin the summary.

Table of contents. This section lists the report's major divisions and subdivisions, including the page number where each begins.

Background. This introduces the report and provides a frame of reference for what follows. It may include historical information leading up to the team's formation and the report's content, and it should lead the audience to the specific goals or questions being addressed.

Procedures. Describe the processes the team followed to collect information, analyze it, and prepare the report. Demonstrating sound research procedures enhances the team's and the report's credibility.

Findings or results. The data obtained are presented without bias or interpretation. Good visuals usually help clarify this information.

Discussion. The findings and results are interpreted and explained in terms of the report's goals. The focus should be on the specific areas or questions identified in the background section.

Conclusions. The interpretations in the discussion section should lead, through logical inferences, to specific conclusions. These are general statements relating to the goals that provide answers to the questions raised.

Recommendations. This section makes specific proposals. Each recommendation states who should do what, by when, from what resources. Frequently, this section appears first; in a short report, it also serves as the summary. In a longer report, the recommendations may begin the executive summary.

Team Involvement

Writing a team report is a challenging job. Forman and Katsky (1986) found that it involves not only all the problems of group process developed throughout this book, but also problems in writing processes such as differing ability levels and expectations. The team must plan well to create the best possible report.

Writing and editing a report through team meetings is well-nigh impossible. The overall content can be determined, and conclusions and recommendations developed, but getting everything down in proper format takes excessive team time. Unless the team has specialized personnel available to do the job, it should find ways to divide the labor of producing the final report. That means developing a work plan and making some decisions about the tone and style of the report.

Developing a Plan   Create an overall plan for the report, including the estimated page length of each section. Who will write which section? Who will put the parts

C A S E   A N A L Y S I S   16.1

The team produced a 168-page final report detailing its procedures, its findings, and its 42 separate recommendations. The writing process began with a subgroup preparing a long outline draft. The task force reviewed and edited the outline, then different team members wrote drafts for various sections.

The members had different styles. The scientists' research orientation was toward written detail, while McDonald's day-to-day operations led those members to a more terse oral style. One member expressed it as the difference between "wordy scientists" and the "one-page memo."

The manuscript was completed by a smaller group that integrated the individual styles, edited the report, and circulated it among other team members. Wordings and rewordings were air-expressed and faxed back and forth until the final copy gained approval.

It took three to four months to work out the final written documents. Previous discussions of issues were rehashed. The team completed the final draft at the last minute to make duplication deadlines. One member speculated that it would have helped if they had given more thought to the written document earlier in the team's life. He thought it might have shortened the writing time if they had recorded meetings or had had a "scribe" take notes and work on a draft of the final report while the task force continued its deliberations.

Issues for Your Consideration:

1. Who were the audiences for the task force report? Which were primary and which were secondary audiences?

2. In what ways would it have helped in writing the final report if the team had visualized it in greater detail as part of the criteria for success in its goal-setting stage?

3. Would a tape recorder at the meetings have affected interactions among the team members? Considering the risks these organizations were taking, could they have used a recorder at the first meeting without impact on the team's processes?

4. Do you think it's unusual for it to take so long to prepare a written report? Must the process lead to rehashing ideas?

5. What issues or concerns arise at this stage, when ideas that had been agreed on when expressed orally or presented as draft proposals during meetings are now to be part of a final written document?

6. Consider the steps and guidelines for written reports in this chapter and put on your consultant's hat. What advice would you give to this team at the beginning of its work about how to go about creating a written report? Critique the description of the process presented here. What changes in procedures, if any, would you recommend? Why?

together and coordinate the editing? Who will type the drafts, polish the copy, proofread, duplicate the report? Who will write cover letters or memos? Who will prepare supplementary materials? Recognize that some pieces, such as the summary and table of contents, cannot be written until the process is nearing completion.

Next, assign tasks. Draw from the expertise on the team. For example, the person who was instrumental in a key part of the background research may be a good candidate to prepare that section. But also recognize that research skills and writing skills may not be correlated; the task has changed, and so have the skills you need. Figure out who writes well, who edits well, who should take responsibility for the final polishing.

To complete the plan, again go back to the key elements: *who* will do *what*, by *when.* Set deadlines, and remember to anticipate the unanticipated.

Make a pact. Agree that every piece and every draft belongs to the entire team. Put all egos on hold, and agree that all drafts are open to rewriting, editing, and polishing by other members. When a writer falls in love with his or her words, and somebody else tries to edit them, the team *and* the report suffer.

Determining Style   Before members go their separate ways to write or edit, make some decisions about the overall tone and style of the report. What degree of formality will it have? Will it use first person (we) or third person (the team)? How should visuals be coordinated with the text? What form will it take? How will it be documented? If everyone understands these issues and incorporates them in his or her writing, then editing and integrating the parts into a cohesive report will be much easier.

Presentation of the Document

When the report is complete, the team must make some decisions about who gets copies and how they will be delivered. Here are some issues, and some thoughts on resolving them.

Prepare a cover letter or memo. Keep it simple. Identify the routine or special function of the report; give honest team sentiment about it, if appropriate; make recommendations for processing it (e.g., meet with team members, plan an oral presentation); and state what the team plans to do next (additional work, further action, or wait for a response).

Disseminate copies to appropriate people. In an organization, every manager or supervisor in the line between the reporting team and the person(s) to whom the report is directed should get a copy. Generally it's good practice to discuss with those to whom the team reports before sending copies to anyone not in the line. Make a list together.

Decide whether to send the report or deliver it in person. The report will get more notice if it's delivered in person, by the whole team or by designated members. Personal delivery should be used only for clear reasons, not for routine reports requiring little or no explanation.

Plan to get feedback. Reports too frequently sit on desks or go directly to files without the team ever hearing a word about their work. The team can hardly demand that its superiors respond, but it can plan other avenues for follow-up. The cover letter and the meeting to deliver the report give the team opportunities to phrase requests tactfully in terms of action *the team* will take, specifying who will do what, and when. For example: "We will contact your office next Friday to see if you have specific concerns the team needs to consider."

Oral Reports

A classic truism in communication is: "A speech is not an essay on its hind legs." Too many people write a report and read it aloud, thereby boring the audience, reducing their credibility, and undermining their efforts. With a team report, you have special opportunities for communication, because you have more people who can be involved. This section suggests ways of planning team involvement, preparing notes, using visuals, handling questions, rehearsing, and making the presentation.

Team Participation

As with a written report, the team needs to plan for each member's participation in the oral report. First, you have to decide which members will actually make presentations. Multiple presenters add variety and interest and demonstrate a wider range of team involvement. Too many presenters, however, makes it too much like musical chairs, with the transitions from one to another dominating the audience's attention.

Again, draw on the expertise of the individuals on the team. Look for different but complementary presentation styles. Those who do not speak can make introductions, handle visuals, or participate in the question-and-answer period. All can help in the rehearsal periods as audience members and questioners. The more all members of the team are involved, the greater the impact of the team's work will be.

Develop a work plan, again specifying who will do what. Assign time limits for each speaker, and set timelines for preparing speaking notes and visuals, arranging for equipment, and holding rehearsal sessions. Make a checklist to ensure that all items are included, and check on progress at each stage.

Notes

Having planned the organizational structure and content of an oral presentation, you need to prepare speaking notes. We strongly recommend that you do *not* write a manuscript for an oral presentation. Once you set precise words on paper, you will have difficulty ever getting away from the script. A manuscript also places extra burdens on the speaker: reading or memorizing takes much more preparation and skill than working from notes, and it usually results in a less effective performance than a well-prepared extemporaneous presentation. Although it's thoroughly prepared and rehearsed, an extemporaneous presentation does not tie you to specific wording; it allows you to be flexible and adaptive to the audience and the situation.

Put your notes on cards, no larger than 4″ × 6″ if you may be speaking without a podium, and no larger than 5″ × 8″ if you're certain you will be using a podium. Larger note cards or thin paper tend to be distracting when moved during the speech.

Use only *key words* in the notes, not full phrases or sentences. Use large print that will be easy to see even if nervousness clouds your vision. Start every new subdivision on a new note card; it helps maintain a better sense of your organization during the actual presentation.

Practice using the notes by letting them serve as reminders while you talk, out loud, about the ideas. You'll find that "talking the speech," rather than writing it, casts it into more natural, oral language—making it more comfortable for your listeners to hear and easier for you to remember and deliver. If, after repeated practice, you find that the key words don't serve your memory well, add something or change the words until they work for you.

Visuals

We have already discussed planning and preparing visuals. To use them well in your presentation, you need to consider: Will the speaker handle his or her own visuals, or will another member of the team reveal each as needed? Where will the focus point or screen be located? Can everyone see it easily? Will audience members need to keep shifting their focus away from the speaker to see the visuals?

Here are few other things to remember when using visuals:

1. Visuals should supplement the speaking, not supplant it. Use visuals to help focus attention on the ideas and to reinforce the oral message.

2. Talk to the audience, not to the visual. A rule to guide you is "Touch-Turn-Talk." Touch—identify the visual area you want the audience to focus on. Turn—redirect your attention to the audience by engaging them with direct, individual eye contact. Talk—only then begin the oral message, not while you're still looking at the visual.

3. Reveal only what you want the audience to focus on. If you have a list of items, disclose only one at a time. When you are finished using a visual, turn it off, cover it, or remove it so the audience doesn't continue to think about it and miss what follows.

Questions and Answers

Questions are the presenter's best friends. Prepare for them with enthusiasm. Martel (1989) gives this advice to people preparing for question and answer periods: "Don't participate in the session until you have a positive attitude regarding how it can help you accomplish both your substance and image goals" (p. 156).

LIGHTS OUT

Four out of 10 top executives admit that they have fallen asleep during office presentations, according to Motivational Systems, a management-development and sales-training organization. . . .

After an exhausting morning of wheeling and dealing, a short snooze during a sales call can provide a much-needed pick-me-up. On the other hand, workplace health and safety authorities warn of . . . the nasty welts produced when Mr. or Ms. Blue Suit executes an R.E.M.-induced full-frontal face-plant onto the desk blotter.

Those whose presentations cause their listeners to break out the No-Doz face even more dire consequences, warns Roger Flax, president of Motivational Systems. "When your audience is tuning out, sales are lost, vital information is poorly communicated to managers and employees, training programs fail, company policies are improperly implemented, and productivity and efficiency suffer."

Considering that 44.5 percent of the 200 vice-presidents polled rated most formal business presentations "boring" or "unbearable," all of

the above probably occur with alarming frequency.

What can speakers do to keep the snoring to a minimum? Flax says the first 15 to 30 seconds of a presentation are critical. "The moment the group's attention and interest start to wander and eyes begin to glaze over, you may have lost your audience for good," he cautions. "Eye contact and rapport must be established immediately. You should stimulate your listeners, introduce your main point, arouse audience interest, and get the adrenaline going."

Excerpted from John Wilcox, "Lights Out," *Training and Development Journal*, September 1989, p. 10. Published by the American Society for Training and Development. Used with permission.

Questions allow you to be sure your message has been understood correctly, let you respond to concerns or objections audience members may have, and provide additional opportunities to enhance the team's credibility. Questions, therefore, help you achieve the report's goals. You need to anticipate questions that may be asked and plan how to respond to them.

Anticipating Questions   Examine the contents of your report and consider your audience. Identify areas where you may expect questions or objections. During rehearsals, each team member can note places where questions may pop up. You should, of course, adapt the presentation to anticipate questions, but the limitations of time and space prohibit covering everything in such detail that there won't be any. As a team, discuss ways to handle the ideas and information during a question-and-answer period at the end of the report.

Team members sometimes develop expertise in specific subject areas, but all should be familiar enough with the report to field most questions. It helps to prepare a concise, easily used, supplementary file with information you may need in answering questions. This might include sources, specific statistical data, synopses of research, or technical details of a plan.

Handling Questions   The speaker's and the team's credibility are enormously enhanced by masterful question-answering. The skills are fairly simple, but impressive in action:

1. Assume that questions are well-intentioned. Even if they aren't, treating them as if they were puts the ball in your court.

2. Listen intently and concentrate fully on the question.
3. Be friendly and cooperative in providing information.
4. Unless a question is both loud and terse, restate it for the audience before you answer it.
5. If the questioner asks a long, involved question, take a moment to analyze it. Restate it more concisely for the audience.
6. If the question really involves two or more questions, separate them and state your intention to answer them separately.
7. If the questioner makes a speech instead of asking a question, don't agree or argue. Listen courteously and then phrase a question from it, or ask the speaker to phrase the question.
8. Answer questions as concisely and directly as possible.
9. If your answer to a question is complicated, organize it into concise chunks and preview the way you intend to answer it.
10. If you have already answered the question, don't mention that fact. Just answer it again.
11. If another member of the team can answer the question better, hand it off—but only if you've agreed on it beforehand.
12. If you don't have an answer, say so; don't fake it. If appropriate, promise to get the answer and get back to the questioner. If it's in your file, another member can look it up as the session proceeds.
13. If the question is idiotic, stupid, or hostile, don't get defensive or sarcastic—stay cool and friendly. Sometimes you can "bridge" the question: start with what the questioner said and move it to your ground. Your credibility increases; hers or his diminishes.

Rehearsal

Now that you have an oral report prepared and a plan for presenting it, you are ready for the next three preparation stages: practice, practice, and practice. Nothing substitutes for good rehearsal. Use the team as a full staff of coaches. Here are some guidelines to help you get the most from your practice time.

Rehearse out loud. Looking over notes and thinking the speech practices only part of the actual presentation. Moving from idea coding to the transmittal step is a significant leap in the communication process. Silent rehearsal is like practicing with only two balls for a three-ball juggling act.

Rehearse in sections. You don't always have to go from beginning to end. It may be more productive to work repetitively on short sections with which you're having difficulty. In ten minutes, you might run through an entire speech once, but could work through a twenty- to thirty-second segment twenty times.

Rehearse at the presentation site if possible. Get the whole team there, and bring friends to serve as audience members. The more closely you can replicate the actual setting, the more your practice helps you adapt to the presentation's complex circumstances.

Rehearse with your visuals. Apply the guidelines presented earlier for using aids. Get a sense of the time it takes to move from one to the other. Among other things, get a feeling for how the visual aids actually help relax you as a speaker; the audience focus is diverted from you from time to time, reducing some tension, and your own movement from audience to visual to notes actually helps your body relax.

Rehearse handling questions. Have other team members or friends ask questions. Practice clear, concise responses. Use the rehearsal to identify potential question areas. Anticipate hostile or trick questions so you can get a feel for your answers.

Rehearse with videotape. No one can give you feedback that substitutes for your own observations, but video replay will be more useful if you can combine your assessment with that of a skilled observer to coach you. Concentrate on what you do well. When you identify things to improve or change, consider specific things to do to replace them. Don't just say, "My hands are awkward," and then glue them to your sides. Awkward might be better.

Rehearse your feelings and responses. Visualize yourself in front of the audience being comfortable and effective. What are you doing? What is the audience doing? How are they responding? Most of us have no difficulty thinking the worst; we focus too little on the best. Create clear, moving pictures—video previews—of yourself succeeding in the presentation and gaining the audience response you desire. Play them back in your mind in full living color; concentrate on your emotional responses as the successful presentation proceeds.

Presentation

Despite extensive preparation, the actual presentation is still likely to be a time of nervousness and anxiety. Having your team there provides moral support. Still, there is a lot at stake: the credibility and reputation of the team and its members will be enhanced or diminished by the audience's responses. The presentation can affect careers in the workplace or grades and friendships in school. Reasonable apprehension is natural in this situation. The challenge is to manage the nervousness and use its energy to enliven your performance. "Get all those butterflies to fly in formation."

The first challenge is to be sure everyone and everything is on hand. Someone should have a checklist, marking off people as they arrive and handouts, visuals, and equipment when they are in place. It's easy to overlook something.

The second challenge is to prepare yourself. Consciously work to relax your throat, shoulders, and neck. Breathe slowly and deeply. Get involved in activities and conversations that occur prior to your speaking turn. Visualize yourself in front of the audience moving successfully through the performance. Most important, focus your thoughts on your purpose—you have a message to share with the audience.

When your turn arrives, move to the front and settle in for a few seconds before starting to speak. Engage individuals in the audience, eye to eye. Smile; be friendly. When you speak, direct your conversation to one person at a time, moving around the room so all are included. Share with them the team's ideas.

Be flexible. One of the strengths of an extemporaneous presentation is that you can adapt. If someone stops you to ask a question that covers one of your points, you can answer the question, skip over the point, and save the time for other items or for more questions. The goal is to have the audience understand and, if appropriate, approve the team's report. If you adapt your presentation—even if you *miss* something you had intended to cover—that's okay as long as you achieve your objective.

Follow-Up and Evaluation

After the presentation of your report—written or oral—the team should examine how well it achieved its goals and what it needs to do next. The practical outcome of your report gives you part of the answer. Did it meet the expectations of your audience? Did you get approval of the report or support for what you proposed? You can enhance your information by using a simple evaluation form at the end of your presentation to get feedback from your audience; it's fairly subtle and anonymous—and it can give you information you might need.

As a team, assess how well you did and plan your next steps. Does the team still have work to do? Is a follow-up report expected? Does the team, or individual members, still have agendas they want addressed? Does the report have consequences that lead the team in new directions?

We know from our own experience that creating an oral or written presentation as a team is an especially challenging and gratifying undertaking. Congratulate yourselves—you deserve it!

Summary

Most teams have reporting responsibilities. Reports may be written, oral, or a combination of the two. The work begins by identifying the report's specific purposes. These goals will be achieved in the minds and actions of the audience, not in the report itself. Therefore, the team needs a clear picture of the audience for the report, including knowledge, attitudes, and values that may affect its response.

The report's content is based on information selected from the team's research, strategically organized to communicate ideas clearly to the audience.

An organizational strategy moves the reader or listener from point to point with appropriate transitions from a purposeful introduction, through a cohesive body, to an effective conclusion.

Although they share many of the same preparation steps, written and oral reports require different approaches after the overall structure has been developed.

A written report moves from the structural plan to a rough draft, followed by extensive editing and rewriting. An oral report requires a set of notes for extemporaneous presentation, followed by disciplined rehearsal. In either case, the final presentation of the document or the performance should be finely tuned.

Team members need to follow up a report with a careful analysis of the end product and the processes by which they produced it. They should seek feedback to assess how well their goals were achieved, and to consider what they will do next.

A team "goes public" through its reports. They are the windows through which others see the team and assess its competence and credibility. As such, they require serious attention.

Exercises

1. As a group, imagine you are preparing both a written and an oral report to be presented to an executive committee. Its members are busy, expert in their fields, but not informed as to the results of your investigation. Brainstorm a list of issues that would affect their reception of your report. What would they want? What would make it clear? What restrictions and goals should you set for the written and oral reports?

2. Listen to an oral report or lecture, and examine the written materials that accompany it. Evaluate the report as to whether it met your expectations, whether it achieved the goals of the project sponsor, whether it met the goals of the communicator(s), and how you responded to it as a listener. What worked? What didn't? If you were coaching the reporter(s), what would you suggest to make it better next time?

3. With a small group of students or a team you're currently on, use the information in this chapter and Form 16.1 (Parts 1, 2, and 3) to plan a written report. Use a real audience, or create a hypothetical one. Draw from material and goals you've created for any of your previous projects in completing this exercise.

4. Using the material from the previous exercise, plan an oral report to accompany the written one for your hypothetical audience. Be sure to plan all aspects of the report, including rehearsal and presentation.

5. Read the Epilogue, and design a way to assess your entire semester's work. If you are currently on a class team, do this exercise together. If not, form a small group in class.

First, make a list of the elements that should have created a good team experience. Then create an assessment method that you can use to evaluate your experience. This can include a form or questionnaire, and/or others methods we've discussed.

Next, send a representative to explain your plan to another team so the members can give you feedback. At the same time, your team will review another team's plan. The representatives then report the other team's responses back to their own teams.

With the feedback from the other team, revise and refine your assessment method. When your work is complete, *use* your method to assess your experience. Discuss the results with your team and talk about what you've learned about teamwork.

Keep a copy of your assessment method (forms and/or other processes) to refer to for your future groups and teams. It will help you make those future experiences satisfying and worthwhile.

FORM 16.1 ▌ PRESENTATION PLANNING GUIDE

Part 1. Analysis

In the left-hand column, fill out the conditions and limitations with which you will be working. In the next column, write in the overall goals of the presentation. In the third column, write the main points that must be made to reach each goal. Draw a line from each goal to each objective that must be reached for that goal. With this information, go to the next planning sheet.

CONDITIONS & LIMITATIONS	GOALS	POINTS TO BE MADE FOR EACH GOAL
Audience		
Audience Expectations		
Time or Page Limits		
Space or Presentation Conditions		
Resources Available		

Part 2. Planning

Based on the information from Part 1, use this "map" to plan your presentation:

PLAN POINTS, SUBPOINTS, SUPPORT VISUALS, AND TRANSITIONS

Choose an *organizational pattern* to connect main points and subpoints logically.

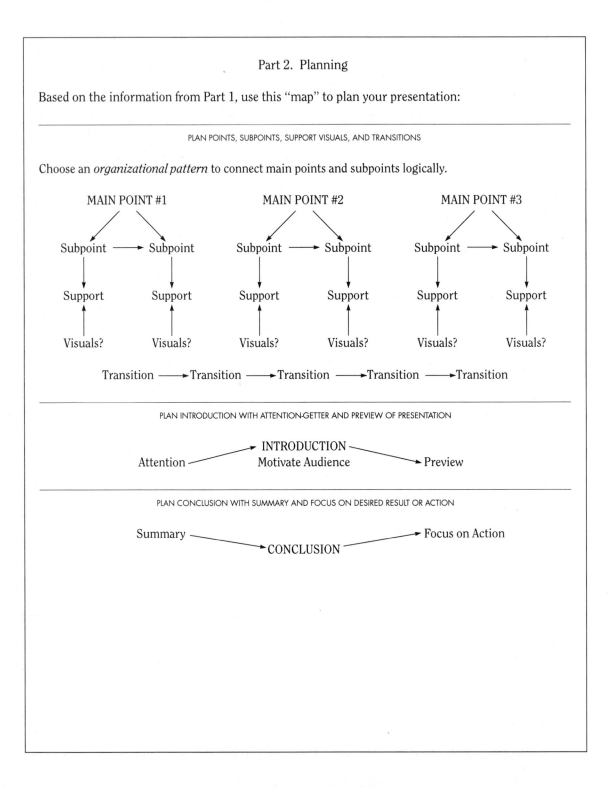

Part 3. Preparation

ASSEMBLE AS INTRODUCTION—BODY—CONCLUSION

ASSIGN RESPONSIBILITIES

For an oral report: Who will present each part?
Who will prepare visuals?
Who will manage visuals during presentation?
Who will handle questions?
Who will handle assessment, follow-up?

For a written report: Who will draft which part?
Who will be responsible for visuals, graphics, etc.?
Who will edit, polish?
Who will be responsible for duplication and distribution?

PREPARE VISUALS, SUPPLEMENTARY MATERIALS, NECESSARY EQUIPMENT, NOTES

PREPARE PERFORMANCE

For an oral report: Make notes.
Talk it out.
Practice.
Coach as a team.

For a written report: Write.
Edit, polish.
Produce.
Present.

Epilogue

"What an experience—I wish it wasn't over!"

"What an experience—I'm glad that's over!"

You've reached the end of this class and this book; we hope that the first statement summarizes your feelings better than the second one. We feel as if we know you; maybe you're a composite, for us, of all the students we've ever known. We want you to feel you've learned something valuable and to know exactly what that something is. We want it to work for you in your life.

To move forward and make what you've learned applicable to your future, we want to think about beginnings, middles, endings—and beginnings again. This is important, not only at the conclusion of your course, but at the end of all work group and team experiences. To help you do that, this epilogue guides you in looking back over your experiences and evaluating them. It gives you a foundation for saying good-bye to present and future groups and teams, and it starts you on your leadership in the future.

Looking Back

As you've used this book, you've seen group communication and teams through a microscope, magnified bit by bit. As you've worked in various groups in your class, you've put those images into action.

Now, we'd like to pull back with a wide-angle lens and take a more *macroscopic* view to get a bigger picture of what you've learned. This will help you see more clearly what you've done and synthesize both your book learning and experiential learnings. Then you can apply them to groups and teams with which you'll work in the future.

Where do we start? When J. Richard Hackman (1990) and his associates analyzed teams in the workplace, they identified three criteria to assess their effectiveness:

The product (outcome, service, decision, project). Did it satisfy the requirements of the team's parent organization or founder? Did it satisfy a set of established criteria (if one existed)?

The processes of the team. Did members' ability to work together increase or decrease? Did processes enhance the members' ability to work together interdependently in the future?

The personal growth and well-being of the members. Did the experience enable people to fulfill their own goals and to develop their learning? (pp. 6–7).

Adopting these criteria, we'll start with the outcomes of your groups and teams, then assess the processes you went through to get there, and finally, evaluate how the experience affected you and other members of the team.

Final Outcomes of the Team

It doesn't hurt to look at your final results from two points of view. One is from the grandstands, and the other is from the goal.

The View from the Stands   Draw back from your involvement and take a seat in the grandstands for a moment. You'll get a broad view of your results. First, identify what your team (or group) accomplished. What desirable results came of the work? Next, scan the field more closely: what do you wish had been better? When you've got this overall view, go a little further back, to the view from the goal.

The View from the Goal   When you started, each member had personal goals (to get a good grade, to learn skills you could apply to your life, to get to know people). As a group, you created goals that you wanted your team to achieve.

Larson and LaFasto (1989), you may remember, noted in the work teams they observed that the best had "clear, elevating" goals. They had mutually focused visions of what they wanted to achieve, and they believed theirs were valuable goals to reach. Ineffective teams' goals had become "unfocused, politicized." Somehow their goals had become insignificant, or they'd been swept away in too many other team or individual goals (p. 27). How about your team?

Remembering your goals and criteria for judging your accomplishments, how did your team do? Did you reach the goal you wanted to reach? Did it meet your criteria? Did you satisfy the requirements of your founder (perhaps your professor in this class)? Assess, as a team, how you feel about that, and what you might do differently next time. It may be that your goals were excellent, or it may be that they became blurred, weren't important enough, or were too dispersed.

First, recognize what you did right. Then, identify what you can do better in your next team to set goals that are clear and worthwhile and to reach them.

Processes of the Team

Of course, excellent achievements also result from excellent processes. To see how well they've worked for you, you'll need to look at three sets of processes and relationships:

Transactional processes that convey meanings about individuals, the team, and the task; establish supportive or defensive climates; and determine the ethics of a team's transactions.

Task processes that define problems, set goals and criteria, collect and analyze information, use creative and critical thinking to analyze problems, develop ideas, analyze them, and make decisions.

Systems and subsystems relationships that a team may have experienced if it worked within a larger organization and/or cooperated with other groups.

Transactional Processes   Much of your experience with groups and teams is reflected in the quality of their transactional processes. These questions may help you focus on that quality:

Shared leadership. Did members take various roles, responsibilities, and functions as needed? Did they guide and encourage transactional processes?

Dialogical ethic. Did members treat one another authentically, equally, inclusively? Did they confirm and support one another? Did they respect one another; appreciate diversity; seek understanding and empathy; enable critical thinking?

Communication. How well did members communicate verbally and nonverbally? Did they use dialogical listening and questioning to clarify, to understand, to negotiate meanings even when people were different?

Climate. Did the climate enable people to be open, supportive, trustworthy, and trusting? Were people able to say what they believed?

Leading. How well did the leader (if you had one) facilitate members' ability to contribute freely; keep processes open and supportive; inspire and strengthen the team in its goals and in its transactions?

Team culture. Did the team develop healthy syntality and strong synergy? Was it cohesive? How did members feel about their image, vision, teamwork? How did they manage problems with groupthink and conformity? Was conflict viewed as positive and managed effectively?

This list is not complete. Maybe you can add some questions that go more directly to the heart of transactional processes as you experienced them. It's *your* insight that makes these concepts real.

Task Processes   Think back over the actual work. How did the task processes help your team progress toward your goals? This list of questions may help you in your assessment:

Preparation. Did members take responsibility for work; get the information and resources the team needed; think and plan ahead for meetings?

Cooperative analysis. Did members engage in vigilant, cooperative critical analysis of goals, criteria, information, problems, and solutions? Did they examine the logic, validity, and truthfulness of sources; causes, effects, inferences, and judgments?

Ethics. Did members vigilantly examine values; issues of right and wrong; probable effects of decisions on others and on team members? Did they examine whether every member's ethics, values, and beliefs were considered in their task processes? Did the team make ethically defensible decisions?

Leading. To what extent did the leader encourage vigilant interaction and decision making; enable members to be open and critical in their thinking; obtain resources necessary for the task? How well did she or he manage meetings and link the team to outside systems and sources as needed?

Meetings. How well were agendas planned and managed? Did meetings accomplish their objectives? Were they efficient, flexible; did they encourage cooperative critical thinking?

Projects and reporting. Did the team make sure every member's input was represented? Were final results carefully prepared and presented? Did the team assess its outcomes?

Again, these questions only touch on the elements of task processes. As you look at them, think about what you know. What would you add?

Systems Relationships If your team functioned within a larger organization, a realistic look at its work includes systems relationships. Some questions to consider are:

Goals and vision. Was your team able to work with the goals and vision of the parent organization? Did your goals contribute to the larger vision?

Support. Was the team supported and rewarded in its work within the system? Did members feel the team was an important component in the larger organization?

Autonomy. How independent was the team able to be in its work? Was it free to set goals; develop solutions; make decisions; assess its work independently? How did its relationship to the larger system affect its transactional and task processes?

Cooperation. How, and in what ways, did your team work with other teams or organizations? Were the relationships effective, well coordinated, mutually beneficial?

We hope all of these questions receive positive answers; but of course, that's unrealistic. No experience is perfect. The point is to find the areas that worked well, and identify those that did not. Then you can make the next experience better.

Members of the Team

If your teamwork has been a success, it also will have affected members in two important ways: their personal growth, and their ability to work interdependently.

Personal Growth and Satisfaction   You can start by assessing your own feelings. In what ways do you feel you've grown from the experience? Maybe you have developed a deeper understanding of people in groups; strengthened your leadership skills; learned how to help a team work together effectively. Perhaps you've developed a new understanding of how differing people—women and men, cultures and subcultures, political right and political left, able-bodied and disabled—contribute to you and you to them. You may have learned to perceive the ethical implications in group communication from a keener perspective. Perhaps learning how to communicate in groups has helped you in other ways—in other classes or in your personal life. What else have you learned?

Have you gained satisfaction from the experience? Was the outcome gratifying? Was it rewarding to contribute your leadership and help to the team when it was needed? Are there ways in which you were satisfied by the processes and/or the outcomes? Knowing what you got from your experiences helps you to use them in the future, so give it some thought.

Think, also, about other members—about how you've seen them develop throughout the team's experience. This, too, provides insights for future leadership. When you set out to help a team achieve success, one of the things you want to facilitate is the members' opportunities for growth and satisfaction in the group.

Interdependence and Future Interaction   Although some groups meet for a brief time and are over, most real work teams are in organizations where the members will work together again, either in the same group or in others. The team experience, if it's been a good one, has given them hands-on training for interdependence.

People who function interdependently understand one anothers' working and communicating styles. They know how to depend on one another, how to help one another. They know what roles to expect of one another in future groups. They have worked out ways of managing conflict and analyzing problems together, and they have developed a dialogical ethic that guides their transactional and task processes.

In reality, as a team's work comes to a close, some people probably are more capable of that kind of interdependence than others. You can judge the team a success if most members have learned to work together interdependently and effectively.

We hope the groups you've worked with during this course have produced quality results; that they have developed good transactional and task processes; and that they have enhanced the growth and future teamwork abilities of the members. We remind you, however, of the cliché "no pain, no gain." Where your experiences have been less than perfect, take heart; they, too, have taught you something invaluable for your future leadership.

What happens now that the group's work is done? Breaking up can be hard to do.

Saying Good-bye

We said earlier that endings, in a sense, are beginnings; the conclusion of one episode is the foundation for the beginning of the next.

Keyton (1991) points out that "exiting is not always the same as saying good-bye" (pp. 14–15). It may be saying good-bye to one group and hello to another one—with much the same membership. As a college student, or as a member of a corporate team, you may have continuing contacts with other members and you may work with them in future groups. Nonetheless, this particular experience is coming to an end, and teams need to close their experiences so people can move on, feeling the experience was complete and knowing they are ready for what comes next.

We suggest that your present and future groups *not*, as many do, just dwindle away. The team needs to meet and think about its time together. You and your group might close your teamwork in two steps, similar to those suggested by Knapp and his colleagues (1973).

First, synthesize your experiences together. This is when you go back and assess your experiences, talk about the highs and lows of your teamwork, and draw some generalizations about it that everyone can share. Often members tell and retell accounts of moments that were funny, or touching, or ridiculous, or triumphant; these become team memories and myths. This is a time for members to resolve issues, to bring the team's perspective together, and to create a sense of completion.

Second, reaffirm one another's work, celebrate your successes, and support one another's abilities to meet future challenges. Make arrangements for future contacts. Part of closing one door may be opening another for friendships, working relationships, or cooperative ventures. Connect the past and the future; people need to see where they've been *and* where they're going.

Moving On

In the first chapter of this book, we talked about how important groups and teams are likely to be in your future life and career. We pointed out that corporations, profit and nonprofit organizations, academic institutions, religious groups—all work extensively with groups and teams.

Please visualize yourself positively in that future. Your leadership can be extremely important, so develop it. What talents, abilities, perspectives, and/or skills in your repertoire can you use to help groups and teams develop excellent processes and produce quality results? How can you strengthen and use those abilities?

What do you want to do better? We suggest that you identify two or three areas you want to develop—skills or approaches you believe will have the greatest impact on your leadership effectiveness. Don't try to take on too many goals at once; it's hard to achieve anything when you're struggling for everything. Start with a short list.

Visualize yourself achieving those objectives, and look for opportunities to practice them. Every time you participate in a classroom group, work on a team of any kind, or volunteer for a committee, you can develop your leadership.

Perhaps your future involves *being* a leader. Maybe someday you will take the lead in important issues and actions. If so, wonderful—we need good leaders.

If you do not choose to be "the leader," however, you still have both responsibilities and opportunities for leader*ship*. Your leadership can influence the quality of your life and work, as well as the quality of others' experiences.

Your leadership can help others in many ways—not only in making work teams function effectively to achieve their goals, important as that is, but by making you more effective in your community, in your religious organization, in your family. It will enable you to achieve goals that are important to you, and may someday help you to overcome problems that others might find insurmountable.

A person who understands both how to share leadership and how to be a leader has choices. You can provide the kind of subtle, quiet leadership that facilitates others in their efforts. You can take the designated leader role and make things happen. You can guide people through dialogically ethical processes in their deliberations and decision making. You can ensure that people—whoever they are, whatever their backgrounds, cultures, genders, beliefs—have opportunities to be part of the processes of teamwork and decision making. You can influence groups so that members respect and value one another, so their decisions and actions are just.

That's what you can accomplish with your leadership. Go forth and do it.

Glossary

Active listening Engaging the speaker mentally, giving nonverbal feedback, silently analyzing and questioning information.

Ad hoc A meeting or group set up to focus specifically on one issue.

Advantages Beneficial side effects that might result from implementing a proposal.

Agenda An ordered list of events to guide a meeting.

Aggressiveness Communicating low regard for others' rights or feelings by directly expressing hostility and/or intent to control their responses.

Applicability Analysis of the degree to which a proposal meets criteria for solving a problem.

Assertiveness Communicating openly, with concern for others' rights and feelings, what one needs or wants them to know.

Assumption An untested belief, often unconscious and usually unstated, that something is a fact.

Authoritarian Leadership style that is directive, controlling, and often relies on coercive or reward power.

Brainstorming A group process for thinking of as many ideas as possible without immediate evaluation.

Breakout sessions Small groups that meet simultaneously during a conference or workshop.

Buzz groups Division of a large audience into small groups for brief discussions, after which they report to the audience at large.

Cause-and-effect reasoning Inferring that one occurrence causes another on the basis of observing a relationship between the two.

Claim The conclusion or argument inferred on the basis of data and reasoning.

Coercive power Ability to punish others as a method of getting them to perform in desired ways.

Cohesiveness The degree to which members are attracted toward one another and the group, making their involvement important to them.

Colloquy A public meeting format involving two types of groups—one of experts, the other of nonex-

perts, or laypeople. The nonexperts use the experts as resources on the topic.

Commitment-strategy organization An organization that reduces layers of authority; commits to quality; adopts methods to make the culture open, receptive, and participative; and encourages and nurtures teamwork.

Communication The process of using verbal and nonverbal cues to negotiate a mutually acceptable meaning between two or more people within a particular context and environment.

Competence Degree of expertness, qualification, authoritativeness, and skill a person demonstrates.

Conference A large meeting that brings together individuals with similar interests to achieve common goals.

Conflict Opposed positions in which two or more people perceive that accomplishing one's goal keeps another's from being achieved.

Conformity Behaving in ways consistent with the group's norms and standards.

Consensus Decisions that represent the agreement of every member.

Control-strategy organization An organization that is status and power driven, hierarchical, and tightly controlling, making cooperative groups and teams difficult to use.

Convention Like a conference, a large meeting that brings together individuals with similar interests to achieve common goals.

Cooperative analysis A process of listening and questioning that makes it possible for team members to think critically, creatively, and analytically and to test the logic and validity of their arguments.

Coorientation Other people's sense that you are similar to them; that you are concerned for their well-being; that you share their interests, values, objectives, and needs.

Coorientational accuracy Correctness of one's understanding of another person's position.

Creative process Finding ways of combining or perceiving relationships of previously unrelated ideas.

Creative team People who bring specific talents together to conduct research, formulate ideas, and carry through an entire original project.

Creative thinking Brain activity that is synthetic, artistic, innovative, global, visionary, intuitive, imaginative.

Credibility Individuals' perceptions of another's competence, objectivity, trustworthiness, coorientation, and dynamism.

Critical thinking Processing information in a logical, linear, rational, mathematical, serial, and organized set of patterns to examine relationships among ideas.

Cybernetic processes Feedback and assessment methods that help open systems with their own development and improvement.

Debate A public meeting format in which speakers take turns advocating opposite sides of an issue before a judge or an audience.

Decision by authority Someone with higher status makes the final decision after hearing the team's report and/or recommendations.

Decision making The culmination of information-gathering and problem-analysis processes to arrive at specific policies or actions to be implemented.

Decision matrix A grid for comparing the merits of different plans by categories of criteria.

Deductive reasoning Drawing a conclusion about a specific case from a general, or universal, statement.

Defensive behavior Hostile responses to feeling threatened or alienated by a situation or by others' behavior.

Delphi technique A method of group analysis that involves a wide range of people without holding meetings.

Democratic Leadership style that makes sure everyone is heard, facilitates discussion and decision making, and shares power.

Designated leader The person charged with organizing, structuring, and empowering team members to achieve the tasks.

Desirability Analysis of value, worthwhileness, and ethics involved in the possible implementation of a proposal.

Deviance Behaving in ways, or expressing opinions, that do not conform to others' expectations.

Dialogic listening A process of "sculpting" meaning through listening, questioning, paraphrasing, and building on each other's ideas.

Disadvantages Undesirable side effects that might result from implementing a proposal.

Drive reduction theories The idea that people are motivated to act in ways that reduce their personal drives or needs.

Dynamism Vigor, intensity, compellingness with which an individual gets and maintains other people's attention.

Emergent leader A person who, over time, fulfills responsibilities and is acknowledged by members to be a leader.

Empathic listening Understanding what others feel and helping identify personal or interpersonal issues that impact on the team.

Ethical dilemma A situation in which the team must apply standards and make decisions between two real choices involving ethical issues.

Ethics Value judgments concerning degrees of right and wrong, goodness and badness, in human conduct.

Expert power Influence based on an individual's expertise, credentials, experience, research, and competence in a given area.

Fallacy An inference from data to claim that circumvents sound, logical reasoning.

Fantasy chaining An imaginative, creative process of linking ideas together like a play.

Fishbone diagram A diagram used in problem analysis for identifying and visualizing cause-and-effect relationships.

Flowchart A diagram, useful in problem analysis, showing the stages, directions, and choices from beginning to end of a process.

Forum A public meeting guided by a moderator in which audience members express and advocate ideas and opinions, ask questions, and seek information.

Games Patterns of behavior that manipulate others through a gimmick leading into a script that results in a payoff for the game player.

Goals The outcomes a team identifies as what it intends to accomplish and toward which it strives.

Governance groups and committees Representatives of larger populations or organizations and subgroups who consider issues, gather information, make proposals, report, make decisions, and/or enact legislation.

Group Two or more persons who are interacting with one another in such a manner that each person influences and is influenced by each other person.

Groupthink A mindlessness in which a cohesive group screens out anything but what it assumes and wants to be true.

Health care team Professionals who coordinate the delivery of all aspects of care and/or rehabilitation to a given patient.

Hidden agenda An individual's disguised personal objectives that guide his or her communication and affect team processes.

Incrementalism Decisions to correct immediate situations create new problems and affect consequent decisions.

Inductive reasoning Drawing a general conclusion from specific instances of an occurrence.

Inference A mental connection from data to a conclusion.

Information gathering Research and inquiry as either sole or partial responsibility of a team or group.

Information power Ability to enable or impede others by sharing or withholding facts.

Instrumental objectives Interim steps the group or team must achieve in order to reach the goals.

Interactive questioning Applying analytical and critcal thinking skills to clarify, probe, analyze, and follow up information expressed by others.

Kinesics Communication through body movement, posture, gestures, and facial expressions.

Laissez-faire Leadership style that is neutral and uninvolved.

Leadership Verbal and nonverbal communication behavior that influences a team's transactional and task processes in achieving members' and the team's needs and goals.

Lecture A presentation by a speaker; often followed by a forum session, with audience participation.

Legitimate power Authority residing in a person's position or office.

Life-cycle theory Leadership style that adapts to a group's maturity, or members' abilities and willingness take responsibility for directing their own behaviors.

Majority vote Results of a ballot in which more than 50 percent of the members who vote favor one candidate or one side of an issue.

Management team Managers who meet to coordinate employee groups, solve problems, make decisions, allocate resources, and so on.

Meaning The understanding an individual has of a concept, based upon experiences, motivations, values, beliefs, and negotiations with others.

Meeting plan A full plan for a public meeting that includes agenda, times, places, responsibilities, and checklists.

Metaphorical thinking A creative process that phrases comparisons between two things as if one thing were the other, thereby suggesting new relationships and ideas.

Midpoint crisis The midpoint of a team's existence, when members recognize that their time is half over, conflicts must be managed, and work must be completed.

Mind locks Assumptions about how people should be or act that close off the ability to think creatively.

Mixed-strategy organization An organization that is shifting from control to commitment and developing approaches to using teams.

Multiple ranking Ranking issues or candidates through several ballots to eliminate candidates until a final decision is reached.

Nominal group technique (NGT) An orderly process for getting full participation in generating and discussing ideas in a group.

Nonverbal communication Cues accompanying language or separate from language that people may interpret as having meaning.

Objectivity Ability to look at both sides of an issue; to suspend personal biases; to be reasonable and dispassionate.

Organizational culture The distinguishing realities, beliefs, values, norms, expectations, and responses that develop as people work together in an organization and that guide their behaviors.

Panel A public meeting format in which several individuals discuss a topic among themselves.

Paper-and-pencil instruments Questionnaires or surveys of a group to ascertain its knowledge or attitudes about a topic.

Paralanguage Communication through the pitch, tone, volume, range, and quality of voice; the pronunciation, articulation, and rate of speech; and in vocalizations such as groaning, sighing, and "uhmming."

Passive-aggression Behavior that expresses anger

and hostility indirectly through strategies that block progress or hurt someone else.

Passivity   Seeming indifferent or agreeable and hiding feelings to avoid dealing with others' responses.

Perception   The process by which people sense, select, and interpret stimuli.

Person-centered messages   Communicating in ways that recognize another's uniqueness, goals, feelings, and concerns.

Personal agenda   The personal needs, wants, or goals an individual brings to working with a group or team.

Plenary sessions   Meetings of all conferees at a conference or convention.

Powerful language   Language style of dominant gender and high-status groups in a society.

Powerless language   Language style of subordinate gender and low-status groups in a society.

Practicality   The feasibility of implementing a proposal.

Primary source   A direct, original source of information, such as a newspaper report, a research study, or an interview.

Principled leader   One who uses ethical standards to facilitate dialogical processes and decision making in a group.

Proactivity   Reaching beyond the moment and creating opportunities; opposite of reactivity.

Problem analysis   Investigation of a problem—its scope, impact, causes, effects—possibly leading to recommendations for solutions.

Project team   People of varied backgrounds and skills who work together to accomplish a specific task from beginning to end.

Proxemics   Communication through uses of and reactions to space between and among people and/or objects.

Punctuated equilibrium   Periods of seeming inertia broken by bursts of energy and change in the development of a team.

Qualifiers   Modifiers that indicate the degree of certainty of a given conclusion.

Quality circle   Employees who work in a group to improve quality in any area of the organization.

Quality improvement   A charge to a group to identify areas where quality can be improved, and find ways to improve it.

Questions of fact   Discussion questions seeking objective, testable, verifiable answers about matters of past or present conditions and data.

Questions of policy   Discussion questions seeking answers to what positions or actions should be adopted.

Questions of prediction   Discussion questions seeking to forecast future conditions of facts, values, and/or policies.

Questions of value   Discussion questions weighing the worthwhileness, ethicality, and relative importance of a concept, act, or policy.

Referent power   Influence inherent in the respect and admiration others have for an individual.

Reflective thinking sequence   Classic analysis of the steps people take in thinking through a problem: sensing a problem, defining it, listing possible solutions, comparing pros and cons, selecting the best solution, implementing it, and reviewing its effectiveness.

Reinforcement theories   Explanations of human behavior as the tendency to continue behaviors that are rewarded and discontinue behaviors that are punished.

Reservation   Recognition of possible arguments against a conclusion, or claim.

Reward power   Ability to provide for others' needs or wants as a method of motivating their performances.

Risk   The chance a team takes in going ahead with an idea that might fail or result in serious damage.

Role-playing   A structured experience in which participants enact a scenario in adopted roles to examine feelings and interactions from a different perspective than their own.

Roles   Sets of behaviors a person uses to fulfill specific expectations of his or her function or character in a situation.

Run-through   A step-by-step review or rehearsal of an entire session.

Secondary source   An information source that paraphrases, repeats, and/or quotes another source.

Self-managing team (SMT)   People who work together and are responsible for all aspects of their efforts, including personnel, budget, work and project planning, coordinating with other teams and departments, and self-assessment.

Self-monitoring   The ability to get feedback and adapt one's behavior in relationship to others' cues.

Self-talk   Messages to yourself about who you are and what you do.

Situational-contingency   Leadership approach that

adapts a leader's style to variations in situations, tasks, purposes, and members.

Social exchange theory An explanation of how an individual chooses a behavior by weighing a prediction of the outcome against his or her minimally acceptable outcome and how it would compare to possible alternatives.

Staff group People who work together in some capacity and meet regularly to discuss information and policies.

Study group People who get together to help one another learn about a given topic.

Subsystem A small group or unit that operates as part of a larger system.

Supportive behavior Communication that reduces defenses and builds open climates by focusing evaluation on problems and issues, not individuals.

Support group People who help one another cope with issues that affect their lives.

Symposium A public meeting format in which a moderator introduces the topic and speakers, each of whom makes a presentation.

Synectics A structured process of metaphorical thinking and group fantasy to create new concepts and solutions from previously unrelated ideas.

Synergy The energy that moves a team; a fusion, or interactive combination, of the drives, needs, motives, and vitality of the members.

Syntality A group's "personality," reflecting the way members interact, the way they share ideas and solve problems, and the way they feel and respond to one another.

Systems theory Describes the systematic, interdependent relationships, processes, and structures of interrelated subsystems and systems.

Task force A group appointed specifically to gather information, solve problems, and/or make recommendations regarding an issue.

T-chart A chart divided into a "T" for comparing the merits of an idea, with "pros" on one side of the vertical divider and "cons" on the other.

Task processes Specific interactions that focus on gathering and sharing information; analyzing problems; designing solutions; analyzing and testing evidence and reasoning; and making, implementing, or evaluating decisions.

Team A diverse group of people who share leadership responsibility for creating a group identity in an interconnected effort to achieve a mutually defined goal within the context of other groups and systems.

Team culture A group's way of being, acting, and doing derived from the larger society, from the parent organization, from the various cultures or subcultures of the members, and from members' interactions.

Team image An identifying set of characteristics unique to the team.

Team vision A mutual understanding that includes but goes beyond goals and objectives to a totality the team visualizes as the result of its work.

Teleconference A meeting by telephone, computer, or video, allowing people to confer from dispersed locations.

Teleconference sessions Programs developed and transmitted to any site capable of receiving the signal; they serve as plenary sessions, addressing a specific theme or interest of conferees.

Terminal objectives A team's final goals.

Transactional processes Give-and-take interactions that carry communication about individuals, the team, and the task processes concurrently.

Transformational leadership Style that elevates, motivates, inspires, and develops members to create the team and to fulfill the vision and goals of the team and the organization.

Trustworthiness Other people's confidence in a person's honesty, sincerity, and consistency of ethical behavior.

Two-thirds vote Results of a ballot showing at least twice the number of votes for an issue as against it.

Value A personal, internal understanding about the worthwhileness and importance of an idea, an action, or way of being.

Vigilance Members' intense dedication to critical thinking and analysis that produces quality choices at every stage of decision making.

Visualization A mental picture of the way a person will feel and act in a situation.

Warrant Rationale behind the inference that links evidence or data to a conclusion, or claim.

Workshops Small groups that convene to learn and develop specific areas of understanding, skills, or creative processes, usually with high involvement by participants.

References

Ancona, D. G. (1990). Outward bound: Strategies for team survival in an organization. *Academy of Management Journal, 33,* 334–365.

Andersen, M. P. (1959). The agree-disagree discussion guide. *Speech Teacher, 8,* 41–48.

Anderson, L. R. (1990). Toward a two-track model of leadership training: Suggestions from self-monitoring theory. *Small Group Research, 21,* 147–167.

Antczak, F. J. (1991). Discursive community and the problem of perspective in ethical criticism. In K. J. Greenberg (Ed.), *Conversations and communication ethics* (pp. 75–85). Norwood, NJ: Ablex.

Argyle, M. (1991). Intercultural communication. In L. A. Samovar & R. E. Porter (Eds.), *Intercultural communication: A reader* (6th ed.) (pp. 32–45). Belmont, CA: Wadsworth.

Argyle, M., & Ingham, R. (1972). Gaze, mutual gaze, and proximity. *Semiotica, 6,* 32–49.

Arnett, R. C. (1987). The status of communication ethics scholarship in speech communication journals from 1915 to 1985. *Central States Speech Journal, 38,* 44–61.

Baker, P. M. (1984). Seeing is behaving: Visibility and participation in small groups. *Environment and Behavior, 16,* 159–184.

Barge, J. K. (1991, November). *Task skills and competence in group leadership.* Paper presented at the meeting of the Speech Communication Association, Atlanta, GA.

Barry, D. (1991, Summer). Managing the bossless team: Lessons in distributed leadership. *Organizational Dynamics,* pp. 31–47.

Bass, B. M. (1990, Winter). From transactional to transformational leadership: Learning to share the vision. *Organizational Dynamics,* pp. 19–31.

Baum, A., Fisher, J. D., & Singer, J. E. (1985). *Social psychology.* New York: Random House.

Beatty, M. J. (1981). Receiver apprehension as a function of cognitive backlog. *Western Journal of Speech Communication, 45,* 277–281.

Benne, K. D., & Sheats, P. (1948). Functional roles of group members. *Journal of Social Issues, 4,* 41–49.

Bennis, W. (1989). *Why leaders can't lead.* San Francisco: Jossey-Bass.

Benoit, W. L., & Benoit, P. J. (1991). Memory for conversational behavior. *The Southern Communication Journal, 56,* 24–34.

Berman, S. J., & Hellweg, S. A. (1989). Perceived supervisor communication competence and supervisor satisfaction as a function of quality circle participation. *The Journal of Business Communication, 26,* 103–119.

Berne, E. (1966). *The structure and dynamics of organizations and groups.* New York: Grove Press.

Blakeslee, S. (1991, September 10). Brain yields new clues on its organization for language. *New York Times,* p. C1.

Bolton, R. (1990). Listening is more than merely hearing. In J. Stewart (Ed.), *Bridges not walls* (5th ed.) (pp. 175–191). New York: McGraw-Hill.

Borden, R. C. (1935). *Public speaking as listeners like it.* New York: Harper & Row.

Borisoff, D., & Merrill, L. (1992). *The power to communicate: Gender differences as barriers* (2nd ed.). Prospect Heights, IL: Waveland.

Bormann, E. G. (1990). *Small group communication: Theory and practice* (3rd ed.). New York: Harper & Row.

Bradley, P. H. (1980). Sex, competence and opinion deviation: An expectation states approach. *Communication Monographs, 47,* 101–110.

Braybrooke, D., & Lindblom, C. E. (1963). *A strategy of decision.* New York: Free Press.

Broome, B. J. (1991). Building shared meaning: Implications of a relational approach to empathy for teaching intercultural communication. *Communication Education, 40,* 235–250.

Brown, L. (1982). *Communicating facts and ideas in business.* Englewood Cliffs, NJ: Prentice-Hall.

Brown, M. T. (1990). *Working ethics: Strategies for decision making and organizational responsibility.* San Francisco: Jossey-Bass.

Buck, R. (1975). Nonverbal communication of affect in children. *Journal of Personality and Social Psy-*

chology, 32, 644–653.

Carbonell, J. L. (1984). Sex roles and leadership revisited. *Journal of Applied Psychology, 69,* 44–49.

Cathcart, C., & Cathcart, R. (1986). Japanese social experience and concept of groups. In L. A. Samovar & R. E. Porter (Eds.), *Intercultural communication: A reader* (5th ed.) (pp. 186–192). Belmont, CA: Wadsworth.

Cattell, R. B. (1948). Concepts and methods in the measurement of group syntality. *Psychological Review, 55,* 48–63.

Clark, R. A. (1979). The impact of selection of persuasive strategies on self-interest and desired liking. *Communication Monographs, 46,* 257–273.

Cody, M. J., Woelfel, M. L., & Jordan, W. J. (1983). Dimensions of compliance-gaining situations. *Human Communication Research, 9,* 99–113.

Condon, E. C. (1976). Cross-cultural interferences affecting teacher-pupil communication in American schools. *International and Intercultural Communication Annual, 3,* 82–86.

Conrad, C. (1991). Communication in conflict: Style-strategy relationships. *Communication Monographs, 58,* 135–155.

Cummings, T. (1978). Self-regulating work groups: A socio-technical synthesis. *Academy of Management Review, 80,* 625–634.

Davis, G. A. (1983). *Creativity is forever.* Dubuque, IA: Kendall/Hunt.

de Bono, E. (1970). *Lateral thinking: Creativity step by step.* New York: Harper & Row.

De Klerk, V. (1991). Expletives: Men only? *Communication Monographs, 58,* 156–169.

Delbecq, A. L., Van de Ven, A. H., & Gustafson, D. H. (1975). *Group techniques for program planning: A guide to Nominal Group and Delphi processes.* Glenview, IL: Scott, Foresman.

DeVito, J. A. (1990). *Messages: Building interpersonal communication skills.* New York: Harper & Row.

Dewey, J. (1910). *How we think.* Boston: D. C. Heath.

Dobbins, G. H., Long, W. S., Dedrick, E. J., & Clemons, T. C. (1990). The role of self-monitoring and gender on leader emergence: A laboratory and field study. *Journal of Management, 16,* 609–618.

Dodd, C. H. (1991). *Dynamics of intercultural communication* (3rd ed.). Dubuque, IA: W. C. Brown.

Dolphin, C. Z. (1988). Variables in the use of personal space in intercultural transactions. *The Howard Journal of Communications, 1,* 23–28.

Dovidio, J. F., & Ellyson, S. L. (1982). Decoding visual dominance: Attributions of power based on relative percentages of looking while speaking and looking while listening. *Social Psychology Quarterly, 45,* 106–115.

Dukerich, J. M., Nichols, M. L., Elm, D. R., & Vollrath, D. A. (1990). Moral reasoning in groups: Leaders make a difference. *Human Relations, 43,* 473–493.

Edwards, B. (1979). *Drawing on the right side of the brain.* Los Angeles: J. P. Tarcher.

Ekman, P., & Friesen, W. V. (1967). Head and body cues in the judgment of emotion: A reformulation. *Perceptual and Motor Skills, 24,* 71–724.

Ekman, P., & Friesen, W. V. (1969). The repertoire of nonverbal behavior: Categories, origins, usage and coding. *Semiotica, 15,* 49–98.

Ekman, P., Friesen, W. V., & Ellsworth, P. C. (1972). *Emotion in the human face: Guidelines for research and an integration of findings.* New York: Pergamon Press.

Elgin, S. H. (1989). *Success with the gentle art of verbal self-defense.* Englewood Cliffs, NJ: Prentice-Hall.

Elmes, M. B., & Gemmill, G. (1990). The psychodynamics of mindlessness and dissent in small groups. *Small Group Research, 21,* 28–43.

Etzioni, A. (1968). *The active society.* New York: Free Press.

Fabun, D. (1968). *You and creativity.* New York: Macmillan.

Fitch-Hauser, M., Barker, D. A., & Hughes, A. (1990). Receiver apprehension and listening comprehension: A linear or curvilinear relationship? *The Southern Communication Journal, 56,* 62–71.

Floyd, J. J. (1985). *Listening: A practical approach.* Glenview, IL: Scott, Foresman.

Forman, J., & Katsky, P. (1986). The group report: A problem in small group or writing processes? *Journal of Business Communication, 23*(4), 23–35.

French, J. R. P., & Raven, B. (1959). The bases of social power. In D. Cartwright (Ed.), *Studies in social power* (pp. 150–167). Ann Arbor: University of Michigan, Institute for Social Research.

Gergen, K. J., Gergen, M. M., & Barton, W. H. (1973). Deviance in the dark. *Psychology Today, 7,* 129–130.

Gersick, C. J. G. (1988). Time and transition in work teams: Toward a new model of group development. *Academy of Management Journal, 31,* 9–41.

Gibb, J. R. (1961). Defensive communication. *Journal of Communication, 11,* 141–148.

Gilligan, C. (1982). *In a different voice.* Cambridge, MA: Harvard University Press.

Gilligan, C., Ward, J. V., Taylor, J. M., & Bardige, B. (Eds.). (1988). *Mapping the moral domain.* Cambridge, MA: Center for the Study of Gender, Education and Human Development, Harvard University Graduate School of Education.

Goleman, D. (1991, September 17). Non-verbal cues are easy to misinterpret. *New York Times,* pp. C1, C9.

Gordon, W. J. J. (1961). *Synectics.* New York: Harper & Row.

Gouran, D. S. (1969). *An investigation to identify the critical variables related to consensus in group discussions of policy* (Project No. 8-F-004). Washington, DC: U.S. Department of Health, Education and Welfare, Office of Education.

Gouran, D. S. (1982). *Making decisions in groups: Choices and consequences.* Glenview, IL: Scott, Foresman.

Gouran, D. S., & Hirokawa, R. Y. (1983). The role of communication in decision-making groups. A functional perspective. In M. S. Mander (Ed.), *Communication in transition* (pp. 168–185). New York: Praeger.

Gudykunst, W. B. (1988). Uncertainty and anxiety. In Y. Y. Kim & W. B. Gudykunst (Eds.), *Theories in intercultural communication* (pp. 123–157). Newbury Park, CA: Sage.

Hackman, J. R. (1982). *A set of methods for research on work teams* (Technical Report No. 1). School of Organization and Management, Yale University, New Haven, CT.

Hackman, J. R. (Ed.). (1990). *Groups that work (and those that don't).* San Francisco: Jossey-Bass.

Hackman, M. Z., & Johnson, C. E. (1991). *Leadership: A communication perspective.* Prospect Heights, IL: Waveland.

Hall, E. T. (1966). *The hidden dimension.* Garden City, NY: Doubleday.

Hastings, C., Bixby, P., & Chaudhry-Lawton, R. (1986). *The superteam solution: Successful teamworking in organisations.* Aldershot, England: Gower.

Hawkins, K. (1991, November). *Consequences of deep interruption for subsequent turn-taking in task-oriented group communication.* Paper presented at the meeting of the Speech Communication Association, Atlanta, GA.

Hellweg, S. A., Samovar, L. A., & Skow, L. (1991). Cultural variations in negotiation styles. In L. A. Samovar & R. E. Porter (Eds.), *Intercultural communication: A reader* (6th ed.) (pp. 185–192). Belmont, CA: Wadsworth.

Hermann, N. (1988). *The creative brain.* Lake Lure, NC: Brain Books.

Hersey, P., & Blanchard, K. H. (1977). *Management of organizational behavior: Utilizing human resources* (3rd ed.). Englewood Cliffs, NJ: Prentice-Hall.

Hersey, P., Blanchard, K. J., & Natemeyer, W. E. (1979). Situational leadership, perception, and the impact of power. *Group & Organization Studies, 4,* 418–428.

Heslin, R., & Patterson, M. L. (1982). *Nonverbal behavior and social psychology.* New York: Plenum.

Hirokawa, R. Y. (1990). The role of communication in group decision-making efficacy: A task-contingency perspective. *Small Group Research, 21,* 190–204.

Hirokawa, R. Y., & Scheerhorn, D. R. (1986). The role of communication in faulty group decision-making. In R. Y. Hirokawa & M. S. Poole (Eds.), *Communication and group decision making* (pp. 63–81). Beverly Hills, CA: Sage.

Hollander, E. P. (1978). *Leadership dynamics: A practical guide to effective relationships.* New York: Free Press.

Hosking, D. M. (1988). Organizing, leadership and skillful process. *Journal of Management Studies, 25,* 147–166.

Howell, J. P., Bowen, D. E., Dorfman, P. W., Kerr, S., & Podsakoff, P. M. (1990, Summer). Substitutes for leadership: Effective alternatives to ineffective leadership. *Organizational Dynamics,* pp. 21–38.

Hunter, J. E., & Boster, F. J. (1987). A model of compliance-gaining message selection. *Communication Monographs, 54,* 63–84.

Ishikawa, K. (1982). *Guide to quality control* (2nd rev. ed.). Tokyo: Asian Productivity Organization.

Jaksa, J. A., & Pritchard, M. S. (1988). *Communication ethics: Methods of analysis.* Belmont, CA: Wadsworth.

Janis, I. L. (1982). *Groupthink* (rev. ed.). Boston: Houghton Mifflin.

Janis, I. L. (1989a). *Crucial decisions: Leadership in policymaking and crisis management.* New York: Free Press.

Janis, I. L. (1989b). *Groupthink: The desperate drive for consensus at any cost.* In J. S. Ott (Ed.), *Classic readings in organizational behavior* (pp. 223–232). Belmont, CA: Wadsworth.

Janis, I. L., & Mann, L. (1977). *Decision making: A psychological analysis of conflict, choice, and commitment.* New York: Free Press.

Johannesen, R. L. (1990). *Ethics in human communication* (3rd ed.). Prospect Heights, IL: Waveland.

Johannesen, R. L. (1992). Perspectives on ethics in persuasion. In C. U. Larson (Ed.), *Persuasion: Reception and responsibility* (6th ed.) (pp. 28–53). Belmont, CA: Wadsworth.

Jones, J. E., & Pfeiffer, J. W. (1973). *The 1973 annual handbook for group facilitators.* San Diego, CA: University Associates.

Katz, N. H., & Lawyer, J. W. (1985). *Communication and conflict: Resolution skills.* Dubuque, IA: Kendall/Hunt.

Kelley, H. H., & Thibaut, J. W. (1978). *Interpersonal relationships.* New York: Wiley.

Kephart, W. M. (1950). A quantitative analysis of intragroup relationships. *American Journal of Sociology, 55,* 544–549.

Keyton, J. (1991, November). *Breaking up is hard to do.* Paper presented at the meeting of the Speech Communication Association, Atlanta, GA.

Kinlaw, D. C. (1991). *Developing superior work teams: Building quality and the competitive edge.* Lexington, MA: Lexington Books.

Kipnis, D., & Schmidt, S. M. (1982). *Profiles of organizational influence strategies: Influencing your subordinates.* San Diego, CA: University Associates.

Kivlighan, D. M., Jr., & Jauquet, C. A. (1990). Quality of group member agendas and group session climate. *Small Group Research, 21,* 205–219.

Knapp, M. L., Hart, R. P., Friedrich, G. W., & Shulman, G. M. (1973). The rhetoric of goodbye: Verbal and nonverbal correlates of human leave-taking. *Speech Monographs, 40,* 182–198.

Kolb, J. A. (1991, November). *Leader behaviors related to team performance in research and non-research teams.* Paper presented at the meeting of the Speech Communication Association, Atlanta, GA.

Kramarae, C. (1981). *Women and men speaking.* Rowley, MA: Newbury House.

Krebs, D., & Adinolf, A. A. (1975). Physical attractiveness, social relations, and personality style. *Journal of Personality and Social Psychology, 31,* 245–253.

Laing, R. D. (1970). *Knots.* London: Tavistock.

Larson, C. E., & LaFasto, F. M. J. (1989). *Teamwork: What must go right/what can go wrong.* Newbury Park, CA: Sage.

Leathers, D. G. (1976). *Nonverbal communication systems.* Boston: Allyn & Bacon.

Legge, W. B. (1971). Listening, intelligence, and school achievement. In S. Duker (Ed.), *Listening: Readings* (pp. 121–133). Metuchen, NJ: Scarecrow.

Levine, T. R., & Wheeless, L. R. (1990). Cross-situational consistency and use/nonuse tendencies in compliance-gaining tactic selection. *The Southern Communication Journal, 56,* 1–11.

Lieberman, D. A. (1991). Ethnocognitivism and problem solving. In L. A. Samovar & R. E. Porter (Eds.), *Intercultural communication: A reader* (6th ed.) (pp. 229–234). Belmont, CA: Wadsworth.

Lumsden, D., Knight, M. E., & Gallaro, D. (1989). Assessing learning outcomes: Opportunities for institutional renewal. *Journal of Staff, Program and Organization Development, 7,* 181–185.

Lumsden, G. (1972). *An experimental study of the effect of verbal agreement on leadership maintenance in problem-solving discussions.* Unpublished doctoral dissertation, Indiana University, Bloomington.

Mabry, E. A. (1989). Developmental aspects of nonverbal behavior in small group settings. *Small Group Behavior, 20,* 190–202.

Maier, N. R. F. (1963). *Problem-solving discussions and conferences: Leadership methods and skills.* New York: McGraw-Hill.

Manz, C. C., & Sims, H. P. (1987). Leading workers to lead themselves: The external leadership of self-managing work teams. *Administrative Science Quarterly, 32,* 106–128.

Manz, C. C., & Sims, H. P. (1991, Spring). Superleadership: Beyond the myth of heroic leadership. *Organizational Dynamics,* pp. 18–35.

Martel, M. (1989). *Mastering the art of Q & A: A survival guide for tough, trick, and hostile questions.* Homewood, IL: Dow Jones-Irwin.

Maslow, A. (1970). *Motivation and personality* (2nd ed.). New York: Harper & Row.

Matsumoto, D. (1991). Cultural influences on facial expressions of emotion. *The Southern Communication Journal, 56,* 128–137.

McClelland, D. C. (1989). That urge to achieve. In J. S. Ott (Ed.), *Classic readings in organizational behavior* (pp. 82–89). Belmont, CA: Wadsworth.

McLuhan, M. (1964). *Understanding media: The extensions of man.* New York: McGraw-Hill.

Mehrabian, A. (1971). *Silent messages.* Belmont, CA: Wadsworth.

Meyers, R. A. (1991, November). *Argument and group decision making research: Implications and applications.* Paper presented at the meeting of the Speech Communication Association, Atlanta, GA.

Michaelson, L. K., Watson, W. E., & Black, R. H. (1989). A realistic test of individual versus group consensus decision making. *Journal of Applied Psychology, 74,* 834–839.

Miller, G. A. (1956). The magic number seven, plus or minus two: Some limits on our capacity for processing information. *Psychological Review, 63,* 81–97.

Mintz, N. (1956). Effects of aesthetic surroundings: II. Prolonged and repeated experiences in a "beautiful" and "ugly" room. *Journal of Psychology, 41,* 247–254.

Murphy, S. (1991, August 4). Letter to the editor. *New York Times Magazine,* p. 8.

Napier, R. W., & Gershenfeld, M. K. (1985). *Groups: Theory and experience.* Boston: Houghton Mifflin.

Natalle, E. J., & Papa, M. J. (1990). Gender and coorientational accuracy in conflict resolution. *International Journal of Group Tensions, 20,* 32–45.

Neale, M. A., & Bazerman, M. H. (1991). *Cognition and rationality in negotiation.* New York: Free Press.

Nemeth, C. J., & Kwan, J. L. (1987). Minority influence, divergent thinking and detection of correct solutions. *Journal of Applied Social Psychology, 17,* 788–799.

Neustadt, R. E., & May, E. R. (1986). *Thinking in time.* New York: Free Press.

Nye, J. L., & Forsyth, D. R. (1991). The effects of prototype-based biases on leadership appraisals: A test of leadership categorization theory. *Small Group Research, 22,* 360–379.

O'Sullivan, M., Ekman, P., Friesen, W., & Scherer, K. (1985). What you say and how you say it: The contribution of speech content and voice quality to judgments of others. *Journal of Personality and Social Psychology, 48,* 54–62.

Ott, J. S. (1989). *The organizational culture perspective.* Pacific Grove, CA: Brooks/Cole.

Pace, R. C. (1990). Personalized and depersonalized conflict in small group discussions: An examination of differentiation. *Small Group Research, 21,* 79–96.

Pace, R. W., & Faules, D. F. (1989). *Organizational communication* (2nd ed.). Englewood Cliffs, NJ: Prentice-Hall.

Pavitt, C., & Sackaroff, P. (1990). Implicit theories of leadership and judgments of leadership among group members. *Small Group Research, 21,* 374–392.

Pearson, J. C., Turner, L. H., & Todd-Mancillas, W. (1991). *Gender and communication* (2nd ed.). Dubuque, IA: W. C. Brown.

Peters, T., & Austin, N. (1985). *A passion for excellence.* New York: Random House.

Pettit, J. D., Vaught, B., & Pulley, K. J. (1990). The role of communication in organizations: Ethical considerations. *Journal of Business Communication, 27,* 223–249.

Pfeiffer, J. W. (1985). *Reference guide to handbooks and annuals* (1985 edition). San Diego, CA: University Associates.

Phillips, J. D. (1948). Report on Discussion 66. *Adult Education Journal, 7,* 181–182.

Potter, D., & Andersen, M. P. (1976). *Small groups: A guide to effective practice* (3rd ed.). Belmont, CA: Wadsworth.

Preiss, R. W., & Wheeless, L. R. (1989). Affective responses in listening: A mega-analysis of receiver apprehension outcomes. *Journal of the International Listening Association, 3,* 71–102.

Putnam, L. L. (1986). Conflict in group decision-making. In R. Y. Hirokawa & M. S. Poole (Eds.), *Communication and group decision-making* (pp. 175–196). Beverly Hills, CA: Sage.

Rifkin, G. (1991, October 8). Market place: Signals of a boom in video meetings. *New York Times,* p. D12.

Robert, H. M., III, & Evans, W. J. (Eds.). (1990). *Robert's rules of order newly revised.* Glenview, IL: Scott, Foresman.

Rogers, C. (1990). *A way of being.* In J. Stewart (Ed.), *Bridges not walls* (5th ed.) (pp. 438–444). New York: McGraw-Hill.

Russo, N. (1967). Connotation of seating arrangement. *Cornell Journal of Social Relations, 2,* 37–44.

Satir, V. (1990). Making contact. In J. Stewart (Ed.), *Bridges not walls* (5th ed.) (pp. 63–68). New York: McGraw-Hill.

Scheidel, T. M., & Crowell, L. (1964). Idea development in small group discussion. *Quarterly Journal of Speech, 50,* 140–145.

Scholtes, P. R. (1988). *The team handbook: How to*

use teams to improve quality. Madison, WI: Joiner Associates.

Schultz, B. (1986). Communication correlates of perceived leaders in the small group. *Small Group Behavior, 17,* 51–65.

Schutz, W. C. (1966). *The interpersonal underworld.* Palo Alto, CA: Science and Behavior Books.

Schwartz, B., Tesser, A., & Powell, E. (1982). Dominance cues in nonverbal behavior. *Social Psychology Quarterly, 45,* 114–120.

Shaw, M. E. (1971). *Group dynamics: The study of small group behavior.* New York: McGraw-Hill.

Shaw, M. E. (1981). *Group dynamics: The psychology of small group behavior* (3rd ed.). New York: McGraw-Hill.

Simon, H. A. (1977). *The new science of management decision* (rev. ed.). Englewood Cliffs, NJ: Prentice-Hall.

Sitaram, K. S., & Cogdell, R. T. (1976). *Foundations of intercultural communication.* Columbus, OH: Charles E. Merrill.

Solomon, C. M. (1990). What an idea: Creativity training. *Personnel Journal, 69*(5), 64–71.

Sommer, R. (1959). Studies in personal space. *Sociometry, 22,* 247–266.

Sprague, J., & Stuart, D. (1992). *The speaker's handbook* (3rd ed.). Fort Worth, TX: Harcourt Brace Jovanovich.

Stewart, L. P., Stewart, A. D., Friedley, S. A., & Cooper, P. J. (1990). *Communication between the sexes: Sex differences and sex-role stereotypes* (2nd ed.). Scottsdale, AZ: Gorsuch Scarisbrick.

Stewart, J., & Thomas, M. (1990). Dialogic listening: Sculpting mutual meanings. In J. Stewart (Ed.), *Bridges not walls* (5th ed.) (pp. 192–210). New York: McGraw-Hill.

Strodtbeck, F., & Hook, L. (1961). The social dimensions of a twelve man jury table. *Sociometry, 24,* 397–415.

Sullivan, J. J., Albrecht, T. L., & Taylor, S. (1990). Process, organizational, relational, and personal determinants of managerial compliance-gaining strategies. *Journal of Business Communication, 27,* 332–355.

Thameling, C. L., & Andrews, P. H. (1991, November). *Majority responses to opinion deviates: A communication analysis.* Paper presented at the meeting of the Speech Communication Association, Atlanta, GA.

Ting-Toomey, S. (1988). Intercultural conflict style: A face-negotiation theory. In Y. Y. Kim & W. B. Gudykunst (Eds.), *Theories in intercultural communication* (pp. 213–235). Newbury Park, CA: Sage.

Toffler, B. L. (1986). *Tough choices: Managers talk ethics.* New York: Wiley.

Toulmin, S. (1958). *The uses of argument.* Cambridge: Cambridge University Press.

Triandis, H. C., Brislin, R., & Hui, C. H. (1988). Cross-cultural training across the individualism-collectivism divide. *International Journal of Intercultural Relations, 12,* 269–298.

Tuckman, B., & Jensen, M. (1977). Stages of small-group development. *Group and Organizational Studies, 2,* 419–427.

Tuppen, C. (1974). Dimensions of communicator credibility: An oblique solution. *Speech Monographs, 41,* 253–266.

Tyler, T. R., Rasinski, K. A., & Spodick, N. (1985). Influence of voice on satisfaction with leaders: Exploring the meaning of process control. *Journal of Personality and Social Psychology, 48,* 72–81.

Verderber, R. F. (1991). *The challenge of effective speaking* (8th ed.). Belmont, CA: Wadsworth.

von Oech, R. (1983). *A whack on the side of the head: How to unlock your mind for innovation.* New York: Warner Books.

Wallace, K. R. (1955). An ethical basis of communication. *The Speech Teacher, 4,* 1–9.

Walton, M. (1986). *The Deming management method.* New York: Putnam.

Walton, R. E., & Hackman, J. R. (1986). Groups under contrasting management strategies. In P. S. Goodman and Associates, *Designing effective work groups* (pp. 168–201). San Francisco: Jossey-Bass.

Watzlawick, P., Beavin, J. H., & Jackson, D. D. (1967). *Pragmatics of human communication.* New York: Norton.

Wharton Applied Research Center. (1981, September 14). *A study of the effects of the use of overhead transparencies on business meetings: Final report.* Philadelphia: University of Pennsylvania.

White, R. K., & Lippett, R. O. (1960). *Autocracy and democracy.* New York: Harper & Row.

Whitehead, J., Jr. (1969). Factors of source credibility. *Quarterly Journal of Speech, 54,* 59–63.

Williams, F. (1987). *Technology and communication behavior.* Belmont, CA: Wadsworth.

Witteman, H. (1991). Group member satisfaction: A

conflict-related account. *Small Group Research, 22,* 24–58.

Wolvin, A. D., & Coakley, C. G. (1991). A survey of the status of listening training in some Fortune 500 corporations. *Communication Education, 40,* 152–164.

Wood, J. T. (1977). Leading in purposive discussions: A study of adaptive behavior. *Communication Monographs, 44,* 152–165.

Wood, W. (1987). Meta-analytic review of sex differences in group performance. *Psychological Bulletin, 102,* 53–71.

Yanes, W. B. (1990, November 9). Forget consensus: Fight it out, stick with decision. *Investor's Daily,* p. 6.

Zajonc, R. (1968). Attitudinal effects of mere exposure. *Journal of Personality and Social Psychology, 9,* 1–29.

Zorn, T. E. (1991). Construct system development, transformational leadership and leadership messages. *The Southern Communication Journal, 56,* 178–193.